W9-AWC-180

AC 61-27C

INSTRUMENT FLYING

HANDBOOK

Revised 1980

REPRINTED BY asa PUBLICATIONS, INC.

DEPARTMENT OF TRANSPORTATION

FEDERAL AVIATION ADMINISTRATION

For sale by the Superintendent of Documents, U.S. Government Printing Office, Washington, D.C. 20402

FOREWORD

General Aviation in the United States has grown tremendously in recent years. The aircraft industry has designed aircraft to satisfy the requirements of business firms, professional people, crop dusters, flight·training schools, and others. Our aviation community is thus expanding to include an ever-broadening spectrum of the American·public.

The Federal Aviation Administration is vitally concerned that this huge air travel potential be exploited in a safe and orderly manner. To this end, development of sound training programs and materials receive high priority among the many activities of the FAA. Since a wide variety of general aviation aircraft possess instrument flight capability—a key factor in achieving greater aircraft utilization—more and more pilots are therefore preparing themselves to "fly the weather."

The *Instrument Flying Handbook* has been developed in response to this increased flight activity and to the continuing requests from individuals and training organizations for an FAA handbook which is oriented to civilian instrument flying. Together with other flight training materials, the handbook emphasizes the concept that an informed pilot is a safe pilot. In this respect, the handbook supports the primary objective of the Federal Aviation Administration—safety in flight.

This handbook, along with the *Airman's Information Manual, Aviation Weather, AC 00-6A*, and *Aviation Weather Services, AC 00-45B* (or other equivalent handbooks on meteorology), will provide the flight student with the basic information needed to acquire an FAA instrument rating. Like any basic text, this one should be supplemented by technical periodicals, textbooks, and training aids, depending upon individual training needs, interests, and objectives. The book is designed for the reader who holds at least a private pilot's certificate and who is knowledgeable in all of the areas discussed in the *Pilot's Handbook of Aeronautical Knowledge (AC 61-23B)*.

In this edition, the repetition of material already published in the *Airman's Information Manual* is held to a minimum. Instead, AIM references are cited throughout the text wherever they are applicable.

The reader must be aware that regulations, air traffic control procedures, charts, and certain other materials referred to in this handbook are subject to change and amendment. Any question regarding currency of these items should be resolved by checking pertinent source materials or the appropriate FAA office.

The *Instrument Flying Handbook*, issued as Advisory Circular 61-27C, was prepared by the Flight Standards Service of the Federal Aviation Administration and supersedes AC 61-27B. Many valuable contributions were provided by other organizations in FAA. Acknowledgement is made to the numerous firms whose equipment or products are illustrated in this publication. The inclusion of such illustrations *does not*, however, constitute an endorsement by the FAA.

Comments regarding this publication should be directed to the U.S. Department of Transportation, Federal Aviation Administration, Flight Standards National Field Office, P.O. Box 25082, Oklahoma City, Okla. 73125.

CONTENTS

I. TRAINING CONSIDERATIONS

Why Get an Instrument Rating?

Not so long ago, flying by instruments was commonly thought of as a special-purpose skill of little value to the nonprofessional pilot. The private pilot flew for pleasure, usually within a few miles of the local airport. Cross-country flights were short by today's standards, and the pilot flew to a destination airport by visual reference to prominent landmarks. The pilot had to rely on visual contact with the ground because there was no other means available for getting safely from one airport to another. This was "contact" flying; "blind" flying was to come.

With the evolution of blind flying instruments, the distinction between contact and instrument flying was sharply defined in the flight training curriculum. During contact flying the student pilot learned to control the airplane by responding to changes that were seen, heard, and felt. It was common practice for the flight instructor to cover the instruments in the student's cockpit, thus forcing the beginner to look for changes in aircraft attitude by references *outside* the cockpit.

Flying by reference to instruments in the early era was considered a "common student error." The pilot controlled airspeed and aircraft attitude by reference to the horizon, by listening for changes in engine RPM, by sensing the sound of the wind through the rigging. The pilot identified a slip or skid in open-cockpit trainers by changes in the feel of the wind. Steep turns were executed by aligning reference points on the aircraft with the horizon and reacting to changes in seat pressure. Even in aircraft equipped with instruments necessary to execute these maneuvers without outside visual reference, the pilot was trained to use the flight instruments as secondary references, if at all. A student of contact flying was taught *not* to use the flight instruments.

The student learned to use flight instruments as the primary means of aircraft control *only* in more advanced training. Ironically, in instrument training the student discovered that much of this training apparently contradicted what had been learned previously as a "contact" pilot. The "swivel neck" habits, necessary during visual flight to ensure separation from other aircraft, became pointless under the hood during simulated instrument flight. Instead of reminders from the instructor to "Look around!" and "Clear the area!" the student heard "Check your airspeed!" and "What does your altimeter tell you?" The seat-of-the-pants sensations, the "sight, sound, and feel" that were so essential to contact flying, had to be ignored by the instrument pilot as the visual sense alone was relied on, regardless of other conflicting sensations. Small wonder that "contact" and "instrument" flying were considered as separate and distinct skills.

To the average nonprofessional pilot, flying meant controlling an aircraft by visual reference to the ground. Blind flying? This was something else—meant for professional airline pilots, military pilots, pioneers, and a few unfortunates who tangled with the weather through carelessness or ignorance. The nonprofessional civilian pilot had neither the equipment to fly safely on instruments nor the need or interest to do so. With the advent of faster and safer aircraft, more reliable flight instruments and radio equipment, and more effective radio aids and ground services, the traditional distinction between visual and instrument flying has undergone corresponding changes.

In sharp contrast to earlier training concepts are the following two quotations from a current military pilot training manual:

> The art of instrument flying, long regarded as a skill apart from contact flying, is now considered the prime method of aircraft control, regardless of weather conditions.
>
> Any instrument flight, regardless of the aircraft used or route flown, is made up of basic maneuvers; the pilot executes these maneuvers by learning to control his flight path by reference to instruments.

High-speed military aircraft cannot be flown safely and effectively without instruments, and mission accomplishment demands all-weather pilot capability. Although this philosophy, basic to military aviation, is neither literally applicable nor desirable in all phases of civil aviation, it reflects important changes affecting civil instrument flight training.

Contact flying and flight by reference to instruments are not taught as distinct and separate skills in unrelated phases of training. Instrument flying is essentially *precision flying*, entirely apart from whether or not the pilot is flying under the hood, in the clouds, or in VFR conditions. As a student pilot, you are flying by reference to instruments when you maintain traffic altitude by reference to the altimeter, when you check the ball of your turn-and-slip indicator to confirm a slip or skid, or when you maintain a predetermined climbing speed by reference to the outside horizon and airspeed indicator.

In terms of precision flying, instrument training begins shortly after your first introduction to the cockpit as a student pilot and continues as long as you maintain an interest in improving your skill.

As your proficiency in the interpretation and use of the instruments progresses, you fly visually, "on the gauges," or by a combination of visual, instrument, and "seat-of-the-pants" references depending upon which source of information best suits your purpose.

From the standpoint of training, instrument flying is a logical extension of visual flying. You learn to use the instruments and navigation equipment, not necessarily to become a weather pilot, but to develop the precision impossible to achieve by visual and other sensory references alone. You learn to fully utilize the potential of your airplane.

Many modern, single-engine airplanes have the capability to go farther, faster, and higher than the airliners of a few years ago. Surveys indicate that the majority of new aircraft sold are equipped for instrument training and for at least limited weather flying. Studies also show that many pilots are operating aircraft loaded with expensive flight and navigation instruments, radio equipment, auto-pilots, and other accessories that for lack of training, they fail to use fully.

Preparation for the instrument rating will better enable you to use the equipment to go when and where you want. Instrument proficiency will aid you in getting in and out of places that are inaccessible to pilots flying by visual flight rules (VFR) and using limited equipment. With or without the rating, as a precision pilot you will fly by reference to instruments. However, without an instrument rating you cannot fly under instrument conditions, as defined by regulations, except in violation of the limitations of your pilot certificate. If you intend to become a career pilot, you cannot advance far professionally without it, except in certain highly specialized commercial operations.

Perhaps you want an instrument rating for the same basic reason you learned to fly in the first place—because you like flying. Maintaining and extending your proficiency, once you have the rating, means less reliance on chance, more on skill and knowledge. Earn the rating, not because you might need it sometime, but because it represents achievement and provides training you will use continually and build upon as long as you fly. But most important, it means greater safety in flying.

Requirements for the Instrument Rating

How much flight time do you need before beginning instrument training? How much total time is required, in flight and on the ground? How much of this time requires direct supervision by a licensed instructor? What assurance do you have that you are getting competent instruction? How do you go about getting training to fly on instruments? Is attendance at an instrument school necessary? What are the advantages of attending an approved school? Can you spread the necessary training over an extended period to fit your spare time from business or other occupations? These are important considerations that should be faced before you begin an extensive and expensive training program. The answers may seem confusing and be misleading unless you take a thorough look at the problems ahead of you.

First, what are the requirements for the issuance of the FAA instrument rating? You will need to carefully review the aeronautical knowledge and experience requirements for the instrument rating as outlined in FAR 61. After completing the instrument rating written test, you are eligible to take the flight test when all experience requirements have been satisfied. It is important to note that the regulations specify *minimum* total and pilot-in-command time requirements. This minimum applies to all applicants, regardless of ability or previous aviation experience. No regulation can be written to specify experience requirements for a particular individual.

The amount of instructional time *needed* is determined not by regulation, but by the individual's ability to achieve a satisfactory level of proficiency. A professional pilot with diversified flying experience may easily attain a satisfactory level of proficiency in the minimum time required by regulation for the issuance of an additional type rating. Your own time requirements will depend upon a variety of factors, including previous flight experience, rate of learning, basic ability, frequency of flight training, type of aircraft flown, quality of ground school training, and quality of flight instruction, to name a few. The total instructional time that *you* will need, and in general the scheduling of such time, is up to the individual most qualified to judge your proficiency, the instructor who supervises your progress and endorses your record of flight training.

Before you decide to acquire instrument flight training, you should ponder the following comments by the chief instructor of an accredited and successful school of aviation:

Any instrument training program should allow sufficient calendar time for the student to assimilate the material involved in preparing for the instrument rating. . . . Emphasis should be placed on acquiring the education rather than acquiring the rating. . . . It is possible to obtain an instrument rating without acquiring an instrument education. A student who acquires the education need have no fear of failing to obtain the rating, however.

These sentiments are shared by many reputable aviation schools offering instrument training, whatever their differences in other respects. You can memorize a prodigious amount of information in a short time, but you will store away very little of it for future use unless you allow time enough to understand it, relate it to what you already know, and apply it with sufficient repetition.

As your flying experience progresses, you will learn increasingly through your own initiative, with or without the benefit of formal training. It is essential, however, that you lay the right foundation. You can do this by attending an instrument training school selected after careful investigation of its curriculum and reputation, or by joining a flying club

which has invested in the necessary equipment and utilizes a competent instructor.

You can accelerate and enrich much of your training by informal study. An increasing number of visual aids and programmed instrument courses are available to the applicant who cannot attend a formal instrument training course. The best course is obviously one that includes a well-integrated flight and ground school curriculum. The importance of close coordination between these two aspects of your education should be apparent from your previous flight experience. The sequential nature of flying requires that each element of knowledge and skill be learned and applied in the right manner at the right time. You can learn volumes of isolated information about flight procedures, basic instrument maneuvers, radio navigation, communications, and Federal Aviation Regulations, yet still have difficulty keeping an airplane right side up.

Until you can plan an orderly instrument flight and have had sufficient dual practice, you can be very easily overwhelmed, not only by the routine revisions of your planning, but by unexpected interruptions that require quick judgment and action. You can learn much of this information while making good use of your VFR time. As a VFR pilot making full use of your equipment and the facilities afforded all flights in controlled airspace, you can polish up communication and navigation techniques so essential to competent instrument flying.

By filing VFR Flight Plans, you can acquire increasing competence in careful flight planning, making en route estimates, revisions, and position reports in coordination with flight control personnel. You can visit FAA Control Towers, Flight Service Stations, and Air Traffic Control Centers to gain a clearer picture of the problems and processes involved in controlling traffic safely under Instrument Flight Rules. Finally, you should clarify some possible misconceptions about what an instrument rating involves.

Holding the instrument rating doesn't necessarily make you a competent weather pilot. The rating certifies only that you have complied with the minimum experience requirements, that you can plan and execute a flight under Instrument Flight Rules via Federal Airways, that you can execute basic instrument maneuvers, and that you have shown acceptable skill and judgment in performing these activities. Your instrument rating permits you to fly into instrument weather conditions with no previous instrument weather experience.

Your instrument rating is issued on the assumption that you have the good judgment to avoid situations beyond your capabilities. The instrument training program that you undertake should help you not only to develop essential flying skills, but also help you develop the judgment necessary to use the skills within your limitations. An instrument course can provide you with experienced instruction and up-to-date information. However, the program that offers tempting shortcuts may help you get the rating, but may leave important gaps in your flight education that could result in serious problems later on.

A clearer picture of your instrument training requirements can be gained by a study of the training curricula of some reputable aviation schools where successful professionals have made it their business to train pilots to a competent level with minimum expenditure of time and money. A representative ground and flight training curriculum is given later in this chapter.

Training for the Instrument Rating

The lack of uniformity existing among the instrument courses available to the prospective student complicates the problem of selecting a training program. For ground school training, you can choose anything from an intensive rote-memory course taking 2 to 5 days (with a "guarantee" to pass the required examinations) to a college-level course scheduling nearly 100 classroom hours over a 32-week period.

Flight training courses likewise vary, ranging from the minimum hours of dual required by regulation to the course offering more than the required hours of flight instruction supplemented by varying amounts of time in procedure trainers. Other courses offer proficiency programs tailored to the pilot's needs, guaranteeing nothing but experienced and reputable instruction—as much or as little as is necessary to achieve and maintain instrument proficiency. If all of these courses prepare the pilot for an instrument rating, why spend 8 months to acquire what allegedly can be accomplished in less than a week? Obviously, there must be some serious basic differences of opinion as to how much you should learn and how long it will take you to learn it.

At one extreme is the argument expressed more or less like this: If holding an instrument rating requires only that you demonstrate proficiency under simulated instrument conditions, you still have weather flying to learn after you have the certificate. Accordingly, why not get the certificate in the cheapest and quickest way possible, with a minimum of ground school and simulated time? Then go out and learn where it really counts—under actual weather conditions.

Many pilots acquire weather proficiency as co-pilots serving with experienced captains. However, an increasing number of nonprofessional pilots become instrument rated without the opportunity for transitioning to weather flying under experienced guidance. If you are one of this group, learning by experience (by yourself) is going to present many difficulties that you can avoid by adequate training.

In contrast to the course offering only the minimum training necessary for the instrument rating is the formal training provided by most flying schools and universities. Such schools base their curricula on a realistic appraisal of the instrument flying environment and its demands on pilot proficiency. More pilots are becoming instrument rated to fly light aircraft in increasingly congested airspace. This is not a "practice" environment, under instrument weather conditions. Air traffic controllers make no distinction between the novice instrument pilot and the veteran, as far as proficiency is concerned.

Unlike the solo VFR pilot who may learn from a constant succession of errors without necessarily becoming involved in a dangerous situation, the instrument pilot (beginner and veteran alike) becomes a serious traffic hazard when uncorrected errors accumulate. The most competent pilot, thoroughly proficient in the best equipment available, can become involved in situations where everything gets complicated at once. At such a time, the pilot must rely on past experience and training. For example, a pilot may fly a light twin for hundreds of hours without an engine malfunction or without making an ADF approach. In terms of actual use of single-engine procedures and training on ADF approaches, time and money have been wasted—except as insurance.

It takes only one harrowing experience to clarify the distinction between minimum practical knowledge and eventual useful information. When an emergency happens, it is too late to wonder why somebody forgot to instruct you as to what to do about it; and it's no consolation whatever that you didn't expect it to happen to you. Your instrument training is never complete; it is adequate when you have absorbed every foreseeable possible detail of knowledge and skill to insure a solution if and when you need it.

The following outline of ground school, procedures trainer, and flight training subjects represents an average of the instrument courses offered by several excellent aviation schools, amplified to include subject material of increasing importance to the instrument pilot. Syllabus organization and points of emphasis differ among schools for various reasons. However, the graduating student should have a sound understanding of the subjects listed, effectively integrated to present a clear operational picture of the following 10 basic components involved in instrument flight under Air Traffic Control:

Aircraft	Weather Information
Pilot	Rules and Procedures
Airport	Communications
Navigation	Ground Control
Aeronautical Information	Air Traffic Control.

Instrument Curriculum

Ground Training

Phase I. The Airplane and Pilot Under Instrument Flight Conditions.

1. Physiological Factors Related to Instrument Flying.
   a. Adjustment to the flight environment.
      (1) Ground habits vs. flight habits.
      (2) Individual differences.
      (3) Importance of physiological factors to the instrument pilot.
   b. Reactions of the body to pressure changes.
      (1) Aerotitis.
      (2) Aerosinusitis.
   c. Reaction of the body to changes in oxygen partial pressure.
      (1) Hypoxia.
      (2) Carbon monoxide.
      (3) Alcohol.
      (4) Hyperventilation.
      (5) Drugs.
   d. Sensations of Instrument Flying.
      (1) Body senses.
      (2) Spatial disorientation.
      (3) Illusions.
2. Aerodynamic Factors Related to Instrument Flight.
   a. Fundamental aerodynamics.
      (1) Airfoils and relative wind.
      (2) Angle of attack.
      (3) Lift/weight, thrust/drag.
      (4) Stalls.
   b. Application of fundamentals to basic maneuvers.
      (1) Straight-and-level flight.
         (a) Airspeed.
         (b) Air density.
         (c) Aircraft weight.
      (2) Climbs/descents.
      (3) Power, airspeed, and vertical speed.
      (4) Power, airspeed, and elevator control.
      (5) Turns.
      (6) Trim.
         (a) Skids/slips.
         (b) Coordination.
3. Flight Instruments.
   a. Source of power.
   b. Function.
   c. Construction.
   d. Operation.
   e. Limitations.
4. Aircraft Control.
   a. Attitude instrument flying.
      (1) Cross-checking (scanning).
      (2) Interpretation.
      (3) Control.
   b. Analysis of basic maneuvers.
      (1) Straight and level.
      (2) Climbs and descents.
      (3) Turns.
      (4) Climbing and descending turns.

5. Basic Radio.
   a. Radio waves, frequency assignment, and characteristics.
   b. Ground facilities and radio class designations.
      (1) VORTAC.
      (2) Marker beacons (Location markers).
      (3) Homing beacons.
      (4) DF facilities.
      (5) ILS.
      (6) Radar.
   c. Airborne equipment.
      (1) Antennas and sources of power.
      (2) Navigation receivers.
         (a) ADF.
         (b) VOR/ILS.
         (c) RNAV.
         (d) Transponder.
      (3) Communications transmitters and receivers.
         (a) Tuning.
         (b) Use.

Phase II. Regulations, Procedures, and Operational Aspects of Instrument Flying.

1. Applicable Regulations and Manuals (FAR, AIM, Airport/Facility Directory, Graphic Notices and Supplemental Data, Notices to Airmen).
2. Aircraft.
   a. Certificates and documents.
   b. Equipment.
      (1) VOR checks-VOT, etc.
      (2) ADF checks.
      (3) Altimeter
      (4) Transponder
      (5) Communication checks
3. Airman.
   a. Pilot certificates and ratings (FAR 61).
   b. Recency of experience.
   c. Instrument rating knowledge, experience, and skill requirements.
      (1) Logging instrument time.
      (2) Simulator time.
      (3) Flight instruction.
4. General Operating and Flight Rules.
   a. FAR 91.
   b. Publications—AIM—chart reading.
5. Air Traffic Control Procedures.
   a. Visual flight on VFR and IFR flight plans.
   b. Instrument flight.
      (1) Airport traffic control.
      (2) En route traffic control.
      (3) Clearances.
      (4) Communications-frequency use.
      (5) IFR reports.
      (6) Special restrictions on air traffic.
         (a) ADIZ.
         (b) Prohibited, restricted, and warning areas.
      (7) Terminal traffic control.

5

c. Composite flight plan.
6. Weather—Fundamentals.
   a. Earth's atmosphere.
   b. Temperature.
   c. Pressure.
   d. Wind.
   e. Moisture.
   f. Stability and instability.
   g. Clouds.
   h. Air masses and fronts.
   i. Turbulence.
   j. Icing.
   k. Thunderstorms.
   l. IFR producers.
7. Navigation.
   a. Dead reckoning—computer.
   b. Radio Navigation—ADF, VOR, RNAV, Radar.
      (1) Orientation.
      (2) Bearings.
      (3) Time/distance from station.
      (4) Course interception.
      (5) Tracking/homing.
      (6) Establishing fixes.
      (7) Station passage.
      (8) Waypoints.
8. Flight Planning and In-flight Procedures.
   a. Departure, destination, and alternate airport data and requirements.
      (1) Landing aids.
      (2) Communications facilities.
      (3) Weather services.
      (4) Airport data.
   b. Charts, route, and altitudes.
      (1) Understanding and use of Enroute Low Altitude Charts.
         (a) Routes.
         (b) Intersections.
         (c) Facilities.
      (2) Minimum IFR altitudes.
   c. Application of weather information to flight planning.
      (1) Sources of weather information—forecaster, FSS, telephone, radio.
      (2) Operational weather data.
         (a) *Weather charts:* surface analysis, weather depiction, radar summary, prognostic, winds and temperatures aloft, freezing level, stability, constant pressure.
         (b) *Weather forecasts:* Area, terminal, winds aloft.
         (c) *Weather reports:* Aviation weather, PIREPs, RAREPs, observed winds aloft.
      (3) Choice of alternate.
   d. En route radio aids.
      (1) Navigation aids.
         (a) Range: VOR (accuracy of VOR radials).
         (b) Location markers.
         (c) Homing facilities.
         (d) D/F facilities (Airport/Facility Directory)
         (e) Radar.
         (f) DME.
      (2) Communications.
         (a) Facilities.
         (b) Frequencies.
   e. Flight log entries and flight plan.
      (1) Reporting points, compulsory and noncompulsory.
      (2) Mileages.
      (3) Time estimates; ETAs between checkpoints, to destination, and alternate airport.
      (4) Groundspeed estimates.
      (5) Winds aloft data.
      (6) Navigation and communications frequencies.
      (7) Magnetic courses.
      (8) Fuel estimates.
      (9) Emergency reference data.
      (10) Methods of filing.
   f. Departure, holding, and arrival procedures.
      (1) Approach procedure charts, en route low altitude charts, area charts, preferred routes, SIDs, STARs.
      (2) Radar—terminal and enroute.
   g. Weather in flight.
      (1) VFR/IFR.
      (2) Weather services—FSS (scheduled and special broadcasts), PIREPS.
      (3) Effects of changing pressure and/or temperature on flight instruments.
      (4) Effects of weather on aircraft performance.
      (5) Procedures to be followed as a result of weather changes.
   h. Changes in flight.
      (1) Deviations from flight plan.
         (a) Time/airspeed tolerances (AIM).
         (b) Initiation or cancellation of IFR flight plan (AIM).
         (c) "VFR on top" operation.
         (d) Change in alternate.
         (e) Change in altitude.
         (f) Change in route.
      (2) Emergency procedures.
         (a) Equipment failure.
            1. Instrument-radar service.
            2. Radio—navigation and/or communications.
            3. Airframe or powerplant.
         (b) Lost procedures.
            1. Emergency pattern for radar identification.
            2. Communications procedure.
            3. VHF/DF.
            4. Radar vectors.
   i. Transitions and Instrument Approaches.
      (1) ADF.
      (2) VOR.
      (3) ILS front and back course.
      (4) RNAV.

(5) Missed approaches.
(6) Radar

Procedures Trainer

Phase I. Basic Instruments.
1. Use of instruments to control attitude, altitude, speed, and direction.
2. Straight-and-level flight.
   a. Pitch control.
   b. Bank control.
   c. Power control.
   d. Trim control.
   e. Change of airspeed and configuration.
3. Turns.
   a. Turns to predetermined headings.
   b. Change of airspeed and configuration.
4. Climbs and descents.
   a. Constant airspeed.
   b. Constant rate.
5. Magnetic compass.
6. Timed turns.
7. Steep turns.

Phase II. Radio Navigation.
1. VOR and ADF.
   a. Orientation.
   b. Time/distance checks.
   c. Interception of predetermined radial or bearing.
   d. Course (radial/bearing) following.
   e. Identification of position.
      (1) Intersections.
      (2) Off-course, including off-course corrections.
      (3) Arrival over station.
   f. Holding and transitions.
2. Instrument approach procedures.
   a. VOR.
   b. ADF.
   c. ILS.
   d. Radar approaches.
3. Departures, routings, and arrivals.
4. ATC procedures.
   a. Clearances.
   b. Position reporting.
   c. Emergencies.

Flight Training

Phase I. Basic Instruments.
1. Preflight procedures.
2. Takeoff procedures.

3. Techniques, procedures, and operating limitations in the use of basic flight instruments.
   a. Altimeter.
   b. Airspeed indicator.
   c. Vertical-speed indicator.
   d. Attitude indicator.
   e. Turn and slip indicator.
   f. Heading indicator.
   g. Magnetic compass.
4. Airwork.
   a. Straight-and-level flight—pitch, bank, and power control.
   b. Turns and turns to predetermined headings, including timed turns.
   c. Climbs and descents (Constant rate).
   d. Climbs and descents (Constant airspeed).
   e. Stalls and maneuvering at approach speeds.
   f. Steep turns.
   g. Recovery from unusual attitudes.

Phase II. Communications, Departures, En route Navigation, and Arrivals Under Instrument Flight Rules.
1. Preparation of flight plan, including use of charts, aircraft performance data, weather services, Airman's Information Manual, Airport/Facility Directory, Notices to Airmen (Class II), and Graphic Notices and Supplemental Data.
2. Arrival estimates—for flight planning and en route revisions.
3. Tuning radio equipment.
   a. Selection of frequencies.
   b. Use of equipment in flight.
4. Orientation by radio (ADF and VOR).
   a. Identification of position.
   b. Time/distance from station.
5. Course following.
6. Identification of position.
   a. Intersections.
   b. Off course, including off-course corrections.
7. Holding
8. Instrument approach procedures.
   a. Use of Area Charts and Instrument Approach Charts.
   b. ADF, VOR, ILS, RNAV, and radar approaches.
   c. Missed approaches.
9. Air Traffic Control Procedures.
   a. Flight Plan.
   b. Clearances.
   c. Emergencies

II. INSTRUMENT FLYING:
COPING WITH ILLUSIONS IN FLIGHT

One purpose in instrument training and in maintaining instrument proficiency is to prevent us from being misled by several types of hazardous illusions that are peculiar to flight. In general, an illusion or false impression occurs when information provided by our sensory organs is misinterpreted or inadequate. Many illusions in flight can be created by complex motions and certain visual scenes that we encounter under adverse weather conditions and at night. Some illusions may lead to spatial disorientation or the inability to determine accurately the attitude or motion of the aircraft in relation to the Earth's surface. Other illusions may lead to landing errors. Spatial disorientation as a result of continued VFR flight into adverse weather conditions is regularly near the top of the cause/factor list in annual statistics on fatal aircraft accidents. Knowledge, good judgment, and proficient instrument flying skills are needed to improve these statistics and help insure safe flying.

This chapter provides the basic knowledge we must have to understand the various illusions encountered in flight, to respect their serious consequences, and to enable us to cope with them effectively.

Sensory Systems for Orientation

We use three sensory systems for orientation: the visual system; the motion sensing system in the inner ear; and the position sensing system involving nerves in the skin, muscles, and joints. These systems work together so effectively when we are on the ground that we seldom have any difficulty with orientation.

Vision is obviously our major sensory organ for orientation while moving about on the ground and during VFR flight. Under VFR conditions, aircraft attitude can be determined by observing the Earth's surface, which usually provides accurate and be-

8

lievable visual information. However, under IFR conditions, aircraft attitude can only be determined accurately by observing and interpreting the flight instruments.

In the absence of reliable visual information from the Earth's surface, we become more aware of information provided by our motion and position sensing systems. Unfortunately, the sensations of motion and position during various flight maneuvers are often quite misleading, and even tend to compel us to believe them rather than information from the flight instruments.

Illusions Leading to Spatial Disorientation

The most hazardous illusions that lead to spatial disorientation are created by information received from our motion sensing system, located in each inner ear. As shown in Figure 2–1, this fluid-filled system consists of three semicircular tubes connected to a sac. Sensory organs in the tubes detect angular acceleration in the pitch, yaw, and roll axes, and a sensory organ in the sac detects gravity and linear acceleration. In flight, our motion sensing system may be stimulated by motion of the aircraft alone, or in combination with head and body movement. Unfortunately, the system is not capable of detecting a constant velocity or small changes in velocity (see Figure 2–1). Nor is it capable of distinguishing between centrifugal force and gravity as shown in Figure 2–2. In addition, the motion sensing system, functioning normally in flight, can produce false sensations. For example, deceleration while turning in one direction can produce the sensation of turning in the opposite direction, an illusion which can be corrected only by overriding the sensations from the inner ear by adequate outside visual references or by proper reading of flight instruments.

The major illusions leading to spatial disorientation are:

"The leans"—A banked attitude, to the left for example, may be entered too slowly to set in motion the fluid in the "roll" semicircular tubes. An abrupt correction of this attitude can now set the fluid in motion and so create the illusion of a banked attitude to the right. The disoriented pilot may make the error of rolling the aircraft back into the original left-banked attitude or, if level flight is maintained, will feel compelled to lean to the left until this illusion subsides.

"Coriolis illusion"—An abrupt head movement made during a prolonged constant-rate turn may set the fluid in more than one semicircular tube in motion, creating the strong illusion of turning or accelerating in an entirely different axis. The disoriented pilot may maneuver the aircraft into a dangerous attitude in an attempt to correct this illusory movement.

"Graveyard spin"—In a prolonged spin the fluid in the semicircular tubes which are in the axis of the spin will cease its motion (see Figure 2–1). The deceleration that occurs during recovery to level flight will again set this fluid in motion, creating an illusion of spinning in the opposite direction. The disoriented pilot may return the aircraft to its original spin.

"Graveyard spiral"—In a prolonged coordinated, constant-rate turn, the fluid in the semicircular tubes in the axis of the turn will cease its movement (see Figure 2–1). An observed loss of altitude in the aircraft instruments and the absence of any sensation of turning may create the illusion of being in a descent with the wings level. The disoriented pilot may pull back on the controls, tightening the spiral and increasing the loss of altitude.

"Somatogravic illusion"—A rapid acceleration during takeoff excessively stimulates the sensory organs for gravity and linear acceleration, and so creates the illusion of being in a nose-up attitude. The disoriented pilot may push the aircraft into a nose-low or dive attitude. A rapid deceleration by quick reduction of the throttle(s) can have the opposite effect, with the disoriented pilot pulling the aircraft into a nose-up or stall attitude.

"Inversion illusion"—An abrupt change from climb to straight-and-level flight can excessively stimulate the sensory organs for gravity and linear acceleration, creating the illusion of tumbling backwards. The disoriented pilot may push the aircraft abruptly into a nose-low attitude, possibly intensifying this illusion.

"Elevator illusion"—An abrupt upward vertical acceleration, as can occur in a helicopter or an updraft, can shift vision downwards (visual scene moves upwards) through excessive stimulation of the sensory organs for gravity and linear acceleration, creating the illusion of being in a climb. The disoriented pilot may push the aircraft into a nose-low attitude. An abrupt downward vertical acceleration, usually in a downdraft, has the opposite effect, with the disoriented pilot pulling the aircraft into a nose-up attitude.

"False horizon"—A sloping cloud formation, an obscured horizon, a dark scene spread with ground lights and stars, and certain geometric patterns of ground lights can provide inaccurate visual information for aligning the aircraft correctly with the actual horizon. The disoriented pilot may place the aircraft in a dangerous attitude.

"Autokinesis"—In the dark, a stationary light will appear to move about when stared at for many seconds. The disoriented pilot could lose control of the aircraft in attempting to align it with the false movements of this light.

Aircraft Maneuvers for Demonstrating Spatial Disorientation

There are a number of controlled aircraft maneuvers that an instructor pilot can perform to give a student pilot experience with spatial disorientation. Each maneuver will normally create a specific illusion. However, *any* false sensation is an effective

Our motion sensing system is located in each inner ear in the approximate position shown.

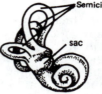

Enlarged, this system is shaped about as shown. It contains fluid and the sensory organs for detecting angular acceleration, and gravity and linear acceleration.

ANGULAR ACCELERATION

The semicircular tubes are arranged at approximately right angles to each other, in the roll, pitch and yaw axes.

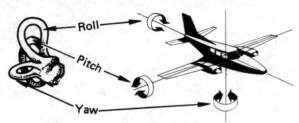

A sensory organ, which consists of small sensory hairs that project into a gelantinous substance, is located in each tube. When the head starts to turn (angular acceleration), or speeds up, slows down, or stops its turning, the sensory hairs in the tube in the axis of turning are temporarily deflected due to the motion of the fluid lagging behind the motion of the tube wall. This causes the sensation of turning.

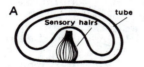

NO TURNING

No sensation

START OF TURN

Sensation of turning as moving fluid deflects hairs.

CONSTANT RATE TURN

No sensation after fluid accelerates to same speed as tube wall

TURN STOPPED

Sensation of turning in opposite direction as moving fluid deflects hairs in opposite direction.

GRAVITY AND LINEAR ACCELERATION

A sensory organ for detecting gravity and linear acceleration is located in the bottom and side of the sac. It consists of small sensory hairs that project upward into a gelatinous substance containing chalk-like crystals. The weight borne by these sensory hairs changes with every head movement with respect to gravity and with every linear acceleration (up, down, left, right, forward, backward), so causing the sensation of tilting the head or body.

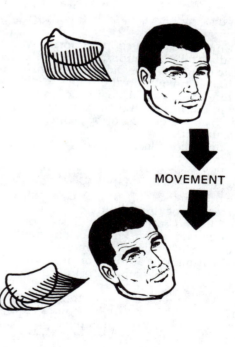

MOVEMENT

FIGURE 2–1. Motion sensing system.

10

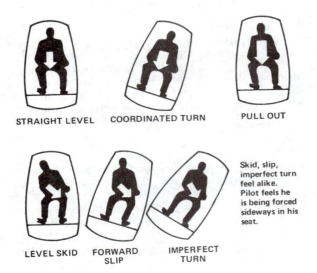

STRAIGHT LEVEL   COORDINATED TURN   PULL OUT

LEVEL SKID   FORWARD SLIP   IMPERFECT TURN

Skid, slip, imperfect turn feel alike. Pilot feels he is being forced sideways in his seat.

FIGURE 2–2. Sensations from centrifugal force.

demonstration of disorientation. Thus, should there be no sensation during any of these maneuvers, the absence of sensation is still an effective demonstration in that it shows inability to detect bank or roll.

"Climbing While Accelerating"—With the student's eyes closed, the instructor maintains approach airspeed in a straight-and-level attitude for several seconds, and then accelerates while maintaining straight-and-level attitude. The usual illusion during this maneuver, without visual references, will be that the aircraft is climbing.

"Climbing While Turning"—With the student's eyes still closed and the aircraft in a straight-and-level attitude, the instructor pilot now executes, with a relatively slow entry, a well-coordinated turn of about 1½ positive G for 90°. While in the turn, without outside visual references, and under the effect of the slight positive G, the usual illusion produced is that of a climb. Upon sensing the climb, the student should immediately open the eyes and see that a slowly-established, coordinated turn produces the same feeling as that of a climb.

"Diving While Turning"—This sensation can be created by repeating the above procedure, with the exception that the student's eyes should be kept closed until recovery from the turn is approximately one-half completed. When the eyes are closed, the usual illusion will be that the aircraft is diving.

"Tilting to Right or Left"—While in a straight-and-level attitude, with the student's eyes closed, the instructor executes a moderate or slight skid to the left with wings level. The usual illusion is that the body is being tilted to the right.

"Reversal of Motion"—This illusion can be demonstrated in any of the three planes of motion. While straight-and-level, with the student's eyes closed, the instructor smoothly and positively rolls the aircraft to approximately a 45° bank attitude while maintaining heading and pitch attitude. The usual illusion is a strong sense of rotation in the opposite direction. After this illusion is noted, the student should open the eyes and observe that the aircraft is in a banked attitude.

"Diving or Rolling Beyond the Vertical Plane"— This maneuver may produce extreme disorientation. While in straight-and-level flight, the student should sit normally, either with eyes closed or gaze lowered to the floor. The instructor starts a positive, coordinated roll toward a 30° or 40° angle of bank. As this is in progress, the student should tilt the head forward, look to the right or left, then immediately return the head to an upright position. The instructor should so time the maneuver that the roll is stopped just as the student returns the head upright. An intense disorientation is usually produced by this maneuver, with the student experiencing the sensation of falling downwards into the direction of the roll.

There are several objectives in demonstrating these various maneuvers.

(i) They indoctrinate student pilots in understanding the susceptibility of the human system to spatial disorientation.

(ii) They demonstrate that judgments of aircraft attitude based on bodily sensations are frequently false.

(iii) They can help to lessen the occurrence and degree of disorientation through a better understanding of the relationship between aircraft motion, head movements, and resulting disorientation.

(iv) They can help to instill a greater confidence in relying on flight instruments for assessing true aircraft attitude.

None of these familiarization maneuvers should be attempted by a student pilot in the absence of an instructor pilot, or at low altitude.

How to Cope with Spatial Disorientation

We can take action to prevent these illusions and their potentially disastrous consequences if we:

1. Always obtain preflight weather briefings.
2. Do not continue flight into adverse weather conditions or into dusk or darkness unless proficient in the use of flight instruments.
3. Ensure that when outside visual references are used, they are reliable, fixed points on the Earth's surface.
4. Avoid sudden head movements, particularly during takeoffs, turns, and approaches to landing.
5. Remember that illness, medication, alcohol, fatigue, sleep loss, and mild hypoxia are likely to increase susceptibility to spatial disorientation.
6. Most importantly, become proficient in the use of flight instruments and rely upon them.

The sensations which lead to illusions during instrument flight conditions are normal perceptions experienced by normal individuals. These undesirable sensations cannot be completely prevented, but they can and must be ignored or sufficiently suppressed by developing absolute reliance upon what the flight instruments are telling us about the attitude of our aircraft.

Practice and experience in instrument flying are necessary to aid us in discounting or overcoming false sensations. As additional proficiency in instrument flying is acquired, we become less susceptible to these false sensations and their effects.

Illusions Leading to Landing Errors

Of the senses, vision is the most important for safe flight. However, various surface features and atmospheric conditions encountered when landing can create illusions of incorrect height above, and distance from, the runway threshold. The major illusions leading to landing errors are:

"Runway width illusion"—A narrower-than-usual runway can create an illusion that the aircraft is at a higher altitude than it actually is (see Figure 2–3), especially when runway length-to-width relationships are comparable. The pilot who does not recognize this illusion will fly a lower approach, with the risk of striking objects along the approach path or landing short. A wider-than-usual runway can have the opposite effect, with the risk of leveling out high and landing hard or overshooting the runway.

"Runway and terrain slopes illusion"—An upsloping runway, upsloping terrain, or both, can create an illusion that the aircraft is at a higher altitude than it actually is (see Figure 2–4). The pilot who does not recognize this illusion will fly a lower approach. A downsloping runway, downsloping approach terrain, or both, can have the opposite effect.

"Featureless terrain illusion"—an absence of surrounding ground features, as when approaching over water, darkened areas, or terrain made featureless by snow, can create an illusion that the

aircraft is at a higher altitude than it actually is. The pilot who does not recognize this illusion will fly a lower approach.

"Atmospheric illusions"—Rain on the windscreen can create an illusion of being at a higher altitude, while atmospheric haze can create an illusion of being at a greater distance from a runway. The pilot who does not recognize these illusions will fly a lower approach. Penetration of fog can create an illusion of pitching up. The pilot who does not recognize this illusion will steepen the approach, often quite abruptly.

"Ground lighting illusions"—Lights along a straight path, such as a road, and even lights on moving trains can be mistaken for runway and approach lights. Bright runway and approach lighting systems, especially where few lights illuminate the surrounding terrain, may create the illusion of less distance to the runway. The pilot who does not recognize this illusion will fly a higher approach.

How to Prevent Landing Errors From Visual Illusions

We can take action to prevent these illusions and their potentially hazardous consequences if we:

1. Anticipate the possibility of visual illusions during approaches to unfamiliar airports, particularly at night or in adverse weather conditions.

2. Conduct aerial visual inspection of unfamiliar airports before landing.

3. Use the fixed and reliable VASI systems for a visual reference, or an electronic glideslope, whenever they are available.

4. Recognize that the chances of being involved in an approach accident are increased when some emergency or other activity distracts from usual procedures.

5. Maintain optimum proficiency in landing procedures.

6. Most importantly, make frequent reference to the altimeter. this instrument should be a primary aid during all approaches—day and night.

A narrower-than-usual runway can
create an illusion that the aircraft
is higher than it actually is, leading
to a lower approach.

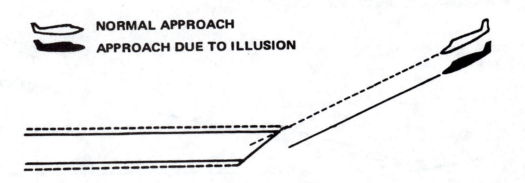

NORMAL APPROACH
APPROACH DUE TO ILLUSION

A wider-than-usual runway can create
an illusion that the aircraft is lower
than it actually is, leading to a
higher approach.

FIGURE 2–3. Runway width illusion.

13

An upsloping runway can create the illusion that the aircraft is higher than it actually is, leading to a lower approach.

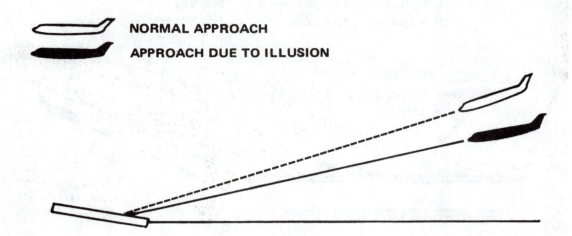

NORMAL APPROACH

APPROACH DUE TO ILLUSION

A downsloping runway can create the illusion that the aircraft is lower than it actually is, leading to a higher approach.

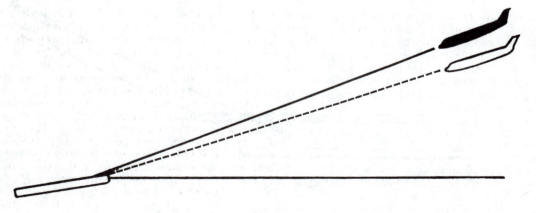

FIGURE 2–4. Runway slope illusion.

14

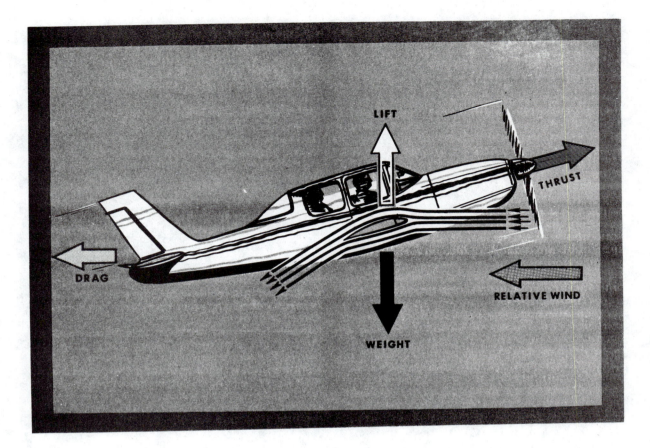

III. AERODYNAMIC FACTORS RELATED TO INSTRUMENT FLYING

You will be concerned in this section with the forces affecting aircraft performance caused by the interaction of air and the aircraft. With an understanding of these forces, you will have a sound basis for predicting how the aircraft will respond to your control. Important as these forces are to the VFR pilot, they must be even more thoroughly understood by the student of instrument flying. You will find, as you learn the basic instrument flying maneuvers, that your understanding of *why* the aircraft reacts in a particular way to your control is the key to your interpretation of information shown on the instrument panel. The importance of these aerodynamic forces and their direct application to your execution of aircraft maneuvers will be evident. Several basic aerodynamic definitions apply to a discussion of these forces.

If a flat plate is moved through the air (Fig. 3–1), the airstream which strikes the plate is forced downward on impact against the plate. The reaction to this downward force produces a resultant force

upward (lift) and a backward force (drag). A rock or a barn door will fly, given an airstream sufficient to produce lift. More efficient is the airfoil, a surface constructed to produce the maximum lift with the minimum drag. Airfoil shapes vary according to the aircraft performance to which the airfoil is designed. The most efficient shape, for the type of aircraft used for civilian instrument training, has a rounded leading edge, smooth cambered surfaces, and a sharp trailing edge.

As the wing moves through the air, the airstream is divided, part of it flowing over one surface while the remainder flows under the other surface (Fig. 3–2). The air flowing over the upper cambered surface, as shown in the diagram, has a longer path to travel and has to flow faster than the air over the opposite surface to reach the trailing edge at the same time. Application of Bernoulli's principle to both Venturi tube and airfoil shows that the air flowing faster exerts the lesser pressure. Because of the resulting differential pressure, the wing is

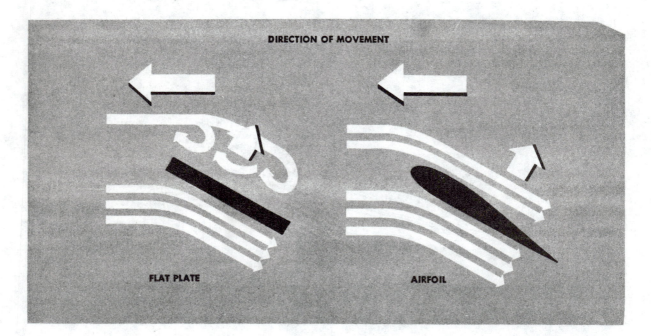

DIRECTION OF MOVEMENT

FLAT PLATE

AIRFOIL

FIGURE 3–1. The airfoil.

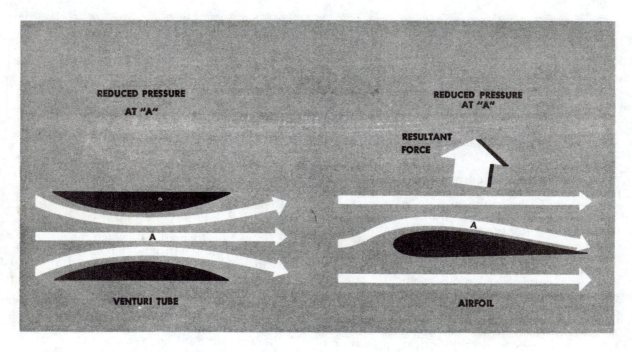

REDUCED PRESSURE
AT "A"

REDUCED PRESSURE
AT "A"

RESULTANT
FORCE

A

A

VENTURI TUBE

AIRFOIL

FIGURE 3–2. Venturi action.

supported by the higher pressure below the lower surface.

Lift is also produced at the leading edge when it is so designed that the approaching airstream divides near the lower part of the airfoil.

The trailing edge of the wing is also designed for efficient airflow. If the trailing edge were rounded, the lower stream of air would tend to curve around into the area of lower pressure along the upper surface, introducing undesirable forces opposing

16

lift on the after part of the airfoil. A sharp trailing edge permits smooth flow of the upper and lower airstreams past the trailing edge.

The lift/drag characteristics which are determined by airfoil design are affected by other basic factors related to control of aircraft performance.

The relative wind (Fig. 3–3) is the motion of the air relative to the chord line of the airfoil. The air can be moving past the airfoil or the airfoil can be moving through the air. The relative wind, as applied to airplanes, is parallel and opposite to the flight path of the aircraft.

The angle of attack is the acute angle measured between the chord line of the wing and the relative wind—not between the chord line and the Earth's surface. The chord line of an airfoil is merely a conveniently chosen reference line in the wing to measure the real or theoretical width of the wing.

A stall is the result of any condition that disrupts the smooth flow of air over the airfoil to the point where sufficient lift is no longer produced by the differential pressure. The wing can stall in any attitude and at any speed. As the angle of attack of the wing is increased, the air particles are forced to make sharper and sharper changes in direction to follow the contour of the wing. With increasing angles of attack, disruption of smooth airflow occurs initially at the trailing edge and moves forward toward the leading edge at higher angles of attack. The wing stalls when the progressive increase in turbulence on the top cambered surface results in a net loss of lift (Fig. 3–4).

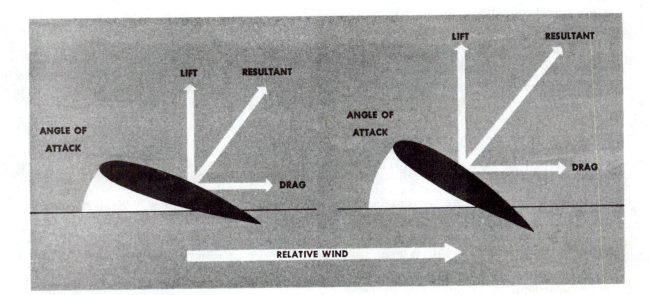

FIGURE 3–3. Relative wind.

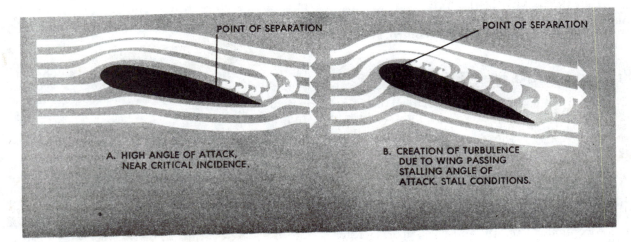

FIGURE 3–4. Angle of attack and stall.

17

Aerodynamic Forces

Lift always acts in a direction perpendicular to the relative wind and to the lateral axis of the aircraft. The fact that lift is referenced to the wing, *not* to the Earth's surface, is the source of many errors in learning flight control. Lift is not always "up." Its direction relative to the Earth's surface changes as you maneuver the aircraft. The magnitude of the force of lift is directly proportional to the density of the air, the area of the wings, and the airspeed. It also depends upon the type of wing and the angle of attack. Lift increases with an increase in angle of attack up to the stalling angle, at which point it decreases with any further increase in angle of attack. In conventional aircraft, lift is therefore controlled by varying angle of attack (attitude) and thrust.

Drag is the total resistance of the air to the movement of the aircraft. Drag acts opposite to the direction of flight of the aircraft and is parallel to the relative wind. Induced drag is the result of the same inherent aerodynamic forces that produce lift. Parasite drag is the resistance to airflow caused by inefficient streamlining, skin friction, and projections into the airstream. Total drag is the sum of induced and parasite drag and is affected by airspeed and air density as well as the other factors noted. Changes in drag, whether induced during attitude changes or the result of gear and/or flap extensions, are reflected in performance changes indicated on your flight instruments.

Thrust in conventional propeller-driven aircraft is the force acting forward with respect to the longitudinal axis of the aircraft. The amount of thrust is determined by the power output of the engine, and for all practical purposes acts parallel to the longitudinal axis. Use of power controls thrust, and therefore lift and performance.

Weight is the force of gravity acting on the aircraft and is always downward toward the center of the Earth regardless of aircraft attitude and flight path. Both the total weight and its distribution affect aircraft flight characteristics. The relationship of these fundamental factors to aircraft performance in various basic flight attitudes and conditions must be understood if you are to control your aircraft with precision.

Straight-and-Level Flight

Straight-and-level flight is a performance term meaning that an aircraft is maintaining a constant indicated altitude and a constant heading. In coordinated, unaccelerated, straight-and-level flight, weight acts downward toward the center of the Earth; lift acts perpendicular to the relative wind and is equal and opposite to weight; drag acts parallel to the relative wind; and thrust acts forward, parallel to the longitudinal axis, and equal and opposite to drag.

In coordinated, straight-and-level, unaccelerated flight, all opposing forces are balanced (Fig. 3–5),

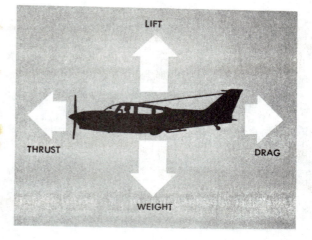

FIGURE 3–5.   Forces in straight-and-level unaccelerated flight.

and as long as the specific flight attitude and thrust are maintained, altitude and heading remain constant. Any variation in these forces requires a different attitude (relationship of the aircraft's longitudinal and lateral axes with the Earth's surface) if the aircraft is to maintain level flight.

Three factors affect attitude in maintaining level flight—airspeed, air density, and aircraft weight.

(1) *Airspeed.*—At a constant angle of attack, any change in airspeed will vary the lift. At low airspeeds, the angle of attack must be proportionately greater to produce the lift necessary for level flight. The aircraft must therefore be flown in a nose-high attitude to maintain level flight at low speeds. At progressively higher airspeeds, the angle of attack necessary to produce sufficient lift for level flight becomes smaller, and the nose of the aircraft is accordingly lowered. Assuming that weight remains constant, any specific airspeed in unaccelerated level flight is associated with a specific thrust and attitude. In other words, if more power is applied than required for level flight, the aircraft will accelerate if held level, or climb if airspeed is held constant.

(2) *Air Density.*—Lift varies directly with changes in air density, which decreases as either altitude, air temperature, or humidity increases. Thus, to maintain level flight at a given true airspeed, the angle of attack of an airfoil must be greater at higher altitudes and/or outside air temperatures than at lower altitudes and/or temperatures. To maintain level flight at high "density altitudes," the aircraft attitude must be relatively nose-high.

(3) *Aircraft Weight.*—For a given weight and airspeed, a specific angle of attack is required to maintain straight-and-level flight. To support heavier loads at a given airspeed, the angle of attack must be relatively greater to provide the necessary lift. To overcome the induced drag resulting from the increased angle of attack, more thrust is also needed to maintain the given airspeed.

Climbs

For all practical purposes, the lift in normal climbs is the same as in level flight at the same airspeed. Though the flight path has changed, the angle of attack of the wing with respect to the flight path remains the same, as does the lift. There is a momentary change, however, as shown in Figure 3–6. In going from straight-and-level flight to a climb, a change in lift occurs when back elevator pressure is applied. Raising the nose increases the angle of attack and momentarily increases the lift. Lift, now greater than weight, causes the aircraft to climb. The flight path is inclined upward, and the angle of attack and lift again stabilize.

If the climb is entered without a change in power setting, the airspeed gradually diminishes because the thrust required to maintain a given airspeed in level flight is insufficient to maintain the same airspeed in a climb. Due to momentum, the change in airspeed is gradual, varying considerably with differences in aircraft size, weight, total drag, and other factors. As the angle of attack changes, a component of the weight acts in the same direction, and parallel to, the total drag of the aircraft, thereby increasing the total drag and decreasing the airspeed. The reduction in airspeed results in a corresponding decrease in drag until the total drag (including the component of weight acting in the same direction) equals the thrust.

The forces are again balanced when the airspeed stabilizes at a value lower than in straight-and-level flight at the same power setting. Lift is equal in magnitude to the component of weight that is perpendicular to the flight path. In a climb, this perpendicular weight component is only part of the weight, the other component acting to increase the total drag. Because the latter component must be balanced by thrust, you must increase thrust (power) to maintain constant airspeed on entering a climb from level flight, the amount of power depending on the change in angle of attack.

Descents

On entering a normal descent from straight-and-level flight without a change in power, a disturbance in balanced forces likewise occurs. As a result of forward pressure on the elevator controls, the angle of attack is reduced and the lift proportionately reduced. The weight being greater than the lift, the aircraft follows a descending flight path. A component of the weight now acts forward along the flight path parallel to the thrust, causing a gradual increase in airspeed as well as an increase in drag. When the angle of attack stabilizes and the lift/weight and thrust/drag forces again balance, the aircraft descends at a constant airspeed. Therefore, to enter a descent from level flight, maintaining a constant airspeed, you must decrease power to prevent an increase in thrust resulting from the forward alignment of the weight component.

Power, Airspeed, and Vertical Speed

In a descent, the component of weight acting forward along the flight path increases as the angle of descent increases and decreases as the angle of descent decreases. The power reduction required to maintain a given airspeed in the descent, depends on the rate of descent desired. For example, a high rate of descent at a specific airspeed, requires a greater power reduction than does a lower rate of descent. The proper combination of pitch attitudes, airspeeds, vertical velocities, and power settings for climbs and descents must be learned for each individual aircraft. Having learned the principles and techniques for the execution of these maneuvers for one aircraft, you can readily apply them to other aircraft.

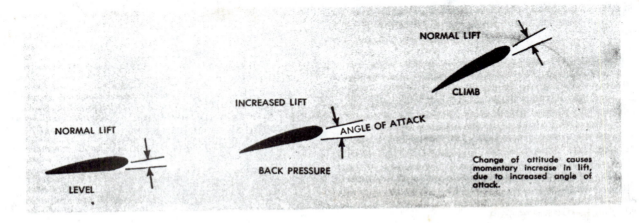

FIGURE 3–6. Climb entry.

Power, Airspeed, and Elevator Control

Rotating the aircraft about the lateral axis is accomplished by forward or aft movement of the elevator control to displace the elevators. The use of the elevators varies with changes in power and airspeed. The slip stream striking the elevators in a downward direction creates a negative angle of attack for the elevators and causes them to exert a negative lift. Changes in power and airspeed vary the amount of downwash and the resulting negative lift exerted by the elevators. As power and airspeed increase, slipstream velocity and downwash lift on the elevators increases. At the same time, lift on the wing increases and the aircraft has a nose-high tendency. Therefore, if the aircraft is trimmed for level flight, an increase in power and airspeed must be accompanied by forward pressure on the controls if you are to remain in level flight.

A decrease in power and/or airspeed has the opposite effect. The negative lift on the elevators and the lift on the wing decrease, resulting in a nose-low tendency. As you reduce power and/or airspeed, you must hold back pressure on the controls to maintain level flight.

Trim

In the simplest terms, trim may be thought of as balance, which is affected by design, loading, atmospheric conditions, and the aerodynamic factors already considered. Aircraft are designed so that weight always acts through a point called the center of gravity, located along the longitudinal axis at some point within specified limits behind the leading edge of the wing. Likewise, lift acts through a point called the center of pressure, located aft of the center of gravity. Since these two points do not coincide, lift and weight exert a twisting force resulting in a normal nose-heaviness. The twisting force is balanced by the negative lift produced by the horizontal stabilizer and elevators. However, as shown earlier, elevator control and the negative lift of the elevators vary with power/airspeed changes, requiring control application as the balanced forces are disturbed. Aircraft balance is affected not only by design and performance factors, but also by the shifting of the center of gravity and the center of pressure in flight, by the rigging of the aircraft, and by the action of torque and P-factor effects in propeller-driven aircraft.

With the application of power in propeller-driven aircraft, torque yaws the nose of the aircraft to the left. This yaw is controlled by the rudder, and the effectiveness of the rudder depends upon the amount of rudder displacement and the airflow. The airflow depends upon the airspeed and slip-stream velocity. Consequently, the nose will also tend to yaw to the left if airspeed is reduced while the power remains constant. Torque control thus depends upon airspeed, technique in the application or reduction of power, and the amount of torque inducing the yaw.

All of the above factors affecting changes in aircraft balance can be counteracted in light aircraft without the use of trim controls. In fact, many pilots commonly neglect proper trim technique and maintain continual control pressures to hold the aircraft in the desired stabilized attitude. This is not only fatiguing, but undesirable for additional reasons to be considered later. Trim devices vary in different aircraft.

In the simplest light aircraft, only an elevator trim control is provided. If such aircraft are used for instrument training, yawing or rolling tendencies must be counteracted by holding aileron and/or rudder pressures to maintain the desired aircraft attitude. With increased aircraft performance, rudder and elevator trim controls are essential, and in high performance or transport-type aircraft, aileron trim control is also necessary. In many light aircraft having no aileron trim control, the left/right fuel selector has a trim function. Wing heaviness on either side, requiring aileron control to maintain attitude, can be corrected by fuel consumption from the heavy side.

Turns

Many of the common misconceptions associated with aircraft performance and pilot control techniques are traceable to ignorance of aerodynamic forces and their varying effects as the aircraft is maneuvered. Our thinking and terminology are oriented to the ground rather than to the air, and these contribute to misunderstandings. For example, we think of "up" and "down" as referenced vertically to the Earth's surface, and the elevators (also a ground-referenced term) as the means of up/down control. Back elevator control pressure should mean "up," and forward elevator, "down." This is true to varying degrees and under certain flight conditions. Under other conditions, back elevator control pressure will fail to produce any "up" result. A related misconception is that because weight always acts downward, lift always acts upward and opposite to weight. This is not always so.

Another mistaken notion is that an aircraft is turned by the rudder(s). This is understandable since the term "rudder" implies a turning function. Further, since the rudder controls rotation about the vertical axis, does it not follow that the aircraft is turned by rudder action? True, you *can* turn an aircraft by moving the rudder. You can also bank the aircraft, or move the nose up, by rudder control, just as you can raise or lower the nose by power changes. Because of these *effects* of control application, misconceptions understandably arise as to the proper *function* of the controls. The fact that the rudder is normally used in turning a conventional aircraft, or that the throttle is used in the execution of climbs and descents simply means that yaw must be controlled in a properly executed turn, and that thrust must be controlled to climb or descend under specified conditions. The interrelated functions of the controls will be clearer as you study the aerodynamics of a turn.

Forces Acting on an Aircraft in Turns

An aircraft, like any moving object, requires a sideward force to make it turn. In a normal turn, this force is supplied by banking the aircraft so that lift is exerted inward as well as upward. The force of lift is thus separated into two components at right angles to each other (Fig. 3–7). The lift acting upward and opposing weight is called the *vertical lift component.* The lift acting horizontally and opposing centrifugal force is called the *horizontal lift component.* The *horizontal lift component* is the sideward force that causes an aircraft to turn. The equal and opposite reaction to this sideward force is centrifugal force. If an aircraft is not banked, no force is provided to make it turn unless the turn is skidded by rudder application. Likewise, if an aircraft is banked, it will turn unless held on a constant heading in a slip. Proper instrument interpretation and aircraft control technique assumes that an aircraft is turned by banking, and that in a banking attitude it should be turning.

Changes in Lift in a Turn

Banking an aircraft in a level turn does not by itself produce a change in the *amount* of lift. However, the division of lift into horizontal and vertical components reduces the amount of lift supporting the weight of the aircraft. Consequently, the reduced vertical component results in the loss of altitude unless the total lift is increased by (1) increasing the angle of attack of the wing, (2) increasing the airspeed, or (3) increasing the angle of attack and airspeed in combination. Assuming a level turn with no change in thrust, you increase the angle of attack by raising the nose until the vertical component of lift is equal to the weight. The greater the angle of bank, the weaker is the vertical lift component, and the greater is the angle of attack for the lift/weight balance necessary to maintain a level turn

Angle of Bank and Rate of Turn

The rate of turn at any given airspeed depends on the amount of sideward force causing the turn; that is, the horizontal lift component. The horizontal lift component varies directly in proportion to bank in a correctly executed turn. Thus, the rate of turn at a given airspeed increases as the angle of bank increases (Fig. 3–8). As the illustration

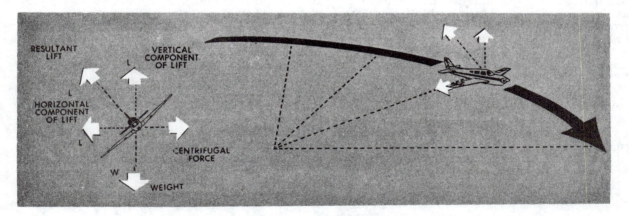

FIGURE 3–7.   Lift components.

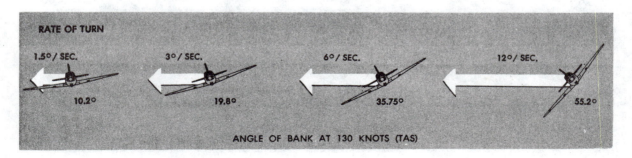

FIGURE 3–8.   Relationship between bank and rate of turn.

21

shows, at 130 knots and approximately 10° of bank, an aircraft completes a 360° turn in 4 minutes. At the same airspeed and approximately 55° of bank, the rate of turn is eight times as great.

Drag Factors in Turns

Drag is induced both by changes in angle of attack and by displacement of the ailerons as the aircraft rolls into, or out of, a turn. As you raise the nose of the aircraft to increase the lift in a level turn, the drag increases directly in proportion to the increase in angle of attack. The resulting decrease in airspeed is, therefore, proportional to the angle of bank. If you wish to maintain constant airspeed in a level turn, you must add power in proportion to the angle of bank used.

If the ailerons alone are used to roll into a turn, the aircraft will tend to yaw in the direction opposite to the direction of turn, the amount of yaw depending upon the amount of aileron displacement and smoothness or abruptness of control technique. Deflection of ailerons increases the lift on the outside wing and decreases the lift on the inside wing. The drag is proportionally increased on the outside wing, resulting in the yawing effect known as "aileron drag" or "adverse yaw." The function of the rudder in a correctly executed entry and recovery from a turn is to counteract this aileron drag. Once the desired bank angle is established and the ailerons are streamlined, no aileron drag exists and the need for rudder control ceases.

Constant Rate Turns

If the airspeed is increased in a turn, the angle of attack must be decreased and/or the angle of bank increased in order to maintain level flight.

As airspeed is increased in a constant-rate level turn, both the radius of turn and centrifugal force increase. This increase in centrifugal force must be balanced by an increase in the horizontal lift com-

ponent, which can be accomplished only by increasing the angle of bank. Thus, to maintain a turn at a constant rate, the angle of bank must be varied with changes in airspeed (Fig. 3–9).

Load Factors and Angle of Bank

A load factor is the ratio of a specified load to the total weight of the airplane. The specified load may be expected in terms of aerodynamic forces, as in turns. In level flight in undisturbed air, the load factor is 1; the wings are supporting only the weight of the airplane. In a coordinated level turn, the wings are supporting not only the weight of the aircraft, but centrifugal force as well. As the bank steepens, the horizontal lift component increases, centrifugal force increases, and the load factor increases (Fig. 3–10). In a coordinated level turn with a 60° bank, the wings support a load equal to twice the weight of the aircraft. To provide the lift to balance this load, the angle of attack must be increased. However, if the load factor becomes so great that an increase in angle of attack cannot provide enough lift to support the load, the wing stalls. Since the stalling speed increases directly with the square root of the load factor, you should be aware of the flight conditions during which the load factor can become critical. Steep turns at low airspeed, structural ice accumulation, and vertical gusts in turbulent air can increase the load factor to a critical level.

Slips and Skids

In straight-and-level, unaccelerated flight, an aircraft points directly along its flight path, except when it is slipping or skidding (Fig. 3–11).

The aircraft may be yawed toward either side of the flight path by rudder action or by incorrect adjustment of the rudder trim tab. The same yawing effect can be caused by inaccurate aileron rigging. If one aileron is deflected slightly downward and the other is aligned properly, the aircraft will

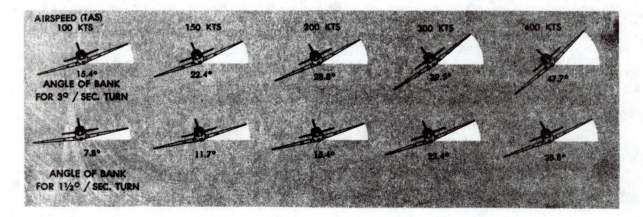

AIRSPEED (TAS)
100 KTS   150 KTS   200 KTS   300 KTS   400 KTS

ANGLE OF BANK
FOR 3° / SEC. TURN
15.4°   22.4°   28.8°   39.5°   47.7°

ANGLE OF BANK
FOR 1½° / SEC. TURN
7.8°   11.7°   15.4°   22.4°   28.8°

FIGURE 3–9. Angle of bank, airspeed, and constant rate turns.

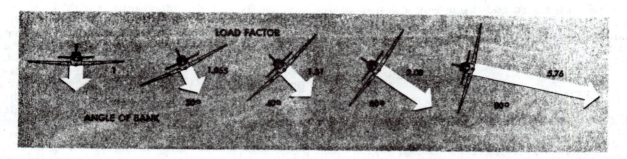

FIGURE 3–10. Relation of load factor to bank.

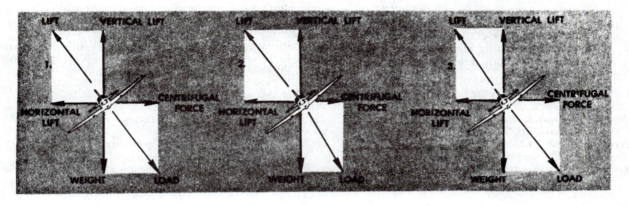

1. Normal turn.
   Centrifugal force equals
   horizontal lift.

2. Slipping turn.
   Centrifugal force less than
   horizontal lift.

3. Skidding turn.
   Centrifugal force greater than
   horizontal lift.

FIGURE 3–11. Forces during normal, slipping, and skidding turns.

tend to yaw in the direction of the down aileron. If the aircraft is in proper trim, with the forces in equilibrium around its pitch, roll, and yaw axes, stabilizing forces will act to maintain this equilibrium. Following a slip or skid, if the aircraft is trimmed for straight-and-level flight and no control forces are held against this stabilizing tendency, the impact of the relative wind against the vertical surfaces will restore the aircraft to proper alignment with the flight path.

To maintain straight flight in propeller-driven aircraft without slipping or skidding, rudder trim must be adjusted following changes in power settings and/or airspeed because the changes in torque effect and the airstream over the vertical tail surfaces varies the directional control. In aircraft having no controllable rudder trim, rudder pressure must be held to maintain directional trim during changes of power and/or airspeed.

Slips.—During a controlled slip, the aircraft is banked, and as noted earlier, the banking normally results in a turn. By application of rudder control opposite the direction of bank, the aircraft is prevented from turning. The banking results in sideways movement of the aircraft with respect to the direction maintained by rudder control.

In a slipping turn—level, climbing, or descending—the aircraft is not turning at the rate appropriate to the bank being used, and the aircraft is yawed toward the outside of the turning flight path. The aircraft is banked too much for the rate of turn, so the horizontal lift component is greater than the centrifugal force. Thus, the ball of the turn-and-slip indicator is displaced in the direction of bank, toward the inside of the turn. Equilibrium between the horizontal lift component and centrifugal force is reestablished either by decreasing the bank, increasing the rate of turn, or a combination of the two changes.

Skids.—A skid occurs in straight-and-level flight when the aircraft yaws either to the right or left, out of alignment with the desired flight path. A skidding turn results from excess of centrifugal force over the horizontal lift component, pulling the aircraft toward the outside of the turn. The rate of turn is too great for the angle of bank, and

23

the ball in the turn-and-slip indicator is displaced toward the outside of the turn. Correction of a skidding turn thus involves a reduction in the rate of turn, an increase in bank, or a combination of the two changes.

Coordination of Rudder and Aileron Controls

Coordination has a very specific meaning as applied to instrument flight techniques. It means using the controls to maintain or establish various conditions of flight with (1) a minimum disturbance of the forces maintaining equilibrium, or (2) the control action necessary to effect the smoothest changes in equilibrium. A controlled slip or skid, for example, requires considerable muscular coordination; the resulting slip or skid, however, is not a coordinated maneuver in the aerodynamic sense.

Coordination of controls during flight by reference to instruments requires that the ball of the turn-and-slip indicator be kept centered, and that available trim control devices be used whenever a change in flight condition disturbs the existing trim. Development of coordinated control technique depends not only on your understanding of the foregoing aerodynamic considerations, but on your attention to the characteristics of the particular type of aircraft in which you train.

Control sensitivities vary considerably in different aircraft and in a given aircraft at various speeds. From experience, you learn that one aircraft is extremely sensitive on rudder control and perhaps noticeably resistant to the movement of elevator control; another aircraft has less than normal lateral stability and tends to overbank; another responds to thrust and drag changes unlike other aircraft. Your application of control pressures must be adapted to each airplane you fly.

Knowing why the aircraft will respond to your control will accelerate your progress in acquiring competent instrument flying techniques.

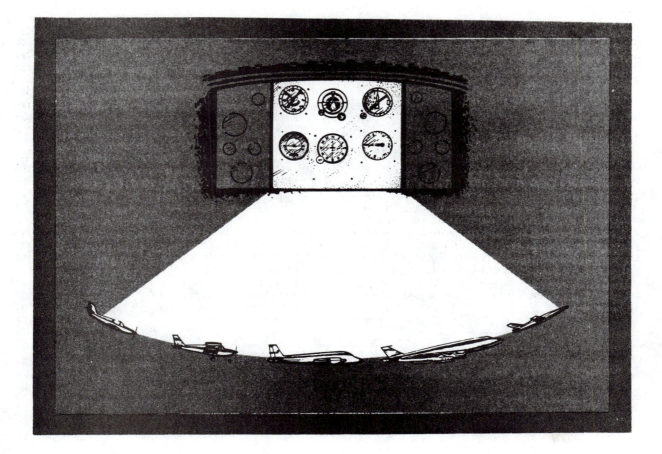

IV. BASIC FLIGHT INSTRUMENTS

If you are among the large group of pilots for whom training cost is a critical consideration, you will be concerned with minimum equipment requirements. The expected cost deters many pilots who have access to aircraft that may be inadequate for weather flying, yet suitable for initial instrument training. An 85-hp light plane will not perform like the latest supercustom light twin, nor will it necessarily take you on instruments where and when you want to go. However, you can acquire substantial basic instrument flying proficiency in any aircraft having the instruments necessary for control of attitude, altitude, speed, and direction. With an altimeter, airspeed indicator, and turn-and-slip indicator (needle/ball or turn coordinator), you have the minimum necessary primary group of instruments. This group is also called the "partial panel" or "emergency panel."

Note that all of the instrument panels shown in Figure 4–1 include the same basic group. Regardless of how elaborately equipped an airplane is, the instrument pilot must know how to use these minimum instruments necessary for aircraft control.

Most of the aircraft currently manufactured for civilian training provide the instruments and equipment required by Federal Aviation Regulation Part 91 for IFR flight. FAR Part 91 also specifies the instruments and equipment needed for daytime Visual Flight Rules and, when applicable, for nighttime Visual Flight Rules.

Pitot Static Instruments

Six basic flight instruments will be discussed in this chapter. The first three to be considered: *pressure altimeter, vertical-speed indicator,* and *airspeed indicator*. Each of these instruments operates in response to pressures through the pitot-static system. Because of the importance of these instruments for safe operation during instrument conditions, you should understand the construction, operation, and use of the pitot-static system and related instruments.

Pitot-static Systems.—Two types of systems are available. Both provide a source of static (atmos-

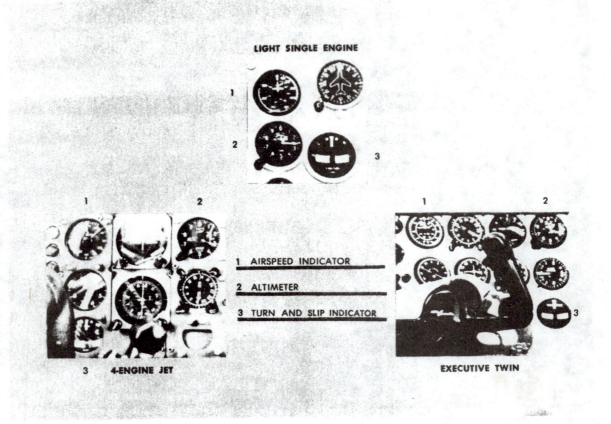

LIGHT SINGLE ENGINE

1 AIRSPEED INDICATOR

2 ALTIMETER

3 TURN AND SLIP INDICATOR

4-ENGINE JET

EXECUTIVE TWIN

FIGURE 4-1.   Partial panel (light single-engine, executive twin, 4-engine jet).

pheric) pressure and impact (ram) pressure to the appropriate instruments. The difference in the systems is largely in the location of the static source (Fig. 4-2).

Of the two systems, the one more recently developed provides for location of the pitot and static sources at separate positions on the aircraft. *Impact pressure* is taken from the pitot tube, mounted parallel to the longitudinal axis and generally in line with the relative wind. The leading edge of the wing, nose section, or vertical stabilizer are the usual mounting positions, where there is a minimum disturbance of air due to motion of the aircraft. Electric heating elements may be installed to remove ice from the pitot head.

Static pressure is taken from the static line attached to the pitot-static head or to a vent or vents mounted flush with the fuselage or nose section. On aircraft using the flush-type static source, there may be two vents, one on each side of the aircraft. These compensate for any possible variation in static pressure on the vents due to erratic changes in aircraft attitude. The vents are connected by a Y-type fitting. Clogging of the pitot opening by ice or dirt (or failure to remove the pitot cover) affects the airspeed indicator only.

Alternate Source of Static Pressure. — In many unpressurized aircraft equipped with a pitot-static tube, an alternate source of static pressure is provided for emergency use. If the alternate source is vented inside the airplane, where static pressure is usually lower than outside static pressure, selection of the alternate source may result in the following instrument indications: the altimeter reads higher than normal; indicated airspeed greater than normal; and the vertical-velocity indicator momentarily shows a climb.

All of these instruments, whether connected to a static source or to both static and pitot lines, operate in response to differences in air pressure that exist within each instrument. The pressure differential is due either to impact and static, or to static and trapped air pressures.

Altitude and Height Measurement

The word "altitude" conveys different meanings to different people involved in aviation. Used by itself, altitude simply means elevation with respect to any assumed reference level. To the aircraft designer, altitude is significant not so much in the sense of height as in the relationship between altitude and air density, which affects aircraft per-

26

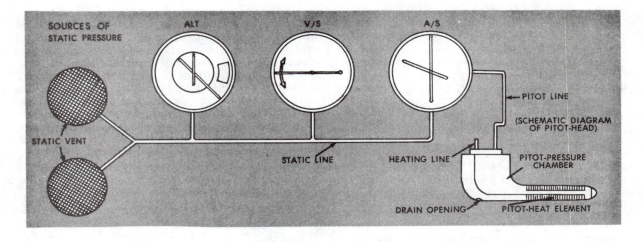

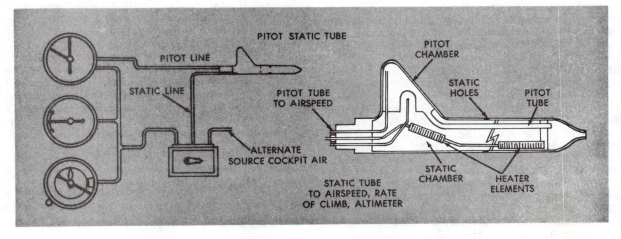

FIGURE 4-2. Pitot-static systems.

formance. To the National Ocean Survey, the surveyed altitude of ground obstructions above sea level is of critical importance, as the pilot depends upon the accuracy of chartered information for ground obstruction clearance. Of special importance is the measurement shown on your altimeter, since this is your immediate source of information in the cockpit. As a pilot, you are concerned with all of these meanings of altitude.

Different terms identify specific meanings of altitude (Fig. 4-3) and various methods of height measurement and computation are necessary to determine them. Altimetry thus involves more than simple measurement of height. Your correct use of the altimeter depends upon your understanding of two basic factors: (1) the reference levels from which height is measured; and (2) the operating principles and limitations of the measuring device. The importance of the reference levels will become apparent as you understand the types of altitude and the pressure altimeter, which is the type of measuring device commonly installed in light aircraft.

Types of Altitude.—Indicated altitude is the altitude read on your altimeter, assuming that the altimeter is correctly adjusted to show the approximate

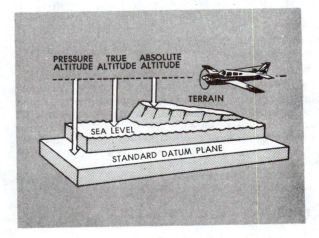

FIGURE 4-3. Types of altitude.

27

height of the aircraft above mean sea level (MSL). Altitudes assigned to aircraft in controlled airspace under Instrument Flight Rules are indicated altitudes, except for flights operating in the high altitude route structure.

Pressure altitude is the altitude read on your altimeter when the instrument is adjusted to indicate height above the Standard Datum Plane. The Standard Datum Plane is a theoretical level where the weight of the atmosphere is 29.92″ of mercury as measured by a barometer. As atmospheric pressure changes, the Standard Datum Plane may be below, at, or above sea level. Pressure altitude is important as a basis for determining aircraft performance as well as for assigning flight levels to aircraft operating at high altitude.

Density altitude is pressure altitude corrected for nonstandard temperature. Under standard atmospheric conditions, each level of air in the atmosphere has a specific density, and under standard conditions, pressure altitude and density altitude identify the same level.

Since aircraft performance data at any level is based upon air density under standard day conditions, such performance data applies to air density levels that may not be identical with altimeter indications. Under conditions higher or lower than standard, these levels cannot be determined directly from the altimeter. For example, your altimeter, set at 29.92″, indicates a pressure altitude of 5,000 feet. According to your aircraft flight manual, your ground run will require 790 feet under standard temperature conditions. However, the temperature is 20° C. above standard, and the expansion of air raises the density levels. Using temperature correction data from tables or graphs or by deriving the density altitude with a computer, you find that the density level is above 7,000 feet, and your ground run will be closer to 1,000 feet.

Absolute altitude is height above the surface. This height may be indicated directly on a radio/radar altimeter, which measures the time interval of a vertical signal bounced from the aircraft to the ground and back. Absolute altitude is essential information for flights over mountainous areas and may be approximately computed from indicated altitude and chart elevation data.

True altitude is true height above sea level. This is a mathematical value determined by computer and therefore based upon standard atmospheric conditions assumed in the computer solution. If the temperature between the surface and the aircraft does not decrease at the standard rate of 2° per 1,000 feet, or if the pressure at flight level is nonstandard, reliance on a computer solution to determine obstruction clearance can be very hazardous.

Pressure Altimeter

The standard pressure altimeter installed in your airplane is far from satisfactory as an accurate instrument for measuring height, though the information it provides is essential for aircraft control and for maintaining terrain clearance and separation from other aircraft under instrument conditions. The limitations of the instrument are due primarily to the fact that its design and operation are based upon its response to conditions that rarely exist. Notwithstanding the limitations, you can use the altimeter as a satisfactory height-measuring instrument if you understand how it responds to nonstandard conditions.

Principle of Operation.—The pressure altimeter operates through the response of trapped air within the instrument to changes in atmospheric pressure. The atmosphere surrounding the earth exerts pressure because of its weight, decreasing at a predictable rate as altitude increases. The pressure altimeter is a barometer that senses changes in atmospheric pressure and, through a gearing mechanism, converts the pressure to an altitude indication in number of feet (Fig. 4–4).

The conversion is based upon a fixed set of values known as the U.S. Standard Atmosphere. As the following table shows, atmospheric conditions are standard when sea level pressure and temperature are 29.92 inches of mercury and 15° C., with a temperature lapse rate (rate of change with increasing altitude) of 2° per 1,000 feet.

U.S. Standard Atmosphere Values

Feet	Pressure (in. of mercury)	Temperature (degrees Centigrade)
16,000	16.21	— 17
15,000	16.88	— 15
14,000	17.57	— 13
13,000	18.29	— 11
12,000	19.03	— 9
11,000	19.79	— 7
10,000	20.58	— 5
9000	21.38	— 3
8000	22.22	— 1
7000	23.09	1
6000	23.98	3
5000	24.89	5
4000	25.84	7
3000	26.81	9
2000	27.82	11
1000	28.86	13
Sea Level	29.92	15

Two essential facts—that conditions are rarely standard and that the altimeter presents you with standard information even when it senses nonstandard conditions—should stress the need for understanding how the altimeter works. The misinformation due to altimeter construction and atmospheric changes must be understood and compensated for.

The basic component of the pressure altimeter is the aneroid wafer (Fig. 4–5). A stack of these hollow, elastic metal wafers expands or contracts as atmospheric pressure changes, and through a shaft and gearing linkage, rotates the pointers on

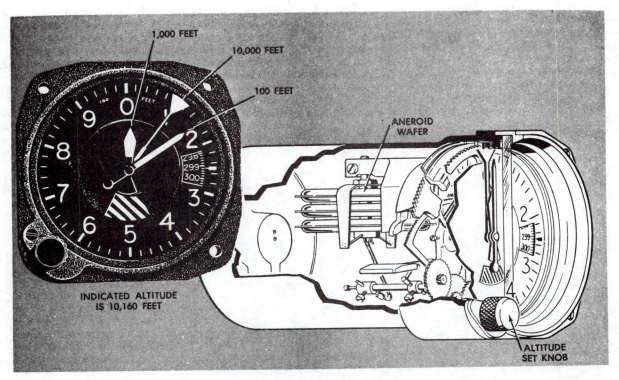

FIGURE 4-4. Altimeter components.

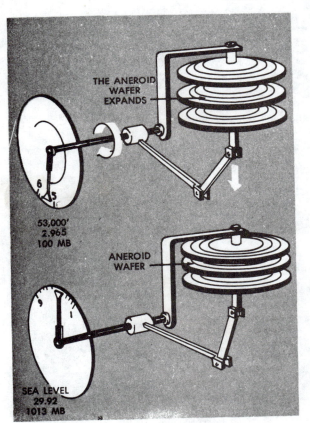

FIGURE 4-5. Operation of the altimeter.

the dial of the instrument. For each pressure level, the aneroid assumes a definite size and causes the hands to indicate height above whatever pressure level is set into the altimeter setting window.

The *altimeter setting dial* provides a means of adjusting the altimeter for nonstandard pressure. For better understanding of the altimeter setting mechanism, assume an altimeter calibrated according to the standard values shown in the previous table, with no provision made for adjusting it for nonstandard conditions. You take off from a sea-level airport where standard conditions exist. On the runway your altimeter reads zero. You land where the field elevation is 2,000 feet and where the surface conditions are also standard. Your altimeter senses 27.82″ Hg and reads 2,000 feet as you land.

Suppose, on the other hand, that the pressure and temperature conditions at the same destination airport had changed to 26.81″ Hg/9° C. Your altimeter on touchdown would sense lower pressure and read 3,000 feet. On an instrument approach under these nonstandard conditions, an unadjusted altimeter would indicate 1,000 feet above the runway level on ground impact. By means of a setting knob, the barometric scale on the altimeter setting dial can be rotated so that the altimeter will read "sea level" when nonstandard pressure exists at sea level.

The scale is calibrated from 28.00″ to 31.00″ to include the extremes in barometric change at sea level. Rotating the setting knob simultaneously rotates the scale and the altimeter hands at a rate of 1″ per 1,000 feet of indicated change of altitude.

29

For practical purposes, this ratio can be considered the standard pressure lapse rate below 5,000 feet. Assume that you adjust your altimeter setting dial to 29.92" on an airport at 1,000-foot elevation, and observe an indicated altitude of 1,300 feet. Disregarding other sources of error, your altimeter must be sensing the pressure for which it is calibrated at 1,300 feet. By rotating the knob, you set the altimeter hands to 1,000 feet and the altimeter setting dial rotates to read 29.62" (1" per 1,000 feet equals 0.1" per 100 feet). Thus, rotation of the altimeter setting dial adjusts the altimeter hands to a desired indication for the size of the aneroid at existing pressure.

Effects of nonstandard conditions can result in a difference of as much as 2,000 feet between true and indicated altitude. Temperature variations ex-

pand or contract the atmosphere and raise or lower the pressure levels that the altimeter is designed to sense. On a warm day, the pressure level where the altimeter will indicate 4,000 feet is higher than it would be under standard conditions; on a cold day the pressure level is lower than standard. Figure 4–6 shows the relationship between indicated and true altitude with temperature variation.

Changes in surface pressure also affect the pressure levels at altitude, as shown in Figure 4–7. At any level, the effect of lower than standard pressure on an uncorrected altimeter is to place the aircraft lower than its altimeter indicates.

The *altimeter setting system* provides you with the means that must be used to correct your altimeter for pressure variations. The system is necessary to ensure safe terrain clearance for instrument ap-

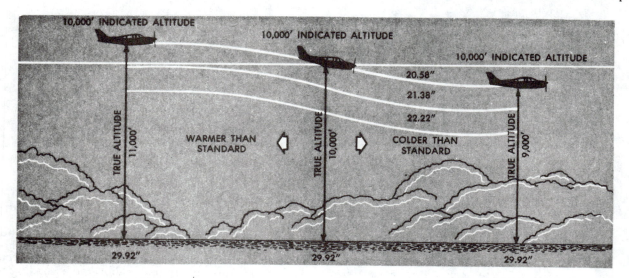

FIGURE 4–6. Nonstandard temperature and altimeter interpretation.

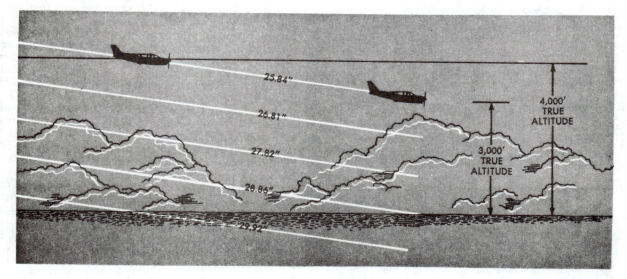

FIGURE 4–7. Nonstandard pressure and altimeter interpretation.

proaches and landings and to maintain vertical separation between aircraft during instrument weather conditions.

Each weather reporting station takes an hourly measurement of atmospheric pressure and, according to the surveyed elevation of the station, corrects the value obtained to sea level pressure. The resulting altimeter setting broadcast by each Flight Service Station is a computed correction for nonstandard surface pressure *only*, for a specific location and elevation. Consequently, altimeter indications based upon a local altimeter setting do not necessarily reflect height above mean sea level except in the vicinity of the reporting station and near the surface.

The setting does not compensate for non-standard conditions aloft, especially for the effect of non-standard temperature. Maintaining the correct reported altimeter settings as you fly cross-country at 5,000 feet indicated altitude does not mean that your aircraft is moving at a constant level of 5,000 feet above mean sea level. However, since instrument flight in controlled airspace is accomplished at assigned indicated altitudes, aircraft separation is maintained because all aircraft using the same altimeter setting are equally affected by nonstandard conditions at various levels. Altimeter settings are provided periodically to aircraft operating IFR in the low altitude structure by the Air Route Traffic Control Centers. These settings should be used during instrument flight below 18,000 feet MSL.

At or above 18,000 feet MSL, the altimeter should be set at 29.92. Refer to FAR 91.81 for details regarding lowest usable flight levels.

Altimeter Errors. Most pressure altimeters are subject to mechanical, elastic, temperature, and installation errors. Although manufacturing and installation specifications, as well as the periodic tests and inspections required by regulations (FAR 43, Appendix E), act to reduce these errors—any scale error should be noted prior to flight. Scale error may be observed in the following manner:

1. Set the current reported altimeter setting on the altimeter setting scale.
2. Altimeter should now read field elevation if you are located on the same reference level used to establish the altimeter setting.
3. Note the variation between the known field elevation and the altimeter indication. If this variation is in the order of plus or minus 75 feet, the accuracy of the altimeter is questionable and the problem should be referred to an appropriately rated repair station for evaluation and possible correction.

Trends in pressure altimeter design are to be seen in Figures 4–8 and 4–9. Both instruments are similar, differing mainly in presentation of the altimeter setting scales. For improved readability, the instruments provide readout of altitude in "thousands" of feet on the drum, while the single needle indicates altitude in "hundreds" of feet.

FIGURE 4–8.

FIGURE 4–9.

Encoding Altimeter

The encoding altimeter (Fig. 4–10) operates in conjunction with the aircraft's ATC transponder which is described on page 123. The transponder is nothing more than a receiver-transmitter which receives a coded interrogation signal from a ground radar site and transmits a coded signal back to the ground site. The interrogation signal from the ground consists of two pulses, either 8 micro-seconds or 21 micro-seconds apart. The transponder receives the pulses and determines the spacing. If

FIGURE 4–10. Encoding altimeter.

the 8 micro-seconds signal is received, the transponder is activated and transmits a "Mode A" signal. If the 21 micro-seconds signal is received, the transponder is activated and will transmit altitude information (a Mode C signal).

In "Mode C" operation, the interrogation signal places the transponder in the altitude reporting mode. When this happens, all codes selected by the transponder are rendered inactive and the encoding altimeter supplies the transponder reply code. This code is related to the aircraft's altitude and is transmitted to the ground site in the same manner as "Mode A." The ground radar alternately interrogates with "Mode A" and "Mode C" signals, thus displaying vertical as well as horizontal and other information on the radar screen, if both "Mode A" and "Mode C" (Mode A/C) are selected. Mode A/C should always be set when flying in an ARTS III environment, above 12,500 feet MSL in controlled airspace (excluding airspace at or below 2,500 feet AGL), or in Terminal Control Areas as specified in FAR Part 91.

There are no specific operating instructions for using an encoding altimeter other than setting it to the local barometric pressure and selecting Mode A/C on the transponder. The computer at the ground radar site as well as the altimeter electronics are referenced to 29.92″ Hg. This means that the altimeter always supplies altitude codes based on 29.92″ Hg regardless of the altimeter's barometric setting. The ground computer automatically computes the difference between the "29.92 altitude" received from the aircraft and the local barometric pressure. It presents the controller the proper "MSL altitude." Since the altimeter electronics are referenced to 29.92″ Hg, changing the altimeter setting does not change the controller's altitude read-out.

Radar Altimeter

The radar altimeter, also known as radio altimeter, provides a continuous indication of aircraft height above the ground. The system is a "down-looking" device which accurately measures the distance between the aircraft and the highest object on the terrain. The time interval between a transmitted and received radio signal is automatically converted into an absolute altitude reading. The radar altimeter shown in Figure 4–11 has a dial type readout. Another type has a digital presentation. A warning light and aural tone are also provided in this model, which alerts the pilot when the aircraft reaches a pre-selected altitude.

FIGURE 4–11. Radar altimeter.

The radar altimeter has three main functions. First, it serves as a ground proximity warning device. Second, it is an accurate cross-check for the barometric altimeter. Third, it gives the pilot rate information on the progress of the final approach and an accurate indication and warning when reaching the "MDA" (Minimum Descent Altitude) or "DH" (Decision Height) during instrument approaches.

All radar altimeters operate on a radio frequency of 4300 MHz.

Vertical-Speed Indicator

The vertical-speed indicator (also called the vertical-velocity or rate-of-climb indicator) is contained within a sealed case, connected to the static pressure line through a calibrated leak. As shown in Figure 4–12, changing pressures expand or contract a diaphragm, connected to the indicating needle through gears and levers. The instrument automatically compensates for changes in temperature. Although the vertical-speed indicator operates from the static pressure source, it is a differential

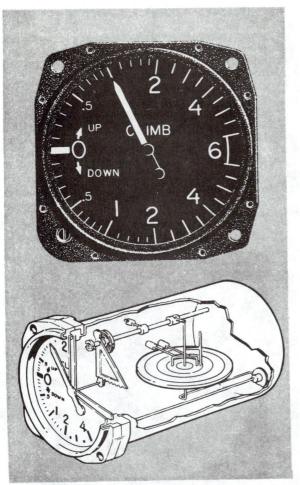

FIGURE 4–12. Vertical-speed indicator components.

pressure instrument. The differential pressure is established between the instantaneous static pressure in the diaphragm and the trapped static pressure within the case.

When the pressures are equalized in level flight, the needle reads zero. As static pressure in the diaphragm changes during entry to a climb or descent, the needle immediately shows a change of vertical direction. However, until the differential pressure stabilizes at a definite ratio, reliable rate indications cannot be read. Because of the restriction in air flow through the calibrated leak, a 6- to 9-second lag is required to equalize or stabilize the pressures.

Limitations in the use of the vertical-speed indicator are due to the calibrated leak. Sudden or abrupt changes in aircraft attitude cause erroneous instrument readings as the air flow fluctuates over the static ports. Both rough control technique and turbulent air result in unreliable needle indications. When used properly, the instrument provides reliable information to establish and maintain level flight and rate climbs or descents.

The *instantaneous vertical-speed indicator* incorporates acceleration pumps to eliminate the limitations associated with the calibrated leak. For example, during climb entry, vertical acceleration causes the pumps to supply extra air into the diaphragm to stabilize the pressure differential without the usual lag time. During the level flight and steady rate climbs and descents, the instrument operates on the same principles as the earlier conventional type.

Adjustment.—The needle of the vertical velocity indicator should indicate zero when the aircraft is on the ground or maintaining a constant pressure level in flight. Most instruments can be adjusted to a zero reading by turning a screw on the lower left corner of the instrument case. If this adjustment cannot be made, you must allow for the error when interpreting the indications in flight.

Airspeed Indicator

The airspeed indicator is constructed to measure the difference between ram pressure from the pitot head and atmospheric pressure from the static source. The instrument (Fig. 4–13) is contained within a sealed case in which is mounted a diaphragm sensitive to pressure changes. The impact pressure line is connected directly to one side of the diaphragm, while the inside of the case is vented to the static source. As the aircraft accelerates or decelerates, expansion or contraction of one side of the diaphragm moves the indicator needle by means of gears and levers. The airspeed dial may show indicated airspeed, true airspeed, Mach (airspeed converted to a decimal fraction of the speed of sound), or a combination of these values calibrated in miles per hour or knots.

Airspeed Errors.—Airspeed, like altitude, is a general term that must be more specifically identified for its application to flying. The instrument is designed to provide speed information under specific limited conditions. Whenever the conditions alter, errors are introduced.

Position error is caused by the static ports sensing erroneous static pressure. The slipstream flow causes disturbances at the static ports preventing actual atmospheric measurement. The error varies with airspeed, altitude, and configuration and may be a plus or a minus value. The error may be determined by reference to an airspeed calibration chart or table. The chart or table may be posted near the airspeed indicator, or included in the Airplane Flight Manual or owner's handbook.

Density error is introduced by changes in altitude and temperature for which the instrument does not automatically compensate. The standard airspeed instrument cannot adjust for variations from sea-level standard atmosphere conditions.

Compressibility error is caused by the packing of air into the pitot tube at high airspeeds, resulting in higher than normal readings. Below approximately 180 knots and at low altitudes the error is negligible.

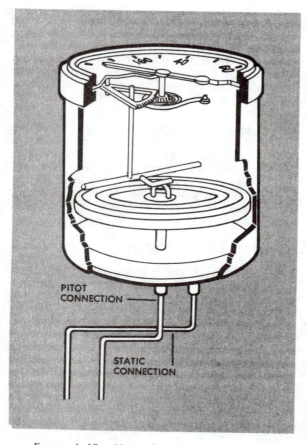

FIGURE 4–13. Airspeed indicator components.

Types of Airspeed

Indicated airspeed is the value read on the face of a standard airspeed indicator. The indicator is calibrated to reflect standard atmosphere adiabatic compressible flow at sea level corrected for airspeed system errors. It can be read in miles per hour or in knots, depending upon the scale of the dial.

Calibrated airspeed is the indicated airspeed of an aircraft, corrected for position and instrument error. Calibrated airspeed is equal to true airspeed in standard atmosphere at sea level.

Equivalent airspeed is the calibrated airspeed of an aircraft corrected for adiabatic compressible flow for the particular altitude. Equivalent airspeed is equal to calibrated airspeed in standard atmosphere at sea level; it is significant to pilots of high speed aircraft, but relatively unimportant to the average light plane pilot.

True airspeed is the airspeed of an aircraft relative to undisturbed air. It is equivalent airspeed corrected for air-density variation from the standard value at sea level. True airspeed increases with altitude when indicated airspeed remains the same.

Mach number is the ratio of true airspeed to the speed of sound.

True Airspeed Indicator

The *true airspeed indicator* combines computer operation and indicator in one instrument to provide both true and indicated airspeed (within the cruising speed range).

Figure 4–14 illustrates the current trend in the design of flight instruments which reduce pilot workload. With the adjusting knob, pressure altitude is set opposite outside air temperature. The needle then shows indicated airspeed in both knots and miles per hour, and true airspeed in m.p.h. More advanced true airspeed indicators contain diaphragms which respond to barometric pressure, free air temperature, and impact pressure. These factors are mechanically resolved to provide true airspeed indications.

FIGURE 4–14. True airspeed indicator.

Mach Indicator

The Mach indicator (Fig. 4–15) is found on more recently developed high performance aircraft. It indicates the ratio of aircraft true airspeed to the speed of sound at flight altitude. The Mach pointer is actuated mechanically by the pressure differential between impact air and static air pressure. In computing a true airspeed from indicated airspeed, air density must be taken into account. This requires a correction for temperature and altitude. With a Mach number, these corrections are unnecessary because the existing temperature at flight level determines the speed of sound at flight level. The Mach number is determined by the speed of sound, which in turn is determined by air density; thus, Mach is always a valid index to the speed of the aircraft.

34

FIGURE 4–15.   Mach indicator.

Gyroscopic Instruments

Of the six basic flight instruments, three (attitude indicator, turn indicator, and heading indicator) are controlled by gyroscopes. Understanding the use of these instruments requires a knowledge of gyroscopic principles, instrument power systems, and the construction and operating details of each instrument. Without the gyroscope and its practical adaptation to flight and navigational instruments, precision all-weather flying would be impossible.

Gyroscopes.—Any rotating body exhibits gyroscopic properties according to Newton's laws of motion. The first law states: A body at rest will remain at rest; or if in motion in a straight line, it will continue in motion in a straight line unless acted upon by an outside force. The second law states: The deflection of a moving body is proportional to the deflective force applied and is inversely proportional to its weight and speed. A gyroscope, or gyro, is a wheel or disc designed to utilize these principles.

Gyroscopic inertia depends upon several design factors:

1. *Weight.*—For a given size, a heavier mass is more resistant to disturbing forces than a lighter mass.

2. *Angular Velocity.*—The higher the rotational speed, the greater the rigidity, or resistance to deflection.

3. *Radius at Which the Weight Is Concentrated.*—Maximum effect is obtained from a mass when its principal weight is concentrated near the rim rotating at high speed.

4. *Bearing Friction.*—Any friction applies a deflecting force to a gyro. Minimum bearing friction keeps deflecting forces at a minimum.

Two types of mounting are used, depending upon how the gyroscopic properties are to be used in the operation of the instrument. A freely or universally mounted gyro is set on three gimbals, with the gyro free to rotate in any plane. Regardless of the position of the gyro base, the gyro tends to remain rigid in space. In the attitude indicator, the horizon bar is gyro-controlled to remain parallel to the natural horizon, and changes in position of the aircraft are shown pictorially (Fig. 4–17).

The semirigid, or restricted, mounting employs two gimbals, limiting the rotor to two planes of rotation. In the turn indicator, the semirigid mounting is used to provide controlled precession of the rotor, and the precessing force exerted on the gyro by the turning aircraft causes the needle to indicate a turn (Fig. 4–18).

Sources of Power For Gyro Operation

The gyroscopic instruments can be operated either by the vacuum system or the electrical system. In some aircraft, all the gyros are either electrically or vacuum motivated; in others, vacuum systems provide the power for the attitude and heading indicators, while the electrical system drives the gyro for operation of the turn needle. Both systems have advantages and disadvantages.

Vacuum (Suction) System.—The vacuum system spins the gyro by sucking a stream of air against the rotor vanes to turn the rotor at high speed, essentially as a water wheel or turbine operates. Air at atmospheric pressure drawn into the instrument through a filter or filters, drives the rotor vanes and is sucked from the instrument case through a line to the vacuum source, and vented into the atmosphere. Either a venturi or a vacuum pump can be used to provide the suction required to spin the rotors of the gyro instruments.

Vacuum values vary with differences in gyro design for optimum rotor speed, ranging approximately from 8,000 to 18,000 rpm in different instruments. The suction for the three indicators is given in inches of mercury (Hg) as follows:

	Minimum	Desired	Maximum
	(inches of mercury)		
Turn Indicator	1.8	1.9	2.1
Attitude Indicator	3.5	4.0	5.0
Heading Indicator	3.5	4.0	5.0

Venturi Tube.—Although the venturi tube is not as common as it was in the past, it can still be used when low cost, and simplicity of installation and operation are desired. A light single-engine airplane suitable for limited instrument training can be equipped with a 2″ venturi (2″ Hg vacuum capacity) to operate a turn needle. With an additional 8″ venturi, power is available for the attitude and heading indicators. A line from the throat of the venturi is connected to the gyros. Throughout the normal range of operating airspeeds, the velocity of air through the venturi creates sufficient suction to spin the gyros. The limitations of the venturi

PRINCIPLES OF THE GYROSCOPE

A gyroscope is a spinning mass or wheel, universally mounted, so that only one point — its center of gravity — is in a fixed position, the wheel being free to turn in any direction around this point.

To simplify this explanation we will illustrate the construction of a demonstrating model step by step.

1.
Picture a rotor and axle, with the rim of the rotor more or less facing you.

2.
Give it a supporting ring, with bearings on which the rotor and its axle can revolve.

3.
Now add an outer ring with bearings at 90° to the rotor bearings, about which the inner ring with its rotor and axle can turn.

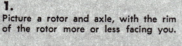

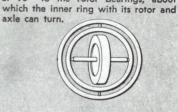

4.
Draw a frame which will support the rotor and its rings on horizontal bearings; this will complete your demonstrating model gyroscope. Disregarding the spin axis, the gyroscope has two degrees of freedom; the assembly can turn about a vertical axis (response axis No. 1) and also about a horizontal axis (response axis No. 2).

5.
When at rest there's nothing unusual about a gyroscope. It's simply a wheel universally mounted. You can point its axle in any direction without altering the geometrical center of the assembly.

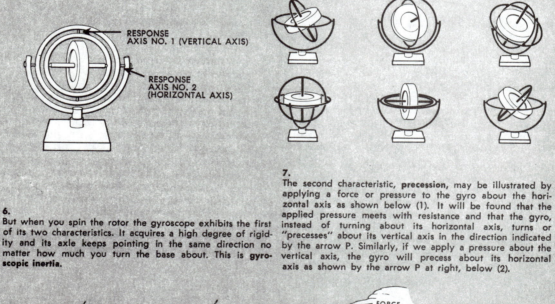

RESPONSE AXIS NO. 1 (VERTICAL AXIS)

RESPONSE AXIS NO. 2 (HORIZONTAL AXIS)

7.
The second characteristic, **precession**, may be illustrated by applying a force or pressure to the gyro about the horizontal axis as shown below (1). It will be found that the applied pressure meets with resistance and that the gyro, instead of turning about its horizontal axis, turns or "precesses" about its vertical axis in the direction indicated by the arrow P. Similarly, if we apply a pressure about the vertical axis, the gyro will precess about its horizontal axis as shown by the arrow P at right, below (2).

6.
But when you spin the rotor the gyroscope exhibits the first of its two characteristics. It acquires a high degree of rigidity and its axle keeps pointing in the same direction no matter how much you turn the base about. This is **gyroscopic inertia.**

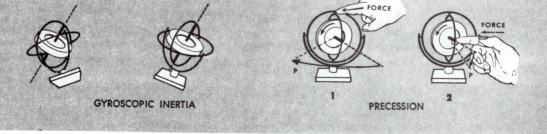

GYROSCOPIC INERTIA

PRECESSION

FIGURE 4–16. Principles of the gyroscope.

FIGURE 4–17. Attitude indicator or gyro-horizon.

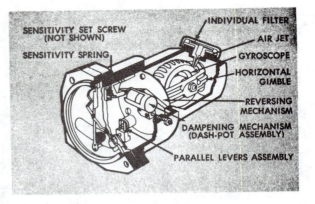

FIGURE 4–18. Turn indicator.

system are clearly evident. The venturi is designed to produce the desired vacuum at approximately 100 mph under standard sea-level conditions. Wide variations in airspeed or air density, or restriction to airflow by ice accretion, will affect the pressure at the venturi throat and thus the vacuum driving the gyro rotors. Further, since the gyro rotors do not reach normal operating speed until after take-off, pre-flight operational checks of venturi-powered gyro instruments cannot be made. For this reason, the system is adequate only for light plane instrument training and limited flying under instrument weather conditions. Aircraft flown throughout a wider range of speed, altitude, and weather conditions require a more effective source of power independent of airspeed and less susceptible to adverse atmospheric conditions.

Engine-Driven Vacuum Pumps.—The vane-type engine-driven pump is the most common source of vacuum for gyros installed in general aviation light aircraft. One type of engine-driven pump is mounted on the accessory drive shaft of the engine, and is connected to the engine lubrication system to seal, cool, and lubricate the pump. The diagram in Figure 4–19 shows the components of a vacuum system with a pump capacity of approximately 10″ Hg at engine speeds above 1000 rpm. Pump capacity and pump size vary in different aircraft, depending on the number of gyros to be operated.

Air-Oil Separator.—Oil and air in the vacuum pump is exhausted through the separator, which separates the oil from the air, vents the air outboard, and returns the oil to the engine sump.

Suction Relief Valve.—Since the system capacity is more than is needed for operation of the instruments, the adjustable suction relief valve is set for the vacuum desired for the instruments. Excess suction in the instrument lines is reduced when the spring-loaded valve opens to atmospheric pressure.

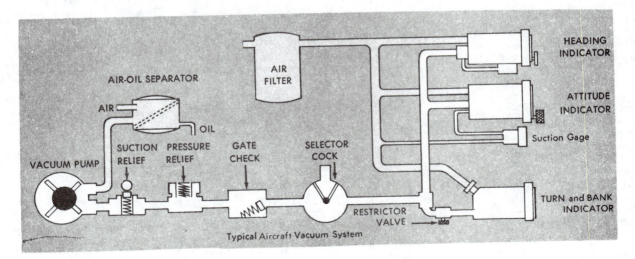

FIGURE 4–19. Pump-driven vacuum system.

Pressure Relief Valve.—Since a reverse flow of air from the pump would close both the gate check valve and the suction relief valve, the resulting pressure could rupture the lines. The pressure relief valve vents positive pressure into the atmosphere.

Gate Check Valve.—The gate check valve prevents possible damage to the instruments by engine backfire, which would reverse the flow of air and oil from the pump.

Selector Cock.—In twin-engine aircraft having vacuum pumps driven by both engines, the alternate pump can be selected to provide vacuum in the event of either engine or pump failure, with a check valve incorporated to seal off the failed pump.

Restrictor Valve.—Since the turn needle operates on less vacuum than that required for other gyro instruments, the vacuum in the main line must be reduced. This valve is either a needle valve adjusted to reduce the vacuum from the main line by approximately one-half, or a spring-loaded regulating valve that maintains a constant vacuum for the turn indicator, unless the main line vacuum falls below a minimum value.

Air Filter.—The master air filter screens foreign matter from the air flowing through all the gyro instruments, which are also provided with individual filters. Clogging of the master filter will reduce airflow and cause a lower reading on the suction gage. In aircraft having no master filter installed, each instrument has its own filter. With an individual filter system, clogging of a filter will not necessarily show on the suction gauge.

Suction gauge.—The suction gauge is a pressure gauge, indicating the difference, in inches of mercury, between the pressure inside the system and atmospheric or cockpit pressure. The desired vacuum, and the minimum and maximum limits, vary with gyro design. If the desired vacuum for the attitude and heading indicators is 5″ and the minimum is 4.6″, a reading below the latter value indicates that the airflow is not spinning the gyros fast enough for reliable operation. In many aircraft, the system provides a suction gauge selector valve, permitting the pilot to check the vacuum at several points in the system.

Another commonly used source of vacuum is the dry vacuum pump, also engine-driven. The pump operates without lubrication, and the installation requires no lines to the engine oil supply, and no air-oil separator or gate check valve. In other respects, the dry pump system and oil lubricated system are the same.

The principal disadvantage of the pump-driven vacuum system relates to erratic operation in high-altitude flying. Apart from routine maintenance of the filters and plumbing, which are absent in the electric gyro, the engine-driven pump is as effective a source of power for light aircraft as the electrical system.

Electrical System.—The electrically driven gyro was designed for military aircraft instruments after

tests showed erratic operation of vacuum-driven gyros at high altitude. At 18,000 feet, in atmospheric pressure approximately half of that at sea level, the vacuum pump is about half as efficient as at sea level. At progressively higher altitudes or extremely low temperatures affecting oil viscosity, the vacuum system will not create enough suction to operate the gyros at desired speed.

The principal value of the electric gyro in light aircraft is its safety factor. In single-engine aircraft equipped with vacuum-driven attitude and heading indicators, the turn needle is commonly operated by an electric gyro. In the event of vacuum system failure and loss of two gyro instruments, the pilot still has a reliable standby instrument for emergency operation. Operated on current directly from the battery, the electric turn indicator is reliable as long as current is available, regardless of generator or vacuum system malfunction. In the electric instrument, the gyro is a small electric motor and flywheel. Otherwise, both electric and vacuum-driven turn-needles are designed to use the same gyroscopic principle of precession. Figure 4–20 shows a typical 12-volt, direct-current light plane electrical system.

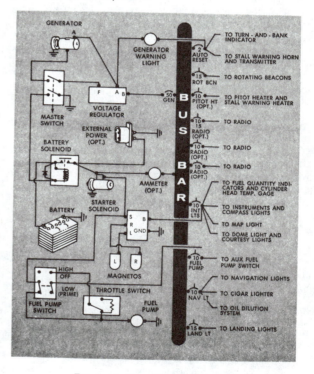

FIGURE 4–20. Electrical system.

Attitude Indicators

The attitude indicator—also referred to as the gyro-horizon, attitude gyro, and artificial horizon—is constructed to show the attitude of your aircraft in relation to the natural horizon when for any reason you must, or choose to, control your aircraft by visual reference inside, rather than outside, the cockpit. Irrespective of variations in instrument design, all attitude indicators relate a gyro-controlled artificial horizon line to some form of pitch and bank reference.

Vacuum-Driven Attitude Indicators.—The cut-away diagram in Figure 4–21 shows the basic components of a typical older type attitude indicator. These instruments are still in common use in general aviation aircraft.

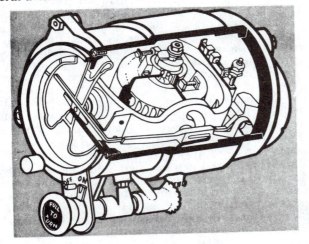

FIGURE 4–21.   Attitude indicator components (vacuum-driven).

The rotor, mounted in a sealed housing, spins in a horizontal plane about the vertical axis. The housing pivots about the lateral axis on a gimbal, which in turn is free to pivot about the longitudinal axis. The instrument case is the third gimbal necessary for universal mounting. The horizon bar is linked to the gyro by a lever, attached to a pivot on the rear of the gimbal frame and connected to the gyro housing by a guide pin.

When the attitude indicator is in operation, gyroscopic rigidity maintains the horizon bar parallel to the natural horizon. When the pitch or bank attitude of the aircraft changes, the miniature aircraft, being fixed to the case, moves with it. These movements of the instrument case with respect to the gyro are shown on the face of the instrument as pitch and bank attitude changes of the miniature aircraft with respect to the horizon bar.

Air is sucked through the filter, then through passages in the rear pivot and inner gimbal ring, then into the housing, where it is directed against the rotor vanes through two openings on opposite sides of the rotor. The air then passes through four equally spaced ports in the lower part of the rotor housing and is sucked out into the vacuum pump or venturi tube.

The chamber containing the ports is the erecting device that returns the spin axis to its vertical alignment whenever a precessing force, such as bearing friction, displaces the rotor from its horizontal plane. The four exhaust ports are each half-covered by a pendulous vane, which allows discharge of equal volumes of air through each port when the rotor is properly erected. Any tilting of the rotor disturbs the total balance of the pendulous vanes, tending to close one vane of an opposite pair while the opposite vane opens a corresponding amount. The increase in air volume through the opening port exerts a precessing force on the rotor hosuing to erect the gyro, and the pendulous vanes return to a balanced condition. See Figures 4–22 and 4–23.

Limits.—The limits of the instrument refer to the maximum rotation of the gimbals beyond which the gyro will tumble. The older type vacuum-driven attitude indicators have bank limits of approximately 100° to 110°, and pitch limits of 60° to 70°. If, for example, the pitch limits are 60° with the gyro normally erected, the rotor will tumble when the aircraft climb or dive angle exceeds 60°. As the rotor gimbal hits the stops, the rotor precesses abruptly, causing excessive friction and wear on the gimbals. The rotor will normally precess back to the horizontal plane at a rate of approximately 8°

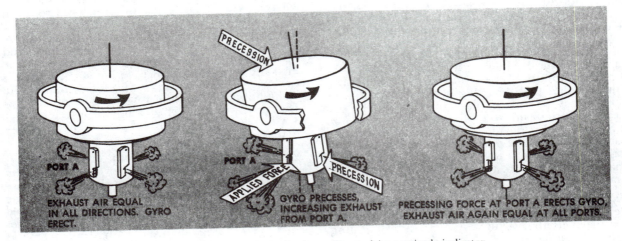

FIGURE 4–22.   Erecting mechanism, vacuum-driven attitude indicator.

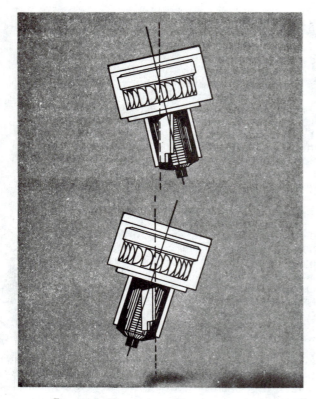

FIGURE 4–23. Action of Pendulous vanes.

per minute. The limits of more recently developed vacuum-driven attitude indicators exceed those given above.

Caging.—Many gyros include a manual caging device, used to erect the rotor to its normal operating position prior to flight or after tumbling, and a flag to indicate that the gyro must be uncaged before use. Turning the caging knob prevents rotation of the gimbals and locks the rotor spin axis in its vertical position. Because the rotor is spinning as long as vacuum power is supplied, normal maneuvering with the gyro caged wears the bearings unnecessarily. Therefore, the instrument should be left uncaged in flight unless the limits are to be exceeded.

In the caged position, the gyro is locked with the miniature aircraft showing level flight, regardless of aircraft attitude. When uncaged in flight, in any attitude other than level flight, the gyro will tend to remain in an unlevel plane of rotation with the erecting mechanism attempting to restore the rotor to a horizontal plane. Therefore, should it be necessary to uncage the gyro in flight, the actual aircraft attitude must be identical to the caged attitude (that is, straight and level), otherwise, the instrument will show false indications when first uncaged.

Errors.—Errors in the indications presented on the attitude indicator will result from any factor that prevents the vacuum system from operating within the design suction limits, or from any force

that disturbs the free rotation of the gyro at design speed. Some errors are attributable to manufacturing and maintenance. These include poorly balanced components, clogged filters, improperly adjusted valves, and pump malfunction. Such errors can be minimized by proper installation and inspection.

Other errors, inherent in the construction of the instrument, are caused by friction and worn parts. These errors, resulting in erratic precession and failure of the instrument to maintain accurate indications, increase with the life of the instrument.

Another group of errors, associated with the design and operating principles of the attitude indicator, are induced during normal operation of the instrument. A skidding turn moves the pendulous vanes from their vertical position, precessing the gyro toward the inside of the turn. After return of the aircraft to straight-and-level, coordinated flight, the miniature aircraft shows a turn in the direction opposite the skid. During a normal turn, movement of the vanes by centrifugal force causes precession of the gyro toward the inside of the turn.

Errors in both pitch and bank indications occur during normal coordinated turns. These errors are caused by the movement of the pendulous vanes by centrifugal force, resulting in the precession of the gyro toward the inside of the turn. The error is greatest in a 180° steep turn. If, for example, a 180° steep turn is made to the right and the aircraft is rolled-out to straight-and-level flight by visual references, the miniature aircraft will show a slight climb and turn to the left. This precession error, normally 3° to 5°, is quickly corrected by the erecting mechanism. At the end of a 360° turn, the precession induced during the first 180° is canceled out by precession in the opposite direction during the second 180° of turn. The slight precession errors induced during the roll-out are corrected immediately by pendulous vane action.

Acceleration and deceleration also induce precession errors, depending upon the amount and extent of the force applied. During acceleration the horizon bar moves down, indicating a climb. Control applied to correct this indication will result in a pitch attitude lower than the instrument shows. The opposite error results from deceleration. Other errors, such as "transport precession" and "apparent precession," relate to rotation of the earth and are of importance to pilots and navigators concerned with high-speed and long-range flight.

The application of the foregoing errors as they affect instrument interpretation will be treated later in Chapter V, "Attitude Instrument Flying—Airplanes."

Electric Attitude Indicators.—In the past, suction-driven gyros have been favored over the electric type for light aircraft because of the comparative simplicity and lower cost. However, the increasing importance of the attitude indicator has stimulated development of improved electric-driven gyros suited to light plane installation. Improvements relating to basic gyro design factors, easier readability, erection characteristics, reduction of induced errors, and instrument limitations are reflected in several available types. Depending upon the particular design improvements, the details among different instruments will vary as to the instrument display and cockpit controls. All of them present, to a varying degree, the essential pitch and bank information for attitude reference.

Electric gyros may be remotely located, with the gyro assembly mounted at some convenient location other than behind the instrument panel, and with the indicator assembly on the instrument panel driven through a servo motor. Another type is a simpler unit incorporating the gyroscope motor in the instrument case integral with the indicator assembly. The H–6B attitude indicator and J–8 gyrohorizon are representative of this type (Figs. 4–24 and 4–25).

J–8 Attitude Indicator.—The J–8 has a vertical seeking gyro, the axis of rotation tending to point toward the center of the earth (Fig. 4–25). The gyro is linked with a horizon bar and stabilizes a kidney-shaped sphere with pitch attitude markings. The sphere, horizon bar, and bank index pointer move with changes of aircraft attitude. Combined readings of these presentations give a continuous pictorial presentation of the aircraft attitude in pitch and roll with respect to the earth's surface.

The gyroscope motor is driven by 115-volt, 400-cycle alternating current. The gyro, turning at 21,000 rpm, is supported by the yoke and pivot assembly (gimbals). Attached to the yoke and pivot assembly is the horizon bar, which moves up and down through an arc of approximately 27°. The kidney-shaped sphere provides a background for the horizon bar and has the words CLIMB and DIVE and a bullseye painted on it. CLIMB and DIVE represent about 60° of pitch. Attached to the yoke and pivot assembly is the bank index pointer

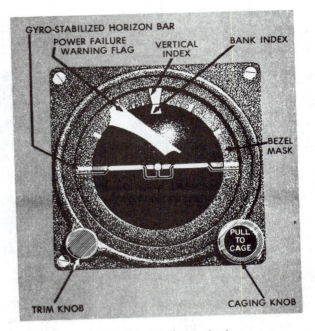

FIGURE 4–24.   H–6b gyro horizon.

which is free to rotate 360°. The dial face of the attitude indicator is marked with 0°, 10°, 20°, 30°, 60°, and 90° of bank, and is used with the bank index pointer to indicate the degree of bank left or right.

Erection and Caging Mechanisms.—The function of the erection mechanism is to keep the gyro axis vertical to the surface of the earth. A magnet attached to the top of the gyro shaft spins at 21,000 rpm. Around this magnet, but not attached, is a sleeve that is rotated by magnetic attraction at ap-

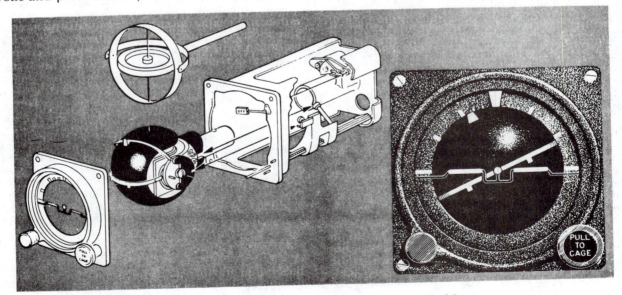

FIGURE 4–25.   Attitude indicator components (electrically-driven).

41

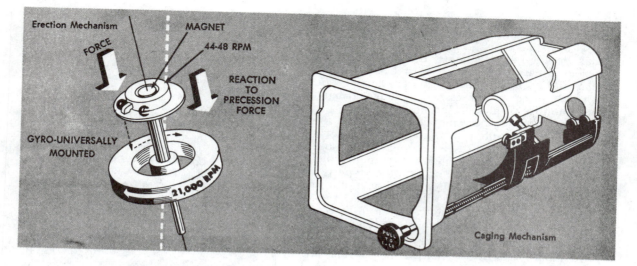

FIGURE 4–26.   Erecting and caging mechanisms of an electric attitude indicator.

proximately 44 to 48 rpm. As illustrated in Figure 4–26, the steel balls revolve. If the pull of gravity is not aligned with the axis of the gyro, the balls will fall to the low side. The resulting precession realigns the axis of rotation vertically.

The gyro can be caged manually by a lever and cam mechanism to provide rapid erection. When the instrument is not getting sufficient power for normal operation, an "OFF" flag appears in the upper right face of the instrument.

The instrument permits 360° of rotation about the pitch and bank axes without tumbling the gyro. The expanded motion of the horizon bar provides sensitive pitch indications near the level flight position.

When the aircraft exceeds the maximum of 27° in pitch up or down, the horizon bar is held in extreme position and the sphere becomes the new reference. A continued increase of climb or dive angle approaching the vertical attitude is indicated by graduations on the sphere. When the aircraft nears vertical, the sphere begins to rotate 180°. As soon as the aircraft departs from the vertical, the instrument again indicates the attitude of the aircraft. This momentary rotation of the sphere is known as controlled precession and should not be confused with gyro tumbling. The attitude of the aircraft about the roll axis is shown by the angle between the horizon bar and the miniature aircraft, and also by the bank index relative to the degree marking on the bezel mask (face plate).

Errors.—Following recovery from unusual attitudes, displacement of the horizon bar in excess of 5° in pitch and/or bank may result. Once the instrument senses gravitational forces, the erection mechanism will immediately begin to correct the precession errors at a rate of 3° to 6° per second. In a normal turn, centrifugal force acting on the erection mechanism will produce normal precession errors in pitch and/or bank up to 5° on return to straight-and-level flight. Acceleration or decel-

eration will also result in precession errors in proportion to the duration and magnitude of the speed change. Following acceleration, the aircraft pitch attitude will be lower than the instrument indication; following deceleration, the aircraft attitude will be higher than the pitch indication until the erection mechanism realigns the gyro.

Trends in Attitude Indicator Design

The value of the attitude indicator is directly related to the readability of the instrument; that is, to the speed and ease with which you can get information from it to determine exact aircraft attitude.

Although the older type attitude indicators are not difficult to interpret in normal flight attitudes, reference to other instruments to confirm the indications observed on the attitude indicator is recommended and particularly when abnormal flight attitudes are experienced. The greater the divergence of the miniature aircraft from the horizon line, the more difficult exact interpretation becomes, yet the extreme attitude is the condition requiring immediate and accurate visual information.

The operation of the bank index can also be confusing. When the aircraft is banked to the right, the index moves left (counterclockwise) and vice versa. Students commonly misinterpret this motion of the bank index and apply aileron control in the wrong direction. Requirements of high performance aircraft have accelerated research to improve readability and reliability of the attitude gyro.

One improved attitude indicator design is shown in Figure 4–27. In this design, the "SLOTTED" bank index has been moved to the upper periphery of the case to improve readability of the angle of bank as read on the graduated scale which is attached to the case. Further bank references are to

FIGURE 4-27. Simplified attitude indicator design.

be seen in the form of converging lines to a point on the horizon. Pitch references are the horizon line and the ground lines parallel to the horizon line.

Several of the attitude indicators being installed in recently manufactured general aviation aircraft are non-tumbling, self-erecting, and have turn errors compensated. They may be either electric or vacuum-driven instruments.

Turn and Slip Indicator

The turn and slip indicator, also referred to as the "needle and ball" and "turn and bank" indicator, was the only available reference for bank attitude before the development of the attitude indicator. Its principal uses in modern aircraft are to indicate trim and to serve as an emergency source of bank information in case the attitude gyro fails.

The turn and slip indicator is actually a combination of two instruments. The needle is gyro-operated to show rate of turn and the ball reacts to gravity and/or centrifugal force to indicate the need for directional trim.

Turn Needle Operation.—The turn needle is operated by a gyro, driven either by vacuum or electricity. Semirigid mounting of the gyro permits it to rotate freely about the lateral and longitudinal axes while restricting its rotation about the vertical axis. The gyro axis is horizontally mounted so that the gyro rotates up and away from the pilot. The gimbal around the gyro is pivoted fore and aft.

Gyroscopic precession causes the rotor to tilt when the aircraft is turned. Due to the direction of rotation, the gyro assembly tilts in the opposite

direction from which the aircraft is turning; this prevents the rotor axis from becoming vertical to the earth's surface. The linkage between the gyro assembly and the turn needle, called the reversing mechanism, causes the needle to indicate the proper direction of turn.

A spring is attached between the instrument case and the gyro assembly to hold the gyro upright when no precession force is applied. Tension on the spring may be adjusted to calibrate the instrument for a given rate of turn. The spring restricts the amount of gyro tilt. Stops prevent the gyro assembly from tilting more than 45° to either side of the upright position. In addition, a damping mechanism prevents excessive oscillation of the turn needle.

Power for the electric gyro may be supplied from either an AC or DC source. When current is supplied directly from the battery, the needle gives reliable indications regardless of malfunction or failure of other components of the electrical system.

Power for the suction-driven turn needle is regulated by a restrictor valve installed between the main suction line and the instrument to produce a desired suction and rotor speed. Since the needle measures the force of precession, excessively high or low vacuum results in unreliable turn needle operation. For a specific rate of turn, low vacuum produces less than normal rotor speed and, therefore, less precession force. Needle deflection is, therefore, less for this specific rate of turn. The reverse is true for the condition of high vacuum.

The turn needle indicates the rate at which the aircraft is turning about the vertical axis in number of degrees per second. Properly understood, the instrument provides bank as well as rate-of-turn information but it tells you nothing about bank attitude unless you understand the relationship between airspeed, angle of bank, and rate of turn discussed in Chapter III, "Aerodynamic Factors Related to Instrument Flying."

Of the two types of turn needle shown in Figure 4-28, the 2-minute turn indicator is the older. If the instrument is accurately calibrated, a single needle-width deflection on the 2-minute indicator means that the aircraft is turning at 3° per second, or standard rate (2 minutes for a 360° turn). On the 4-minute indicator, a single needle-width deflection shows when the aircraft is turning at 1½° per second, or half standard rate (4 minutes for a 360° turn). From a comparison of the indexes on the two instruments, you can see why the 4-minute instrument was developed: The half standard-rate (one-needle width deflection) turn used by high-speed aircraft is more easily read on the 4-minute indicator.

Slip Indicator (Ball) Operation.—This part of the instrument is a simple inclinometer consisting of a sealed, curved glass tube containing kerosene and a black agate or common steel ball bearing which is free to move inside the tube. The fluid provides a dampening action, insuring smooth and easy movement of the ball. The tube is curved so that

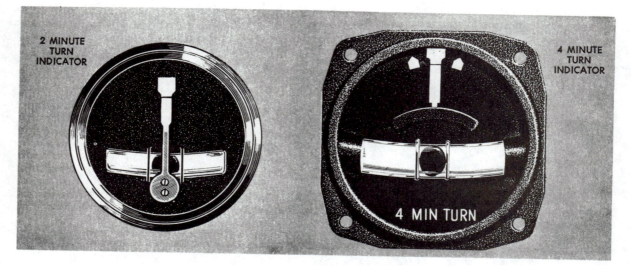

FIGURE 4–28.   Turn indicators (2- and 4-minute).

in a horizontal position the ball tends to seek the lowest point. A small projection on the left end of the tube contains a bubble of air which compensates for expansion of the fluid during changes in temperature. Two strands of wire wound around the glass tube fasten the tube to the instrument case and also serve as reference markers to indicate the correct position of the ball in the tube. During coordinated straight-and-level flight, the force of gravity causes the ball to rest in the lowest part of the tube, centered between the reference wires.

Figure 4–29 shows the forces acting on the ball during turns. During a coordinated turn these forces are in balance, allowing the ball to remain in the center of the tube. When the forces acting on the ball become unbalanced, the ball moves away from the center of the tube.

In a skid, the rate of turn is too great for the angle of bank, and excessive centrifugal force causes the ball to move to the outside of the turn. To correct to coordinated flight calls for increasing the bank or decreasing the rate of turn or a combination of both.

In a slip, the rate of turn is too slow for the angle of bank, and the lack of centrifugal force causes the ball to move to the inside of the turn. To return to coordinated flight requires decreasing the bank or increasing the rate of turn, or a combination of both. The ball is thus used to check for coordinated flight. It is actually a "balance" indicator since it shows the relationship between the angle of bank and the rate of turn. Note that in each instance shown in Figure 4–29, the aircraft is turning at half standard rate, regardless of the position of the ball.

Errors.—Errors in turn needle indications are due to (1) insufficient or excessive rotor speed; or (2) inaccurate adjustment of the calibrating spring.

Turn Coordinator

Recent years have seen the development of a new type of turn indicator, referred to as a "Turn Coordinator" or "Pictorial Turn Indicator." In place of the conventional turn needle indication of rate-of-turn, both instruments pictured in Figure 4–30, display a movement of the aircraft on the roll axis that is proportional to the roll rate. When the roll rate is reduced to zero, the instrument provides an indication of the rate-of-turn. This new design features a realignment of the gyro in such a manner that it senses aircraft movement about the yaw and roll axes and pictorially displays the resultant motion as described above. Both instruments also possess a dampening feature that provides a more stable indication than the conventional turn and slip indicator. The conventional inclinometer (ball) is common to both instruments. It should be clearly understood that the miniature aircraft of the turn coordinator displays *only* rate of roll and rate of turn. It does *not* directly display the bank angle of the aircraft.

Heading Indicators

Many types of heading or directional indicators are used in modern aircraft. Most of them are complex gyro-controlled systems designed to compensate automatically for errors inherent in older north-seeking instruments.

The heading indicator commonly used in light aircraft is the relatively simple directional gyro, which has no direction-seeking properties and must be set to headings shown on the magnetic compass. Knowledge of the magnetic compass is thus essential to proper use of the directional gyro. The mag-

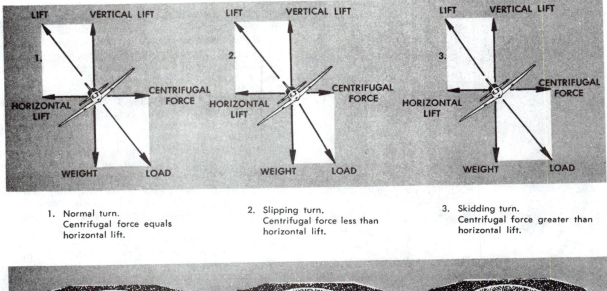

1. Normal turn.
   Centrifugal force equals
   horizontal lift.

2. Slipping turn.
   Centrifugal force less than
   horizontal lift.

3. Skidding turn.
   Centrifugal force greater than
   horizontal lift.

FIGURE 4–29. Coordinated, slipping, and skidding turn indications.

FIGURE 4–30. Pictorial turn indicators.

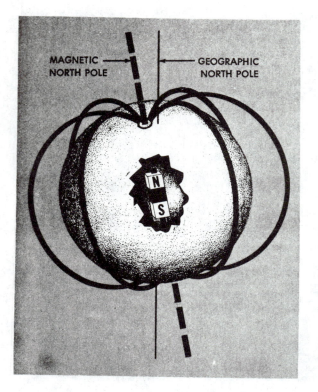

FIGURE 4–31. Magnetic and geographic poles.

netic compass is also important as a standby, or emergency, directional indicator since it requires no aircraft source of power for operation. In order to use the magnetic compass effectively, you must understand some basic properties of magnetism and their effect on the instrument.

Magnetic Attraction.—A magnet is a piece of metal that has the property of attracting another metal. The force of attraction is greatest at the poles or points near each end of the magnet; and the least attraction is in the area halfway between the two poles. Lines of force flow from each of these poles in all directions, bending around and flowing toward the other poles to form a magnetic field. Such a magnetic field surrounds the Earth, with the lines of force oriented approximately to the north and south magnetic poles (Fig. 4–31).

In flight, allowance must be made for the difference in locations of the geographic and magnetic poles if your course reference is the geographic (true) pole, because the aircraft compass is oriented to the magnetic pole. Lines of equal magnetic declination or "variation" are called isogonic lines, and are plotted in degrees of east and west variation on aeronautical charts. A line connecting points of zero degrees variation is called the agonic line. These lines are replotted periodically on aeronautical charts to correct any change which may have occurred as a result of the shifting of the poles, or any changes caused by local magnetic disturbances. Figure 4–32 shows the irregular pattern of the lines of equal variation in the United States.

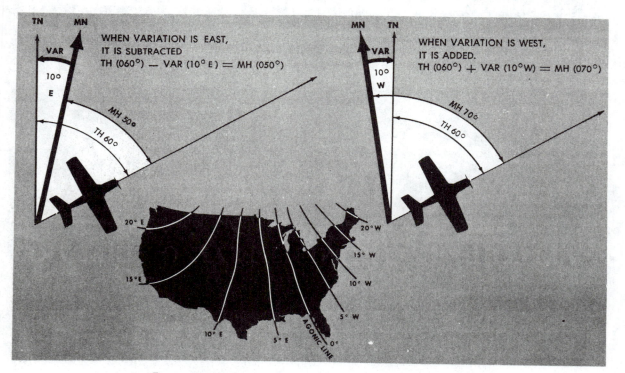

FIGURE 4–32. Lines of equal variation in the United States.

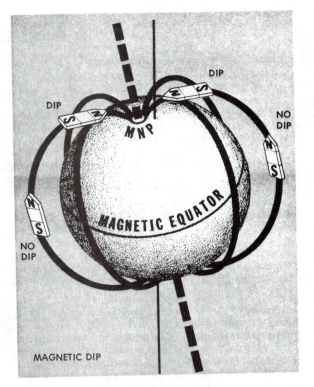

FIGURE 4–33. Magnetic dip.

Magnetic Dip.—A number of compass errors are caused by deflection of the aircraft compass needles as they seek alignment with the earth's magnetic lines of force. Note in Figure 4–33 how lines of force in the earth's magnetic field are parallel to the earth's surface at the magnetic equator, and curve increasingly downward closer to the magnetic poles. A magnetic needle will tend to assume the

same direction and position as the line of force. Thus, the needle will be parallel with the Earth's surface at the magnetic equator, but will point increasingly downward as it is moved closer to the magnetic pole. This characteristic is known as magnetic dip. You should understand the relationship between latitude and magnetic dip to be able to effectively use the standby compass either for normal or emergency operations.

Compass Construction.—The magnetic compass is a simple self-contained instrument (Fig. 4–34). Two steel magnetized needles are mounted on a float, with a compass card attached around the float. The needles are parallel, with their northseeking end pointed in the same direction. The compass card has letters for cardinal headings—N.E.S.W. Each 30° interval of direction is represented by a number from which the last zero is omitted. Between the numbers, the card is graduated for each 5°. The float assembly, consisting of the magnetized needles, compass card, and float, is mounted on a pedestal and sealed in a chamber filled with an acid-free white kerosene.

This fluid serves two purposes. Due to buoyancy, part of the weight of the card is taken off the pivot that supports the card. The fluid also decreases oscillation and lubricates the pivot point on the pedestal. The pedestal is the mount for the float assembly and compass card. The float assembly is balanced on the pivot, which allows free rotation of the card and allows it to tilt at an angle up to 18°. At the rear of the compass bowl, a diaphragm is installed to allow for any expansion or contraction of the liquid, thus preventing the formation of bubbles or possible bursting of the case.

A glass face is on one side of the compass, and mounted behind the glass is a lubber or reference line by which compass indications are read. Two small compensating magnets are located in the top

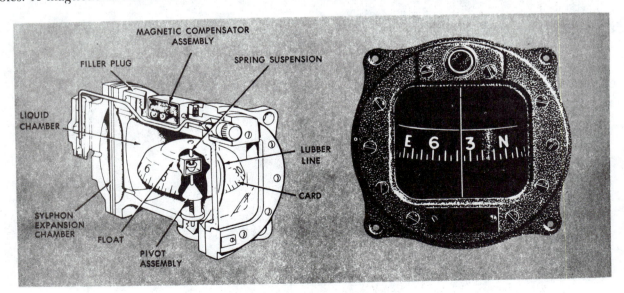

FIGURE 4–34. Magnetic compass.

of the compass case to counteract deviation. These are adjustable by two set screws labeled N—S and E—W.

Compass Errors.—*Variation.*—The angular difference between true and magnetic north is referred to as magnetic variation. Figure 4-32 shows how variation is applied to true heading to derive magnetic heading.

· *Deviation.*—The compass needles are affected not only by the earth's magnetic field, but also by magnetic fields generated when aircraft electrical equipment is operated and by metal components in the aircraft. These magnetic disturbances within the aircraft, called deviation, deflect the compass needles from alignment with magnetic north. Deviation varies according to the electrical components in use, and the magnetism changes with jolts from hard landings and installation of additional radio equipment.

To reduce this deviation, each compass is checked and compensated periodically by adjustment of the N—S/E—W magnets. The errors remaining after "swinging" the compass are recorded on a compass correction card mounted in the airplane. To fly compass headings, you refer to the compass correction card for corrected headings to steer.

Magnetic dip is the tendency of the compass needles to point down as well as to the magnetic pole. The resultant error is known as dip error, greatest at the poles and zero at the magnetic equator.

Since the compass card is designed to respond only to the horizontal plane of the earth's magnetic field, it turns freely only in the horizontal plane. Any movement of the card from the horizontal results in dip errors. Discussion of these errors is limited to the northern hemisphere; the errors are reversed in the southern hemisphere.

Northerly turning error (Fig. 4-35) is the most pronounced of the dip errors. Due to the mounting of the magnetic compass, its center of gravity is below the pivot point on the pedestal and the card is well balanced in the fluid. When the aircraft is banked, the card is also banked as a result of centrifugal force. While the card is in the banked attitude, the vertical component of the Earth's magnetic field causes the north-seeking ends of the compass to dip to the low side of the turn, giving an erroneous turn indication. This error is most apparent on headings of north and south. When making a turn from a heading of north, the compass briefly gives an indication of a turn in the opposite direction. When making a turn from south, it gives an indication of a turn in the correct direction but at a much faster rate than is actually occurring.

Acceleration error is also due to the dip of the earth's magnetic field. Because of the pendulous-type mounting, the aft end of the compass card is tilted upward when accelerating, and downward when decelerating during changes of airspeed. This deflection of the compass card from the horizontal results in an error which is most apparent on headings of east and west. When accelerating on either an east or west heading (Fig. 4-36), the error appears as a turn indication toward north. When decelerating on either of these headings, the compass indicates a turn toward south. The word

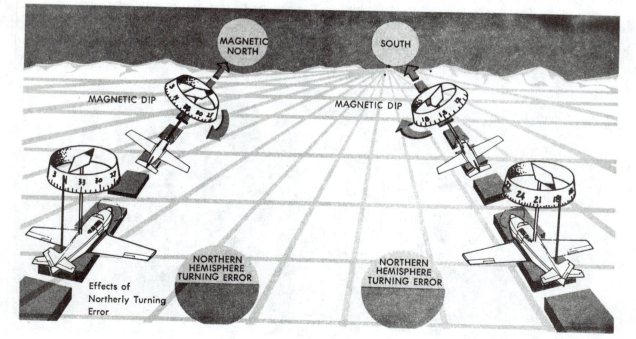

FIGURE 4-35. Northerly turning error.

48

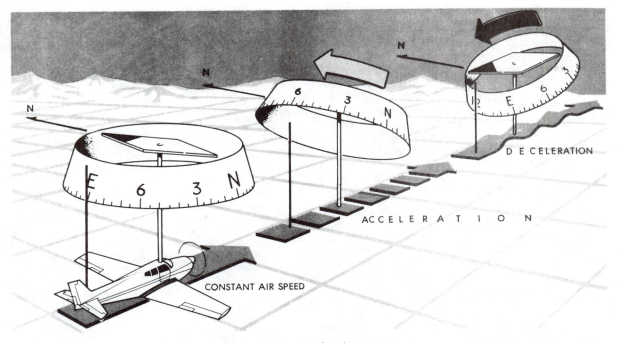

FIGURE 4-36. Acceleration error.

"ANDS" (Acceleration—North/Deceleration—South) may help you to remember the acceleration error.

Oscillation error results from erratic movement of the compass card which may be caused by turbulence or rough control technique. During oscillation, the compass is affected by all of the factors discussed. With proper training, the instrument can be effectively used despite the errors.

Vacuum-Driven Heading Indicator

The diagramatic illustrations (Figs. 4-37 and 4-38) depict the principal components of the older type vacuum-driven heading indicator still used in many general aviation aircraft.

The vacuum-drive heading indicator is the simplest of many types of gyro-controlled directional

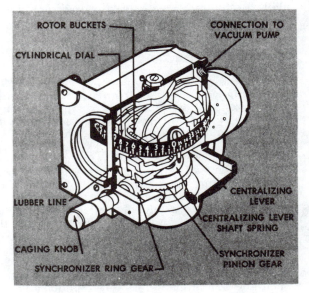

FIGURE 4-37. Heading indicator components (vacuum-driven).

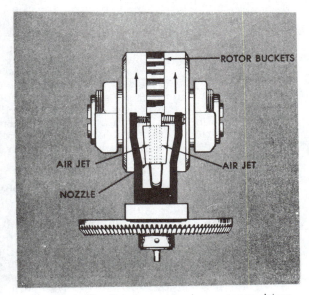

FIGURE 4-38. Erecting mechanism—vacuum-driven heading indicator.

indicators designed to provide stable heading reference. Within limits, the directional gyro is not affected by the factors that induce errors in the magnetic compass.

The operation of the heading indicator (Fig. 4–37) depends upon the principle of rigidity in space of a universally mounted gyroscope. The rotor turns in a vertical plane. Fixed at right angles to the plane of the rotor (to the vertical gimbal) is a circular compass card. Since the rotor remains rigid in space, the points on the card hold the same position in space relative to the vertical plane. As the instrument case revolves about the vertical gimbal, the card provides clear and accurate heading references.

The source of power for the gyro is the engine-driven vacuum pump (or venturi) which sucks air from the rear of the instrument case. This causes air under atmospheric pressure to pass through the filtering system, thence through an air bearing into the hollow vertical gimbal ring. The air then passes through the air nozzle and jets, striking the rotor at a point just above the plane of the horizontal gimbal.

The speed of the rotor may vary from 10,000 to 18,000 rpm, depending on instrument design. For proper operation, the suction gauge reading can be as low as 3.5 and as high as 5.0 inches of mercury, with 4.0 the desired suction. Limits for adjustment of the vacuum are 3.75 and 4.25, or as specified in your aircraft operating hand-book.

Erecting Mechanism.—During flight, precessing forces displace the rotor from the vertical plane. To compensate for precession and to provide better airflow distribution against the rotor buckets, the air is divided by two parallel jets at the tip of the nozzle (Fig. 4–38).

Each jet strikes the buckets at points equidistant from the center of the buckets when the rotor is perpendicular in its normal rotating plane. When the gyro precesses, both jets strike one side of the buckets and cause the plane of the rotor to again become parallel to the flow of air from the jets.

Limitations.—The design of the vacuum-driven directional gyro imposes limitations on rotation about the gimbals preventing operation of the instrument in abnormal flight attitudes. If the plane of rotation of the rotor were able to become parallel to the base of the case, it would lose its ability to hold the card in a stationary position, since its axis would be in line with the vertical gimbal and the card would tend to spin with the rotor. The stop, or limiting factor, in the instrument is the caging arm. In the uncaged position, the caging arm rests on the bottom of the vertical gimbal ring and in that position restricts the movement of the vertical gimbal ring about the rotor or the horizontal gimbal. The caging arm is held against the bottom of the vertical gimbal ring by means of a small spring so that rough air cannot cause it to fly up and tumble the instrument. Beyond the normal operating limits—55° of pitch and bank—when the horizontal

gimbal touches the stop, the precessional force causes the card to spin rapidly. This may be corrected by caging, resetting, and uncaging the instrument.

Errors.—The chief cause of precession, causing the card to creep or drift, is bearing friction. Normal movement of the gimbal rings produces friction, which is increased if the bearings are worn, dirty, or improperly lubricated. Other sources of precession error include unbalanced gyro components and the effect of the earth's rotation. The latter effect depends upon the position of the instrument in relation to the earth, and is not appreciable unless a flight involves considerable change in latitude.

An apparent error frequently results from misuse of the magnetic compass when the directional gyro is set. Unless magnetic deviations are applied, the indicator may appear to drift several degrees after a turn is completed. Another common error results from failure to maintain straight-and-level flight while reading the magnetic compass for the heading to set in the directional gyro. Errors in the magnetic compass induced by attitude changes are thus duplicated in the heading indicator.

The instrument should be checked at least every 15 minutes during flight and reset to the correct heading. An error of no more than 3° in 15 minutes is acceptable for normal operations.

Caging Mechanism.—The heading indicator can be adjusted by pushing in on the caging knob to mesh pinion and ring gears, thereby permitting rotation of the vertical gimbal and card. (Another type of caging mechanism utilizes friction between rubber and metal rings.) After setting, the gyro is uncaged by pulling out the caging knob to release the gimbals from the caging mechanism. Before setting the instrument during ground operations, allow 5 minutes after engine starting for the gyro to reach operating speed.

Azimuth Heading Indicator

The heading indicator shown in Figure 4–39 is representative of the instruments found in the more recent general aviation aircraft. This instrument is a refinement of the older vacuum-driven heading indicator and is considered easier to interpret.

The gyro assembly is identical to that of the type already discussed. However, instead of the horizontally mounted compass card, an azimuth card is mounted on the face of the instrument. The card, geared to the vertical gimbals, rotates as the aircraft turns. The aircraft heading is shown under the pointer on the nose of the miniature aircraft, inscribed on the glass cover of the instrument face. In addition to the nose index, additional 45°, 90°, and 180° indices are painted on the glass. Errors, pitch and bank limitations, and method of caging vary with the particular model. Certain models are non-tumbling and self-erecting.

FIGURE 4–39. Azimuth directional gyro.

Remote Indicating Compass

Remote indicating compasses have been developed to compensate for the errors and to reduce the limitations of the older type heading indicators. The pictorial navigation indicator and the slaving control and compensator unit, the two panel mounted components of a typical system, are shown in Figure 4–40. The pictorial navigation indicator is commonly referred to as a horizontal situation indicator (HSI), which is described on page 53.

The heading indicator of the pictorial navigation indicator is a remote indicating compass. The slaving control and compensator unit has a pushbutton that provides the pilot a means of selecting either the "slaved gyro" or "free gyro" mode. The slaving control and compensator unit also has a slaving meter and two manual heading drive butttons. The slaving meter indicates the difference between the displayed heading and the magnetic heading. A right deflection indicates a clockwise error of the compass card; a left deflection indicates a counterclockwise error. Whenever the aircraft is in a turn and the card rotates, the slaving meter will show a full deflection to one side or the other. When the system is in "free gyro" mode, the compass card may be adjusted by depressing the appropriate heading drive button.

The magnetic slaving transmitter and directional gyro unit are illustrated in Figure 4–41. The magnetic slaving transmitter is mounted remotely, usually in a wingtip, to eliminate the possibility of magnetic interference. It contains the flux valve which is the direction sensing device of the system. Its operation is diagramatically illustrated in Figure

FIGURE 4–40. Pictorial navigation indicator; slaving control and compensator unit.

4-42. The flux valve picks up the lines of force concentrated in any one spoke segment of the unit. Note in the illustration how the concentration of lines of flux change from number 1 to numbers 2 and 3 as the aircraft changes heading from north to west. This concentration of lines of magnetic force, after being amplified, is relayed to the directional gyro unit, which is also remotely mounted. These signals operate a torque motor in the directional gyro unit. The torque motor precesses the gyro unit until it is aligned with the transmitter signal. The magnetic slaving transmitter is connected electrically to the heading indicator of the pictorial navigation indicator on the instrument panel.

There are a number of designs of the remote indicating compass, therefore only basic features of the system are covered here. As an instrument pilot, you should become familiar with the characteristics of the equipment in your aircraft.

51

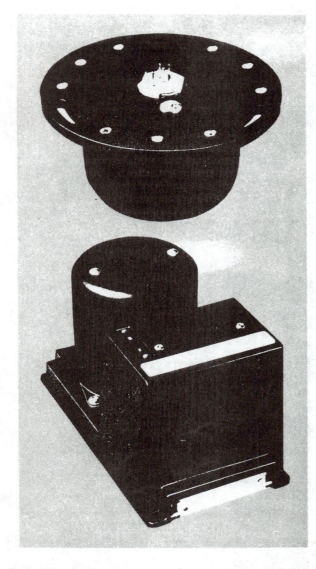

FIGURE 4–41. Magnetic slaving transmitter and directional gyro unit.

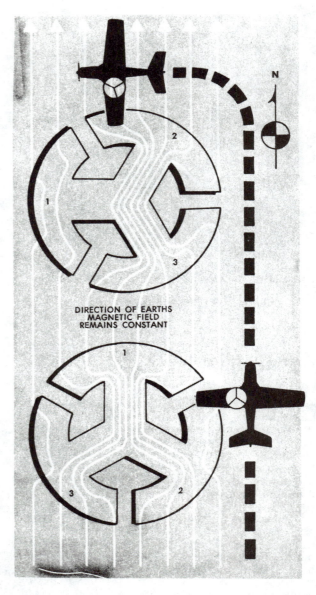

DIRECTION OF EARTHS
MAGNETIC FIELD
REMAINS CONSTANT

FIGURE 4–42. Operation of flux valve unit.

Radio Magnetic Indicator (RMI)

The radio magnetic indicator, or RMI, is beginning to appear on the instrument panels of modern general aviation aircraft. This instrument, shown in Figure 4–43, consists of a rotating compass card, a double-barred bearing indicator, and a single-barred bearing indicator. The compass card, actuated by the aircraft's compass system, rotates as the aircraft turns. The magnetic heading of the aircraft is always directly under the index at the top of the instrument, assuming no compass deviation error. The bearing pointers display ADF or VOR magnetic bearings to the selected station. In most installations, the double-barred bearing indicator gives the magnetic bearing to the VOR or VORTAC to which the receiver is tuned, and the single-barred indicator is an ADF needle which gives the magnetic bearing to the selected low frequency facility. The tail of the double-barred indicator tells you the radial you are on, and the tail of the single-barred indicator tells you your magnetic bearing from a low frequency station. Some RMI installations have selector switches which permit the pilot to use both indicators in conjunction with dual VOR receivers or both indicators as ADF needles. When used with area navigation equipment, the RMI can be set up to indicate either the bearing to the "waypoint" or to the VOR/DME station used to establish the "waypoint."

FIGURE 4–43. Radio magnetic indicator (RMI).

deviations from the course selected with the course indicating arrow. It moves left or right to indicate deviation from the centerline in the same manner that the angular movement of a conventional VOR/LOC needle indicates deviation from course. The desired course is selected by rotating the course indicating arrow in relation to the azimuth card by means of the course set knob. This gives you a pictorial presentation. The fixed aircraft symbol and course deviation bar display the aircraft relative to the selected course as though you were above the aircraft looking down. The TO-FROM indicator is a triangular shaped pointer. When the indicator points to the head of the course arrow, it indicates that the course selected, if properly intercepted and flown, will take the aircraft to the selected facility, and vice versa. The glide slope deviation pointer indicates the relation of the aircraft to the glide slope. When the pointer is below the center position, the aircraft is above the glide slope and an increased rate of descent is required.

In some installations, the azimuth card is a remote indicating compass; in others, such as the one described here, the heading must be checked against the magnetic compass occasionally and reset with the heading set knob.

Horizontal Situation Indicator (HSI)

The horizontal situation indicator (Fig. 4–44) is a combination of two instruments, the vertical azimuth card heading indicator and VOR/ILS indicator. The aircraft heading displayed on the rotating azimuth card under the upper lubber line is 105°. The course indicating arrow head shown is set to 061°; the tail indicates the reciprocal, 241°. The course deviation bar operates with a VOR/LOC navigation receiver to indicate left or right

Integrated Flight System (Flight Director System)

Further advances in attitude instrumentation combine the gyro horizon with other instruments, thereby reducing the number of separate instruments to which the pilot must devote attention. An integrated flight system consists of electronic components which compute and indicate the aircraft attitude required to attain and maintain a preselected flight condition. "Command" indicators tell

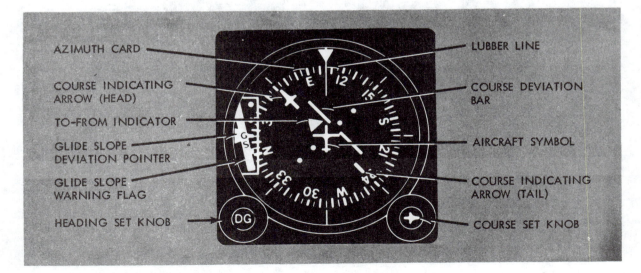

FIGURE 4–44. Horizontal situation indicator (HSI).

the pilot in which direction and how much to change aircraft attitude to achieve the desired result. The computed command indications relieve the pilot of many of the mental calculations required for instrument flight.

The flight director/autopilot system described in this paragraph is typical of that installed in some of the more complex general aviation airplanes. The components installed in the instrument panel include the mode controller, flight command indicator, pictorial navigation indicator (horizontal situation indicator), and annunciator panel. These units are illustrated in Figure 4–45. The mode controller contains six pushbutton switches for turning on the flight director and selection of all modes, a switch for autopilot engagement, a trim switch, and a preflight test button. The flight command indicator displays information regarding pitch and roll attitude, pitch and roll commands, and decision height (when used with a radar altimeter). The

pictorial navigation indicator displays slaved gyro magnetic heading information, VOR/LOC/RNAV course deviation, and glideslope deviation indications. The annunciator panel displays all vertical and lateral flight director/autopilot modes, including all "armed" modes prior to capture. simply stated, it tells the pilot when the selected mode has been received and accepted by the system, and if an "armed" mode is selected, when capture has been initiated. It also has integral marker beacon lights and a trim failure warning.

Since compact, low cost integrated flight systems are presently available, the future pilot of sophisticated private, business, and executive aircraft as well as the airline and military pilot will be using one of these systems as standard equipment. A flight control guidance system which consists of either an automatic pilot with an approach coupler or a flight director system is required for Category II operations.

Pictorial Navigation Indicator

Annunciator Panel

Mode Controller

Flight Command Indicator

Figure 4–45. Integrated flight system.

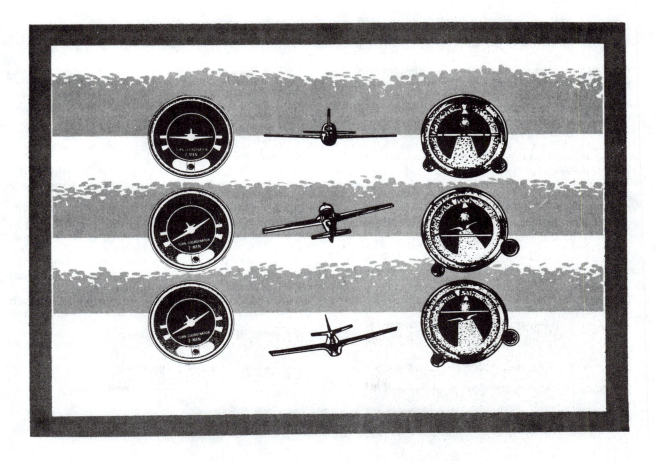

V. ATTITUDE INSTRUMENT FLYING-AIRPLANES

NOTE: The instrument maneuvers presented in Chapter V are based on an airplane equipped with a turn coordinator. If the airplane flown has a turn needle, the descriptions apply if "turn needle" is substituted for "miniature aircraft of the turn coordinator."

Attitude instrument flying may be defined in general terms as the control of an airplane's spatial position by the use of instruments rather than by outside visual reference.

Any flight, regardless of the airplane used or route flown, consists of basic maneuvers. In visual flight, you control airplane attitude with relation to the natural horizon by using certain reference points on the airplane. In instrument flight, you control airplane attitude by reference to the flight instruments. A proper interpretation of the flight instruments will give you essentially the same information that outside references do in visual flight. Once you learn the role of all instruments in establishing and maintaining a desired airplane attitude, you are better equipped to control the airplane in emergency situations involving failure of one or more key instruments.

There are at least two basic methods in use for learning attitude instrument flying. Both methods involve the use of the same instruments, and both use the same responses for attitude control. They differ in their reliance on the attitude indicator and consequently on the use and interpretation of other instruments.

One method presents the problem of attitude control essentially from this standpoint: airplane performance depends upon how you control the attitude and thrust relationship of the airplane. The first group of instruments presents existing performance information. The altimeter, for example, shows the altitude, or altitude changes, resulting from power and attitude control. The airspeed indicator, vertical-speed indicator, heading indicator, and turn coordinator likewise tell you what the airplane is doing with respect to speed, vertical movement, direction, rate of direction change and trim. This group of instruments is therefore referred to as the performance instruments.

The second group of instruments presents information necessary to determine the power and attitude necessary for maintaining or changing airplane performance. The attitude indicator and tachometer (or manifold pressure gauge and tachometer in combination) show you what pitch, bank, and power combination is controlling the performance shown on the other instruments. These are called control instruments.

The third group shows you where your flight path is with respect to the earth's surface, and therefore these are called navigation instruments.

Another basic method for presenting attitude instrument flying, groups the instruments as they relate to control function as well as airplane performance. All maneuvers involve some degree of motion about the lateral (pitch), longitudinal (bank/roll), and vertical (yaw) axes. Attitude control is accordingly stressed in this handbook in terms of *pitch control, bank control, power control,* and *trim control* (Fig. 5–1). Instruments are therefore grouped as they relate to control function and airplane performance as follows:

Pitch Instruments

Attitude Indicator
Altimeter
Airspeed Indicator
Vertical-Speed Indicator

Bank Instruments

Attitude Indicator
Heading Indicator
Turn Coordinator

Power Instruments

Manifold Pressure Gauge (MP)
Tachometer/RPM
Airspeed Indicator
Engine Pressure Ratio (EPR)—Jet

For any maneuver or condition of flight, the pitch, bank, and power control requirements are most clearly indicated by certain key instruments. Those instruments which provide the most pertinent and essential information will be referred to as primary instruments. Supporting instruments back up and supplement the information shown on the primary instruments. Straight-and-level flight at a constant airspeed, for example, means that an exact altitude is to be maintained with zero bank (constant heading) at a constant airspeed. The pitch instrument, bank instrument, and power instru-

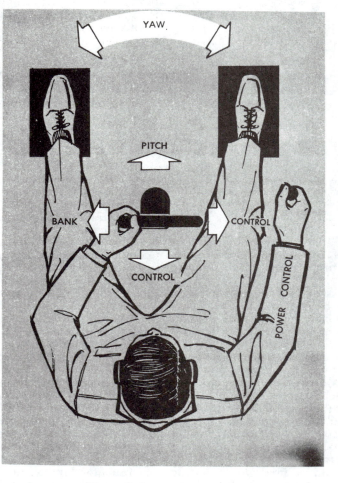

FIGURE 5–1. Attitude control.

56

ment which tell you whether you are maintaining this flight condition are the:

1. *Altimeter*—which supplies the most pertinent altitude information and is therefore primary for pitch.

2. *Heading Indicator*—which supplies the most pertinent bank or heading information ("banking" means turning) and is therefore primary for bank.

3. *Airspeed Indicator*—which supplies the most pertinent information concerning performance in level flight in terms of power output, and is therefore primary for power.

This concept of primary and supporting instruments in no way lessens the value of any particular flight instrument. The attitude indicator is the basic attitude reference. It is the only instrument which portrays instantly and directly the actual flight attitude. It should always be used, when available, in establishing and maintaining pitch and bank attitudes. The specific use of primary and supporting instruments will be better understood as the basic instrument maneuvers are presented in detail.

You will find the terms "direct indicating instrument" and "indirect indicating instrument" used in the following pages. A "direct" indication is the true and instantaneous reflection of airplane pitch and bank attitude by the miniature aircraft relative to the horizon bar of the attitude indicator. The altimeter, airspeed indicator, and vertical-speed indicator give "indirect" indications of pitch attitude at a given power setting. The heading indicator and turn needle give "indirect" indications of bank attitude.

Included in the appendix of this handbook is a reproduction of the *Instrument Flight Instructor Lesson Guide (Airplanes)* which is correlated with the material which follows.

Fundamental Skills

During attitude instrument training, you must develop three fundamental skills involved in all instrument flight maneuvers: *instrument cross-check, instrument interpretation,* and *aircraft control.* Although you learn these skills separately and in deliberate sequence, a measure of your proficiency in precision flying will be your ability to integrate these skills into unified, smooth, positive control responses to maintain any prescribed flight path.

Cross-Check.—The first fundamental skill is cross-checking (also called "scanning" or "instrument coverage"). Cross-checking is the continuous and logical observation of instruments for attitude and performance information. In attitude instrument flying, the pilot maintains an attitude by reference to instruments that will produce the desired result in performance. Due to human error, instrument error, and airplane performance differences in various atmospheric and loading conditions, it is impossible to establish an attitude and have performance remain constant for a long period of time. These variables make it necessary for the pilot to constantly check the instruments and make appropriate changes in airplane attitude.

As a beginner, you may cross-check rapidly, looking *at* the instruments without knowing exactly what you are looking *for*. With increasing experience in basic instrument maneuvers and familiarity with the instrument indications associated with them, you will learn what to look for, when to look for it, and what response to make. As proficiency increases, you scan primarily from habit, suiting your scanning rate and sequence to the demands of the flight situation. You can expect to make many of the common scanning errors, both during training and at any subsequent time, if you fail to maintain basic instrument proficiency through practice.

The following cross-check faults are frequent problems:

1. *Fixation,* or staring at a single instrument, usually occurs for a good reason, but with poor results. For instance, you may find yourself staring at your altimeter which reads 200 feet below assigned altitude, wondering how the needle got there. While you gaze at the instrument, perhaps with increasing tension on the controls, a heading change occurs unnoticed, and more errors accumulate.

Another common fixation is likely when you initiate an attitude change. For example, you establish a shallow bank for a 90° turn and stare at the heading indicator throughout the turn, instead of maintaining your cross-check of other pertinent instruments. You know that the aircraft is turning and that you need not recheck the heading indicator for approximately 25 seconds after turn entry, yet you can't take your eyes off the instrument. The problem here may not be entirely due to cross-check error. It may be related to difficulties with one or both of the other fundamental skills. You may be fixating because of uncertainty about reading the heading indicator (interpretation) or because of inconsistency in rolling out of turns (control).

2. *Omission* of an instrument from your cross-check is another likely fault. It may be caused by failure to anticipate significant instrument indications following attitude changes. For example, on your roll out from a 180° steep turn, you establish straight and level flight with reference to the attitude indicator alone, neglecting to check the heading indicator for constant heading information. Because of precession error, the attitude indicator will temporarily show a slight error, correctable by quick reference to the other flight instruments.

3. *Emphasis* on a single instrument, instead of on the combination of instruments necessary for attitude information, is an understandable fault during initial stages of training. You naturally tend to rely on the instrument that you understand most readily, even when it provides erroneous or inadequate information. Until completely accurate and infallible instruments are devised, reliance on a single instrument is poor technique. For example, you can maintain reasonably close altitude control with the attitude indicator, but you cannot hold altitude

with precision without including the altimeter in your cross-check.

Instrument Interpretation.—The second fundamental skill, instrument interpretation, requires the most thorough study and analysis. It begins with your understanding of each instrument's construction and operating principles. Then you must apply this knowledge to the performance of the airplane you are flying, the particular maneuvers to be executed, the cross-check and control techniques applicable to that airplane, and the flight conditions in which you are operating. For example, (Fig. 5–2), using full power in a light airplane for a 5-minute climb from near sea level, the attitude indicator shows the miniature aircraft two bar widths (twice the thickness of the miniature aircraft wings) above the artificial horizon. The airplane is climbing at 500 feet per minute as shown on the vertical-speed indicator, and at an airspeed of 90 knots, as shown on the airspeed indicator. With the power available in this particular airplane and the attitude selected by the pilot, the performance is shown on the instruments.

Now set up the identical picture on the attitude indicator in a modern jet executive airplane. With the same airplane attitude as shown in the first example, the vertical-speed indicator in the jet reads 2,000 feet per minute, and the air-speed indicates 300 knots. As you learn the performance capabilities of the airplane in which you are training, you will interpret the instrument indications appropriately in terms of the attitude of the airplane. If the pitch attitude is to be determined, the airspeed indicator, altimeter, vertical-speed indicator, and attitude indicator provide the necessary information. If the bank attitude is to be determined, the heading indicator, turn coordinator, and attitude indicator must be interpreted.

For each maneuver, you will learn what performance to expect and the combination of instruments that you must interpret in order to control airplane attitude during the maneuver.

Aircraft Control.—The third fundamental instrument flying skill is aircraft control. With the instruments substituted for outside references, the necessary control responses and thought processes are the same as those for controlling airplane performance by means of outside references. Knowing the desired attitude of the airplane with respect to the natural and artificial horizon, you maintain the attitude or change it by movement of the appropriate controls.

Aircraft control is composed of three components: pitch control, bank control, and power control.

1. *Pitch control* is controlling the rotation of the airplane about the lateral axis by movement of the elevators. After interpreting the pitch attitude from the proper flight instruments, you exert control pressures to effect the desired pitch attitude with reference to the horizon.

2. *Bank control* is controlling the angle made by the wing and the horizon. After interpreting the bank attitude from the appropriate instruments, you exert the necessary pressures to move the aile-

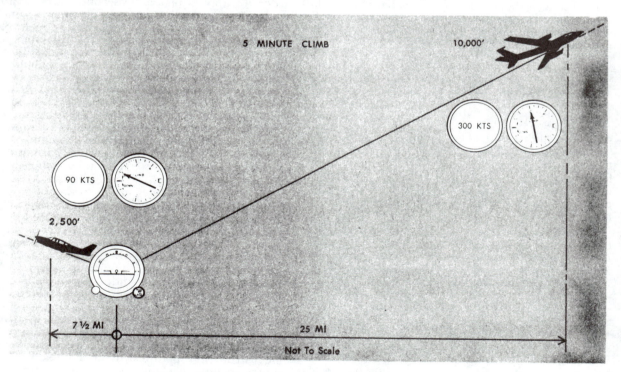

FIGURE 5–2. Power and attitude equal performance.

58

rons and roll the airplane about the longitudinal axis.

3. *Power control* is used when interpretation of the flight instruments indicates a need for a change in thrust.

Trim is used to relieve all possible control pressures held after a desired attitude has been attained. An improperly trimmed airplane requires constant control pressures, produces tension, distracts your attention from cross-checking, and contributes to abrupt and erratic attitude control. The pressures you feel on the controls must be those *you* apply while controlling a planned change in airplane attitude, not pressures held because you let the airplane control you.

Preflight Instrument Check

Before any flight, especially a flight into instrument conditions, a thorough check should be made of all instruments and equipment in the airplane. Your airplane flight handbook lists the items to be checked. They may vary as to sequence and content from the checks shown below.

Before Starting Engine.—Although the following pre-start check might seem a waste of time, it can reveal conditions or defects which would make starting inadvisable.

1. Appropriate handbooks, en route charts, approach charts, computer, and flight log.
2. Radio equipment—switches off.
3. Suction gauge—proper markings.
4. Pitot cover—removed.
5. Airspeed indicator—proper reading.
6. Heading indicator—uncaged if applicable.
7. Attitude indicator—uncaged if applicable.
8. Turn coordinator—miniature aircraft level, ball approximately centered (level terrain).
9. Vertical-speed indicator—zero indication.
10. Magnetic compass—full of fluid.
11. Clock—wind and set to the correct time.
12. Engine instruments—proper markings and readings.
13. De-icing and anti-icing equipment—availability and fluid quantity.

After Starting Engine.—Make the following checks.

1. *Suction Gauge or Electrical Indicators.*—Check the source of power for the gyro instruments. The suction developed should be appropriate for the instruments in that particular aircraft. If the gyros are electrically driven, check the generators and inverters for proper operation.
2. *Pitot Head.*—Heat checked.
3. *Magnetic Compass.*—Check the card for freedom of movement and be sure that the bowl is full of fluid. Determine compass accuracy by comparing the indicated heading against a known heading while the airplane is stopped or taxiing straight. Remote Indicating Compasses should also be checked against known headings.
4. *Heading Indicator.*—Allow 5 minutes after starting engines for the gyro rotor of the vacuum-operated heading indicator to attain normal operating speed. Before taxiing, or while taxiing straight, set the heading indicator to correspond with the magnetic compass heading. Be sure the instrument is fully uncaged if it has a caging feature. Before takeoff, recheck the heading indicator. If your magnetic compass and deviation card are accurate, the heading indicator should show the known taxiway or runway direction when the airplane is aligned with them (within 5°).

Electric gyros should also be set and checked against known headings. Allow 3 minutes for the electric gyro to attain operating speed. A gyrosyn (slaved gyro) compass should be checked for slaving action and its indications compared with those of the magnetic compass.

5. *Attitude Indicator.*—Allow the same times as noted above for gyros to attain normal rotor speed. If the horizon bar erects to the horizontal position and remains at the correct position for the attitude of the airplane, or if it begins to vibrate after this attitude is reached and then slowly stops vibrating altogether, the instrument is operating properly. If the horizon bar fails to remain in the horizontal position during straight taxiing, or tips in excess of 5° during taxi turns, the instrument is unreliable.

Adjust the miniature aircraft with reference to the horizon bar for the particular airplane while on the ground. For some tricycle-geared airplane, a slightly nose-low attitude on the ground will give a level flight attitude at normal cruising speed.

6. *Altimeter.*—With the altimeter set to the current reported altimeter setting, note any variation between the known field elevation and the altimeter indication. If the variation is in the order of plus or minus 75 feet, the accuracy of the altimeter is questionable and the problem should be referred to an appropriately rated repair station for evaluation and possible correction.

7. *Turn Coordinator.*—During taxi turns, check the miniature aircraft for proper turn indications. The ball should move freely. While taxiing straight, the miniature aircraft should be level.

8. *Vertical-Speed Indicator.*—The instrument should read zero. If it does not, tap the panel gently. If it stays off the zero reading and is not adjustable, the ground indication will have to be interpreted as the zero position in flight.

9. *Carburetor Heat.*—Check for proper operation and return to cold position.

10. *Engine Instruments.*—Check for proper readings.

11. *Radio Equipment.*—Check for proper operation and set as desired.

12. *De-Icing and Anti-Icing Equipment.*—Check operation.

Basic Maneuvers

Instrument flying techniques differ according to airplane type, class, performance capability, and instrumentation. The procedures and techniques that follow will, therefore, need to be modified for application to different types of airplanes. Recommended procedures, performance data, operating limitations, and flight characteristics of a particular airplane are available in your airplane flight manual or owner's handbook for study before practicing the flight maneuvers.

The flight maneuvers discussed here assume a single-engine, propeller-driven light airplane with retractable gear and flaps and a panel with instruments representative of those discussed earlier under "Basic Flight Instruments." The sequence of maneuvers in the training curriculum, as well as the time necessary for their mastery, is also flexible. The instrument takeoff, for example, is not required on the flight check for the instrument rating. Whether or not it is worth your study and practice depends upon the flight instruments you have available and the weather conditions in which you expect to fly. With the exception of the instrument takeoff, all of the maneuvers can be performed on "partial panel," with the attitude gyro and heading indicator covered or inoperative.

Straight-and-Level Flight

Pitch Control.—The pitch attitude of an airplane is the angle between the longitudinal axis of the airplane and the actual horizon. In level flight, the pitch attitude varies with airspeed and with load. For training purposes, the latter factor can normally be disregarded in light airplanes. At a constant airspeed, there is only one specific pitch attitude for level flight. At low cruise speeds, the level flight attitude is nose-high (Fig. 5–3); at high cruise speeds, the level flight attitude is nose-low

FIGURE 5–3. Pitch attitude and airspeed in level flight—low cruise speed.

60

(Fig. 5–4). Figure 5–5 shows the attitude at normal cruise speeds.

The pitch instruments are the *attitude indicator*, the *altimeter*, the *vertical-speed indicator*, and the *airspeed indicator*.

The *attitude indicator* gives you a *direct* indication of pitch attitude. You attain the desired pitch attitude by raising or lowering the miniature aircraft in relation to the horizon bar by means of elevator control. This corresponds to the way you adjust pitch attitude in contact flight by raising or lowering the nose of the airplane in relation to the natural horizon. However, unless the airspeed is constant, and until you have established and identified the level flight attitude for that airspeed, you have no way of knowing whether level flight, as indicated

on the attitude indicator, is resulting in level flight as shown on the altimeter, vertical-speed indicator, and airspeed indicator. With the miniature aircraft of the attitude indicator properly adjusted on the ground before takeoff, it will show approximately level flight at normal cruise speed when you complete your level-off from a climb. If further adjustment of the miniature aircraft is necessary, the other pitch instruments must be used to maintain level flight while the adjustment is made. Caging and uncaging the attitude indicator in flight, as well as the limitations of the instrument, have been discussed in Chapter IV, "Basic Flight Instruments."

In practicing pitch control for level flight, using only the attitude indicator, restrict the displacement of the horizon bar to a bar width up or down, a

FIGURE 5–4. Pitch attitude and airspeed in level flight—high cruise speed.

61

FIGURE 5–5. Pitch attitude and airspeed in level flight—normal cruise speed.

half-bar width, then a one-and-one-half bar width. Half-, two-, and three-bar-width nose-high attitudes are shown in Figures 5–6, 5–7, and 5–8.

Your instructor will demonstrate these normal pitch corrections while you compare the indications on the attitude indicator with the airplane's position with respect to the natural horizon. Note that pitch attitude changes for corrections to level flight by reference to instruments are much smaller than those commonly used for contact flight. Note especially that, with the airplane correctly trimmed for level flight, the elevator displacement and the control pressures necessary to effect these standard pitch changes are usually very slight. Just how much elevator control pressure to use is a problem you must solve for yourself, with a few helpful hints.

First, you cannot feel control pressure changes with a tight grip on the controls. Relaxing and learning to control "with your eyes and your head" instead of your muscles usually takes considerable conscious effort during early stages of instrument training.

Second, make the pitch changes smooth and small, yet with a positive pressure. Practice these small corrections until you can make pitch corrections up or down, "freezing" (holding constant) the one-half, full, and one-and-one-half bar widths on the attitude indicator.

Third, with the airplane properly trimmed for level flight, momentarily release all of your pressure on the elevator control when you become aware of tenseness. This will remind you that the airplane

62

FIGURE 5–6. Pitch correction for level flight—half-bar
width.

FIGURE 5–8. Pitch correction for level flight—three-bar
width.

FIGURE 5–7. Pitch correction for level flight—two-bar
width.

is stable and, except under turbulent conditions, will maintain level flight if you leave it alone. One of your most difficult initial training problems will be to resist the impulse to move the controls, even when your eyes tell you that no control change is called for.

At a constant thrust, any deviation from level flight (except in turbulent air) must be the result of a pitch change. The *altimeter,* therefore, gives you an *indirect* indication of the pitch attitude in level flight, assuming constant power. Since the

altitude should remain constant when the airplane is in level flight, any deviation from the desired altitude shows the need for a pitch change. If you are gaining altitude (Fig. 5–9), the nose must be lowered (Fig. 5–10). How much? And how can it be done by reference to the altimeter alone?

The *rate* of movement of the altimeter needle is as important as its *direction* of movement in maintaining level flight without the use of the attitude indicator. An excessive pitch deviation from level flight results in a relatively rapid change of altitude; while a slight pitch deviation causes a slow change. Thus, if the altimeter needle moves rapidly clockwise, assume a considerable nose-high deviation from level flight attitude. Conversely, if the needle moves slowly counter-clockwise to indicate a slightly nose-low attitude, assume that the pitch correction necessary to regain the desired altitude is small. As you add the altimeter to the attitude indicator in your cross-check, you will learn to recognize the rate of movement of the altimeter needle for a given pitch change as shown on the attitude indicator.

If you are practicing precision control of pitch in an airplane without an attitude indicator, make small pitch changes by visual reference to the natural horizon, and note the rate of movement of the altimeter. Note the pitch change giving the slowest steady rate of change on the altimeter. Then practice small pitch corrections until you can control them by interpretation and control of the rate of needle movement.

Your instructor may demonstrate an excessive nose-down deviation (indicated by rapid movement of the altimeter needle) and then, as an example, show you the result of improper corrective technique. The normal impulse is to make a large pitch correction in a hurry, but this inevitably leads to

NOSE HIGH   ALTITUDE HIGH

FIGURE 5–9. Using the altimeter for pitch interpretation—altitude increase.

LOWER NOSE TO
CORRECT ALTITUDE ERROR

FIGURE 5–10. Pitch correction following altitude increase.

overcontrolling: the needle slows down, then reverses direction, and finally indicates an excessive nose-high deviation. The result is tension on the controls, and erratic control response and increasingly extreme control movements. The correct technique, which is slower and smoother, will return the airplane to the desired attitude more quickly, with positive control and no confusion.

When a pitch error is detected, corrective action should be taken promptly, but with light control pressures and with two distinct changes of attitude: first is a change of attitude to stop the needle movement, second is a change of attitude to return to the desired altitude.

When you observe needle movement indicating an altitude deviation, apply just enough elevator pressure to slow down the rate of needle movement. If it slows down abruptly, ease off some of the pressure until the needle continues to move, but slowly. Slow needle movement means that your airplane attitude is close to level flight. Add a little more corrective pressure to stop the direction of needle movement. At this point you are in level flight; a reversal of needle movement means that you have passed through it. Relax your control pressures carefully as you continue to cross-check, since changing airspeed will cause changes in the effectiveness of a given control pressure. Next, adjust the pitch attitude with elevator pressure for the rate of change of altimeter needle movement that you have correlated with normal pitch corrections, and return to the desired altitude.

As a rule of thumb, for errors of less than 100 feet, (Fig. 5–11) use a half-bar-width correction (Fig. 5–12). For errors in excess of 100 feet (Fig. 5–13), use an initial full-bar-width correction (Fig. 5–14).

Practice predetermined altitude changes using the altimeter alone, then in combination with the attitude indicator.

The *vertical-speed indicator* gives an *indirect* indication of pitch attitude and is both a trend and a rate instrument. As a trend instrument, it shows immediately the initial vertical movement of the airplane, which, disregarding turbulence, can be considered a reflection of pitch change. To maintain level flight, use the vertical-speed indicator in conjunction with the altimeter and attitude indicator. Note any "up" or "down" trend of the needle from zero and apply a very light corrective elevator pressure. As the needle returns to zero, relax the corrective pressure. If your control pressures have been smooth and light, the needle will react immediately and slowly, and the altimeter will show little or no change of altitude.

Used as a rate instrument, the lag characteristics of the vertical-speed indicator must be considered.

Lag refers to the delay involved before the needle attains a stable indication following a pitch change. Lag is directly proportional to the speed and magnitude of a pitch change. If a slow, smooth pitch change is initiated, the needle will move, with minimum lag, to a point of deflection corresponding to the extent of the pitch change and then stabilize as the aerodynamic forces are balanced in the climb or descent. A large and abrupt pitch change will produce erratic needle movement and also introduce greater time delay (lag) before the needle stabilizes. Students are cautioned not to "chase the needle" when flight through turbulent conditions produces such erratic needle movements.

In using the vertical-speed indicator as a rate instrument and combining it with the altimeter and attitude indicator to maintain level flight, keep this in mind: the amount the altimeter has moved from the desired altitude governs the rate at which you

ERROR LESS THAN 100 FEET

FIGURE 5–11. Altitude error—less than 100 feet.

65

FIGURE 5–12. Pitch correction—less than 100 feet.

FIGURE 5–13. Altitude error—greater than 100 feet.

should return to that altitude. A rule of thumb is to make an attitude change that will result in a vertical speed rate that is approximately double your error in altitude. For example, if off altitude 100 feet, your rate of return should be approximately 200 feet per minute. If off more than 100 feet, the correction should be correspondingly greater, but should never exceed the optimum rate

66

FIGURE 5–14. Pitch correction—greater than 100 feet.

of climb or descent for your airplane at a given airspeed and configuration. A deviation of more than 200 feet per minute from the desired rate of return is considered overcontrolling. For example, if you are attempting to return to an altitude at a rate of 200 feet per minute, a rate in excess of 400 feet per minute indicates overcontrolling. While returning to an altitude, the vertical-speed indicator is the primary pitch instrument. Occasionally, the vertical-speed indicator is slightly out of calibration and may indicate a climb or descent when the airplane is in level flight. If you cannot adjust the instrument, you must take the error into consideration when using it for pitch control. For example, if the needle indicates a descent of 200 feet per minute while in level flight, use this indication as the zero position.

The *airspeed indicator* presents an *indirect* indication of the pitch attitude. At a constant power setting and pitch attitude, the airspeed remains constant (Fig. 5–15). As the pitch attitude lowers, airspeed increases (Fig. 5–16), and the nose should be raised. As the pitch attitude rises, the airspeed decreases (Fig. 5–17), and the nose should be lowered. A rapid change in airspeed indicates a large pitch change, and a slow change of airspeed indicates a small pitch change. The apparent lag in airspeed indications with pitch changes varies greatly among different airplanes and is due to the time required for the airplane to accelerate or decelerate when the pitch attitude is changed. There is no appreciable lag due to the construction or operation of the instrument. Small pitch changes, smoothly executed, result in an immediate change of airspeed.

Pitch control in level flight is a question of scanning and interpretation of the instrument panel for whatever information the instruments present that will enable you to visualize and control pitch attitude. Regardless of individual differences in scanning technique, all pilots should use the instruments that give the best information for controlling the airplane in any given maneuver. They also check the other instruments to aid in maintaining the important, or *primary*, instruments at the desired indication.

As noted previously, the primary instrument is the one that gives the most pertinent information for any particular maneuver. It is usually the one that you should hold at a constant indication. Which instrument, for example, is primary for pitch control in level flight? This question should be considered in the context of specific airplane, weather conditions, pilot experience, operational conditions, and other factors. Attitude changes must be detected and interpreted instantly for immediate control action in high-performance airplanes. On the other hand, a reasonably proficient instrument pilot in a slower airplane may rely more on the altimeter for primary pitch information, especially if it is determined that too much reliance on the attitude indicator fails to provide the necessary precise attitude information. Whether the pilot decides to regard the altimeter as primary, or the attitude indicator as primary is a question of which approach best helps control attitude.

67

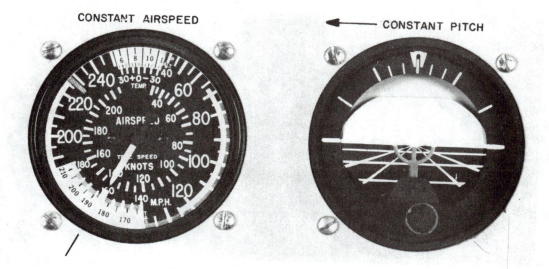

FIGURE 5–15.   Constant power plus constant pitch equals constant airspeed.

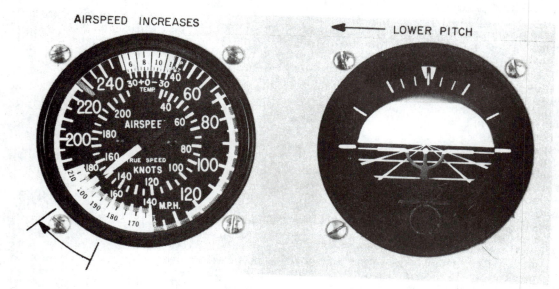

FIGURE 5–16.   Constant power plus decreased pitch equals increased airspeed.

68

FIGURE 5–17.   Constant power plus increased pitch equals decreased airspeed.

In this handbook, the *altimeter* is normally considered as the primary pitch instrument during level flight.

Bank Control.—The bank attitude of an airplane is the angle between the lateral axis of the airplane and the natural horizon. To maintain a straight-and-level flight path, you must keep the wings of the airplane level with the horizon (assuming that the airplane is in coordinated flight). Any deviation from straight flight resulting from bank error should be corrected by *coordinated* aileron and rudder pressure.

The instruments used for bank control are the *attitude indicator*, the *heading indicator*, and the *turn coordinator* (Fig. 5–18).

The *attitude indicator* shows any change in bank attitude *directly* and instantly. On the standard attitude indicator, the angle of bank is shown pictorially by the relationship of the miniature aircraft to the artificial horizon bar, and by the alignment of the pointer with the banking scale at the top of the instrument. On the face of the standard 3″ instrument, small angles of bank can be difficult to detect by reference to the miniature aircraft, especially if you lean to one side or move your seating position slightly. The position of the scale pointer is a good check against the apparent miniature aircraft position. Disregarding precession error, small deviations from straight coordinated flight can be readily detected on the scale pointer. The banking index may be graduated as shown in Figure 5–19, or it may lack the 10° and 20° indexes. Refer to Chapter IV on "Basic Flight Instruments" for ap-

plication of bank control techniques to types of attitude indicators other than the one illustrated here. Caging and uncaging, as well as the banking limitations of various types are covered in that chapter.

The instrument depicted in Figure 5–19 has a scale pointer that moves in the *same* direction of bank shown by the miniature aircraft. If, however, your airplane is equipped with the type attitude indicator shown in Figure 4–25 on page 41, you may be bothered by the fact that the scale pointer moves in a direction *opposite* to the direction of bank shown by the miniature aircraft. A bank indication of 30° to the right of the zero, or nose position, indicates a 30° left banking attitude. Errors due to the construction of this instrument are common and understandable, but the obvious advantage of the attitude indicator is that you get an immediate indication of both pitch and bank attitude in a single glance. Even with the precession errors associated with many attitude indicators, the quick attitude presentation requires less visual effort and time for positive control than do the other flight instruments.

The bank attitude of an aircraft in coordinated flight is shown *indirectly* on the *heading indicator*, since banking results in a turn and change in heading. A rapid movement of the heading indicator needle (or azimuth card in a directional gyro) indicates a large angle of bank, whereas a slow movement of the needle or card reflects a small angle of bank, assuming the same airspeed in both instances. If you note the rate of movement of the heading indicator for given degrees of bank shown on the attitude indicator, you will learn to look for

FIGURE 5-18.   Instruments used for bank control.

important bank information on the heading indicator, especially when precession error in the attitude indicator requires a precise check of heading information to maintain straight flight.

When you note deviations from straight flight on the heading indicator, make your correction to the desired heading by using an angle of bank no greater than the number of degrees to be turned. In any case, limit your bank corrections to a bank angle no greater than that required for a standard-rate turn. Use of larger bank angles requires a very high level of proficiency, and normally results in overcontrolling and erratic bank control. For heading indicator limitations, refer to the chapter on "Basic Flight Instruments."

The *miniature aircraft of the turn coordinator* gives you an *indirect* indication of the bank attitude of the airplane. When the miniature aircraft is level, the airplane is in straight flight. When the miniature aircraft is in a stabilized deflection, the airplane is turning in the direction indicated. Thus, if the ball is centered, a left deflection of the miniature aircraft means the left wing is low and the airplane is in a left turn. Return to straight flight is accomplished by coordinated aileron and rudder pressure to level the miniature aircraft. You must observe the miniature aircraft closely to detect small deviations from the desired position. When the instrument is used to maintain straight flight, control pressures must be applied very lightly and smoothly.

The *ball of the turn coordinator* is actually a separate instrument, conveniently located under the miniature aircraft because the two instruments are used

70

FIGURE 5–19. Bank interpretation with the attitude indicator.

FIGURE 5–20. Slip indication.

together. The ball instrument indicates the quality of the turn. If the ball is off center, the airplane is slipping or skidding, and the miniature aircraft under these conditions is erroneous in its indications of bank attitude. Figures 5–20 and 5–21 show the instrument indications for slips and skids, respectively. If the wings are level and the airplane is properly trimmed, the ball will remain in the center, and the airplane will be in straight flight. If the ball is not centered, the airplane is improperly trimmed (or you are holding rudder pressure against proper trim).

To maintain straight-and-level flight with proper trim, note the direction of ball displacement. If the ball is to the left of center and the left wing is low, apply left rudder pressure (or release right rudder pressure if you are holding it) to center the ball and correct the slip. At the same time apply right aileron pressure as necessary to level the wings, cross-checking the heading indicator and attitude indicator as you center the ball. If the wings are level and the ball is displaced from center, the airplane is skidding. Note the direction of ball displacement and use the same corrective technique as for an indicated slip. Center the ball (left ball/left rudder, right ball/right rudder), use aileron as necessary for bank control, and retrim.

To trim the airplane, using only the turn coordinator, use aileron pressure to level the miniature aircraft and rudder pressure to center the ball. Hold these indications with control pressures, gradually releasing them as you apply rudder trim sufficient to relieve all rudder pressure. Apply aileron trim if available to relieve aileron pressure. With a full instrument panel, maintain a wings-level attitude by reference to all available instruments while you trim the airplane.

FIGURE 5–21. Skid indication.

Power Control.—Power produces thrust which, with the appropriate angle of attack of the wing overcomes the forces of gravity, drag, and inertia to determine airplane performance.

Power control must be related to its effect on altitude and airspeed, since any change in power setting results in a change in the airspeed or the altitude of the airplane. At any given airspeed, the power setting determines whether the airplane is in level flight, in a climb, or in a descent. If you

71

increase the power while in straight-and-level flight and hold the airspeed constant, the airplane will climb; and if you decrese the power while holding the airspeed constant, the airplane will descend. On the other hand, if you hold *altitude* constant, the power applied will determine the airspeed.

The relationship between altitude and airspeed determines the need for a change in pitch or power. If the airspeed is off the desired value, always check the altimeter before deciding that a power change is necessary. If you think of altitude and airspeed as interchangeable, you can "trade" altitude for airspeed by lowering the nose, or convert airspeed to altitude by raising the nose. If your altitude is higher than desired and your airspeed low (Fig. 5–22), or vice versa, a change in pitch alone may return the airplane to the desired altitude and airspeed. If both airspeed and altitude are high (Fig. 5–23) or if both are low, then a change in both pitch and power is necessary in order to return to the desired airspeed and altitude.

For changes in airspeed in straight-and-level flight, pitch, bank, and power must be *coordinated* in order to maintain constant altitude and heading. When power is changed to vary airspeed in straight-and-level flight, a single-engine propeller-driven airplane tends to change attitude around all axes of movement. Therefore, to maintain constant altitude and heading, you will need to apply various control pressures in proportion to the change in power. When you add power to increase airspeed, the pitch instruments will show a climb unless you apply forward elevator control pressure as the airspeed changes. When you increase power, the airplane tends to yaw and roll to the left unless you apply counteracting aileron and rudder pressures.

FIGURE 5–22. Airspeed low and altitude high (lower pitch).

FIGURE 5–23. Airspeed and altitude high (lower pitch and reduce power).

72

The increased speed of cross-check required to keep ahead of these changes varies with the type of airplane and its torque characteristics, the extent of power and speed change involved, and your technique in making the power change.

Power control and airspeed changes are much easier when you know in advance the approximate power settings necessary to maintain various airspeeds in straight-and-level flight. However, to change airspeed any appreciable amount, common procedure is to underpower or overpower on initial power changes to accelerate the rate of airspeed change. (For small speed changes, or in airplanes that decelerate or accelerate rapidly, overpowering or underpowering is unnecessary.)

Consider the example of an airplane which requires 23 inches of manifold pressure to maintain a normal cruising airspeed of 140 knots, and 18 inches of manifold pressure to maintain an airspeed of 100 knots. The reduction in airspeed from 140 knots to 100 knots while maintaining straight-and-level flight, is discussed below and illustrated in Figures 5–24, 5–25, and 5–26.

Instrument indications, prior to the power reduction, are shown in Figure 5–24. While the basic attitude is established and maintained on the attitude indicator, specific pitch, bank, and power control requirements are detected on these primary instruments:

    Altimeter—Primary Pitch
    Heading Indicator—Primary Bank
    Airspeed Indicator—Primary Power

Supporting pitch and bank instruments are shown in the illustrations. Although not shown, the supporting power instrument is the manifold pressure gauge (or tachometer if the propeller is fixed pitch).

As you make a smooth power reduction to approximately 15″ Hg (underpower), the manifold pressure gauge becomes the primary power instrument (Fig. 5–25). With practice, you will be able to change a power setting with only a brief glance at the power instrument, by sensing the movement of the throttle, the change in sound, and the changes in the feel of control pressures.

As the thrust decreases, increase the speed of your cross-check and be ready to apply left rudder, back elevator, and aileron control pressure the instant the pitch and bank instruments show a deviation from altitude and heading. As you become

FIGURE 5–24. Straight-and-level flight (normal cruising speed).

FIGURE 5–25. Straight-and-level flight (airspeed decreasing).

proficient, you will learn to cross-check, interpret, and control the changes with no deviation of heading and altitude. Assuming smooth air and ideal control technique, as airspeed decreases, a proportionate increase in airplane pitch attitude is required to maintain altitude. Similarly, effective torque control means counteracting yaw with rudder pressure.

As the power is reduced, the altimeter is primary for pitch, the heading indicator is primary for bank, and the manifold pressure gauge is momentarily primary for power (at 15″ Hg in this example). Control pressures should be trimmed off as the airplane decelerates. As the airspeed approaches the desired airspeed of 100 knots, the manifold pressure is adjusted to approximately 18″ Hg and becomes the supporting power instrument. The airspeed indicator again becomes primary for power (Fig. 5–26).

Practice of airspeed changes in straight-and-level flight provides an excellent means of developing increased proficiency in all three basic instrument skills, and brings out some common errors to be expected during training in straight-and-level flight.

Having learned to control the airplane in a "clean" configuration (minimum drag conditions), you can increase your proficiency in cross-check and control by practicing speed changes while extending or retracting the flaps and landing gear.

While practicing, be sure you comply with the airspeed limitations specified in your Aircraft Flight Handbook for gear and flap operation.

Sudden and pronounced attitude changes may be necessary in order to maintain straight-and-level flight as the landing gear is extended and the flaps are lowered in some airplanes. The nose tends to pitch down with gear extension, and when flaps are lowered, lift increases momentarily (at partial flap settings) followed by a marked increase in drag as the flaps near maximum extension.

Control technique varies according to the lift and drag characteristics of each airplane. Accordingly, knowledge of the power settings and trim changes associated with different combinations of airspeed and gear and flap configurations will reduce your instrument cross-check and interpretation problems.

For example, assume that in straight-and-level flight, an airplane indicates 145 knots with power at 22″ manifold pressure/2,300 rpm, gear and flaps up. After reduction in airspeed, with gear and flaps fully extended, straight-and-level flight at the same altitude requires 25″ manifold pressure/2,500 rpm. Maximum gear extension speed is 125 knots; maximum flap extension speed is 105 knots. Airspeed reduction to 95 knots, gear and flaps down, can be made in the following manner:

1. Increase rpm to 2,500, since a high power setting will be used in full drag configuration.

74

FIGURE 5–26. Straight-and-level flight (reduced airspeed stabilized).

2. Reduce manifold pressure to 10". As the airspeed decreases, increase cross-check speed.

3. Make trim adjustments for an increased angle of attack and decrease in torque.

4. As you lower the gear at 125 knots, the nose may tend to pitch down and the rate of deceleration increases. Increase pitch attitude to maintain constant altitude, and trim off some of the back elevator pressures. If you lower full flaps at this point, your cross-check, interpretation, and control must be very rapid. A less difficult technique is to stabilize the airspeed and attitude with gear down before lowering the flaps.

5. Since 18" manifold pressure will hold level flight at 95 knots with the gear down, increase power smoothly to that setting as the airspeed indicator shows approximately 100 knots, and retrim. The attitude indicator now shows approximately two-and-a-half-bar width nose high in straight-and-level flight.

6. Actuate the flap control and simultaneously increase power to the predetermined setting (25") for the desired airspeed, and trim off the pressures necessary to hold constant altitude and heading. The attitude indicator now shows a bar-width nose low in straight-and-level flight at 95 knots.

When you can consistently maintain constant altitude and heading with smooth pitch, bank, power,

and trim control during these pronounced changes in trim, you will have developed a high level of proficiency in the basic skills involved in straight-and-level flight.

Common Errors.—*Heading errors* usually result from the following faults:

1. Failure to cross-check the heading indicator, especially during changes in power or pitch attitude.

2. Misinterpretation of changes in heading, with resulting corrections in the wrong direction.

3. Failure to note, and remember, a preselected heading.

4. Failure to observe the *rate* of heading change and its relation to bank attitude.

5. Overcontrolling in response to heading changes, especially during changes in power settings.

6. Anticipating heading changes with premature application of rudder control.

7. Failure to correct small heading deviations. Unless *zero* error in heading is your goal, you will find yourself tolerating larger and larger deviations. Correction of a 1° error takes a lot less time and concentration than correction of a 20° error.

8. Correcting with improper bank attitude. If you correct a 10° heading error with a 20° bank correction, you can roll past the desired heading

before you have the bank established, requiring another correction in the opposite direction. Don't multiply existing errors with errors in corrective technique.

9. Failure to note the cause of a previous heading error and thus repeating the same error. For example, your airplane is out of trim, with a left-wing low tendency. You repeatedly correct for a slight left turn, yet do nothing about trim.

10. Failure to set the heading indicator properly, or failure to uncage it.

Pitch errors usually result from the following faults:

1. Improper adjustment of the miniature aircraft of the attitude indicator to the wings-level attitude. Following your initial level-off from a climb, check the attitude indicator and make any necessary adjustment in the miniature aircraft for level flight indication at normal cruise airspeed.

2. Insufficient cross-check and interpretation of pitch instruments. For example, the airspeed indication is low. Believing that you are in a nose-high attitude, you react with forward pressure without noting that a low power setting is the cause of the airspeed discrepancy. Increase your cross-check speed to include *all* relevant instrument indications *before* you make a control response.

3. Uncaging the attitude indicator (if it has a caging feature) when the airplane is not in level flight. The altimeter and heading indicator must be stabilized with airspeed indication at normal cruise when you pull out the caging knob, if you expect the instrument to read straight-and-level at normal cruise airspeed.

4. Failure to interpret the attitude indicator in terms of the existing airspeed.

5. Late pitch corrections. Students commonly like to leave well enough alone. When the altimeter shows a 20-foot error, there is a reluctance to correct it, perhaps because of fear of overcontrolling. If overcontrolling is the error, the more you practice small corrections and find out the cause of overcontrolling, the closer you will be able to hold your altitude. If you tolerate a deviation for fear of "rocking the boat," your errors will increase.

6. Chasing the vertical-speed indications. This tendency can be corrected by proper cross-check of other pitch instruments, as well as by increasing your understanding of the instrument characteristics.

7. Using excessive pitch corrections for the altimeter deviation. Rushing a pitch correction by making a large pitch change generally aggravates the existing error and saves neither time nor effort.

8. Failure to maintain established pitch corrections. This is a common error associated with cross-check and trim errors. For example, having established a pitch change to correct an altitude error, you tend to slow down your cross-check, waiting for the airplane to stabilize in the new pitch attitude. To maintain the attitude, you must continue to cross-check and trim off the pressures that you are holding.

9. Fixations during cross-check. After initiating a heading correction, for example, you become preoccupied with bank control and neglect to notice a pitch error. Likewise, during an airspeed change, unnecessary gazing at the power instrument is common. Bear in mind that a small error in power setting is of less consequence than large altitude and heading errors. The airplane will not decelerate any faster while you stare at the manifold pressure gauge than while you continue your cross-check.

Power errors usually result from the following faults:

1. Failure to know the power settings and pitch attitudes appropriate to various airspeeds and airplane configurations.

2. Abrupt use of throttle.

3. Failure to "lead" the airspeed when making power changes. For example, during an airspeed reduction in level flight, especially with gear and flaps extended, adjust the throttle to maintain the slower speed *before* the airspeed reaches the desired speed. Otherwise, the airplane will decelerate to a speed lower than that desired, resulting in further power adjustments. How much you lead the airspeed depends upon how fast the airplane responds to power changes.

4. Fixation on airspeed or manifold pressure instruments during airspeed changes, resulting in erratic control of both airspeed and power.

Trim errors usually result from the following faults:

1. Improper adjustment of seat or rudder pedals for comfortable position of legs and feet. Tension in the ankles makes it difficult to relax rudder pressures.

2. Confusion as to operation of trim devices, which differ among various airplane types. Some trim wheels are aligned appropriately with the airplane's axes; others are not. Some rotate in a direction contrary to what you expect.

3. Faulty sequence in trim technique. Trim should be used, not as a substitute for control with the wheel (stick) and rudders, but to relieve pressures already held to stabilize attitude. As you gain proficiency, you become familiar with trim settings, just as you do with power settings. With little conscious effort, you trim off pressures continually as they occur.

4. Excessive trim control. This induces control pressures that must be held until you retrim properly. Use trim frequently and in small amounts.

5. Failure to understand the cause of trim changes. If you do not understand the basic aerodynamics related to the basic instrument skills, you will be "behind the airplane" continually.

Straight Climbs and Descents

Climbs.—For a given power setting and load condition, there is only one attitude that will give the most efficient rate of climb. The airspeed and the

76

climb power setting that will determine this climb attitude are given in the performance data found in your airplane flight handbook. Details of the technique for entering a climb vary according to airspeed on entry and the type of climb (constant airspeed or constant rate) desired. (Heading and trim control are maintained as discussed under straight-and-level flight).

Entries.—To enter a constant airspeed climb from *cruising* airspeed, raise the miniature aircraft to the approximate nose-high indication appropriate to the predetermined climb speed. The attitude will vary according to the type airplane you are flying. Apply light back elevator pressure to initiate and maintain the climb attitude. The pressures will vary as the airplane decelerates. Power may be advanced to the climb power setting simultaneously with the pitch change, or after the pitch change is established and the airspeed approaches climb speed. If the transition from level flight to climb is smooth, the vertical-speed indicator will show an immediate trend upward, continue moving slowly, and will stop at a rate appropriate to the stabilized airspeed and attitude. (Primary and supporting instruments for the climb entry are shown in Figure 5-27.)

Once the airplane stabilizes at a constant airspeed and attitude, the airspeed indicator is primary for pitch and the heading indicator remains primary

for bank (Fig. 5–28). You will monitor the "Tach or MP" as the primary power instrument to ensure that the proper climb power setting is being maintained. If the climb attitude is correct for the power setting selected, the airspeed will stabilize at the desired speed. If the airspeed is low or high, make an appropriate small pitch correction.

To enter a constant airspeed climb from *climb* airspeed, first complete the airspeed reduction from cruise airspeed to climb speed in straight-and-level flight. The climb entry is then identical to entry from cruising airspeed, except that power must be increased simultaneously to the climb setting as the pitch attitude is increased. Climb entries on partial panel are more easily and accurately controlled if you enter the maneuver from climbing speed.

The technique for entering a constant rate climb is very similar to that used for entry to a constant airspeed climb from climb airspeed. As the power is increased to the approximate setting for the desired rate, simultaneously raise the miniature aircraft to the climbing attitude for the desired airspeed and rate of climb. As the power is increased, the airspeed indicator is primary for pitch control until the vertical speed approaches the desired value. As the vertical-speed needle stabilizes, it becomes primary for pitch control and the air-

FIGURE 5-27. Climb entry for constant airspeed climb.

77

| PRIMARY PITCH | SUPPORTING PITCH AND BANK | |
| SUPPORTING BANK | PRIMARY BANK | SUPPORTING PITCH |

FIGURE 5-28. Stabilized climb at constant airspeed.

speed indicator becomes primary for power control (Fig. 5-29).

Pitch and power corrections must be quickly and closely coordinated. For example, if the vertical speed is correct, but the airspeed is low, add power. As the power is increased, the miniature aircraft must be lowered slightly to maintain constant vertical speed. If the vertical speed is high and the airspeed is low (Fig. 5-30), lower the miniature aircraft slightly and note the increase in airspeed to determine whether or not a power change is also necessary. Familiarity with the approximate power settings helps to keep your pitch and power corrections at a minimum.

Leveling off.—To level off from a climb and maintain an altitude, it is necessary to start the level-off before reaching the desired altitude. The amount of lead varies with rate of climb and pilot technique. If your airplane is climbing at 1,000 feet per minute (fpm), it will continue to climb at a decreasing rate throughout the transition to level flight. An effective practice is to lead the altitude by 10 percent of the vertical speed shown (500 fpm/50-foot lead, 1,000 fpm/100-foot lead).

To level off at *cruising* airspeed, apply smooth, steady forward elevator pressure toward level flight

attitude for the speed desired. As the attitude indicator shows the pitch change, the vertical-speed needle will move slowly toward zero, the altimeter needle will move more slowly, and the airspeed will show acceleration (Fig. 5-31). Once the altimeter, attitude indicator, and vertical-speed indicator show level flight, constant changes in pitch and torque control will have to be made as the airspeed increases. As the airspeed approaches cruising speed, reduce power to the cruise setting. The amount of lead depends upon the rate of acceleration of your airplane.

To level off at *climbing* airspeed, the nose is lowered to the pitch attitude appropriate to that airspeed in level flight. Power is simultaneously reduced to the setting for that airspeed as the pitch attitude is lowered. If your power reduction is at a rate proportionate to the pitch change, the airspeed will remain constant.

Descents.—A descent can be made at a variety of airspeeds and attitudes by reducing power, adding drag, and lowering the nose to a predetermined attitude. Sooner or later the airspeed will stabilize at a constant value. Meanwhile, the only flight instrument providing a positive attitude reference, by itself, is the attitude indicator. Without the at-

78

| PRIMARY POWER | SUPPORTING PITCH AND BANK | |
| SUPPORTING BANK | PRIMARY BANK | PRIMARY PITCH |

FIGURE 5–29. Stabilized climb at constant rate.

titude indicator, as during a partial panel descent, the airspeed indicator, the altimeter, and the vertical-speed indicator will be showing varying rates of change until the airplane decelerates to a constant airspeed at a constant attitude. During the transition, changes in control pressure and trim, as well as cross-check and interpretation, must be very accurate if you expect to maintain positive control.

Entry.—The following method for entering descents is effective either with or without an attitude indicator. First, reduce airspeed to your selected descent airspeed while maintaining straight-and-level flight, then make a further reduction in power (to a predetermined setting). As the power is adjusted, simultaneously lower the nose to maintain constant airspeed, and trim off control pressures.

During a constant *airspeed* descent, any deviation from the desired airspeed calls for a pitch adjustment. For a constant *rate* descent, the entry is the same, but the vertical-speed indicator is primary for pitch control (after it stabilizes near the desired rate), and the airspeed indicator is primary for power control. Pitch and power must be closely coordinated, as in climbs, when corrections are made (Fig. 5–32).

Leveling off.—The level-off from a descent must be started before you reach the desired altitude. The amount of lead depends upon the rate of descent and control technique. With too little lead, you will tend to overshoot the selected altitude unless your technique is rapid. Assuming a 500-fpm rate of descent, lead the altitude by 100–150 feet for a level-off at airspeed higher than descending speed. At the lead point, add power to the appropriate level flight cruise setting (Fig. 5–33). Since the nose will tend to rise as the airspeed increases, hold forward elevator pressure to maintain the vertical speed at the descending rate until approximately 50 feet above the altitude, then smoothly adjust the pitch attitude to the level flight attitude for the airspeed selected.

To level off from a descent at descent airspeed, lead the desired altitude by approximately 50 feet, simultaneously adjusting the pitch attitude to level flight and adding power to a setting that will hold the airspeed constant (Fig. 5–34). Trim off the control pressures and continue with the normal straight-and-level flight cross-check.

Common errors result from the following faults:

1. Overcontrolling pitch on climb entry. Until you know the pitch attitudes related to specific

79

FIGURE 5–30. Airspeed low and vertical speed high—reduce pitch.

power settings used in climbs and descents, you will tend to make larger than necessary pitch adjustments. One of the most difficult habits to learn during instrument training is to *restrain* the impulse to disturb a flight attitude until you know what the result will be. Overcome your inclination to make a large control movement for a pitch change, and learn to apply small control pressures smoothly, cross-checking rapidly for the results of the change, and continuing with the pressures as your instruments show the desired results at a rate that you can interpret. Small pitch changes can be easily controlled, stopped, and corrected; large changes are more difficult to control.

2. Failure to vary the rate of cross-check during speed, power, or attitude changes on climb or descent entries.

3. Failure to maintain a new pitch attitude. For example, you raise the nose to the correct climb attitude, and as the airspeed decreases, you either overcontrol and further increase the pitch attitude, or allow the nose to lower. As control pressures change with airspeed changes, cross-check must be increased and pressures readjusted.

4. Failure to trim off pressures. Unless you trim, you will have difficulty determining whether con-

trol pressure changes are induced by aerodynamic changes or by your own movements.

5. Failure to learn and use proper power settings.

6. Failure to cross-check *both* airspeed and vertical-speed *before* making pitch or power adjustments.

7. Improper pitch and power coordination on slow-speed level offs, owing to slow cross-check of airspeed and altimeter indications.

8. Failure to cross-check the vertical-speed indicator against the other pitch control instruments, resulting in "chasing" the vertical speed.

9. Failure to note the rate of climb or descent to determine the lead for level offs, resulting in overshooting or undershooting the desired altitude.

10. "Ballooning" (allowing the nose to pitch up) on level offs from descents, resulting from failure to maintain descending attitude with forward elevator pressure as power is increased to the level-flight cruise setting.

11. Failure to recognize the approaching straight-and-level flight indications as you level off. Until you have positively established straight-and-level flight, maintain an accelerated cross-check.

PRIMARY POWER AS A/S
APPROACHES DESIRED VALUE

SUPPORTING PITCH
AND BANK

PRIMARY PITCH

SUPPORTING BANK

PRIMARY BANK

SUPPORTING PITCH

FIGURE 5–31. Level-off at cruising airspeed.

Turns

Standard Rate Turns.—To enter a standard-rate level turn, apply coordinated aileron and rudder pressures in the desired direction of turn. Students commonly roll into turns at a much too rapid rate. During initial training in turns, base your control pressures on your rate of cross-check and interpretation. There is nothing to be gained by maneuvering an airplane faster than your capacity to keep up with the changes in instrument indications.

On the roll-in, use the attitude indicator to establish the approximate angle of bank, then check the miniature aircraft of the turn coordinator for a standard-rate turn indication. Maintain the bank for this rate of turn, using the miniature aircraft of the turn coordinator as the primary bank reference and the attitude indicator as the supporting bank instrument (Fig. 5–35). Note the exact angle of bank shown on the banking scale of the attitude indicator when the turn coordinator indicates a standard rate turn.

During the roll-in, check the altimeter, vertical-speed indicator, and attitude indicator for the pitch adjustments necessary as the vertical lift component decreases with increase in bank. If constant air-

speed is to be maintained, the airspeed indicator becomes primary for power, and the throttle must be adjusted as drag increases. As the bank is established, trim off the pressures applied during pitch and power changes.

To recover to straight-and-level flight, apply coordinated aileron and rudder pressures opposite the direction of turn. If you strive for the same rate of roll-out that you use to roll into the turn, you will encounter fewer problems in judging the lead necessary to roll out on exact headings, especially on partial panel maneuvers. As you initiate the turn recovery, the attitude indicator becomes the primary bank instrument. When the airplane is approximately level, the heading indicator is the primary bank instrument as in straight-and-level flight. Pitch, power, and trim adjustments are made as changes in vertical lift component and airspeed occur. The ball should be checked throughout the turn, especially if control pressures are held instead of being trimmed off.

Some airplanes are very stable during turns, and slight trim adjustments permit "hands off" flight while the airplane remains in the established attitude. Other airplanes require constant rapid cross-check and control during turns to correct over-

81

PRIMARY POWER

SUPPORTING PITCH
AND BANK

SUPPORTING BANK

PRIMARY BANK

PRIMARY PITCH

FIGURE 5–32. Constant rate descent, airspeed high—reduce power.

SUPPORTING PITCH
AND BANK

ADD POWER
AT 100'—150'
LEAD

SUPPORTING BANK

PRIMARY BANK

PRIMARY PITCH

FIGURE 5–33. Level-off airspeed higher than descent airspeed.

FIGURE 5–34. Level-off at descent airspeed.

FIGURE 5–35. Standard rate turn, constant airspeed.

83

banking tendencies. Due to the interrelationship of pitch, bank, and airspeed deviations during turns, your cross-check must be fast to prevent an accumulation of errors.

Turns to Predetermined Headings.—As long as an airplane is in a coordinated bank, it continues to turn. Thus, the roll-out to a desired heading must be started before the heading is reached. The amount of lead varies with the relationship between the rate of turn, angle of bank, and rate of recovery. For small changes in heading, using an angle of bank not exceeding the number of degrees to be turned, lead the desired heading by one-half the number of degrees of bank used. For example, if you maintain a 10° bank during a change in heading, start the roll-out 5° before reaching the desired heading. For larger changes in leading, the amount of lead will vary since the angle of bank for a standard-rate turn varies with the True Airspeed. Practice with a lead of one-half the angle of bank until you have determined the precise lead suitable to your technique. If your rates of roll-in and roll-out are consistent, you can readily determine the precise amount of lead suitable to your particular roll-out technique by noting the amount that you consistently undershoot or overshoot the headings.

Timed Turns.—A timed turn is a turn in which the clock and the turn coordinator are used to change heading a definite number of degrees in a given time. For example, using a standard-rate turn (3° per second), an airplane turns 45° in 15 seconds; using a half-standard-rate turn, the airplane turns 45° in 30 seconds.

Prior to performing timed turns, the turn coordinator should be calibrated to determine the accuracy of its indications (Fig. 5–36). Establish a standard rate turn as indicated by the turn coordinator and as the sweep second hand of the clock passes a cardinal point (12, 3, 6, 9), check the heading on the heading indicator. While holding the indicated rate of turn constant, note the indicated heading changes at 10-second intervals. If the airplane turns more or less than 30 degrees in that interval, a larger or smaller deflection of the miniature aircraft of the turn coordinator is necessary to produce a standard-rate turn. When you have calibrated the turn coordinator during turns in each direction, note the corrected deflections, if any, and apply them during all timed turns.

You use the same cross-check and control technique in making timed turns that you use to execute turns to predetermined headings, except that you substitute the clock for the heading indicator. The

FIGURE 5–36. Turn coordinator calibration.

84

miniature aircraft of the turn coordinator is primary for bank control, the altimeter is primary for pitch control, and the airspeed indicator is primary for power control. Start the roll-in when the clock second hand passes a cardinal point, hold the turn at the calibrated standard-rate indication (or half-standard-rate for small changes in heading), and begin the roll-out when the computed number of seconds has elapsed. If the rates of roll-in and roll-out are the same, the time taken during entry and recovery need not be considered in the time computation.

NOTE: The arrow above the heading indicator in Fig. 5–36 and the following instrument panel illustrations portrays the apparent movement of the miniature aircraft relative to the compass card.

If you practice timed turns with a full instrument panel, check the heading indicator for the accuracy of your turns. If you execute the turns without the gyro heading indicator, use the magnetic compass at the completion of the turn to check turn accuracy, taking compass deviation errors into consideration.

Compass Turns.—In most light airplanes, the magnetic compass is the only direction-indicating instrument independent of other airplane instruments and power sources. Because of its operating characteristics, called compass errors, pilots are prone to use it only as a reference for setting the heading indicator, but a knowledge of magnetic compass characteristics will enable you to use the instrument to turn your airplane to correct headings and maintain them. The construction and operation of the magnetic compass was discussed in Chapter IV. This information should be thoroughly understood before practicing compass turns.

Bear in mind the following points when making turns to magnetic compass headings or when using the magnetic compass as a reference for setting the heading indicator:

1. If you are on a northerly heading and you start a turn to the east or west, the indication of the compass lags, or shows a turn in the opposite direction.

2. If you are on a southerly heading and you start a turn toward the east or west, the compass indication precedes the turn, showing a greater amount of turn than is actually occurring.

3. When you are on an east or west heading, the compass indicates correctly as you start a turn in either direction.

4. If you are on an easterly or westerly heading, acceleration results in a northerly turn indication; deceleration results in a southerly turn indication.

5. If you maintain a north or south heading, no error results from diving, climbing, or changing airspeed.

With an angle of bank between 15° and 18°, the amount of lead or lag to be used when turning to northerly or southerly headings varies with, and is approximately equal to, the latitude of the locality

over which the turn is being made. When turning to a heading of north, the lead for roll-out must include the number of degrees of your latitude, *plus* the lead you normally use in recovery from turns. During a turn to a south heading, maintain the turn until the compass *passes* south the number of degrees of your latitude, *minus* your normal roll-out lead (Fig. 5–37).

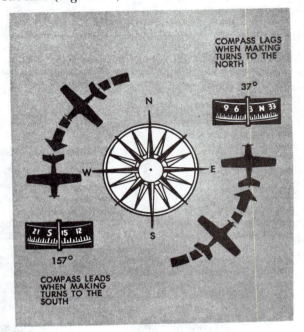

FIGURE 5–37. Northerly and southerly turn error.

For example, when turning from an easterly direction to north, where the latitude is 30°, start the roll-out when the compass reads 37°, (30° plus one-half the 15° angle of bank, or whatever amount is appropriate for your rate of roll-out). When turning from an easterly direction to south, start the roll-out when the magnetic compass reads 203°, (180° plus 30° minus one-half the angle of bank). When making similar turns from a westerly direction, the appropriate points at which to begin your roll-out would be 323° for a turn to north, and 157° for a turn to south.

When turning to a heading of east or west from a northerly direction, start the roll-out approximately 10° to 12° before the east or west indication is reached. When turning to an east or west heading from a southerly direction, start the roll-out approximately 5° before the east or west indication is reached. When turning to other headings, the lead or lag must be interpolated.

Abrupt changes in attitude or airspeed and the resulting erratic movements of the compass card make accurate interpretations of the instrument very difficult. Proficiency in compass turns depends on knowledge of the compass characteristics, smooth control technique, and accurate bank and pitch control.

Steep Turns.—For purposes of instrument flight training in conventional airplanes, any turn greater than a standard-rate may be considered steep (Fig. 5–38). The exact angle of bank at which a normal turn becomes steep is unimportant. What is important is that you learn to control the airplane with bank attitudes in excess of those you normally use on instruments. Practice in steep turns will not only increase your proficiency in the basic instrument flying skills, but also enable you to react smoothly, quickly, and confidently to unexpected abnormal flight attitudes under instrument flight conditions.

Pronounced changes occur in the effects of aerodynamic forces on aircraft control at progressively steepening bank attitudes. Skill in cross-check, interpretation, and control is increasingly necessary in proportion to the amount of these changes, though the techniques for entering, maintaining, and recovering from the turn are the same in principle for steep turns as for shallower turns.

Enter a steep turn exactly as you do a shallower turn, but prepare to cross-check rapidly as the turn steepens. Because of the greatly reduced vertical lift component, pitch control is usually the most difficult aspect of this maneuver. Unless immediately noted and corrected with a pitch increase, the loss of vertical lift results in rapid movement of the altimeter, vertical-speed, and airspeed needles. The faster the rate of bank change, the more suddenly the lift changes occur. If your cross-check is fast enough to note the immediate need for pitch

FIGURE 5–38. Steep left turn.

changes, smooth, steady back elevator pressure will maintain constant altitude. However, if you overbank to excessively steep angles without adjusting pitch *as* the bank changes occur, pitch corrections require increasingly stronger elevator pressure. The loss of vertical lift and increase in wing loading finally reach a point where further application of back elevator pressure tightens the turn without raising the nose. (The effect of abrupt elevator control on wing loading and its effect on airplane stalling speeds during steep turns was discussed in Chapter III.)

How do you recognize overbanking and a low pitch attitude? What should you do to correct it? If you observe a rapid downward movement of the altimeter needle or vertical-speed needle, together with an increase in airspeed, despite your application of back elevator pressure, you are in a diving spiral (Fig. 5–39). Immediately shallow the bank with smooth and coordinated aileron and rudder pressures, hold or slightly relax elevator pressure, and increase your cross-check of attitude indicator, altimeter, and vertical-speed indicator. Reduce power if the airspeed increase is rapid. When the

vertical speed trends upward, the altimeter needle will move slower as the vertical lift increases. When you note that the elevator is effective in raising the nose, hold the bank attitude shown on the attitude indicator and adjust elevator control pressures smoothly for the nose-high attitude appropriate to the bank maintained. If your pitch control is consistently late on your entries to steep turns, roll out immediately to straight-and-level flight and analyze your errors. Practice shallower turns until you can keep up with the attitude changes and control responses required, then steepen the banks as you develop quicker and more accurate control technique.

The power necessary to maintain constant airspeed increases as the bank and drag increase. With practice, you quickly learn the power settings appropriate to specific bank attitudes, and can make adjustments without undue attention to airspeed and power instruments. During training in steep turns, as in any other maneuver, attend to "first things first." If you keep pitch relatively constant, you have more time to cross-check, interpret, and control for accurate airspeed and bank control.

Figure 5–39.   Diving spiral.

87

During recovery from steep turns to straight-and-level flight, elevator and power control must be coordinated with bank control in proportion to the changes in aerodynamic forces. Back elevator pressures must be released, and power decreased. The common errors associated with steep turns are the same as those discussed later in this section; however, remember, errors are more exaggerated, more difficult to correct, and more difficult to analyze unless your rates of entry and recovery are consistent with your level of proficiency in the three basic instrument flying skills.

Climbing and Descending Turns.—To execute climbing and descending turns, combine the technique used in straight climbs and descents with the various turn techniques. The aerodynamic factors affecting lift and power control must be considered in determining power settings, and the rate of cross-check and interpretation must be increased to enable you to control bank as well as pitch changes.

Change of Airspeed in Turns.—Changing airspeed in turns is an effective maneuver for increasing your proficiency in all three basic instrument skills. Since the maneuver involves simultaneous changes in all components of control, proper execution requires rapid cross-check and interpretation as well as smooth control. Proficiency in the maneuver will also contribute to your confidence in the instruments during attitude and power changes involved in more complex maneuvers.

Pitch and power control techniques are the same as those used during changes in airspeed in straight-and-level flight.

As discussed in Chapter III, the angle of bank necessary for a given rate of turn is proportional to the true airspeed. Since the turns are executed at standard-rate, the angle of bank must be varied in direct proportion to the airspeed change in order to maintain a constant rate of turn. During a reduction of airspeed, you must decrease the angle of bank and increase the pitch attitude to maintain altitude and a standard rate turn.

The altimeter and turn coordinator indications should remain constant throughout the turn. The altimeter is primary for pitch control and the miniature aircraft of the turn coordinator is primary for bank control. The manifold pressure gauge (or tachometer) is primary for power control while the airspeed is changing. As the airspeed approaches the new indication, the airspeed indicator becomes primary for power control.

Two methods of changing airspeed in turns may be used. In the first method, airspeed is changed after the turn is established (Fig. 5–40); in the second method, the airspeed change is initiated simultaneously with the turn entry. The first method is easier, but regardless of the method used, the rate of cross-check must be increased as you reduce power. As the airplane decelerates, check the altimeter and vertical-speed indicator for needed pitch changes and the bank instruments for needed

FIGURE 5–40. Change of airspeed in turn.

bank changes. If the miniature aircraft of the turn coordinator shows a deviation from the desired deflection, change the bank. Adjust pitch attitude to maintain altitude. When the airspeed approaches that desired, it becomes primary for power control and the manifold pressure gauge (or tachometer) is adjusted to maintain the desired airspeed. Trim is important throughout the maneuver to relieve control pressures.

Until your control technique is very smooth, frequent cross-check of the attitude indicator is essential to keep from overcontrolling and to provide approximate bank angles appropriate to the changing airspeeds.

Common Errors During Turns.—*Pitch errors* result from the following faults:

1. Preoccupation with bank control during turn entry and recovery. If it takes 5 seconds to roll into a turn, check the pitch instruments as you initiate bank pressures. If your bank control pressure and rate of bank change are consistent, you will soon develop a sense of timing that tells you how long an attitude change will take. During the interval, you check pitch, power, and trim—as well as bank—controlling the total attitude instead of one factor at a time.

2. Failure to understand or remember the necessity for changing the pitch attitude as the vertical lift component changes, resulting in consistent loss of altitude during entries.

3. Changing the pitch attitude before it is necessary. This fault is very likely if your cross-check is slow and your rate of entry too rapid. The error occurs during the turn entry due to a mechanical and premature application of back elevator control pressure.

4. Overcontrolling the pitch changes. This fault is commonly applied to the previous one.

5. Failure to properly adjust the pitch attitude as the vertical lift component increases during the roll-out, resulting in consistent gain in altitude on recovery to headings.

6. Failure to trim during turn entry and following turn recovery (if turn is prolonged).

7. Failure to maintain straight-and-level cross-check after roll-out. This error commonly follows a perfectly executed turn.

8. Erratic rates of bank change on entry and recovery, resulting in failure to cross-check the pitch instruments with a consistent technique appropriate to the changes in lift.

Bank and heading errors result from the following faults:

1. Overcontrolling, resulting in overbanking on turn entry, overshooting and undershooting headings, as well as aggravated pitch, airspeed, and trim errors.

2. Fixation on a single bank instrument. On a 90° change of heading, for example, leave the heading indicator out of your cross-check for approximately 20 seconds after establishing a standard-rate turn, since at 3° per second you won't approach the

lead point until that time has elapsed. Make your cross-check selective; check what needs to be checked at the appropriate time.

3. Failure to check for precession of the horizon bar following recovery from a turn. If the heading indicator shows a change in heading when the attitude indicator shows level flight, the airplane is turning. If the ball is centered, the attitude gyro has precessed; if the ball is not centered, the airplane may be in a slipping or skidding turn. Center the ball with rudder pressure, check the attitude indicator and heading indicator, stop the heading change if it continues, and retrim.

4. Failure to use the proper degree of bank for the amount of heading change desired. Rolling into a 20° bank for a heading change of 10° will normally overshoot the heading. Use the bank attitude appropriate to the amount of heading change desired.

5. Failure to remember the heading you are turning to. This fault is likely when you rush the maneuver.

6. Turning in the wrong direction, due either to misreading or misinterpretation of the heading indicator or to confusion as to location of points on the compass. Turn in the shortest direction to reach a given heading, unless you have a specific reason to turn the long way around. Study the compass rose until you can visualize at least the positions of the eight major points around the azimuth. A number of memory "gimmicks" can be used to make quick computations for heading changes. For example, to turn from a heading of 305° to a heading of 110°, do you turn right or left for the shortest way around? Subtracting 200 from 305 and adding 20, you get 125° as the reciprocal of 305°; therefore, execute the turn to the right. Likewise, to figure the reciprocal of a heading less than 180°, add 200 and subtract 20. If you can compute more quickly using multiples of 100's and 10's than by adding or subtracting 180° from the actual heading, the method suggested above may save you time and confusion.

7. Failure to check the ball of the turn coordinator when interpreting that instrument for bank information. If the roll rate is reduced to zero, the miniature aircraft of the turn coordinator indicates only direction and rate of turn. Unless the ball is centered, you cannot assume that the turn is resulting from a banked attitude.

Power and airspeed errors result from the following faults:

1. Failure to cross-check the airspeed indicator as you make pitch changes.

2. Erratic use of power control. This may be due to improper throttle friction control, to inaccurate throttle settings, chasing the airspeed readings, abrupt or overcontrolled pitch and bank changes, or failure to recheck the airspeed to note the effect of a power adjustment.

3. Poor coordination of throttle control with pitch and bank changes, associated with slow cross-check or failure to understand the aerodynamic factors related to turns.

Trim errors result from the following faults:

1. Failure to recognize the need for a trim change may be due to slow cross-check and interpretation. For example, a turn entry at a rate too rapid for your cross-check leads to confusion in cross-check and interpretation, with resulting tension on the controls.

2. Failure to understand the relationship between trim and attitude/power changes.

3. Chasing the vertical-speed needle. Overcontrolling leads to tension and prevents you from sensing the pressures to be trimmed off.

4. Failure to trim following power changes.

Errors During Compass Turns.—In addition to the faults discussed above, the following errors connected with compass turns should be noted:

1. Faulty understanding or computation of lead and lag.

2. Fixation on the compass during the rollout. Until the airplane is in straight-and-level, unaccelerated flight, there is no point in reading the indicated heading. Accordingly, after you initiate the roll-out, cross-check for straight-and-level flight *before* checking the accuracy of your turn.

Unusual Attitudes and Recoveries

An unusual attitude is any airplane attitude not normally required for instrument flight. Unusual attitudes may result from a number of conditions, such as turbulence, disorientation, instrument failure, confusion, preoccupation with cockpit duties, carelessness in cross-checking, errors in instrument interpretation, or lack of proficiency in aircraft control. Since unusual attitudes are not intentional maneuvers during instrument flight, except in training, they are often unexpected, and the reaction of an inexperienced or inadequately trained pilot to an unexpected abnormal flight attitude is usually instinctive rather than intelligent and deliberate. This individual reacts with abrupt muscular effort, which is purposeless and even hazardous in turbulent conditions, at excessive speeds, or at low altitudes. However, with practice, the techniques for rapid and safe recovery from unusual attitudes can be learned.

When an unusual attitude is noted on your cross-check, the immediate problem is not how the airplane got there, but what it is doing and how to get it back to straight-and-level flight as quickly as possible.

Recognizing Unusual Attitudes.—As a general rule, any time you note an instrument rate of movement or indication other than those you associate with the basic instrument flight maneuvers already learned, assume an unusual attitude and increase the speed of cross-check to confirm the attitude, instrument error, or instrument malfunction. Nose-high attitudes (Fig. 5–41) are shown by the rate and direction of movement of the altimeter needle, vertical-speed needle, and airspeed needle, as well as the immediately recognizable indication

of the attitude indicator (except in extreme attitudes). Nose-low attitudes (Fig. 5–42) are shown by the same instruments, but in the opposite direction.

Recovery From Unusual Attitudes.—In moderate unusual attitudes, the pilot can normally reorient himself by establishing a level flight indication on the attitude indicator. However, the pilot should not depend on this instrument for these reasons: If the attitude indicator is the spillable type, its upset limits may have been exceeded; it may have become inoperative due to mechanical malfunction; even if it is the non-spillable type instrument and is operating properly, its indications are very difficult to interpret in extreme attitudes. As soon as the unusual attitude is detected, the recovery should be initiated primarily by reference to the airspeed indicator, altimeter, vertical-speed indicator, and turn coordinator.

Nose-High Attitudes.—If the airspeed is decreasing or below the desired airspeed, increase power (as necessary in proportion to the observed deceleration), apply forward elevator pressure to lower the nose and prevent a stall, and correct the bank by applying coordinated aileron and rudder pressure to level the miniature aircraft and center the ball of the turn coordinator, The corrective control applications are made almost simultaneously but in the sequence given above. A level pitch attitude is indicated by the reversal and stabilization of the airspeed indicator and altimeter needles. Straight coordinated flight is indicated by the level miniature aircraft and centered ball of the turn coordinator.

Nose-Low Attitudes.—If the airspeed is increasing, or is above the desired airspeed, reduce power to prevent excessive airspeed and loss of altitude. Correct the bank attitude with coordinated aileron and rudder pressure to straight flight by referring to the turn coordinator. Raise the nose to level flight attitude by smooth back elevator pressure. All components of control should be changed simultaneously for a smooth, proficient recovery. However, during initial training (or when your technique is rusty) a positive, confident recovery should be made "by the numbers," in the sequence given above. A very important point to remember is that the instinctive reaction to a nose-down attitude is to pull back on the elevator control. The possible result of this control response in a steep diving turn has been discussed previously.

After initial control has been applied, continue with a fast cross-check for possible overcontrolling, since the necessary initial control pressures may be large. As the rate of movement of altimeter and airspeed indicator needles decreases, the attitude is approaching level flight. When the needles stop and reverse direction, the aircraft is passing through level flight. As the indications of the airspeed indicator, altimeter, and turn coordinator stabilize, incorporate the attitude indicator into the cross-check. The attitude indicator, and turn co-

FIGURE 5-41. Unusual attitude—nose high.

ordinator should be checked to determine bank attitude and corrective aileron and rudder pressures applied. The ball should be centered. If it is not, skidding and slipping sensations can easily aggravate disorientation and retard recovery. If you enter the unusual attitude from an assigned altitude (either by your instructor or Air Traffic Control if operating under Instrument Flight Rules), return to the original altitude *after* stabilizing in straight-and-level flight.

Common errors associated with unusual attitudes include the following faults:

1. Failure to keep the airplane properly trimmed. A cockpit interruption when you are holding pressures can easily lead to inadvertent entry into unusual attitudes.

2. Disorganized cockpit. Hunting for charts, logs, computers, etc., can seriously detract from your attention to the instruments.

3. Slow cross-check and fixations. Your impulse is to stop and stare when you note an instrument discrepancy, *unless* you have trained enough to develop the skill required for immediate recovery.

4. Attempting to recover by sensory sensations other than sight. The discussion of disorientation in Chapter II indicates the importance of trusting your instruments.

5. Failure to *practice* basic instrument skills once you have learned them. All of the errors noted in connection with basic instrument skills are aggravated during unusual attitude recoveries until the elementary skills have been mastered.

91

AIRSPEED INCREASING DIVING RIGHT TURN LOSING ALTITUDE

FIGURE 5–42. Unusual attitude—nose low.

Instrument Takeoff

However remote you may consider the chance of your making an IFR departure under completely "blind" weather conditions, your competency in instrument takeoff will provide the proficiency and confidence necessary for use of flight instruments during departures under conditions of low visibility, rain, low ceilings, or disorientation at night. A sudden rapid transition from "visual" to "instrument" flight can result in serious disorientation and control problems.

Instrument takeoff techniques vary with different types of airplanes, but the method described below is applicable whether the airplane is single- or twin-engine; tricycle-gear or conventional-gear.

Align the airplane with the centerline of the runway with the nosewheel or tailwheel straight. (Your instructor may align the airplane if he has been taxiing while you perform the instrument check under a hood or visor.) Lock the tailwheel, if so equipped, and hold the brakes firmly to avoid creeping while you prepare for takeoff. Set the heading indicator with the nose index on the 5°

mark nearest the published runway heading, so that you can instantly detect slight changes in heading during the takeoff. Make certain that the instrument is uncaged (if it has a caging feature) by rotating the knob after uncaging and checking for constant heading indication. If you use an electric heading indicator with a rotatable needle, rotate the needle so that it points to the nose position, under the top index. Advance the throttle to an RPM that will provide partial rudder control. Release the brakes, advancing the power smoothly to takeoff setting. During the takeoff roll, hold the heading constant on the heading indicator by the use of rudder. In multiengine, propeller-driven airplanes, also use differential throttle to maintain direction. The use of brakes should be avoided, except as a last resort, as it usually results in overcontrolling and extending the take-off roll. Once you release the brakes, any deviation in heading must be corrected instantly.

As the airplane accelerates, cross-check both heading indicator and airspeed indicator rapidly. As flying speed is approached (approximately 15–25 knots below takeoff speed), apply elevator control smoothly for the desired takeoff attitude on the attitude indicator. This is approximately a 2-bar-width climb indication for most light airplanes.

Continue with a rapid cross-check of heading indicator and attitude indicator as the airplane leaves the ground. Do not pull it off; let it fly off while you hold the selected attitude constant. Maintain pitch and bank control by reference to the attitude indicator, and make coordinated corrections in heading when so indicated on the heading indicator. Cross-check the altimeter and vertical-speed indicator for a positive rate of climb (steady clockwise rotation of the altimeter needle at a rate that you can interpret with experience, and a stable rate of climb appropriate to the airplane shown on the vertical-speed indicator).

When the altimeter shows a safe altitude (approximately 100 feet), raise the landing gear and flaps, maintaining attitude by reference to the attitude indicator. Because of control pressure changes during gear and flap operation, overcontrolling is likely unless you note pitch indications accurately and quickly. Trim off control pressures necessary to hold the stable climb attitude. Check the altimeter, vertical-speed indicator, and airspeed for a smooth acceleration to predetermined climb speed (altimeter and airspeed increasing, vertical-speed stable). At climb speed, reduce power to climb setting (unless full power is recommended for climb by your airplane flight handbook) and trim.

Throughout the instrument takeoff, cross-check and interpretation must be rapid, and control positive and smooth. During liftoff, gear and flap retraction, and power reduction, the changing control reactions demand rapid scanning, adjustment of control pressures, and accurate trim changes.

Common errors during the instrument takeoff include the following:

1. Failure to perform an adequate cockpit check before the takeoff. Ridiculous as it seems, students have attempted instrument takeoffs with inoperative airspeed indicators (pitot tube obstructed), gyros caged, controls locked, and numerous other oversights due to haste or carelessness.

2. Improper alignment on the runway. This may result from improper brake application, allowing the airplane to creep after alignment, or from alignment with nosewheel or tailwheel cocked. In any case, the result is a built-in directional control problem as the takeoff starts.

3. Improper application of power. Abrupt application of power complicates directional control. Add power with a smooth, uninterrupted motion.

4. Improper use of brakes. Incorrect seat or rudder pedal adjustment, with your feet in an uncomfortable position, frequently causes inadvertent application of brakes and excessive heading changes.

5. Overcontrolling rudder pedals. This fault may be caused by late recognition of heading changes, tension on the controls, misinterpretation of the heading indicator (and correcting in the wrong direction), failure to appreciate changing effectiveness of rudder control as the aircraft accelerates, and other factors. If heading changes are observed and corrected instantly with small movement of the rudder pedals, swerving tendencies can be reduced.

6. Failure to maintain attitude after becoming airborne. If you react to "seat-of-the-pants" sensations when the airplane lifts off, your pitch control is guesswork. You may either allow excessive pitch up, or apply excessive forward elevator pressure, depending on your reaction to trim changes.

7. Inadequate cross-check. Fixations are likely during trim changes, attitude changes, gear and flap retractions, and power changes. Once you check an instrument or apply a control, continue the cross-check and note the effect of your control during the next cross-check sequence.

8. Inadequate interpretation of instruments. Failure to understand instrument indications *immediately* indicates that further study of the maneuver is necessary.

Basic Instrument Flight Patterns

After you have attained a reasonable degree of proficiency in basic maneuvers, you can apply your skills to the various combinations of individual maneuvers. The following practice patterns, and those described in pages 265 and 266 of the Appendix are directly applicable to operational instrument flying problems to be discussed in later chapters.

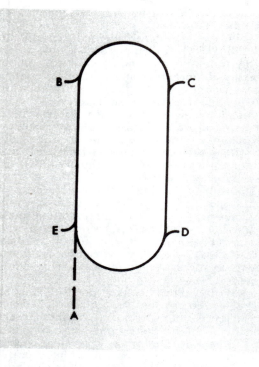

FIGURE 5-43.   Holding pattern (entire pattern in level flight).

Steps—
1. Time 3 minutes straight-and-level flight from A to B. During this interval, reduce airspeed to holding speed (maximum 175 knots). Use any airspeed appropriate for your airplane.
2. Start 180° standard-rate turn at B. Roll out at C on the reciprocal of your heading at A.
3. Time 1 minute straight-and-level flight from C to D.
4. Start 180° standard-rate level turn at D, rolling out on original heading.

NOTE.—This pattern is an exercise combining use of the clock with basic maneuvers. Holding procedures are covered in Chapter XII.

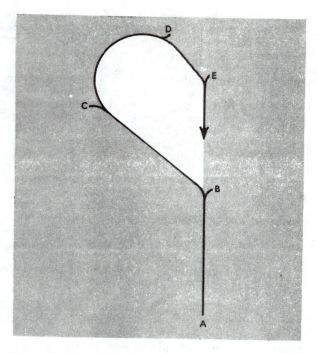

FIGURE 5-44.   Standard procedure turn (entire pattern in level flight).

Steps—
1. Start timing at A for 2 minutes from A to B.
2. At B, turn 45° (standard-rate). After roll-out, fly 1 minute to C.
3. At C, turn 180°.
4. At completion of turn, time 45 seconds to E.
5. Start turn at E for 45° change of heading to reciprocal of heading at beginning of maneuver.

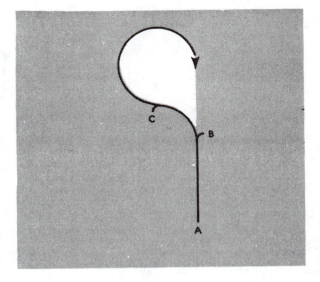

FIGURE 5-45. 80/260 procedure turn (entire pattern in level flight).

Steps—
1. Start timing at A for 2 minutes from A to B.
2. At B, enter a left standard rate turn for a heading change of 80°.
3. At the completion of the 80° turn at C, immediately turn right for a heading change of 260°, rolling out on the reciprocal of the entry heading.

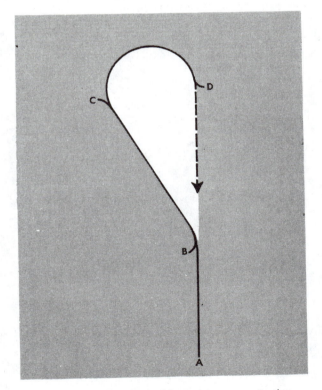

FIGURE 5-46. Teardrop holding pattern entry (entire pattern in level flight).

Steps—
1. Start timing at A for 2 minutes from A to B. Reduce airspeed to holding speed in this interval.
2. At B, enter standard-rate turn for 30° change of heading. Time 1 minute from B to C.
3. At C, enter standard rate turn for a 210° change of heading, rolling out on the reciprocal of the original entry heading.

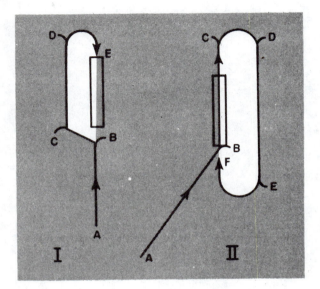

FIGURE 5-47. Patterns applicable to circling approaches (runways are imaginary).

Pattern I — Steps—
1. At A, start timing for 2 minutes from A to B; reduce airspeed to approach speed.
2. At B, make a standard rate turn to the left for 45°.
3. At the completion of the turn, time for 45 seconds to C.
4. At C, turn to the original heading; fly 1 minute to D, lowering the landing gear and flaps.
5. At D, turn right 180°, rolling out at E on the reciprocal of the entry heading.
6. At E, enter a 500 fpm rate descent. At the end of a 500-foot descent, enter a straight constant airspeed climb, retracting gear and flaps.

Pattern II — Steps—
1. At A, start timing for 2 minutes from A to B; reduce airspeed to approach speed.
2. At B, make a standard rate turn to the left for 45°.
3. At the completion of the turn, time for 1 minute to C.
4. At C, turn right for 180°; fly for 1½ minutes to E, lowering the landing gear and flaps.
5. At E, turn right for 180°, rolling out at F.
6. At F, enter a 500 fpm rate descent. At the end of a 500-foot descent, enter a straight constant airspeed climb, retracting gear and flaps.

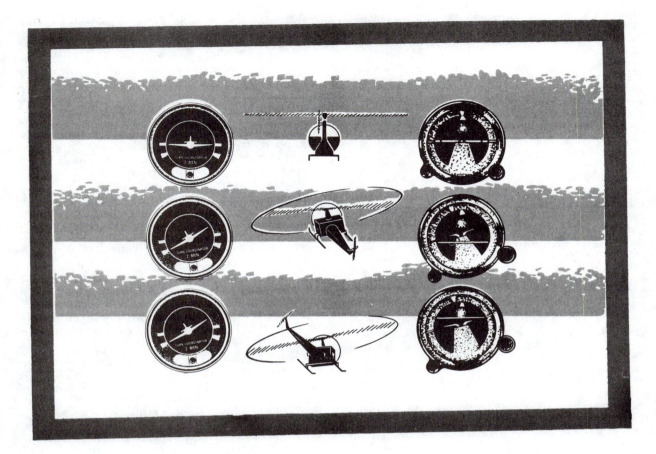

VI. ATTITUDE INSTRUMENT FLYING—
HELICOPTERS

NOTE: The instrument maneuvers presented in Chapter VI are based on a helicopter equipped with a turn coordinator. If the helicopter flown has a turn needle, the descriptions apply if "turn needle" is substituted for "miniature aircraft of turn coordinator."

This chapter describes the performance of basic instrument maneuvers in helicopters. These maneuvers are covered in the same sequence as in the preceding chapter on attitude instrument flying in airplanes. With a few exceptions, the material presented in the first part of the preceding chapter from page 55 through the first column of page 59, is applicable to both airplanes and helicopters. Although the flight maneuvers described in this chapter assume a turbine engine powered single-rotor helicopter, the descriptions can be made to apply to a reciprocating engine powered helicopter by minor changes in terminology. For example, during power control in a reciprocating engine powered helicopter, references should be made to "manifold pressure" rather than "torque."

Helicopter Control

As in airplanes, attitude instrument flying in helicopters is essentially visual flying with the flight instruments substituted for the various reference points on the helicopter and the natural horizon. Control changes required to produce a given attitude by reference to instruments are identical to those used in helicopter VFR flight, and the pilot's thought processes are the same. Unlike airplanes, in helicopters both lift and thrust originate from a single source, the main rotor(s). The helicopter's *pitch attitude* is controlled by changing the angle of attack of the main rotor disc with cyclic. In straight-and-level flight, pitch attitude changes result in airspeed changes and also cyclic climbs and descents. *Power control* in a helicopter is accomplished by changing the angle of attack of the individual rotor blades by means of collective pitch. In level flight, changes of power (collective pitch) result in altitude changes if airspeed is held constant, or airspeed changes if altitude is held constant. When making power changes, you must understand and apply the principles of torque; e.g., when power is increased, the helicopter tends to pitch up and yaw right; when power is decreased, the helicopter tends to pitch down and yaw left. Because of this torque effect, you must frequently cross-check the ball of the turn coordinator to ensure proper torque correction (pedal trim).

As in airplanes, aircraft control in helicopters includes pitch attitude control, bank attitude control, power control, and trim.

1. *Pitch attitude control* is controlling the movement of the helicopter about its lateral axis. After interpreting the helicopter's pitch attitude by reference to the pitch instruments (attitude indicator, altimeter, airspeed indicator, and vertical-speed indicator), cyclic control adjustments are made to affect the desired pitch attitude with reference to the natural horizon. In this chapter, the pitch attitudes illustrated are approximate and will vary with the particular helicopter flown.

2. *Bank attitude control* is controlling the angle made by the lateral tilt of the rotor and the natural horizon, or, the movement of the helicopter about its longitudinal axis. After interpreting the helicopter's bank instruments (attitude indicator, heading indicator, and turn coordinator), cyclic control adjustments are made to attain the desired bank attitude.

3. *Power control* is the application of collective pitch. In straight-and-level flight, changes of collective pitch are made to correct altitude, if the error is more than 100 feet or the airspeed is off more than 10 knots. If the error is less than that amount, a slight cyclic climb or descent should be used.

As a helicopter instrument pilot, you should know the approximate power settings required for your particular helicopter, in various load configurations and flight conditions. For example, on an average day a light single-rotor turbine engine helicopter with the pilot, one passenger, and a full fuel load, requires approximately 62% torque for straight-and-level flight at 90 knots. During flight, minor adjustments from this basic setting should be made to achieve the desired performance.

4. *Trim* in helicopters refers to the use of the cyclic centering button (if the helicopter is so equipped) to relieve all possible cyclic pressures. Trim also refers to the use of pedal adjustment to center the ball of the turn coordinator. Pedal trim is required during all power changes.

The proper adjustment of collective pitch and cyclic friction will help you relax during instrument flight. Friction should be adjusted to minimize overcontrolling and to prevent creeping, but not applied to such a degree that control movement is limited.

Straight-and-Level Flight

Straight and level unaccelerated flight consists of maintaining the desired altitude, heading, airspeed, and pedal trim.

Pitch Control.—The pitch attitude of a helicopter is the angular relation of its longitudinal axis and the natural horizon. If available, the attitude indicator is used to establish the desired pitch attitude. In level flight, pitch attitude varies with airspeed and center of gravity. For training purposes, center of gravity can normally be disregarded in a light single-rotor helicopter. At a constant altitude and a stabilized airspeed, the pitch attitude is approximately level (Fig. 6–1). The flight instruments for pitch control are the *attitude indicator, altimeter, vertical-speed indicator,* and *airspeed indicator* (Fig. 6–2).

FIGURE 6–1. Airspeed and pitch attitude in level flight.

98

FIGURE 6–2. Instruments used for pitch control.

The *attitude indicator* gives a *direct* indication of the pitch attitude of the helicopter. In visual flight, you attain the desired pitch attitude by using cyclic to raise and lower the nose of the helicopter in relation to the natural horizon. During instrument flight, exactly the same procedure is followed in raising or lowering the miniature aircraft in relation to the horizon bar.

You may note some delay between control application and resultant instrument change. This is the normal control lag in the helicopter and should not be confused with instrument lag. The attitude indicator may show small misrepresentations of pitch attitude during maneuvers involving acceleration, deceleration, or turns. This precession error can be detected quickly by cross-checking the other pitch instruments.

If the miniature aircraft is properly adjusted on the ground, it may not require readjustment in flight. If, however, the miniature aircraft is not on the horizon bar after level-off at normal cruising airspeed, adjust it as necessary while maintaining level flight with the other pitch instruments. Once the miniature aircraft has been adjusted in level flight at normal cruising airspeed, leave it unchanged so it will give an accurate picture of pitch attitude at all times.

When making initial pitch attitude corrections to maintain altitude, the changes of attitude should be small and smoothly applied. The initial movement of the horizon bar should not exceed one bar

high or low (Fig. 6–3). If further change is required, an additional correction of one-half bar will normally correct any deviation from the desired altitude. This correction (one and one-half bars) is normally the maximum for pitch attitude corrections from level flight attitude. Make corrections of this magnitude, then cross-check the other pitch

FIGURE 6–3. Initial pitch correction at normal cruise—one bar width.

instruments to determine whether the pitch attitude change is sufficient. If more correction is needed to return to altitude, or if the airspeed varies more than 10 knots from that desired, adjust power.

The *altimeter* gives an *indirect* indication of the pitch attitude of the helicopter in straight-and-level flight. Since the altitude should remain constant in level flight, deviation from the desired altitude shows a need for a change in pitch attitude and, if necessary, power. When losing altitude, raise the pitch attitude and, if necessary, add power; when gaining altitude, lower the pitch attitude and, if necessary, reduce power.

The *rate* at which the altimeter moves helps in determining pitch attitude. A very slow movement of the altimeter indicates a small deviation from the desired pitch attitude; while a fast movement of the altimeter indicates a large deviation from the desired pitch attitude. Make any corrective action promptly, with small control changes. Also, remember that movement of the altimeter should always be corrected by two distinct changes. The first is a change of attitude to stop the altimeter; and the second, a change of attitude to return smoothly to the desired altitude. If the altitude and airspeed are more than 100 feet and 10 knots low, respectively, apply power along with an increase of pitch attitude; if the altitude and airspeed are high by more than 100 feet and 10 knots, reduce power along with a lowered pitch attitude.

There is a small lag in the movement of the altimeter; however, for all practical purposes, consider that the altimeter gives an immediate indication of a change, or a need for change in pitch attitude.

Since the altimeter provides the most pertinent information regarding pitch in level flight and is the instrument which should be held constant, it is considered primary for pitch.

The *vertical-speed indicator* gives an *indirect* indication of pitch attitude of the helicopter and should be used in conjunction with the other pitch instruments to attain a high degree of accuracy and precision. The instrument indicates zero when in level flight. Any movement of the needle from the zero position shows a need for an immediate change in pitch attitude to return it to zero. If the airspeed varies from that desired by more than 10 knots, a coordinated power change is also required. Always use the vertical-speed indicator in conjunction with the altimeter in level flight. If a movement of the vertical-speed indicator is detected, immediately use the proper corrective measures to return it to zero. The altimeter will usually indicate that there has been little or no change in altitude. If you do not zero the needle of the vertical-speed indicator immediately, the results will show on the altimeter as a gain or loss of altitude.

The initial movement of the vertical-speed needle is instantaneous and indicates the trend of the vertical movement of the helicopter. It must be realized that a period of time is necessary for the vertical-speed indicator to reach its maximum point

of deflection after a correction has been made. This time element is commonly referred to as "lag." The lag is directly proportional to the speed and magnitude of the pitch change. If you employ smooth control techniques and make small adjustments in pitch attitude, lag is minimized and the vertical-speed indicator is easy to interpret. Over-controlling can be stopped by neutralizing the controls, allowing the pitch attitude to stabilize, and then readjusting the pitch attitude by utilizing the indications of the other pitch instruments.

Occasionally, the vertical-speed indicator may be slightly out of calibration and thus indicate a slight climb or descent when the aircraft is in level flight. If it cannot be readjusted properly, this error must be taken into consideration when using the vertical-speed indicator for pitch control. For example, an improperly set vertical-speed indicator may indicate a descent of 100 feet per minute when the helicopter is in level flight. That reading of the instrument would, therefore, indicate level flight, and any deviation from that reading would indicate a change in attitude.

The *airspeed indicator* gives an *indirect* indication of helicopter pitch attitude. With a given power setting and pitch attitude, the airspeed will remain constant. If the airspeed increases, the nose is too low and should be raised; if the airspeed decreases, the nose is too high and should be lowered. A rapid change in airspeed indicates a large change in pitch attitude, and a slow change in airspeed indicates a small change in pitch attitude. There is very little lag in the indications of the airspeed indicator. When making attitude changes and some lag is noticed between control application and change of airspeed, cyclic control lag is responsible. Generally, a departure from the desired airspeed, due to an inadvertent pitch attitude change, will also result in a change in altitude. For example, an increase in airspeed due to a low pitch attitude will result in a decrease in altitude. Correction of pitch attitude will regain both airspeed and altitude.

Bank Control.—The bank attitude of a helicopter is the angular relation of its lateral axis and the natural horizon. To maintain a straight course in visual flight, you must keep the lateral axis of the helicopter level with the natural horizon. Assuming the helicopter is in coordinated flight, any deviation from a laterally level attitude produces a turn.

The flight instruments used for bank control are the *attitude indicator, heading indicator,* and the *turn coordinator* (Fig. 6–4). The heading indicator is considered *primary* for bank in level flight.

The *attitude indicator* gives a *direct* indication of the bank attitude of the helicopter. For instrument flight, the miniature aircraft and the horizon bar of the attitude indicator are substituted for the actual helicopter and the natural horizon. Any change in bank attitude of the helicopter is indicated instantly by the miniature aircraft. For proper interpretations of this instrument, you should imagine being in the miniature aircraft. If the helicopter is properly trimmed and the rotor tilts, a turn begins.

FIGURE 6–4. Instruments used for bank control.

The turn can be stopped by leveling the miniature aircraft with the horizon bar. The ball should always be kept centered through proper pedal trim.

The angle of bank is indicated by the pointer on the banking scale at the top of the instrument (Fig. 6–5). Small bank angles which may not be seen by observing the miniature aircraft, can easily be determined by referring to the banking scale pointer.

FIGURE 6–5. Bank interpretation with the attitude indicator.

Pitch and bank attitudes can be determined simultaneously on the attitude indicator. Even though the miniature aircraft is not level with the horizon bar, pitch attitude can be established by observing the relative position of the miniature aircraft and the horizon bar.

If the attitude indicator has a caging feature, the instrument should be caged and uncaged only in straight-and-level flight as indicated by the other bank instruments, otherwise it will show a false indication. The attitude indicator may show small misrepresentations of bank attitude during maneuvers which involve turns. This precession error can be immediately detected by closely cross-checking the other bank instruments during these maneuvers. Precession normally is noticed when rolling out of a turn. If, on the completion of a turn, the miniature aircraft is level and the helicopter is still turning, make a small change of bank attitude to center the turn needle and stop the movement of the heading indicator.

In coordinated flight, the *heading indicator* gives an *indirect* indication of the helicopter's bank attitude. When a helicopter is banked, it turns. When the lateral axis of the helicopter is level, it flies straight. Therefore, when the heading indicator shows a constant heading, the helicopter is level laterally. A deviation from the desired heading indicates a bank in the direction the helicopter is turning. A small angle of bank is indicated by a slow change of heading; a large angle of bank is

101

indicated by a rapid change of heading. If a turn is noticed, apply opposite cyclic until the heading indicator indicates the desired heading, simultaneously checking the ball for centered position. Make the correction to the desired heading using an angle of bank no larger than the number of degrees to be turned. This correction should not exceed the angle of bank required for a standard rate turn.

During coordinated flight, the *miniature aircraft* of the *turn coordinator* gives an indirect indication of the bank attitude of the helicopter. When the miniature aircraft is displaced from level, the helicopter is turning in the direction of the displacement. Thus, if the miniature aircraft is displaced to the left, the helicopter is turning left. Leveling the miniature aircraft with cyclic will produce straight flight. A close observation of the miniature aircraft is necessary to accurately interpret small deviations from the desired position.

Cross-check the *ball* of the turn coordinator to determine that the helicopter is in coordinated flight. If the rotor is laterally level and torque is properly compensated by pedal pressure, the ball will remain in the center. To center the ball, level the helicopter laterally by reference to the other bank instruments, then center the ball with pedal trim. Torque correction pressures vary as power changes are made. Always check the ball following such changes.

Common Errors During Straight-and-Level Flight.

1. Failure to maintain altitude.
2. Failure to maintain heading.
3. Overcontrolling pitch and bank during corrections.
4. Failure to maintain proper pedal trim.
5. Failure to cross-check all available instruments.

Power Control.—Establishing specific power settings is accomplished through collective pitch adjustments—RPM is controlled automatically in a turbine engine helicopter. Once a desired power setting is established, frequent attention to the torque meter is necessary. At any given airspeed, a specific power setting determines whether the helicopter is in level flight, in a climb, or in a descent. For example, cruising airspeed maintained with cruising power will result in level flight. If you increase the power setting and hold the airspeed constant, the helicopter will climb. Conversely, if you decrease power and hold the airspeed constant, the helicopter will descend. As a rule of thumb, in a turbine engine helicopter a 10 percent change in the torque value required to maintain level flight will result in a climb or descent of approximately 500 feet per minute, if the airspeed remains the same.

If the altitude is held constant, power determines the airspeed. For example, at a constant altitude, cruising power results in cruising airspeed. Any deviation from the cruising power setting results in a change of airspeed. When power is added to increase airspeed, the nose of the helicopter pitches up and yaws to the right; when power is reduced to decrease airspeed, the nose pitches down and yaws to the left. The yawing effect is most pronounced in single-rotor helicopters, and is absent in helicopters with counter rotating rotors. To counteract the yawing tendency of the helicopter, apply pedal trim during power changes.

To maintain a constant altitude and airspeed in level flight, coordinate pitch attitude and power control. The relationship between altitude and airspeed determines the need for a change in power and/or pitch attitude. If the altitude is constant and the airspeed is high or low, change the power to obtain the desired airspeed. During the change in power, make an accurate interpretation of the altimeter; then counteract any deviation from the desired altitude by an appropriate change of pitch attitude. If the altitude is low and the airspeed is high, or vice versa, a change in pitch attitude alone may return the helicopter to the proper altitude and airspeed. If both airspeed and altitude are low, or if both are high, a change in both power and pitch attitude is necessary.

To make power control easy when changing airspeed, it is necessary to know the approximate power settings for the various airspeeds which will be flown. When the airspeed is to be changed any appreciable amount, adjust the power so that the torque is approximately 5 percent over or under that setting necessary to maintain the new airspeed. As the power approaches the desired setting, include the torque meter in the cross-check to determine when the proper adjustment has been accomplished. As the airspeed is changing, adjust the pitch attitude to maintain a constant altitude. A constant heading should be maintained throughout the change. As the desired airspeed is approached, adjust power to the new cruising power setting and further adjust pitch attitude to maintain altitude. Overpowering and underpowering torque approximately 5 percent is the normal procedure. This results in a change of airspeed at a moderate rate, which allows ample time to adjust pitch and bank smoothly. The instrument indications for straight-and-level flight at normal cruise, and during the transition from normal cruise to slow cruise, are illustrated in Figures 6–6 and 6–7. After the airspeed has stabilized at slow cruise, the attitude indicator will show an approximate level pitch attitude.

The altimeter is the primary pitch instrument during level flight, whether flying at a constant airspeed, or during a change in airspeed. Altitude should not change during airspeed transitions. The heading indicator remains the primary bank instrument. Whenever the airspeed is changed any appreciable amount, the torque meter is momentarily the primary instrument for power control, and it should be adjusted to indicate an exact power setting. When the airspeed approaches that desired, the airspeed indicator again becomes the primary instrument for power control.

FIGURE 6–6. Straight-and-level flight (normal cruising airspeed).

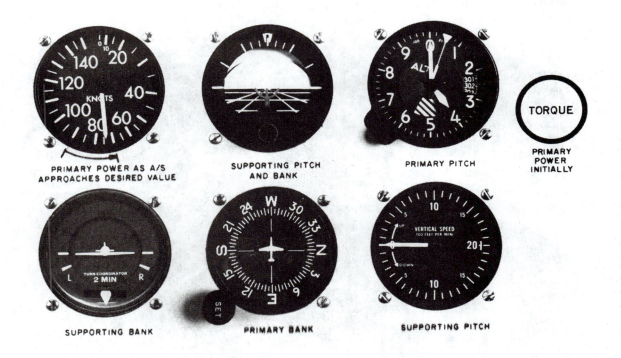

FIGURE 6–7. Straight-and-level flight (airspeed decreasing).

103

The cross-check of the pitch and the bank instruments to produce straight-and-level flight should be combined with the power control instruments. With a constant power setting, a normal cross-check should be satisfactory. When changing power, however, the speed of the cross-check must be increased to cover the pitch and bank instruments adequately. This is necessary to counteract any deviations immediately.

Common Errors During Airspeed Changes.
1. Improper use of power.
2. Overcontrolling pitch attitude.
3. Failure to maintain heading.
4. Failure to maintain altitude.
5. Improper pedal trim.

Straight Climbs and Descents (Constant airspeed and constant rate)

Climbs.—For any power setting and load condition, there is only one airspeed which will give the most efficient rate of climb. To determine this, you should consult the climb data for the type helicopter being flown. The technique varies according to airspeed on entry and the type of climb (constant airspeed or constant rate) desired.

Entries.—To enter a **constant airspeed climb** from cruise airspeed (if climb speed is lower than cruise speed), simultaneously increase torque to the climb power setting and adjust pitch attitude to the approximate climb attitude. The increase in power causes the helicopter to start climbing and only very slight back cyclic pressure need be applied to complete the change from level to climb attitude. The attitude indicator should be used to accomplish the pitch attitude change. If the transition from level flight to a climb is smooth, the vertical-speed indicator will show an immediate upward trend and will stop at a rate appropriate to the stabilized airspeed and attitude. Primary and supporting instruments for climb entry are illustrated in Figure 6–8.

When the helicopter stabilizes on a constant airspeed and attitude, the airspeed indicator becomes primary for pitch. The torque meter continues to be primary for power and should be monitored closely to determine that the proper climb power setting is being maintained. Primary and supporting instruments for a stabilized constant airspeed climb are shown in Figure 6–9.

If cruise and climb airspeeds are the same, the climb pitch attitude, shown by the attitude indicator, will be nearly the same as the cruise pitch attitude.

The technique and procedures for entering a **constant rate climb** are very similar to those previously described for a constant airspeed climb. For training purposes, a rate climb is entered from climb airspeed. The rate used will be the one that is appropriate for the particular helicopter flown. Normally, in helicopters with low rates of climb, 500 feet per minute is appropriate. In helicopters capable of high climb rates, use a rate of 1,000 feet per minute.

FIGURE 6–8. Climb entry—constant airspeed climb.

FIGURE 6-9. Stabilized climb—constant airspeed.

To enter a rate climb, increase torque to the approximate setting for the desired rate. As power is applied, the airspeed indicator is primary for pitch until the vertical speed approaches the desired rate. At this time, the vertical-speed indicator becomes primary for pitch. Change pitch attitude by reference to the attitude indicator to maintain the desired vertical speed. When the vertical-speed indicator becomes primary for pitch, the airspeed indicator becomes primary for power. Primary and supporting instruments for a stabilized constant rate climb are illustrated in Fig. 6–10. Adjust torque to maintain desired airspeed. Pitch attitude and power corrections should be closely coordinated. To illustrate this, if the vertical speed is correct, but the airspeed is low, add power. As the power is increased, it may be necessary to lower the pitch attitude slightly to avoid increasing the vertical rate. Adjust the pitch attitude smoothly to avoid overcontrolling. Small power corrections (approximately 5 percent torque) usually will be sufficient to bring the airspeed back to the desired indication.

Leveling off.—The level off from a **constant airspeed climb** must be started before reaching the desired altitude. Although the amount of lead varies with the helicopter and pilot technique, the most important factor is vertical speed. Normally, the lead for each 500 feet per minute rate of climb is 50 feet. When the proper altitude lead is reached, the altimeter becomes primary for pitch. Adjust the

pitch attitude to level flight attitude for that airspeed. Cross-check the altimeter and vertical speed to determine whether level flight has been attained at the desired altitude. To level off at cruise airspeed (if this speed is higher than climb airspeed), leave the torque at climb power setting until the airspeed approaches cruise airspeed, then reduce torque to cruise power setting.

The level off from a **constant rate climb** is accomplished in the same manner as the level off from a constant airspeed climb.

Descents.—A descent may be performed at any normal airspeed the helicopter is capable of, but the airspeed must be determined prior to entry. The technique is determined by type of descent (constant airspeed or constant rate).

Entries.—If your airspeed is higher than descending airspeed and you wish to make a **constant airspeed descent** at descending airspeed, reduce torque to the descending power setting and maintain a constant altitude. When you approach the descending airspeed, the airspeed indicator becomes primary for pitch and the torque meter continues to be primary for power. The helicopter will begin to descend as the airspeed is held constant. For a **constant rate descent,** reduce the torque to the approximate setting for the desired rate. If the descent is started at descending airspeed, the airspeed indicator is primary for pitch until the ver-

FIGURE 6–10.   Stabilized climb—constant rate.

tical speed approaches the desired rate. At this time, the vertical-speed indicator becomes primary for pitch and the airspeed indicator becomes primary for power. Coordinate power and pitch attitude control as was described earlier for constant rate climbs.

Leveling off.—The level off from a **constant air-speed descent** may be made at descending airspeed or at cruise airspeed (if this is higher than descending airspeed). As in a climb level off, the altitude lead depends on rate of descent and control technique. For a level off at descending airspeed, this lead should be approximately 50 feet for each 500 feet per minute rate of descent. At the altitude lead, simultaneously advance the torque to the setting necessary to maintain descending airspeed in level flight. At this point, the altimeter becomes primary for pitch and the airspeed indicator becomes primary for power.

To level off at an airspeed higher than descending airspeed, increase the torque approximately 100 to 150 feet prior to reaching the desired altitude. The power setting should be that which is necessary to maintain the desired airspeed in level flight. Hold the vertical speed constant until approximately 50 feet above the desired altitude. At this point, the altimeter becomes primary for pitch and the airspeed indicator becomes primary for power. The level off from a **constant rate descent** should be accomplished in the same manner as the level off from a constant airspeed descent.

Common Errors During Straight Climbs and Descents.
1. Failure to maintain heading.
2. Improper use of power.
3. Poor control of pitch attitude.
4. Failure to maintain proper pedal trim.
5. Failure to level off on desired altitude.

Turns

Standard Rate Turns.—Turns made by reference to instruments should be made at a definite rate. Turns described in this section are those which do not exceed a standard rate of three degrees per second as indicated by the turn coordinator. True airspeed determines the angle of bank necessary to maintain a standard rate turn. At 70 knots true airspeed, approximately 12 degrees of bank are required to maintain a standard rate turn; at 90 knots true airspeed, approximately 15 degrees of bank are required.

To enter a turn, apply lateral cyclic in the direction of the desired turn. The entry should be accomplished smoothly, using the attitude indicator to establish the approximate bank angle. When the turn coordinator indicates a standard rate turn, it becomes primary for bank. The attitude indicator now becomes supporting for bank. During level turns, the altimeter is primary for pitch and the airspeed indicator is primary for power. Primary and supporting instruments for a stabilized stand-

106

PRIMARY POWER   PRIMARY BANK INITIALLY
SUPPORTING PITCH   PRIMARY PITCH   TORQUE

SUPPORTING POWER

PRIMARY BANK AS
TURN IS ESTABLISHED   SUPPORTING PITCH

FIGURE 6–11.   Standard rate turn—constant airspeed.

ard rate turn are illustrated in Figure 6–11. If an increase in torque is required to maintain airspeed, slight forward cyclic pressure may be required since the helicopter tends to pitch up as collective pitch angle is changed. Apply pedal trim as required to keep the ball centered.

To recover to straight-and-level flight, apply cyclic in the direction opposite the turn. The rate of roll-out should be the same as the rate of roll-in. As you initiate the turn recovery, the attitude indicator becomes primary for bank. When the helicopter is approximately level, the heading indicator becomes primary for bank as in straight-and-level flight. The airspeed indicator and ball should be cross-checked closely to maintain desired airspeed and pedal trim.

Turns to Predetermined Headings.—As was stated earlier, turning and banking in coordinated flight are the same. A helicopter will turn as long as its lateral axis is tilted; therefore, the recovery must start before the desired heading is reached. The amount of lead varies with the rate of turn and the individual pilot's rate of recovery.

As a guide, when making a 3 degree per second rate of turn, use a lead of one-half the angle of bank. Use this lead until you are able to determine the exact amount required by your particular technique. The bank angle should never exceed the number of degrees to be turned. As in any standard rate turn, the rate of recovery should be the same as the rate of entry. During turns to predetermined headings, cross-check the primary and supporting pitch, bank, and power instruments closely.

Timed Turns, Compass Turns, and Changes of Airspeed in Turns.—The procedures for performing these maneuvers in a helicopter and an airplane are essentially the same. See the descriptions in Chapter V.

Steep Turns.—Any turn greater than a standard rate is considered a steep turn. In helicopters, steep turns should be limited to one and a half times a standard rate turn as indicated by the turn coordinator. A steep turn is seldom necessary or advisable in instrument weather conditions, but it is an excellent maneuver to increase your ability to react quickly and smoothly to rapid changes of attitude.

Regardless of the bank angle used, the entry and recovery techniques are the same as for any turn. You will find it more difficult to control pitch because of the greater decrease of vertical lift as the bank increases. With some attitude indicators, precession while in a steep turn adds to the difficulty of maintaining the desired attitude. There is a tendency to lose altitude and/or airspeed in steep turns because of the decrease of vertical lift. Therefore, to maintain a constant altitude and airspeed, additional power will be required. You should not initiate a correction, however, until the instruments indicate the need for a correction.

107

FIGURE 6–12. Steep left turn.

Refer to the attitude indicator when making a correction even though precession of the instrument is evident. Note the need for a correction on the altimeter and vertical-speed indicator, check the indications on the attitude indicator, and make the necessary change. After you have made this change, again check the altimeter and vertical-speed indicator to determine whether or not the correction was adequate. The primary and supporting instruments for a stabilized steep turn are illustrated in Figure 6–12.

The recovery should be smooth with a normal rate of roll-out. As the helicopter rolls out of the turn, vertical lift will increase and there will be a tendency to climb. Also, there will be a tendency for the airspeed to increase. Necessary corrections should be made as soon as the need is indicated by the instruments.

Climbing and Descending Turns.—For climbing and descending turns, the techniques described earlier for straight climbs and descents and those for standard rate turns are combined. For practice, start the climb or descent and turn simultaneously. The primary and supporting instruments for a stabilized constant airspeed left climbing turn are illustrated in Figure 6–13. The level off from a climbing or descending turn is the same as the level off from a straight climb or descent. To recover to straight-and-level flight, you may: (1) stop the turn, then level off; (2) level off, then stop the turn; or

(3) stop the turn and level off simultaneously. During climbing and descending turns, keep the ball of the turn coordinator centered with pedal trim.

Common Errors During Turns.
 1. Failure to maintain desired rate of turn.
 2. Failure to maintain altitude in level turns.
 3. Failure to maintain desired airspeed.
 4. Variation of rate of entry and recovery.
 5. Failure to use proper lead in turns to headings.
 6. Failure to properly compute time during timed turns.
 7. Failure to use proper leads and lags during compass turns.
 8. Improper use of power.
 9. Failure to use proper pedal trim.

Unusual Attitudes and Recoveries

Any maneuver not required for normal helicopter instrument flight is an unusual attitude and may be caused by any one or a combination of such factors as turbulence, disorientation, instrument failure, confusion, preoccupation with cockpit duties, carelessness in cross-checking, errors in instrument interpretation, or lack of proficiency in aircraft control. Due to the instability characteristics of the helicopter, unusual attitudes can be extremely critical. As soon as you detect an unusual attitude, make a recovery to straight-and-level

108

FIGURE 6-13. Stabilized left climbing turn—constant airspeed.

flight as soon as possible with a minimum loss of altitude.

To recover from an unusual attitude, correct bank and pitch attitude, and adjust power as necessary. All components are changed almost simultaneously, with little lead of one over the other. If the helicopter is in a steep climbing or descending turn, correct bank, pitch, and power. The bank attitude should be corrected by referring to the turn coordinator and attitude indicator (if available). Pitch attitude should be corrected by referring to the altimeter, airspeed indicator, vertical-speed indicator, and attitude indicator (if available). Adjust power by referring to the airspeed indicator and torque meter.

Since the displacement of the controls used in recoveries from unusual attitudes may be greater than those for normal flight, care must be taken in making adjustments as straight and level flight is approached. The instruments must be cross-checked closely to avoid overcontrolling.

Common Errors During Unusual Attitude Recoveries.

1. Failure to make proper pitch correction.
2. Failure to make proper bank correction.
3. Failure to make proper power correction.
4. Overcontrol of pitch and/or bank attitude.
5. Overcontrol of power.
6. Excessive loss of altitude.

Instrument Takeoff

The procedures and techniques described here should be modified as necessary to conform with those set forth in the operating instructions for the particular helicopter flown.

Adjust the miniature aircraft of the attitude indicator as appropriate for the aircraft being flown. After the helicopter is aligned with the runway or takeoff pad, to prevent forward movement of a helicopter equipped with a wheel-typed landing gear, set the parking brakes or apply the toe brakes. If the parking brake is used, it must be unlocked after the takeoff has been completed. Apply sufficient friction to the collective pitch control to minimize overcontrolling and to prevent creeping. Excessive friction should be avoided since this will limit collective pitch movement.

After checking all instruments for proper indications, start the takeoff by applying collective pitch and a predetermined power setting (normally 10 percent torque above hover power—but not exceeding maximum allowable power). Add power smoothly and steadily to gain airspeed and altitude simultaneously, and to prevent settling to the ground. As power is applied and the helicopter becomes airborne, pedals are used initially to maintain the desired heading. At the same time, apply forward cyclic to begin the acceleration to climbing

109

FIGURE 6–14. Instrument indications during instrument takeoff.

airspeed. During the initial acceleration, the pitch attitude of the helicopter, as read on the attitude indicator, should be one to two bar widths low. The primary and supporting instruments after becoming airborne are illustrated in Figure 6–14. As the airspeed increases to the appropriate climb airspeed, adjust pitch gradually to climb attitude (see Figure 6–9). As climb airspeed is reached, reduce power to the climb power setting and transition to a fully coordinated straight climb.

During the initial climb-out, minor heading corrections should be made with pedals only until sufficient airspeed is attained to transition to fully-coordinated flight. Throughout the instrument takeoff, instrument cross-check and interpretations must be rapid and accurate, and aircraft control positive and smooth.

Common errors during instrument takeoffs.
1. Failure to maintain heading.
2. Overcontrolling pedals.
3. Failure to use required power.
4. Failure to adjust pitch attitude as climbing airspeed is reached.

Autorotations

Both straight-ahead and turning autorotations should be practiced by reference to instruments. This training will ensure that you can take prompt corrective action to maintain positive aircraft control in the event of power failure.

To enter autorotation, reduce collective pitch smoothly to maintain a safe rotor RPM and apply pedal trim to keep the ball of the turn coordinator centered. The pitch attitude of the helicopter should be approximately level as shown by the attitude indicator. The airspeed indicator is the primary pitch instrument and should be adjusted to the recommended autorotation speed. The heading indicator is primary for bank in a straight-ahead autorotation. In a turning autorotation, a standard rate turn should be maintained by reference to the miniature aircraft of the turn coordinator.

A practice instrument autorotation must be terminated in a power recovery performed in accordance with the procedure recommended for the helicopter being flown.

Common Errors During Autorotations.

1. Uncoordinated entry due to improper pedal trim.
2. Poor airspeed control due to improper pitch attitude.
3. Poor heading control in straight-ahead autorotations.
4. Failure to maintain proper rotor RPM.
5. Failure to maintain standard rate turn during turning autorotations.

110

VII. ELECTRONIC AIDS TO INSTRUMENT FLYING

Until comparatively recent times, navigation and voice communications were distinctly separate aspects of cross-country flight. The pilot had to be almost entirely self-dependent. Although ground facilities were sometimes available to provide useful local weather information, the pilot was the BOSS. The pilot had full responsibility for the flight and therefore made all the decisions. Today the pilot is still boss of the aircraft, but modern air travel involves more decisions and responsibilities than can possibly be handled in the cockpit. While the pilot navigates, flight progress is coordinated by radio with a vast team of experts who are also responsible for decisions affecting the flight.

Navigation and communications are thus closely interrelated components of cross-country instrument flight in controlled airspace. The electronic ground and airborne aids, the operational procedures, and the rules are interdependent. Knowledge of the basic radio principles applicable to both communications and navigation equipment will increase your understanding of their use and limitations.

Basic Radio Principles

Wave Transmission.—Whether transmitted by sound, light, or electricity, energy moves in waves. A wave is a pulse of energy traveling through a medium by means of vibrations from particle to particle. For example, when a stone is dropped into the water, the energy of motion disturbs the water, causing the water to rise and fall. Energy waves travel outward from the source of disturbance, but the water itself does not move outward. This rise and fall above and below the normal undisturbed level can be pictured as a curved line (Fig. 7–1).

The *amplitude* of a wave is the linear distance measuring the extreme range of fluctuation from the highest or lowest point to the midpoint between them (BH, ID, FJ). A *cycle* is the interval between any two points measuring the completion of a single wave movement, referenced from any point on the wave to the corresponding point on the succeeding wave (A to E, B to F, C to G). *Wavelength* is the linear distance of a cycle, measured in units appropriate to the size of a wave (A to E). The *frequency*

111

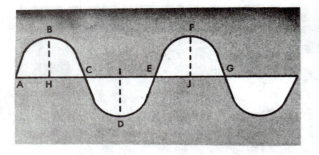

FIGURE 7–1. Wave transmission.

of a wave is the number of cycles completed in one unit of time. If 10 cycles are completed in one second, the wave frequency is 10 cycles per second. Since radio wave cycles per unit of time involve very high numbers, radio frequencies are expressed in kilo Hertz* (thousands of cycles per second) or Mega Hertz (millions of cycles per second). Thus, a frequency of 1,000 Hz equals 1 kHz, and 1,000 kHz equals 1 MHz.

*The Federal Aviation Administration, in conformance with worldwide practice, has formally adopted the term "Hertz" as the basic unit of frequency, meaning cycle or cycles per second. The standard abbreviations Hz (Hertz); kHz (kilo Hertz); and MHz (Mega Hertz) are therefore used in this publication.

Current is the flow of electrons through a conductor. Direct current (DC) flows only in one direction. Alternating current (AC) flows in one direction during a given time interval, then in the opposite direction for the same interval, reversing continuously. An alternating current can be represented as a continuous change of direction of flow of electrons from positive to negative (Fig. 7–2).

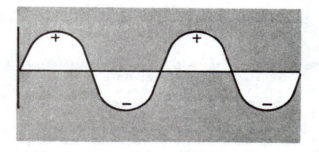

FIGURE 7–2. Alternating current.

Radio Waves.—When an electric current flows through a wire, a magnetic field is generated around the wire. When alternating current flows through a wire, the magnetic field alternately builds up and collapses. Radio waves are produced by sending a high-frequency alternating current through a conductor (antenna). The frequency of the wave radiated by the antenna is equal to the frequency, or number of cycles per second, of the alternating current. The velocity of the radiated wave is 186,000 miles per second.

Frequency Bands.—Radio frequencies extend from approximately 20 kilo Hertz to over 30,000 Mega Hertz. Since different groups of frequencies within this range produce different effects in transmission, radio frequencies are classified into groups or frequency bands, according to these differences.

Band	Frequency Range
Low-frequency (L/F)	30 to 300 kHz
Medium-frequency (M/F)	300 to 3000 kHz
High-frequency (H/F)	3000 kHz to 30 MHz
Very high frequency (VHF)	30 to 300 MHz
Ultra high frequency (UHF)	300 to 3000 MHz

Characteristics of Radio Wave Propagation.—All matter has a varying degree of conductivity or resistance to radio waves. The Earth itself acts as the greatest resistor to radio waves. Radiated energy that travels near the ground induces a voltage in the ground that subtracts energy from the wave, decreasing the strength (attenuating) of the wave as the distance from the antenna becomes greater. Trees, buildings, and mineral deposits affect attenuation to varying degrees. Radiated energy in the upper atmosphere is likewise affected as the energy of radiation is absorbed by molecules of air, water, and dust. The characteristics of radio wave propagation varying according to the frequency of the radiated signal, determining the design, use, and limitations of both ground and airborne equipment.

Low-Frequency Radio Wave Propagation.—A radio wave radiates from an antenna in all directions. Part of the energy travels along the ground (ground wave) until its energy is dissipated. The remainder of the transmitted energy travels upward into space (sky wave) and would be lost if it were not reflected in the ionosphere by highly charged particles (ions) caused by the Sun's radiation. Reflection of radio signals back to the Earth permits reception of the signals at varying distances from the transmitter. The distance is determined by the height and density of the ionosphere and the angle at which the radiated wave strikes the ionosphere. The height and density of the ionosphere varies with the time of day, seasons, and latitude since its composition is determined by solar radiation. See Figure 7–3.

The distance between the transmitting antenna and the point where the sky wave first returns to the ground is called the *skip distance* (Fig. 7–3). The distance between the point where the ground wave can no longer be received and the sky wave returned is called the *skip zone*. Since solar radiation varies the position and density of the ionosphere, great changes in skip distance occur at dawn and dusk when fading of signals is more prevalent.

High-Frequency Wave Propagation (3,000 kHz to 30 MHz).—The attenuation of the ground wave at frequencies above approximately 3,000 kHz is so great that the ground wave is of little use except at very short distances. The sky wave must be utilized, and since it reflects back and forth from sky to ground, it may be used over long distances (12,000 miles, for example).

Very High Frequency Propagation (30 to 300 MHz).—At frequencies above about 30 MHz, there

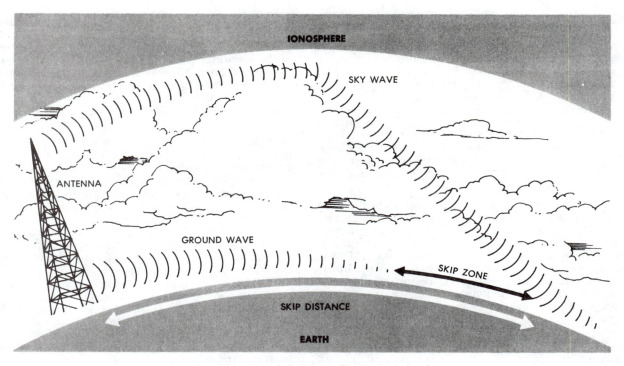

FIGURE 7–3. Low-frequency radio wave propagation.

is practically no ground wave propagation and ordinarily no reflection from the ionosphere. Thus, use of VHF signals is possible only if the transmitting and receiving antennas are raised sufficiently above the surface of the Earth to allow the use of a direct wave. This type of radiation is known as "line-of-sight" transmission. Accordingly, the use of VHF/UHF radio waves is limited by the position of the receiver in relation to the transmitter (Fig. 7–4).

When using airborne VHF/UHF equipment, it is of the utmost importance that this limitation be understood. The range of VHF/UHF transmission increases with altitude, and may be approximately determined by the following simple method: Multiply the square root of the aircraft altitude in feet by 1.23 to find the VHF/UHF transmission range in nautical miles. For example, an aircraft flying 3,600 feet above flat terrain will receive VHF/UHF signals approximately 74 nautical miles from the transmitter.

Static Disturbance to Reception of Radio Waves

Static, whether it originates away from the aircraft in lightning discharges or from electrostatic discharges from the aircraft surfaces, distorts the radio wave and interferes with normal reception of both communications and navigation signals. Low-frequency airborne equipment is particularly subject to static disturbance. Signals in the higher frequency bands are static-free.

Precipitation static occurs when static electricity is generated on various aircraft surfaces in flight and is discharged onto other surfaces or into the air. An aircraft generally accumulates little or no static charge when flying in clear atmosphere. But an aircraft flying in particle-laden air may encounter precipitation static because of charged particles that (1) adhere to the aircraft, (2) create a charge through frictional contact, or (3) divide into

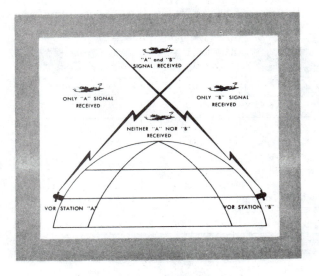

FIGURE 7–4. Line-of-sight transmission.

113

charged fragments on impact with the aircraft surfaces.

At the lower altitudes and in moderate to heavy rain, precipitation static is common. It is often accompanied by St. Elmo's Fire, a corona discharge which lights up the aircraft surface areas where maximum static discharge occurs.

Precipitation static is also common in very high clouds or in dust storms, where high winds pick up and carry substantial amounts of solid particles. It can also result from atmospheric electric fields in thunderstorm clouds. Ice crystal static is encountered in cirrus clouds, or in altostrautus and nimbostratus clouds in the winter.

Frequency Interference.—Omni and localizer receivers used for en route navigation and instrument approaches are susceptible to interference from FM radios, which operate in the VHF frequency range. The frequency oscillations in a portable FM radio operated in an aircraft will be picked up by the aircraft navigation receivers, distorting the navigation receiver information.

Additional irregularities in radio wave propagation, of particular significance in their effect on low-frequency receivers, will be discussed in connection with the use of the radio compass.

Transmission and Reception of Radio Signals

Some of the radio signal transmission characteristics related to ground and airborne equipment and its use are shown in Figure 7–5.

Basic Communication Equipment.—In order to transmit messages from one location to another by radio, the following basic equipment is needed (Fig. 7–6):
1. A transmitter to generate radio frequency (r-f) waves.
2. A microphone (or key) to control these energy waves.

3. A transmitting antenna suitable for radiation of the radio frequencies used.
4. A suitable receiving antenna to intercept some of the radio frequency waves.
5. A receiver to change the intercepted radio frequency waves into audio frequency waves.
6. A speaker, or earphones, to change the audio frequency waves into audible sound.

Basic Navigation Equipment.—In order to transmit navigation signals from a ground facility to airborne navigation instruments, the following basic equipment is needed:
1. Signal-forming components to determine the character of the radio frequency signals generated.
2. A transmitter, to generate the radio frequency waves.
3. Transmitting antennas, suitable for radiation of the radio frequency signals used.
4. A receiving antenna, or antennas, to intercept the radio frequency signals.
5. Aircraft receiver components, to select and interpret the navigation signals.
6. Instruments and devices for visual-audio presentation of radio navigation information.

The simplified diagram in Figure 7–7 shows how the navigation and communications equipment, both ground and airborne, are related.

Modifying the Radiated Signal.—In order to use the radiated signal for communicating information, it is necessary that the signal be modified by the information to be transmitted. The modification can be done either by interrupting the signal (as in morse code), or by *modulating* the signal (Fig. 7–8). An unmodulated signal is called a *continuous wave* (cw). A modulated signal is commonly called a *modulated carrier wave* (mcw). Figure 7–9 illustrates a continuous wave, an amplitude modulated wave, and a frequency modulated wave.

Receiving the Radiated Signals.—Radio waves set up currents in receiving antennas, just as an alternating current is set up in any conductor placed near another conductor that carries alternating cur-

BAND	RANGE		POWER REQUIRED	ANTENNA LENGTH REQUIREMENT
	DAY	NIGHT		
L-f	Long	Long	Very high	Long
M-f	Medium	Long	High to medium	Long
H-f (3 to 10 MHz)	Short	Medium to long	Medium	Medium
H-f (10 to 30 MHz)	Long	Short	Low	Short
V-h-f	Short	Short	Low	Very short

Long range: over 1,500 miles. Medium range: 200 to 1,500 miles. Short range: under 200 miles.

FIGURE 7–5. Transmission characteristics of radio signals.

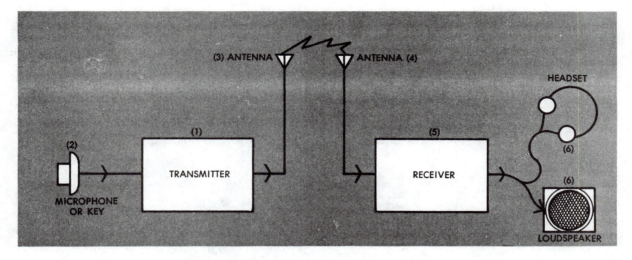

FIGURE 7–6. Basic communication equipment.

rent. *Tuning* is the selection of the desired signal (frequency) and rejection of the undesired signals (Fig. 7–10). The tuning circuit in the receiver is adjusted to resonance at the frequency of the desired signal. Other frequencies are rejected by the tuning circuit, and the selected signal is allowed to flow to an *amplifier* which increases the strength of the signal. If the signal being received is a modulated carrier wave, the useful information which it carries must be detected. This process is called *demodulation* and is accomplished by the *detector*.

Radio Navigation Systems

In the broad sense of the term, radio navigation includes any method by which a pilot follows a predetermined flight path over the Earth's surface by utilizing the properties of radio waves. The navigation can be conducted by any one or any combination of the following three basic systems:

1. Self-contained airborne systems entirely independent of ground facilities. The Doppler radar navigation system currently used for long overwater and transpolar flights is an example.

2. Ground facilities that continuously monitor and determine the exact aircraft position, on the basis of which the pilot is given navigational guidance by radio communications. Ground-controlled radar navigation is becoming increasingly important to instrument flight operations. Long range radar operated by Air Route Traffic Control Centers (ARTCC) can provide continuous navigational guidance to aircraft operating along most of the routes between major metropolitan terminals.

3. A combination of ground and airborne equipment, by means of which the ground facilities transmit signals to airborne instruments. The pilot determines and controls ground track on the basis of the instrument indications.

The navigation systems in common use today are a combination of VOR (very high frequency om-

nidirectional range), and additional electronic aids and ground-controlled radar.

Very High Frequency Omnirange

The VOR, or omnirange, is the primary navigation facility for civil aviation in the National Airspace System. As a VHF facility, it eliminates atmospheric static interference and other limitations associated with the older low-frequency facilities that VOR has replaced. The VOR generates directional information and transmits it by ground equipment to the aircraft, providing 360 magnetic courses TO or FROM the VOR station. These courses are called *radials* and are oriented FROM the station (Fig. 7–11). For example, aircraft A (heading 180°) is inbound on the 360 radial; after crossing the station, the aircraft is outbound on the 180 radial at A-1. Aircraft B is shown crossing the 225 radial. Similarly, at any point around the station, an aircraft can be located somewhere on a VOR radial.

Principles of Operation.—VOR operation is based upon the principle that the phase difference between two AC voltages may be used to determine azimuth location. The principle may be more readily visualized by imagining two light signals, both at the same geographic position. The first light is a flashing (reference) signal, visible from any point around the compass. The second light is a narrow beam (variable signal) that rotates continuously at a specific rate. Thus, if you are at any point around the circle, you will see the rotating beam only at the instant it sweeps past your position. Assume that the reference light flashes only when the rotating (variable) beam passes through magnetic north to indicate that the two signals are "in phase." If the rotating beam completes one revolution per minute, you can determine your bearing to the light sources from any point around the com-

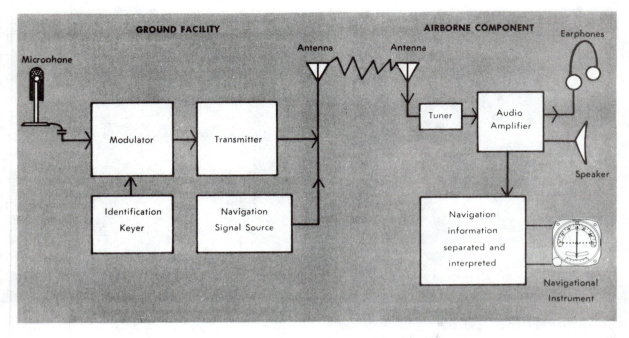

FIGURE 7-7. Basic navigation equipment.

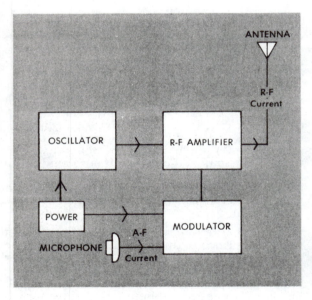

FIGURE 7-8. Amplitude modulation.

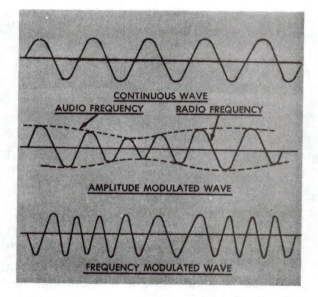

FIGURE 7-9. Wave modulation.

pass rose by noting the time interval between your observations of flashing and beam signals. For example, if the two signals are in phase at north (flashing), and you see the rotating beam 20 seconds later, the variable signal has made 20/60 of a revolution. Thus, you must be viewing the beam from a position on the 120 radial (20/60 times 360°, equals 120°), as shown in Figure 7-12. In terms of azimuth, the refernece and variable signals are 120° "out of phase."

VOR Transmitter.—The VOR transmitter uses the same principle of phase comparison, rotating a signal electrically at 1,800 revolutions per minute. There are two navigation signal components contained in the transmitted signal. One of these signals has a constant phase at all points around the VOR and is called the *reference* signal. In all directions other than magnetic north, the two signals are out of phase. The omni receiver measures the phase

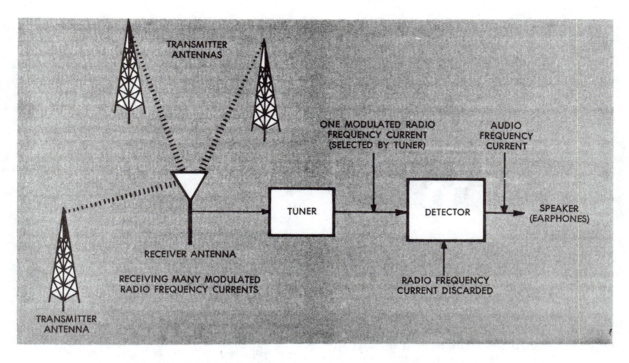

FIGURE 7–10. Transmission and reception of radio signals.

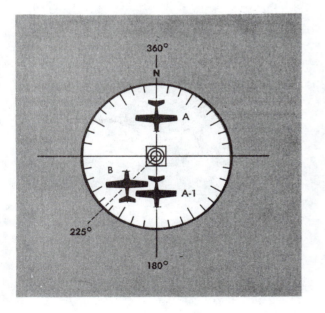

FIGURE 7–11. VOR radials.

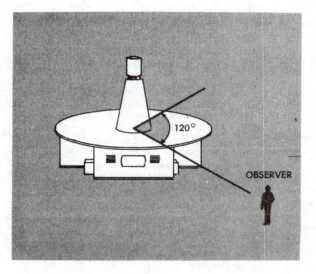

FIGURE 7–12. Variable and reference phase relationship—VOR.

difference electronically and presents the information to indicate bearing.

In addition to the navigation signals radiated by the VOR, provision is also made for voice transmission and automatic identification of the facility on the same radio frequency.

The VOR ground equipment is easily identified from the air as a small low building topped with a flat white disc upon which are locate the antennas and a fiberglass antenna shelter (Fig. 7–13).

The equipment includes an automatic monitoring system that is activated when the signal is interrupted or the phasing is changed. The monitor automatically turns off defective equipment, turns on the standby transmitter, and sounds an alarm in the control room, ensuring continuous reliable service to the users.

FIGURE 7-13. VOR transmitter.

VOR Class Designations and Frequencies.— Omniranges are classified according to their operational uses. The standard VOR facility has a power output of approximately 200 watts, with a maximum usable range depending upon the aircraft altitude, class of facility, location and siting of the facility, terrain conditions within the usable area of the facility, and other factors. Above and beyond certain altitude and distance limits, signal interference from other VOR facilities and signal weakening make the signal unreliable. Areas of confusion between VOR stations can be recognized by an aural squeal and oscillation of the visual indicators in the aircraft.

VOR facilites operate within the 108.0–117.95 MHz frequency band. Frequency assignment between 108.0 and 112.0 MHz is even tenth decimals to preclude any conflict with ILS localizer frequency assignment. Between 112.0 and 117.95 MHz the frequency assignment may be either even or odd tenth decimals. H–VORs and L–VORs have a normal usable distance of 40 nautical miles below 18,000 feet. T–VORs are short-range facilities which have a power output of approximately 50 watts and a usable distance of 25 nautical miles at 12,000 feet and below. T–VORs are used primarily in terminal areas, on or adjacent to airports, for instrument approaches.

VOR Irregularities.—Minor irregularities in VOR signals consist of course shifting, and may be slightly affected by the altitude of the aircraft. Slow movement of the deviation needle on the aircraft instrument is called *course bends;* fast deviations of the needle are called *course scalloping.* When preparing to fly over unfamiliar routes, you can check for VOR irregularities by referring to the appropriate flight-planning publications. These occasional defects are identified by FAA technical specialists to provide pilots with information on the current status of all VOR facilities. En route radials

published as usable will not be displaced more than 2.5° from the theoretical location of the radial (allowable tolerance—1.5° for radials published for VOR approaches).

VOR Facility Information Itemized.—
1. Frequency range—108–117.95 MHz.
2. Course information—all directions: radials named FROM the VOR.
3. Coverage—at least 40 miles at normal minimum IFR altitudes.
4. Identification—standard 3-letter code every 5 seconds, or a combination of code and voice identification, with voice every 15 seconds.
5. Voice communication—the VOR can be used for normal voice communication without interference with the navigation information being radiated.
6. Heading insensitivity—the VOR information received by an aircraft is not influenced by aircraft attitude or direction of flight.

VOR Receiving Equipment

VOR signals can be received by a variety of airborne equipment. Tuning equipment and visual indicators representative of current design are shown in Figure 7–14. Irrespective of differences in dial design, method of tuning, separation of receiver components, and multipurpose designs, all VOR receivers have at least the essential components shown in the NAV/COMM receiver illustrated in the figure.

FIGURE 7-14. VOR receiver.

The components of a VOR receiver can be described as follows:
1. *Frequency selector.*—The frequency selector may be a knob or knobs or "crank," manually rotated to select any of the frequencies between 108.0–117.95 MHz.
2. *Course selector.*—By turning the OBS (Omni Bearing Selector), the desired course is selected. This may appear in a window or under an index.
3. *Course deviation indicator* (CDI).—The deviation indicator is composed of a dial, and a needle hinged to move laterally across the dial. The needle centers when the aircraft is on the selected radial or its reciprocal (Fig. 7–15). Full needle deflection

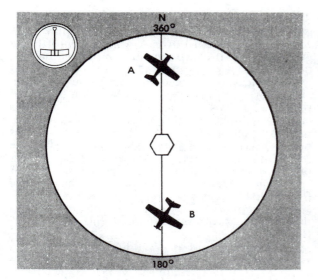

FIGURE 7–15. · Course deviation indicator.

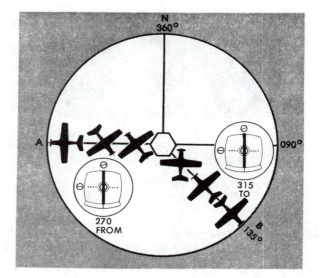

FIGURE 7–16. To/From indicator.

from the center position to either side of the dial indicates the aircraft is 10° or more off course. assuming normal needle sensitivity.

4. *TO/FROM indicator*, also called "sense indicator" and "ambiguity indicator." The TO/FROM indicator shows whether the selected course will take the aircraft TO or FROM the station. It does *NOT* indicate whether the *aircraft* is *heading* to or from the station (Fig. 7–16).

5. *Flags,* or other signal strength indicators. The device to indicate a usable or an unreliable signal may be an "OFF" flag that retracts from view when signal strength is sufficient for reliable instrument indications, or insufficient signal strength may be indicated by a blank TO/FROM window.

VOR flight procedures will be discussed in Chapter VIII, "Using the Navigation Instruments." VOR approach procedure charts are described in Chapter X, "The Federal Airways System and Controlled Airspace."

Distance Measuring Equipment (DME)

Used in conjunction with the nationwide VOR system, distance measuring equipment (DME) has made it possible for you to know the exact geographic position of your aircraft immediately by observation of your VOR and DME indicating equipment. Without DME, you can determine your position by triangulation methods using a single VOR receiver, dual VOR receivers, or a combination of VOR receiver(s) and low-frequency equipment. With DME and VOR equipment in combination, direct reading instruments tell you the distance and bearing to or from the station.

DME Equipment and Operating Principle.—The aircraft transmits an *interrogating signal,* made up of a pair of RF pulses, which is received by the DME *transponder* antenna at the ground facility. The signal triggers ground receiver equipment, and a second pair of pulses is generated and transmitted through the DME transponder antenna back to the interrogating aircraft. The airborne DME interrogating and indicating equipment measures the elapsed time between the second interrogating and reply pulses and converts this time measurement into a mileage, groundspeed, or time readout on the instrument panel. The mileage readout is the direct distance from the aircraft to the DME ground facility and is commonly referred to as slant-range distance. The difference between a measured distance on the surface and the DME slant-range distance is known as slant-range error and is smallest at low altitude and long range. This error is greatest when the aircraft is directly over the ground facility, at which time the DME receiver will display altitude in nautical miles above the facility. Slant-range error is negligible if the aircraft is one mile or more from the ground facility for each 1,000 feet of altitude above the elevation of the facility. Lightweight DME equipment is reported by manufacturers to be accurate within plus or minus one-half mile or three percent of the distance, whichever is greater. Operation of the airborne equipment is simple, as illustrated in Figure 7–17. This model features a selector switch and digital readout which allows the pilot to obtain distance, groundspeed, or time-to-facility.

Area Navigation

Area navigation (RNAV) allows a pilot to fly a selected course to a predetermined point without the need to overfly ground-based navigation facilities. RNAV systems include doppler radar, inertial navigation system (INS), very low frequency (VLF),

FIGURE 7–17. DME indicator.

and the course line computer. The course line computer is the RNAV system which the general aviation pilot is most likely to use.

The course line computer is based on azimuth and distance information generated by the present VORTAC system. It is also called the "Rho-Theta" system. Rho (distance) is derived from the distance measuring feature of the VORTAC, and Theta (bearing) information is derived from the azimuth feature. As shown in Figure 7–18, the value of side (A) is the measured DME distance to the VORTAC. Side (B), the distance from the VORTAC to the waypoint, and angle (1), the bearing from the VORTAC to the waypoint, are set in the cockpit control. The bearing from the VORTAC to the aircraft, angle (2), is measured by the VOR receiver. The airborne computer compares angles (1) and (2) and determines angle (3). With this information, the computer, by means of simple trigonometric functions, continuously solves for side (c), which is the distance in nautical miles and magnetic course from

the aircraft to the waypoint. This is presented as guidance information on the cockpit display.

Advisory Circular 90–45A, which sets forth the guidelines for the implementation of area navigation, defines a waypoint as, " . . . a predetermined geographical position used for route-definition and/or progress-reporting purposes that is defined relative to a VORTAC station position." Waypoints are also defined by latitude and longitude coordinates for the use of airborne self-contained systems not dependent on VORTAC inputs. With the course line computer, the pilot effectively moves or off-sets the VORTAC to a desired location. A "phantom station" is created by setting the distance (Rho) and the bearing (Theta) of the waypoint from a convenient VORTAC, in the appropriate windows of the waypoint selector or "off-set control" (Figure 7–19).

The advantages of the VORTAC area navigation system stem from the ability of the airborne computer to, in effect, locate the VORTAC wherever convenient, if it is within reception range (Figure 7–20). A series of these "phantom stations" or waypoints make up an RNAV route. A number of RNAV routes have been established in the high altitude structure. High altitude RNAV routes are depicted on the "RNAV En Route High Altitude Charts." In addition to the published routes, you may fly a random RNAV route under IFR if it is approved by ATC. RNAV Standard Instrument Departures (SIDs) and Standard Terminal Arrival Routes (STARs) are contained in the SID and STAR booklets.

RNAV approach procedure charts. such as that

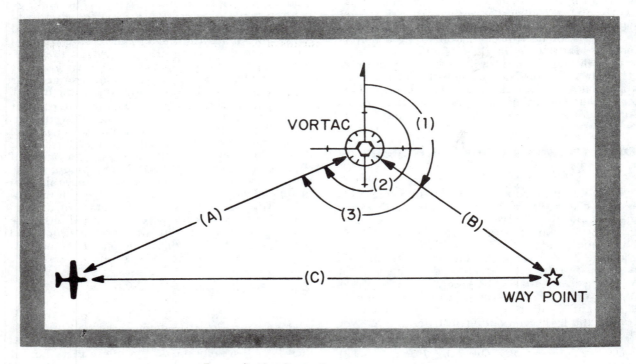

FIGURE 7–18. Course line computer geometry.

FIGURE 7–19 Waypoint selector or "off-set control

depicted in Figure 7–21, are also available. You will note that the waypoint identification boxes contain the following information: waypoint name, coordinates, frequency, identifier, radial-distance (facility to waypoint), and reference facility elevation. The initial approach fix (IAF), final approach fix (FAF), and missed approach point (MAP) are labeled. Since these are non-precision approaches, minimums appropriate to such approaches apply. To fly either an RNAV route or to execute an RNAV approach, under IFR, your aircraft *must* have RNAV equipment which meets the standards set forth in FAA Advisory Circular 90–45A.

Although cockpit displays of guidance information vary, the displacement of a vertical reference means distance from a selected track in nautical miles and not angular displacement. The guidance instrument in one model, Figure 7–22, resembles a conventional VOR course deviation indicator. The familiar CDI needle serves as a course line computer indicator in the CLC (course line computer) mode. A lateral deflection of the needle indicates nautical miles right or left of the selected course. Each dot on the horizontal scale may have any value such as .5, 1, 2, or 10 nautical miles. A DME indicator gives distance to the waypoint.

Vertical as well as horizontal guidance is provided in some installations. For example, one manufacturer has designed an Ascent Descent Director (ADD), which combined with the basic two-dimensional RNAV system, provides vertical guidance information similar to a glide slope. With this equipment, a waypoint can be selected not only at a desired surface location but also at a desired altitude. Thus, you can fly a pre-determined vertical profile to a pre-selected point in space.

Radar Systems

The FAA first began installing radar equipment at airports in the late 1940s. Further development of radar systems and their expanded use in the Air Traffic Control system have greatly modified and simplified instrument flying procedures. There are three basic types of radar systems: ASR (airport surveillance radar), PAR (precision approach radar), and ASDE (airport surface detection equipment).

Fundamental Principles of Radar.—Radar is based upon the precise timing of a returning RF echo from a target and the displaying of this information to the radar operator in such a manner that the distance and bearing to this target can be instantly determined. The radar transmitter must be capable of delivering extremely high power levels toward the airspace under surveillance, and the associated radar receiver must be able to detect extremely small signal levels of the returning echoes.

These requirements can be better appreciated when you realize that the effective size of a small airplane is comparable to a small doorway. The radar system may be expected to detect and display this plane from what small fraction of energy is reflected from this surface at ranges up to 200 miles under optimum conditions. By means of a Microwave Link Relay System (Fig. 7–23), an unlimited number of radar transmitter sites can be remoted from the control center to provide navigational guidance along the air routes.

Primary Radar.—The surveillance system provides the controller with a map-like presentation upon which appears all the radar echoes of aircraft within detection range of the radar facility. By means of electronically generated range marks and azimuth-indicating devices, the controller can locate each radar target with respect to the radar facility, or can locate one radar target with respect to another. From direct-reading counters on his control panel, the controller determines the bear-

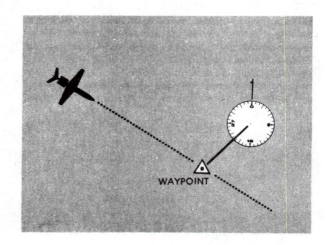

FIGURE 7–20. Aircraft/VORTAC/waypoint relationship.

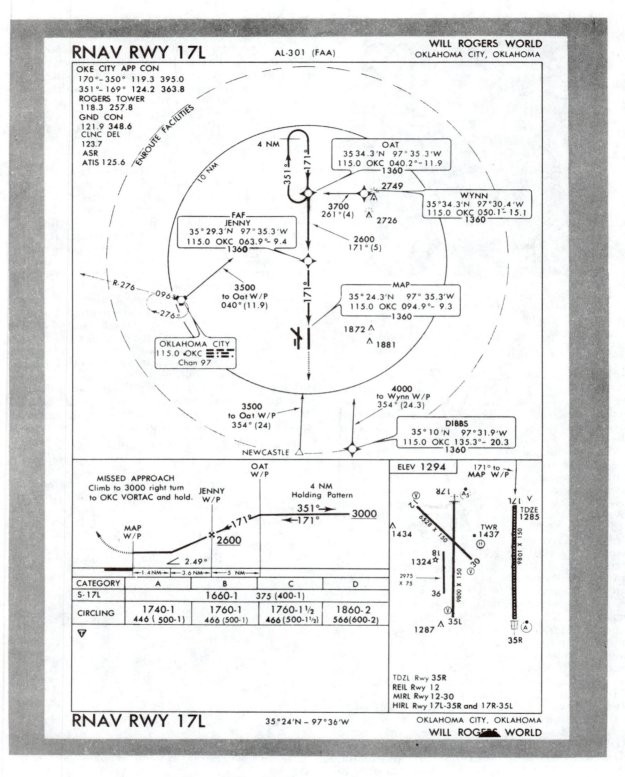

FIGURE 7–21.   RNAV approach procedure chart.

122

FIGURE 7-22. RNAV guidance instrument.

ing and range of one aircraft target with respect to another.

Another device, a video mapping unit, generates an actual airway or airport map and presents it on the radar display equipment. Using the video mapping feature, the air traffic controller not only can view the aircraft targets, but will see these targets in

relation to runways, navigation aids, and hazardous ground obstructions in the area.

The essential difference between Airport Surveillance Radar and Air Route Surveillance Radar is in the equipment required to provide greater maximum usable ranges. Airport surface detection equipment (ASDE) is also a surveillance system, but it scans the ground, rather than the air, for targets. At many major terminals, runways or taxiways may be as far as 2 miles from the controller's position. During all weather conditions, the ASDE equipment permits the controller to have radar-visual access to all parts of the airport although he may not be able (optically) to see the far ends of the airport (Fig. 7-24).

Use of the FAA primary radar facilities will be fully discussed in Chapter XI, "Air Traffic Control."

Secondary Radar.—The surveillance radar system cannot identify one specific radar target found within a display presenting perhaps a dozen or more targets. This problem can be solved with Air Traffic Control Radar Beacon System (ATCRBS) equipment, which is becoming more prevalent in business aircraft installations. The ground equipment is an *interrogating unit,* with the beacon antenna mounted so as to scan with the surveillance antenna. The interrogating equipment transmits a coded pulse sequence that actuates the aircraft *transponder.* The transponder answers the coded sequence by transmitting a pre-selected coded sequence back to the ground equipment, providing positive aircraft identification as well as other special data. Figure 7-25 shows the ASR antenna with the associated interrogating unit on top.

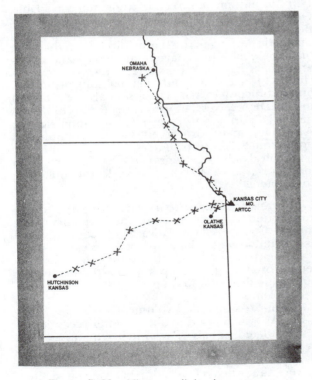

FIGURE 7-23. Microwave link relay system.

FIGURE 7-24. ASDE radar.

FIGURE 7–25.   ASR and beacon antenna.

Low-Frequency Nondirectional Homing Beacons

The low-frequency nondirectional radio beacon, or homing, facility was one of the earliest electronic navigation aids adopted by the FAA. Homing beacons are installed at various locations to provide either navigation fixes or homing points. The typical homing beacon facility incorporates a low-frequency transmitter and an associated antenna system that provides a non-directional radiation pattern. The transmitter, operating in the frequency range between 200–415 kHz, is amplitude-modulated with a 1,020 Hz audio tone to provide coded identification.

Types of "H" Facilities.—There are four types of nondirectional homing facilities in use:

1. HH facilities have a power output of 2,000 or more watts and a reception range of 75 nautical miles; they are generally used with overwater routes.

2. H facilities have a power output of 50 to 1999 watts and a reception range of 50 nautical miles.

3. MH facilities have a power output of less than 50 watts and a reception range of 25 nautical miles.

4. ILS compass locator facilities have a power output of less than 25 watts and a reception range of 15 nautical miles. They are designated as LOM (Outer Locator) and LMM (Middle Locator), appropriate to the outer and middle beacon sites where they are located.

Principles of ADF Receiver Operation.—The automatic direction finder (ADF) used with the non-directional homing beacon is a radio receiver that determines the bearing from the aircraft to the transmitting station. Use of the "H" facility requires a directional antenna for reception of the signals. A directional antenna is one that conducts radio signals more efficiently in one direction than in others.

A single-wire vertical antenna ("sense" antenna) is nondirectional in that it conducts received or transmitted signals with equal efficiency in all directions. A loop of wire, or two wires suitably connected, have important directional characteristics for transmission or reception.

Directional antennas for ADF receivers are usually in the form of loops, which extract a portion of the signal energy. The position of the plane of the loop in reference to the station determines the induced voltages in the sides of the loop and the strength of the signal received through the antenna. Maximum signal strength is received when there is a maximum difference in the induced voltages in the sides of the loop (Fig. 7–26). Minimum signal strength (or null) exists when equal voltages are induced in both sides of the loop simultaneously and no current passes through the receiver.

Sense Antenna.—A sense antenna is also necessary for the operation of automatic direction finding equipment because the loop antenna, although it senses direction by comparison of voltages, cannot sense whether the station is behind or ahead, or to the left or right. This characteristic of loop reception is called *ambiguity.* By combining the properties of the loop antenna with those of a sense antenna, the direction of the incoming signal is resolved so that the ADF indicator continuously shows the relative bearing of the transmitting station to which tuned.

ADF Receiving Equipment.—Several different types of automatic direction finders are available. One type indicates only relative bearing to the station; another indicates both relative bearing and magnetic bearing to the station directly on the same dial. Some indicators have rotating dials and pointers, others have fixed dials. The receiver may include a tuning meter, and a manual control position on the function switch. The essentials are common to all ADF receivers, however, regardless of design detail. In addition to receiving navigation signals, ADF equipment also receives voice communications from L/MF transmitters.

A typical older type light plane ADF receiver and indicator (Fig. 7–27) may include the following components:

1. *Frequency band selector,* permitting the use of any ground transmitter, within the frequency range shown. Commercial broadcasting stations as well as the nondirectional homing beacons can be used.

2. *Function switch,* to select either the sense antenna for tuning, or loop antenna for manual or automatic direction finding.

3. Tuning crank.

4. On-off switch and volume control.

5. CW switch, used to obtain better reception of unmodulated signals. The switch actuates a signal in the receiver which is added to the incoming signals producing a continuous tone. On some receivers, the switch is labelled "BFO," meaning "Beat Frequency Oscillator."

FIGURE 7–27. Older type ADF receiver.

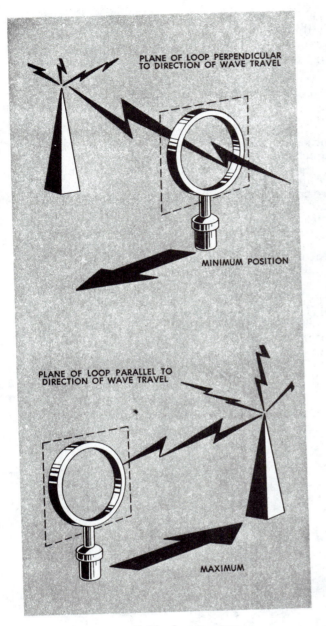

FIGURE 7–26. Loop antenna.

FIGURE 7–28. Modern ADF receiver.

6. Loop switch which is operative when function switch is in "Loop" position. It is used to rotate the loop left or right to more accuately tune in weak stations and also to identify the aural null position of the incoming signal.

The modern crystal-controlled ADF receiver with digital tuning (Fig. 7–28) eliminates manual tuning and the tuning meter. In the model shown, any frequency from 200 kHz to 1699 kHz, in increments of 1 kHz, may be selected. When the function switch is set to ADF, the bearing pointer of the indicator shows the relative bearing to the station. During ANT operation, audio is received from the

station tuned and the bearing pointer is automatically stowed at the 90° position.

NDB (ADF) flight procedures will be discussed in Chapter VIII, "Using the Navigation Instruments." NDB approach procedure charts are described in Chapter X, "The Federal Airways System and Controlled Airspace."

125

VHF Direction Finding Ground Equipment

Direction finding ground facilities use a cluster of vertical antennas which feed a rotating goniometer (angle-measuring device), causing an indicator to point towards an aircraft whose signal is being received. Used directly with ASR radar to locate and direct lost aircraft, the bearing information is presented both by a pointer and by a bright straight line on the radar display, starting from the location of the DF antenna and passing through the radar target representing the transmitting aircraft. Other than a VHF transmitter, no additional airborne equipment is needed to actuate the ground equipment. VHF direction finding procedures are covered in the *Airman's Information Manual*.

Instrument Landing System

Although called an instrument landing system, the ILS (Fig. 7-29) provides a number of ground facilities, either as part of the basic system or associated with it, for several different types of in-strument *approaches* to be discussed in a later chapter.

Ground Components

An instrument landing system consists of the following components:

1. *A localizer radio course* to furnish horizontal guidance to the airport runway.

2. *A glide slope radio course* to furnish vertical guidance along the correct descent angle to the proper "touchdown" point on the runway.

3. *Two VHF marker beacons* (outer and middle) are normally installed on the front course. They provide accurate radio fixes along the approach path to the runway. At some locations, a third marker beacon may be employed on the front course to indicate the point at which the decision height should occur on a Category II ILS. A marker beacon may be installed on the back course to indicate the back course final approach fix.

4. *Approach lights* are normally installed on the ILS runway to provide means for transition from instrument to visual flight.

The following supplementary elements, though not specific components of the system, may be in-

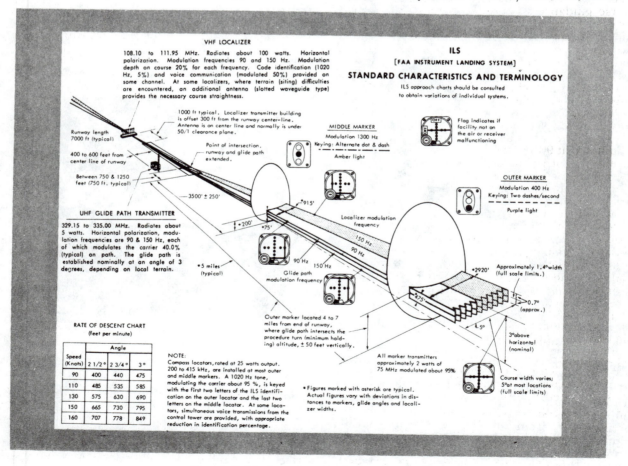

FIGURE 7-29 Instrument landing system (ILS).

126

corporated into the system to increase safety and utility.

1. *Compass locators* to provide transition from en route NAVAIDS to the ILS system; to assist in holding procedures, tracking the localizer course, identifying the marker beacon sites; and to provide a final approach fix for ADF approaches.

2. *Distance measuring equipment* (DME) co-located with the glide slope transmitter to provide positive distance-to-touchdown information.

3. *Supplementary lighting systems* to facilitate transition from instrument to outside visual references during the final stage of the approach.

Localizer

The localizer antenna array is located on the extended centerline of the instrument runway of an airport, remote enough from the opposite approach end of the runway to prevent the array from being a collision hazard.

This unit radiates a field pattern which develops a course down the centerline of the runway toward the middle and outer markers, and a similar course along the runway centerline in the opposite direction. These courses are called the "front" and "back" courses, respectively. The localizer provides course guidance throughout the descent path to the runway threshold from a distance of 18 nautical miles from the antenna between an altitude of 1,000 feet above the highest terrain along the course line and 4,500 feet above the elevation of the antenna site.

The radiated field pattern is modulated at two different frequencies. The right side of this pattern, looking along the normal approach path from the outer marker toward the runway, is modulated at 150 Hz. The left side of the radiated pattern is modulated at 90 Hz. The on-course path is formed by equi-signal points between the two modulated sides of the pattern, and becomes increasingly narrow as the transmitter is approached.

The localizer course width is defined as the angular displacement at any point along the course between a full "fly-left" and a full "fly-right" indication on the aircraft course deviation indicator (CDI or localizer needle). The localizer signal is adjusted to produce an angular width between 3° and 6°, as necessary, to provide a linear width of approximately 700 feet at the runway approach threshold. In addition, the FAA localizer provides a full "fly-left" or full "fly-right" to an aircraft well outside the on-course area, preventing the possibility of a "false course."

ILS Identification.—Each localizer facility is identified by a 3-letter coded designator transmitted at frequent regular intervals. The identification is always preceded by the coded letter "I" to identify the received signal as originating at the ILS facility. For example, the ILS localizer at Springfield, Mo., transmits the identifier "ISGF." The localizer includes a voice feature on its frequency for use by the associated Air Traffic Control facility in issuing approach and landing instructions. The frequency band of the localizer equipment is 108.10 to 111.95 MHz.

Glide Slope

The term "glide slope" means the complete radiation pattern generated by the glide slope facility. The term "glide path" means that portion of the glide slope that intersects the localizer. The glide slope equipment is housed in a building approximately 750 to 1,250 feet from the approach end of the runway, between 400 and 600 feet to one side of the centerline. The course projected by the glide slope equipment is essentially the same as would be generated by a localizer operating on its side, with the upper side of the course modulated at 90 Hz and the lower side at 150 Hz. The glide slope projection angle is normally adjusted to 2.5 to 3 degrees above horizontal so that it intersects the middle marker at about 200 feet and the outer marker at about 1,400 feet above the runway elevation. At locations where standard minimum obstruction clearance cannot be obtained with the normal maximum glide slope angle, the glide slope equipment is displaced inward from the standard location if the length of the runway permits.

Unlike the localizer, the glide slope transmitter radiates signals only in the direction of the final approach on the "front course." The system provides no vertical guidance for approaches on the "back course." The glide path is normally 1.4° thick. At 10 nautical miles from the point of touchdown, this represents a vertical distance of approximately 1,500 feet, narrowing to a few feet at touchdown.

False Courses.—In addition to the desired course, glide slope facilities inherently produce additional courses at higher vertical angles; the angle of the lowest of these "false courses" will occur at approximately 12.5°. However, if your approach is conducted at the altitudes specified on the appropriate approach chart, these false courses will not be encountered.

Marker Beacons

Two VHF marker beacons, outer and middle, are normally used in the FAA ILS system. A third beacon, the inner, is used where Category II operations are certified. Also, a marker beacon may be installed to indicate the final approach fix on the ILS back course.

These beacons have a power output of 3 watts or less and operate on a frequency of 75 MHz. The radiation patterns are fan-shaped with an elliptical cross-section with its minor axis parallel to the approach path and its major axis at right angles to the approach path.

The *Outer Marker* (OM) is located on the front course 4 to 7 miles from the airport and indicates a position at which an aircraft, at the appropriate altitude on the localizer course, will intercept the glide path. The outer marker is modulated at 400 Hz. It is identified by continuous dashes at the rate of 2 per second, and a purple marker beacon light.

The *Middle Marker* (MM) is located approximately 3,500 feet from the landing threshold on the centerline of the localizer front course. The middle marker is modulated at 1300 Hz. It is identified by alternate dots and dashes at the rate of 95 dot/dash combinations per minute, and an amber marker beacon light.

The *Inner Marker* (IM), where installed, is located on the front course between the middle marker and the landing threshold. It indicates the point at which an aircraft is at the decision height on the glide path during a Category II ILS approach. The inner marker is modulated at 3000 Hz. It is identified by continuous dots at the rate of 6 per second, and a white marker beacon light.

The *Back Course Marker* (BCM), where installed, indicates the back course final approach fix. The back course marker is modulated at 3000 Hz and identified with 2 dots at a rate of 72 to 75 2-dot combinations per minute, and a white marker beacon light.

Compass Locators.—Compass Locators are low-powered nondirectional radio beacons which operate between 200 and 415 KHz. When used in conjunction with an ILS front course, the compass locator facilities are co-located with the Outer and Middle Marker facilities (shown as LOM and LMM on instrument approach charts). The coding identification of the Outer Locator consists of the *first* two letters of the station identifier; for example, the Outer Locator at Love Field, Dallas, Tex., (DAL) is identified as "DA." The Middle Locator at DAL is identified by the *last* two letters "AL."

Approach Lighting Systems

Normal approach and letdown on the ILS is divided into two distinct stages: the "instrument" approach using only radio guidance, and the "visual" stage, when visual contact with the ground is necessary for accuracy and safety. The most critical period of an instrument approach, particularly during low ceiling/visibility conditions, is at the point when you must decide whether to land or execute a missed approach.

The purpose of the approach lighting system is to provide you with lights that will penetrate the atmosphere far enough from touchdown to give you directional, distance, and glide path information for safe visual transition. Checking the *Airport/Facility Directory* for the particular type of lighting facilities at your destination airport is an important flight planning detail for any instrument flight. With reduced visibility, rapid orientation to a strange runway can be difficult, especially during a circling approach to an airport with minimum lighting facilities, or to a large terminal airport located in the midst of distracting lights.

The approach lighting system shown in Figure 7–30 is a common installation as you would see it when properly aligned from the runway end. The same approach lighting system in Figure 7–30 is a common installation as you would see it when

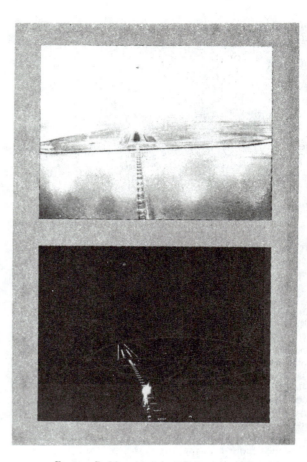

FIGURE 7–30. Approach light system.

properly aligned from the runway end. The same approach is illustrated under day and night conditions.

A high-intensity flasher system is installed at many large airports. The flashers consist of a series of very brilliant blue-white bursts of light flashing in sequence along the approach lights, giving the effect of a ball of light traveling towards the runway.

Runway End Identifier Lights (REIL) are installed for rapid and positive identification of the approach end of an instrument runway. The system consists of a pair of synchronized flashing lights, one of which is located laterally on each side of the runway threshold facing the approach area.

The Visual Approach Slope Indicator (VASI) gives visual descent guidance information during the approach to a runway. The standard VASI consists of light bars that project a visual glide path which provides safe obstruction clearance within the approach zone. The normal glide slope angle is 3°; however, the angle may be as high as 4.5° for proper obstacle clearance. On runways served by ILS, the VASI angle normally coincides with the electronic

128

glide slope angle. Course guidance is obtained by alignment with the runway lights.

The standard VASI installation consists of either 2-, 4-, 6-, 12-, or 16-light units arranged in downwind and upwind light bars. Some airports serving long-bodied aircraft have 3-bar VASIs which provide two visual glide paths to the same runway. The first glide path encountered is the same as provided by the standard FAA VASI. The second glide path is about 1/4° higher than the first and is designed for the use of pilots of long-bodied aircraft.

The basic principle of VASI is that of color differentiation between red and white. Each light projects a beam having a white segment in the upper part and a red segment in the lower part. The light units of a standard FAA 2-bar VASI are arranged so you will see them as illustrated in Figure 7–31.

From a position above the glide path you will see both bars as white. Moving down to the glide path, you will see the color of the upwind bars change from white to pink to red. When you are on the proper glide path, you will overshoot the downwind bars and undershoot the upwind bars. Thus you will see the downwind bars as white and the upwind bars as red. From a position below the glide path you will see both light bars as red. Moving up to the glide path, you will see the color of the downwind bars change from red to pink to white. When below the glide path, as indicated by a distinct red signal, a safe obstruction clearance may not exist.

As you approach the runway threshold, the visual glide path will separate into individual lights. At this point, you should continue the approach by reference to the runway touchdown zone.

ILS Receiving Equipment

For reception of electronic signals from all of the ILS transmitting facilities described, your airborne equipment will include the following receivers:
1. Localizer receiver.
2. Glide slope receiver.
3. Marker beacon receiver.
4. ADF receiver.
5. DME receiver.

Use of the ILS does not require all of these components, however. For example, an instrument approach on the ILS system may be made with only localizer and marker beacon receivers (sometimes called a "localizer approach"); with only localizer and ADF receivers; or with an ADF receiver only, using the locator as a primary approach aid. The authorized landing minimums will of course vary according to the ground and airborne equipment available and operating properly.

Localizer Receiver.—The typical light-plane VOR receiver is also a localizer receiver with common tuning and indicating equipment. Some receivers have separate function selector switches. Otherwise, tuning of VOR and localizer frequencies is accomplished with the same knobs and switches,

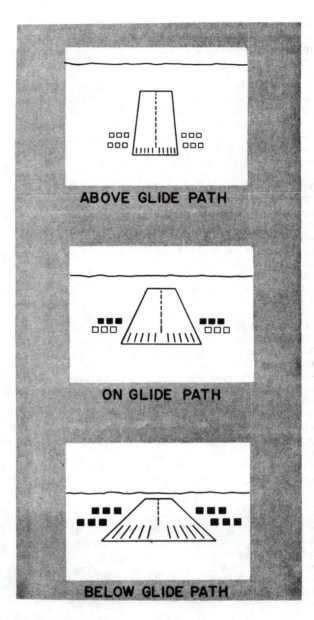

ABOVE GLIDE PATH

ON GLIDE PATH

BELOW GLIDE PATH

FIGURE 7–31. Standard FAA 2-bar VASI.

and the CDI indicates "on course" as it does on a VOR radial.

Glide Slope Receiver.—Though some glide slope receivers are tuned separately, in a typical installation the glide slope is tuned automatically to the proper frequency when the localizer is tuned in. Each of the 40 localizer channels in the 108.10 to 111.95 MHz band is paired with a corresponding glide slope frequency of the 40 UHF glide slope

129

channels available (see AIM). Although all of these 40 frequency pairs are not presently being utilized, they will be in the future.

Localizer/Glide Slope Indicator.—When the localizer indicator also includes a glide-slope needle, the instrument is often called a crosspointer indicator. The crossed horizontal (glide-slope) and vertical (localizer) needles are free to move through standard 5-dot deflections to indicate position on the localizer course and glide path. See Figure 7–32.

The *localizer needle* indicates, by deflection, whether the aircraft is right or left of the localizer centerline, regardless of the position or heading of the aircraft. Rotation of the omni bearing selector has no effect on the operation of the localizer needle. When the aircraft is inbound on the front course or outbound on the back course, the needle is deflected toward the on-course (A, Fig. 7–33) and you turn toward the needle to correct your track. Conversely, when the aircraft is inbound on the back course or outbound on the front course, you turn away from the direction of needle deflection to reach the center of the localizer course (B, Fig. 7–33). With an ADF tuned to the outer compass locator, orientation on the localizer course is simplified (C, Fig. 7–33). The problem of orientation with respect to both the localizer course and VOR radials will be discussed in Chapter VIII, "Using the Navigation Instruments."

The localizer course is very narrow, normally 5°. This results in high needle sensitivity. With this course width, a full-scale deflection shows when the aircraft is 2.5° to either side of the centerline. This sensitivity permits accurate orientation to the landing runway. With no more than a ¼-scale deflection maintained, your aircraft will be aligned with the runway. High needle sensitivity also tends to enourage overcontrolling, until you learn to apply correct basic flying techniques for smooth control of the aircraft.

Deflection of the *glide slope needle* indicates the position of the aircraft with respect to the glide path (Fig. 7–34). When the aircraft is above the glide path, the needle is deflected downward. When the aircraft is below the glide path, the needle is deflected upward.

When the aircraft is on the glide path, the needle is horizontal, overlying the reference dots. Since the glide path is much sharper than the localizer course (approximately 1.4° from full "up" to full "down" deflection), the needle is very sensitive to displacement of the aircraft from on-path alignment. With the proper rate of descent established on glide slope interception, very small corrections keep the aircraft aligned.

The localizer and glide slope *warning flags* disappear from view on the indicator when sufficient voltage is received to actuate the needles. The flags show when an unstable signal or receiver malfunction occurs.

ILS flight procedures will be discussed in Chapter VIII, "Using the Navigation Instruments." ILS approach procedure charts are described in Chapter X, "The Federal Airways System and Controlled Airspace." Additional information on the FAA ILS system appears in the *Airman's Information Manual* under the heading, AIR NAVIGATION RADIO AIDS.

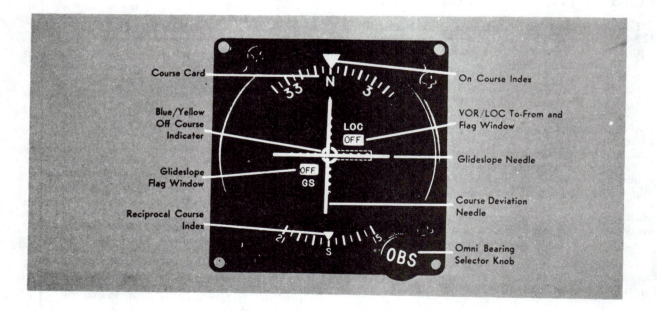

FIGURE 7–32. Localizer-glide slope indicator.

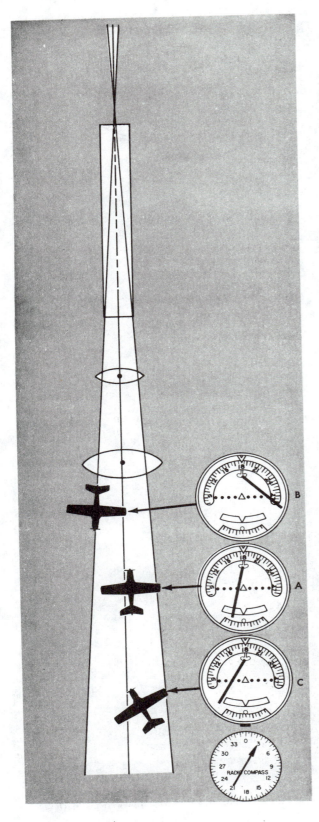

FIGURE 7–33. Localizer receiver indications.

SDF and LDA

These navaids are similar to a standard ILS localizer and are used for nonprecision instrument approaches. Both transmit signals within the frequency range of 108.10 MHz and 111.95 MHz. You will use essentially the same pilot techniques and procedures in executing SDF and LDA approaches that you use in no-glide-slope localizer approaches. Back course approaches may be associated with either SDF or LDA.

The SDF (Simplified Directional Facility) (Fig. 7–35) provides a final approach course similar to the ILS localizer described earlier in this chapter. A clear understanding of the ILS localizer and the additional factors given in the following paragraphs completely describe the operational characteristics and use of the SDF.

The SDF course may or may not be aligned with the runway and the course may be wider than a standard ILS localizer, resulting in less precision. Usable off-course indications are limited to 35° either side of the course centerline. Instrument indications in the areas between 35° and 90° are not controlled and should be disregarded.

The SDF antenna may be offset from the runway centerline. Because of this, the angle of convergence between the final approach course and the runway bearing should be determined by reference to the instrument approach chart. This angle is usually not more than 3°. You should always note this angle since the approach course originates at the antenna site, and an approach continued beyond the runway threshold would lead the aircraft to the SDF offset position rather than along the runway centerline.

The SDF signal emitted from the transmitter is fixed at either 6° or 12° as necessary to provide maximum flyability and optimum course quality. Identification consists of a three letter identifier transmitted in code on the SDF frequency. The identifier for Ponca City Muni SDF is AYQ.

The LDA (localizer-type directional aid) (Fig. 7–36) is of comparable utility and accuracy to a localizer but is not part of a complete ILS. The LDA course width is between 3° and 6° and thus provides a more precise approach course than the similar SDF installation which may have a course width of 6° or 12°. The LDA course is not aligned with the runway; however, straight-in minima may be published where the angle between the runway centerline and the LDA course does not exceed 30°. If this angle exceeds 30°, only circling minima are published. The procedure depicted in Figure 7–36 is an example of this condition. The identifier is three letters preceded by "I," transmitted in code on the LDA frequency.

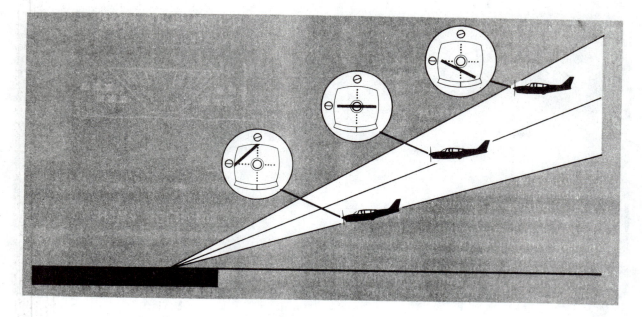

FIGURE 7–34. Glide slope receiver indications.

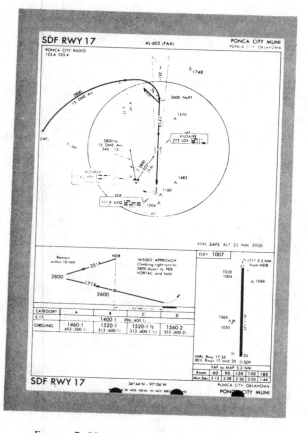

FIGURE 7–35. SDF approach procedure chart.

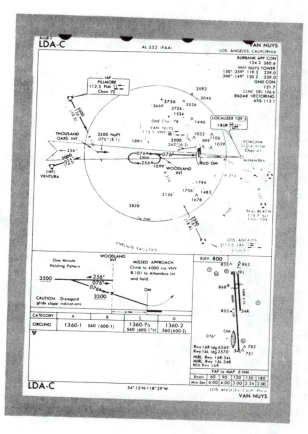

FIGURE 7–36. LDA approach procedure chart.

132

VIII. USING THE NAVIGATION INSTRUMENTS

VOR Receiver

One VOR receiver, used correctly and operating properly, will provide positive and accurate course guidance between most airports on or off Federal Airways. Dual VOR receivers will reduce your en-route workload considerably. VOR in combination with DME will provide the navigational information that, without these aids, requires constant division of attention between basic aircraft control, computation, navigation, and coordination with Air Traffic Control.

There are several common misconceptions about Omni, including the notions that the VOR receiver *automatically* solves your problems of course orientation and drift correction; that a "TO" indication always means that your aircraft is heading toward the station; that you always turn toward the direction of needle displacement to intercept a desired course; or that a fluctuating TO/FROM indication necessarily means station passage. As you will see, each component of the VOR indicator and tuning apparatus operates in relation to the other

components. The indicator provides precisely the information you set it up to measure, *the position of your aircraft antenna with respect to a selected magnetic course to or from the VOR transmitter*. Correctly used, omni simplifies your navigation problems and reduces the time and effort necessary for their solution.

The following discussion assumes the VOR receiver illustrated in Figure 8–1; it may differ in minor details from many of the several designs in common use.

Tuning.—The ON/OFF/Volume Control turns on the navigation receiver and controls the audio volume. The volume control has no effect on the operation of the VOR indicator. With the volume set at a comfortable level and the "ID" tone control adjusted, the station is identified by code or automatic voice transmission. Positive identification of the VOR station is important since a Flight Service Station (FSS) may transmit messages simultaneously over a number of "remoted" VOR facilities. If you hear "Jonesville Area Radio" transmitting

FIGURE 8-1. VOR/Localizer receiver.

CDI shows full deflection, rotate the OBS knob until the CDI centers and a positive "TO" or "FROM" is indicated. The needle will eventually center by rotation of the OBS and dial in either direction.

To center the needle quickly, note the "TO" or "FROM" indication. With a "TO" indication, rotate the OBS *toward* the deflection, counterclockwise with a left deflection and clockwise with a right deflection. With a "FROM" indication, rotate the OBS away from the deflection to center the CDI.

Receiver Checks.—VOR receiver checks are required as specified in Federal Aviation Regulation Part 91.

In addition to the receiver tolerance checks in the Regulation, *course sensitivity* may be checked by noting the number of degrees of change in the course selected as you rotate the OBS to move the CDI from center to the last dot on either side. This should be between 10° and 12°.

Competent pilots check their VOR receivers frequently and carefully, not only for maximum permissible tolerance limits, but for errors indicated in a specific instrument. For example, the tolerance limit between the two indicated bearings on a dual VOR receiver check is 4°. Assume that you are checking your receivers at a designated check point on the ground, located on the 090 radial of "X" VOR. The OBS on your #1 receiver shows 094, needle centered; the OBS on #2 receiver shows 098, needle centered. Add a possible 2° deviation of the actual location of the 090 radial from its theoretical location, and assume further that your #2 receiver course sensitivity check shows a 15° change. After adding up the possible cumulative errors, an experienced pilot would not rely on the #2 receiver for accurate navigation information.

Orientation

CDI Interpretation.—With your receiver properly tuned and checked, rotate the OBS knob until the needle centers. Assume that the needle centers with the 180° course under the index (Fig. 8–2). Your aircraft can be on any heading and at any point over the north/south reference line shown, except over the station or close to it. Approaching inbound from point "I" to point "S", the CDI will deviate from side to side as the aircraft passes directly over the station where no signal is received. Likewise a centered CDI with any other course shown under the index locates your aircraft over either the selected radial or its reciprocal.

TO/FROM Interpretation.—With a course of 180° selected under the index, a "TO" indication shows, regardless of heading, whenever your aircraft is located within the approximate hemispherical area north of the 90/270 reference line. A "FROM" indication appears when the aircraft is located south of the approximate 90/270 reference line. Movement across the 90/270 area is indicated by an ambiguous TO/FROM signal. In this area, the

a weather broadcast, you may be tuned to Jonesville Omni or to any of a number of VOR stations remoted from Jonesville FSS. If no station identification signal is heard, the facility has been taken over by maintenance for tune-up or repair.

Frequency Selection.—The left knob selects Mega Hertz; the right knob selects tenth-Mega Hertz and Kilo Hertz. This model covers the 200-channel VOR/LOC frequency range of 108.00 MHz through 117.95 MHz with 50 kHz spacing. Aeronautical charts show VOR frequencies as well as the coded identification.

Omni-Bearing Selector (OBS).—The OBS knob drives the omni-bearing indicator dial for selection of any desired radial under the course index, with the reciprocal of the course shown under the lower index. With the receiver warmed up and a usable signal received, the "OFF" flag will disappear, and the course deviation indicator (CDI) will move to a stable position. If a steady flag does not appear in either the "TO" or "FROM" window and the

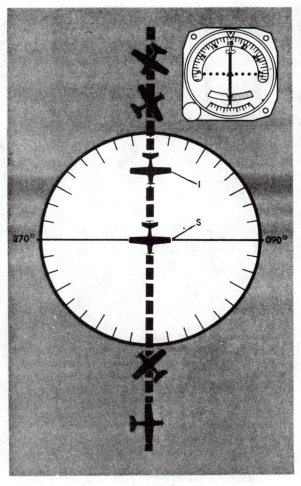

FIGURE 8–2. CDI interpretation.

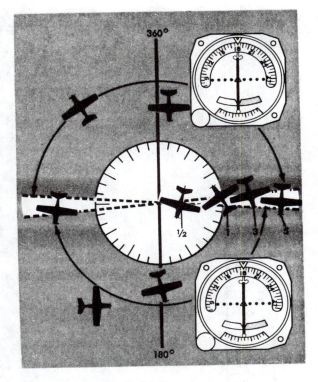

FIGURE 8–3. To/From interpretation.

resultant of the opposing reference and variable signals, which actuate the TO/FROM indicator, is insufficient to produce a positive "TO" or "FROM" indication. At a speed of 150 knots, the approximate times to cross this area at various distances from the station (Fig. 8–3) are as follows:

Distance from station (in nautical miles)	Width (zone of confusion at 3000 AGL) (time in seconds)
½	8
1	10
3	25
5	50

Likewise, with any given course under the index, a "TO" will show whenever your aircraft is located in the hemispherical area approximately 90° on either side of the selected course. "FROM" will show in the other hemisphere. Note that the course index is at the *bottom* of the dial shown in Figure 8–4.

CDI and TO/FROM Interpretation.—As Figure 8–4 shows, the position of the CDI tells you that: You

are on a specific radial (or its reciprocal); or you are to the right or left of it; *with respect to the* course selected.

Movement of the CDI, in conjunction with heading information, tells you:

1. Of impending station passage.
2. Wind drift.
3. Approximate distance from the VOR station. Drift correction and time/distance checks will be discussed later in this chapter.

The TO/FROM indicator locates you in one of two hemispherical areas, depending on the course selected, or in an area of weak signal strength.

To determine the radial on which you are located:

1. Note the TO/FROM reading.
2. If the reading is "FROM', center the CDI by rotation of the OBS knob opposite the direction of CDI deflection. When the needle centers, read the radial under the course selector index.
3. If the reading is "TO", rotate the OBS knob in the direction of CDI deflection until "FROM" appears and proceed as in the previous step.

To determine the inbound course to the station from your present position:

1. Read the inbound magnetic course directly from the reciprocal window, following determination of the radial (if your indicator has no reciprocal window, compute the inbound course arithmetically).
2. Rotate the reciprocal to the opposite course index to change the "FROM" to a "TO" reading,

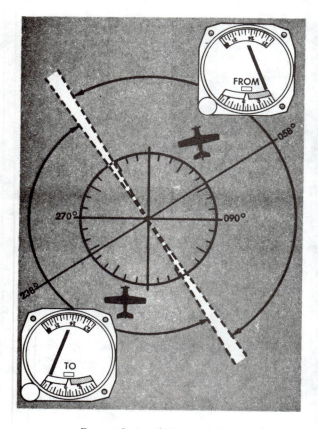

FIGURE 8–4. VOR orientation.

and the needle will center, provided your aircraft has not moved to another radial. If so, recenter the needle with small adjustments, unless you are close to the station and crossing radials rapidly.

3. To "home" to the station, turn to the heading indicated by the course index. Continue to recenter the needle and adjust the heading as necessary. Since homing does not involve drift correction, the aircraft follows a curved path to the station in a crosswind condition.

Tracking a Course — VOR

Tracking, in contrast to homing, involves drift correction sufficient to maintain a direct course to or from a transmitting station. The course selected for tracking inbound is the course shown under the course index with the TO/FROM indicator showing "TO". If you are off course to the left, the CDI is deflected right; if you are off course to the right, the CDI is deflected to the left. Turning toward the needle returns the aircraft to the course centerline and centers the needle.

To track inbound with the wind unknown, proceed in the following steps (Fig. 8–5). Outbound tracking procedures are the same.

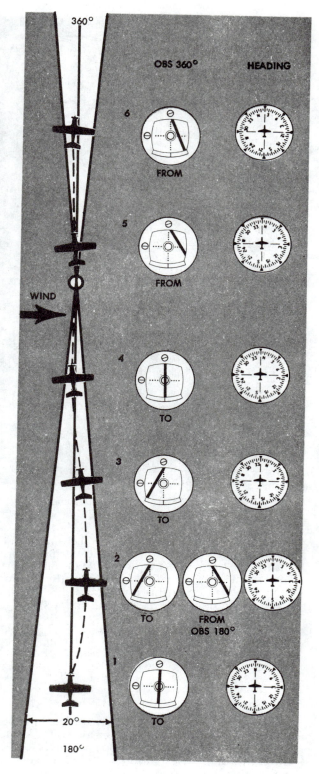

FIGURE 8–5. VOR tracking.

1. With the CDI centered, maintain the heading corresponding to the selected course.

2. As you hold the heading, observe the CDI for deflection to left or right. Direction of CDI deflection from centerline shows the direction of the crosswind component. The illustration shows a left deflection, therefore left crosswind.

(Note the indications with the *reciprocal* of the inbound course set on the OBS. The indicator correctly shows "FROM", and the aircraft to the left of the centerline with *reference to the selected course*. Sometimes called "reverse sensing" this CDI deflection indicates a turn *away* from the needle for direct return to the course centerline, and illustrates the importance of correlating heading and course selection. VOR tracking can be accomplished with "reverse sensing," but errors in orientation can easily result.)

3. Turn 20° toward the needle and hold the heading correction until the needle centers.

4. Reduce the drift correction to 10° left of the course setting, and note whether this drift-correction angle keeps the CDI centered. Subsequent left or right needle deflection indicates an excessive or insufficient drift-correction angle, requiring further bracketing. With the proper drift-correction angle established, the CDI will remain centered until the aircraft is close to the station. Approach to the station is indicated by flickering of the TO/FROM indicator and CDI as the aircraft flies into the "cone of confusion" (no-signal area). Station passage is shown by complete reversal of the TO/FROM indicator. The extent of the cone of confusion, an inverted cone, increases with altitude. Thus, flight through the cone of confusion varies from a few seconds at low levels to as much as 2 minutes at high altitude.

5 and 6. Following station passage and TO/FROM reversal, correction to course centerline is still toward the needle. Note that the extent of CDI deflection is, by itself, no indication of the amount of aircraft displacement from the course centerline. A large CDI deflection immediately following station passage calls for no heading correction until the CDI stabilizes; at 20 miles out, a two-dot deflection may require a large correction angle for return to centerline.

The rate of movement of the CDI during course bracketing is thus an approximate index of distance from the station. For accurate radial interception and course following, the data given in Figure 8–6 may be helpful.

Assuming a receiver with normal course sensitivity and full-scale deflection at 5 dots:

Aircraft displacement from course is approximately *200 ft. per dot per nautical mile*. For example, at 30 nautical miles from the station, one dot deflection indicates approximately one nmi displacement of the aircraft from the course centerline.

Time/Distance Checks by VOR.—Time and distance from a VOR station can be determined by several

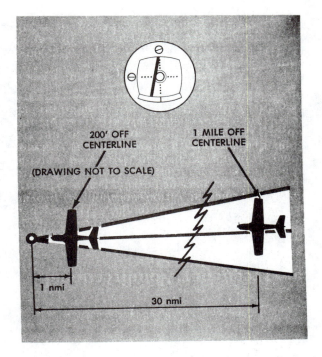

FIGURE 8–6. CDI deflection and aircraft displacement from course.

methods involving practical application of formulas or elementary geometry. These time/distance computations are approximations since wind drift is not considered in the solutions.

Wing-Tip Bearing Change.—The formula solution is applied to the elapsed time for a predetermined change in azimuth, or relative bearing, from the aircraft to a station located at 90° from the aircraft heading (Fig. 8–7).

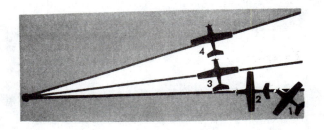

FIGURE 8–7. Time-distance check (VOR); wing-tip bearing change.

Determine time/distance to station by the following steps. After tuning and identifying the VOR station:

1. Determine the radial on which you are located.

137

2. Turn inbound and re-center the needle if necessary.

3. Turn 80° right, or left, of the inbound course, rotating the OBS to the nearest 10° increment *opposite* the direction of turn.

4. Maintain heading. When the CDI centers, note the time.

5. Maintaining the same heading, rotate the OBS 10° in the same direction as in step 3, above.

6. Note the elapsed time when the CDI again centers.

7. Time/distance from the station is determined from the following formulas:

(a) Time to station $= \dfrac{60 \times \text{minutes flown between bearing change}}{\text{degrees of bearing change}}$

(b) Distance to station $= \dfrac{\text{TAS} \times \text{minutes flown}}{\text{degrees of bearing change}}$

By analysis of the time formula, above, you can derive the following rules of thumb:

Degrees of bearing change:	*Time to station*
10	6 × time (in minutes) of bearing change
5	12 × time (in minutes) of bearing change
20	3 × time (in minutes) of bearing change

Even more simply, for a 10° bearing change, note the elapsed time in seconds. One-tenth of this time is the time in minutes to the station. For example, if a 10° wing-tip bearing change takes 80 seconds, you are 8 minutes from the station. The amount of bearing change flown should vary, depending upon the distance of the aircraft from the station and groundspeed crossing radials.

Isosceles Triangle Method (Fig. 8–8).—Time/distance to station can also be found by application of the isosceles triangle principle (i.e., if two angles of a triangle are equal, two of the sides are also equal), as follows:

1. With the aircraft established on a radial, inbound, rotate the OSB 10° to the left.

2. Turn 10° to the right and note the time.

3. Maintain constant heading until the CDI centers, and note the elapsed time.

4. Time to station is the same as the time taken to complete the 10° change of bearing.

Course Interception—VOR

If your desired course is not the one that you are flying, you must orient yourself with respect to the VOR station and the course to be flown and work out a course interception problem. The following steps may be used to intercept a predetermined course, either inbound or outbound: (Steps 1–3 may be omitted if you turn directly to intercept course without initially turning to parallel the desired course.)

1. Turn to a heading to parallel the desired course, in the same direction as the course to be flown.

2. Determine the difference between the radial to be intercepted and the radial on which you are located.

3. Double the difference to determine the interception angle which will be not less than 20° or greater than 90°.

4. Rotate the OBS to the desired radial or inbound course.

5. Turn to the interception heading.

6. Hold this magnetic heading constant until the CDI centers, indicating that the aircraft is on course. (With practice in judging the varying rates of closure with the course centerline, you learn to lead the turn to prevent overshooting the course.)

7. Turn to the magnetic heading corresponding to the selected course, and follow tracking procedures inbound or outbound.

Course interceptions are illustrated in Figures 8–9 and 8–10 with instrument indications shown at various stages.

Application of Basic VOR Procedures (Fig. 8–11).— Assume that you are tracking inbound on the 247 radial of VOR "A", using a single VOR receiver. You expect to hold at intersection "H" and transition from VOR "A" to the Outer Compass Locator for a localizer approach on the instrument landing system shown.

Plotting Position (VOR).—Since magnetic bearings are read directly from the VOR indicator, you can easily establish a fix on the 247 radial of VOR "A" by identifying the intersecting radial of VOR "B"

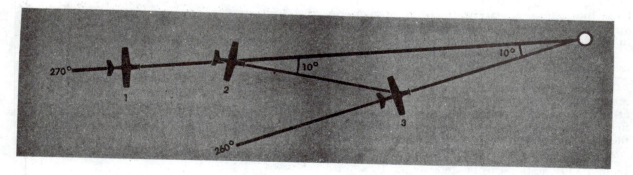

FIGURE 8–8. Time-distance check (VOR); isosceles triangle method.

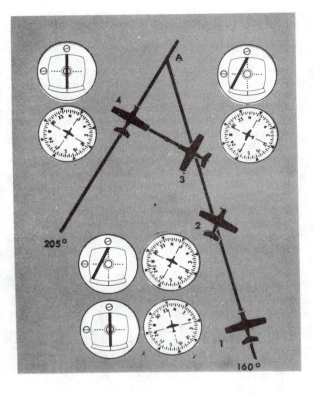

FIGURE 8-9. Course interception (VOR).

Intercept the 205 radial of VOR A, inbound—
1. Present position, inbound on 160 radial.
2. Turn right to parallel inbound course. (205° plus 180° equals 025°) Difference between 160 and 205 equals 45°. (double 45 for interception angle of 90°) Turn to 295° (205° plus 90°).
3. Maintain heading of 295° until 205 radial is intercepted (OBS 025, needle centered).
4. Track inbound on 205 radial.

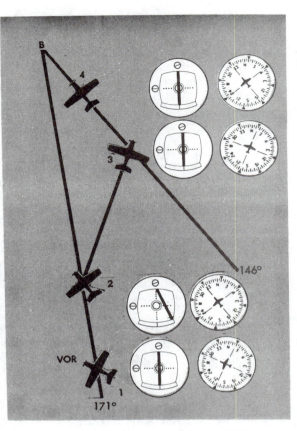

FIGURE 8-10. Course interception (VOR).

Intercept the 146 radial of VOR B, inbound—
1. Present position, crossing 171 radial.
2. Turn right to parallel inbound course. (146° plus 180° equals 326°) Difference between 146 and 171 equals 25°. (double 25 for interception angle of 50°) Turn to 016° (326° plus 50°).
3. 146 radial is intercepted when CDI centers with OBS at 326; turn to inbound heading of 326.
4. Track inbound on 146 radial.

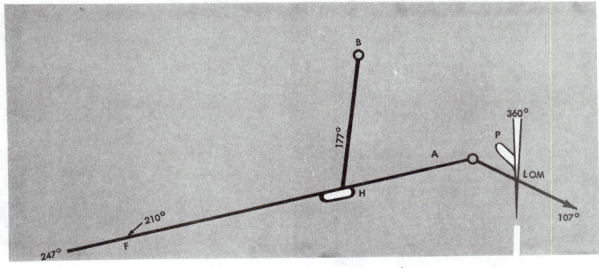

FIGURE 8-11. Application of VOR procedures.

139

and plotting your position on the Enroute Chart. At point "F", your receiver will read "FROM" with the OBS set on 210 and the CDI centered. With your position established and time noted, the distance from "F" to the holding fix "H" can be measured on the Enroute Chart and your ETA at "H" confirmed or revised.

Holding (VOR).—If your VOR equipment is limited to one receiver, it is especially important that you establish your inbound heading for accurate course following while you orient yourself to the 177 radial of VOR "B". To prevent overshooting the fix for holding entry, your position checks and tuning will have to be done accurately and quickly. You can easily misinterpret your position with respect to the 177 radial if you fail to set the OBS correctly. When establishing a fix or intersection by means of VOR stations on either side of your course, the TO/FROM indicator will read "FROM" and the CDI will *always* be deflected *toward* the station as you approach the fix, if the OBS is set with the *radial* (not the reciprocal) under the index (Fig. 8–12).

Roll into a standard-rate turn to the right as the CDI centers. As you roll out on the outbound heading, check the CDI to determine the position of the 177 radial. Then tune in VOR "A", setting the OBS on 067.

Transition and Localizer Approach

Where radar vectors are available on approach control frequencies, you will normally be vectored to the final approach course without executing a procedure turn. Assume in this instance that you are doing your own navigating. Over VOR "A", note the time of reversal from a "TO" to a "FROM" indication, and turn to transition from the outer fix to the outer compass locator (LOM) on the 107 radial. Transition bearings and distances are shown on approach charts enabling you to estimate time from outer fixes to final approach fixes. Position over the LOM can be established with either an ADF receiver or marker beacon receiver. When the ADF needle or marker beacon receiver indicates passage over the final approach fix, turn left to intercept and track outbound on the localizer front course. See Figure 8–13.

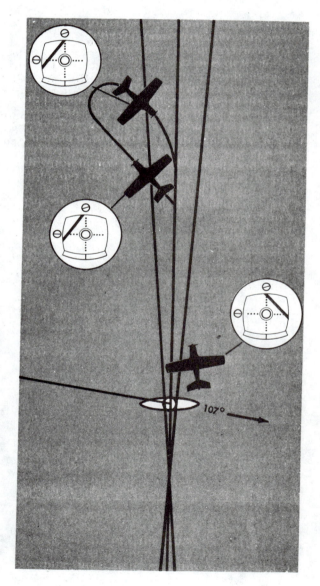

FIGURE 8–13. Transition to localizer course.

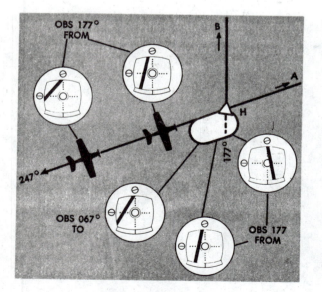

FIGURE 8–12. Holding; VOR receiver indications.

Because of the narrow localizer course width, overcontrolling of heading corrections is a common error during localizer course tracking. Unless the CDI shows a full deflection, heading corrections in 5° increments (or less) should keep you close to the centerline. The sooner you establish the correct drift-correction angle, the easier it will be to track without chasing the localizer needle.

Time from the LOM to procedure turn entry depends upon the type of procedure turn to be executed, type of aircraft, wind velocity, and distance restrictions shown on the approach chart. CDI deflections during a standard procedure turn on the front course are illustrated in Figure 8–13. When turning inbound into the localizer course, cross-check of the CDI should be frequent to prevent overshooting the course centerline. If your interception angle is 45° as shown, start the turn to the inbound course as soon as the CDI moves from the full deflection position.

Once you have reached the localizer centerline, maintain the inbound heading until the CDI moves off center. Drift corrections should be small and reduced proportionately as the course narrows. By the time you reach the outer marker, your drift correction should be established accurately enough on a well executed approach to permit completion of the approach with heading corrections no greater than 2°.

The heaviest demand on pilot technique occurs during descent from the outer marker to the middle marker, when you maintain the localizer course, adjust pitch attitude to maintain the proper rate of descent, and adjust power to maintain proper airspeed. Simultaneously, the altimeter must be checked and preparation made for visual transition to land or for a missed approach. The need for accurate instrument interpretation and aircraft control can be appreciated, in the complete ILS, by noting the relationship between CDI/glide path needle indications and aircraft displacement from the localizer and glide path centerlines. See Figures 8–14 and 8–15.

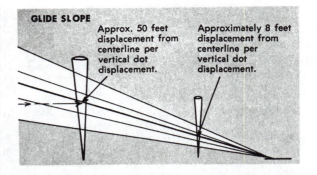

FIGURE 8–15. Glide slope receiver indications and aircraft displacement.

VOR Procedures Using the RMI

A brief description of the RMI was given earlier in this handbook on page 52. This section covers RMI procedures as they relate to tracking a course and intercepting a course. The procedures given are similar to those previously described on pages 136 through 138 using the CDI. In the RMI illustrations, only the double–barred bearing pointer is displayed.

Tracking a Course.—Follow these steps (Fig. 8–16) when tracking inbound. A similar procedure is used when tracking outbound.

1. Your heading is 360°, you are on the 360° course (inbound on the 180° radial), and the bearing pointer indicates 360°.

2. As you maintain a constant heading of 360°, the bearing pointer indicates you have drifted off course approximately 10° to the right. This indicates a left crosswind component.

3. Turn left 20° to a heading of 340°.

4. The aircraft has returned to course and the bearing pointer again indicates 360°. If you maintain the present heading of 340° you will fly through the course. If you return to the original heading of 360°, you will drift off course to the right again.

5. Reduce the drift correction to 10° left. The aircraft heading is now 350°. This correction may hold the desired course, or it may be too small or too large. If the course is not maintained, further bracketing will be required.

Intercepting an Inbound Course.—Follow these steps (Fig. 8–17) when intercepting an inbound course. A similar procedure is used when intercepting an outbound course. The first three steps may be omitted if you turn directly to the interception heading.

1. Determine the inbound course to be intercepted, then turn to a heading that parallels it. In this example, the 360° course is to be intercepted.

2. After paralleling the inbound course, note the deflection of the bearing pointer. In this example, the deflection is 30° left.

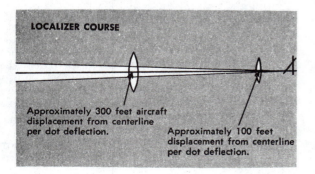

FIGURE 8–14. Localizer receiver indications and aircraft displacement.

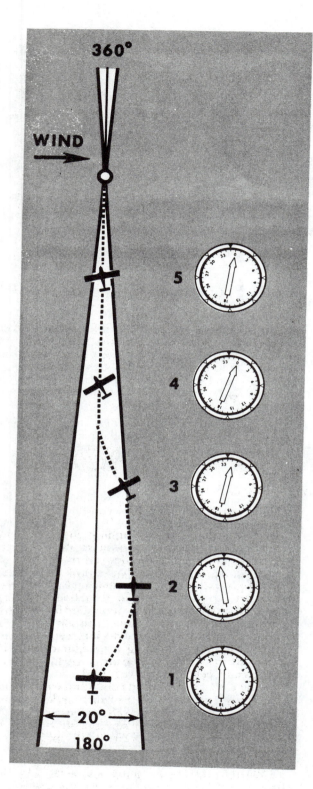

FIGURE 8-16. VOR tracking with RMI.

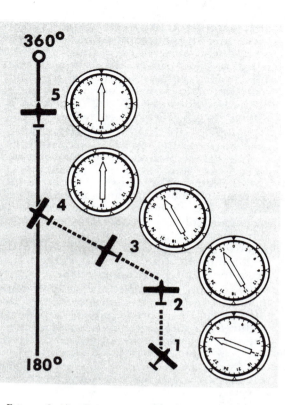

FIGURE 8-17. VOR course interception with RMI.

3. Double the number of degrees deflection to determine the interception angle. The angle should not be less than 20° nor greater than 90°. Turn to the interception heading. In this example, it is 300°.

4. Hold the interception heading until the bearing pointer indicates the desired course, 360°. At this point you have intercepted the course.

5. Turn to the desired course (this turn should be started before reaching the course unless the rate of interception is very slow).

DME Arc Procedures

The FAA is publishing an increasing number of instrument approach procedures which incorporate DME arcs. The procedures and techniques given here for intercepting and maintaining such arcs are applicable to any facility which provides DME information. Such a facility may or may not be collocated with the facility that provides final approach guidance.

It is recognized that the pilot, particularly in a single pilot operation, is too busy during an instrument approach to use formulas for the computation of leads for arc and radial interception, therefore, none are given.

Unless you are highly proficient in the use of the airborne equipment and in performing arc procedures, it is recommended that DME arcs be flown

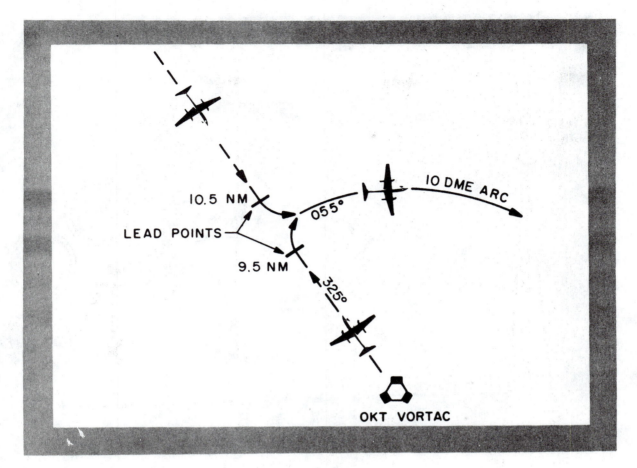

FIGURE 8–18.   DME arc interception.

in IFR weather conditions only when RMI equipment is available.

Refer to Figure 8–18 and follow these steps to intercept the 10 DME arc when inbound on the 325 radial:

1. Track inbound on the OKT 325° radial, frequently checking the DME mileage readout.

2. Since a .5 nautical mile lead is satisfactory for groundspeeds of 150 knots or less, start the turn to the arc at 10.5 miles. At higher groundspeeds, use a proportionately greater lead.

3. Continue the turn for approximately 90°. The roll-out heading will be 055° in no-wind conditions.

4. During the last part of the intercepting turn, monitor the DME closely. If it appears that the arc is being overshot, roll out of the turn early. If the arc is being undershot, continue past the originally-planned rollout point.

The procedure for intercepting the 10 DME arc when outbound is basically the same, the leadpoint being 10 miles minus .5 miles or 9.5 miles.

When flying a DME arc such as that illustrated in Figure 8–19, it is important that you keep a continuous mental picture of your position relative to the facility. Since the wind drift correction angle is constantly changing throughout the arc, wind orientation is important. In some cases, wind can be used in returning to the desired track. Arcs of large radii are easier to fly because of their "flat" curve. High airspeeds require more pilot attention because of the higher rate of deviation and correction. Maintaining the arc is simplified by keeping slightly inside the curve. Thus, the arc is always turning toward the aircraft and interception may be accomplished by holding a straight course. If you are outside the curve, the arc is "turning away" and a greater correction is required.

With an RMI, in a no-wind condition, you should theoretically be able to fly an exact circle around the facility by maintaining a relative bearing of 90° or 270°. In actual practice, a series of short legs are flown. To maintain the arc (Fig. 8–19), proceed as follows:

1. With the RMI bearing pointer on the wingtip reference (90° or 270° position) and the aircraft at the desired DME range, maintain a constant heading and allow the bearing pointer to move 5° to 10° behind the wingtip. This will cause the range to increase slightly.

143

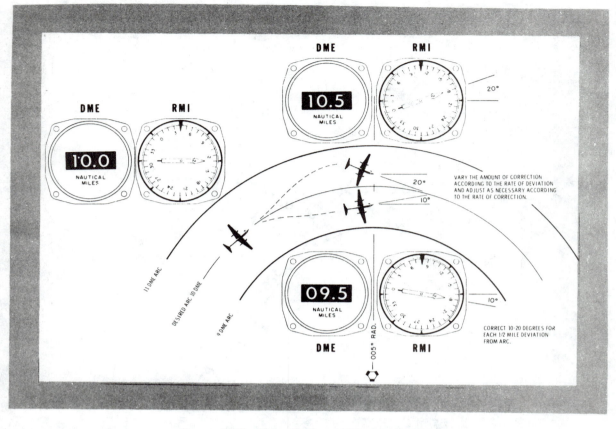

FIGURE 8–19.   Using DME and RMI to maintain arc.

2. Next, turn toward the facility to place the bearing pointer 5° to 10° ahead of the wingtip reference, then maintain heading until the bearing pointer is again behind the wingtip. Continue this procedure to maintain the approximate arc.

3. If a crosswind is drifting you away from the facility, turn the aircraft until the bearing pointer is ahead of the wingtip reference. If a crosswind is drifting you toward the facility, turn until the bearing pointer is behind the wingtip.

4. As a guide in making range corrections, change the relative bearing 10° to 20° for each 1/2 mile deviation from the desired arc. For example, in no-wind conditions, if you are 1/2 mile outside the arc and the bearing pointer is on the wingtip reference, turn the aircraft 20° toward the facility to return to the arc (Fig. 8–19).

Without an RMI, orientation is more difficult since you do not have a direct azimuth reference. However, the procedure can be flown using the OBS and CDI for azimuth information and the DME for arc distance. Refer again to Figure 8–18, and follow these steps:

1. If the rollout on the 055° heading places the aircraft on the arc, the DME will read 10.0 miles.

2. Set the OBS to 335°; when the CDI centers, you are crossing the 335 radial.

3. If the CDI reads right of center and the DME reads 10.5 miles, you are outside (left) of the arc and approaching the 335 radial. Correct heading to the right and monitor the DME for closure with the arc. If you are inside (right) of the arc, maintain heading to intercept the arc.

4. As the 10 DME arc and the 335 radial are achieved, set the OBS ahead 20° to 355° and turn to a heading 100° from the 335 radial (to a no-wind heading of 075°). Hold this heading until the 355 radial is crossed or the arc is intercepted. At this point, set the OBS ahead 20° and turn to a heading 100° from the radial you have just crossed. This technique will maintain a track slightly inside the 10 DME arc in no-wind conditions.

When intercepting a radial from a DME arc, the lead will vary with arc radius and groundspeed. For the average general aviation aircraft flying arcs such as those depicted on most approach charts at speeds of 150 knots or less, the lead will be under 5°. There is no essential difference between intercepting a radial from an arc and intercepting it from a straight course. With an RMI, the rate of bearing movement should be monitored closely while flying

144

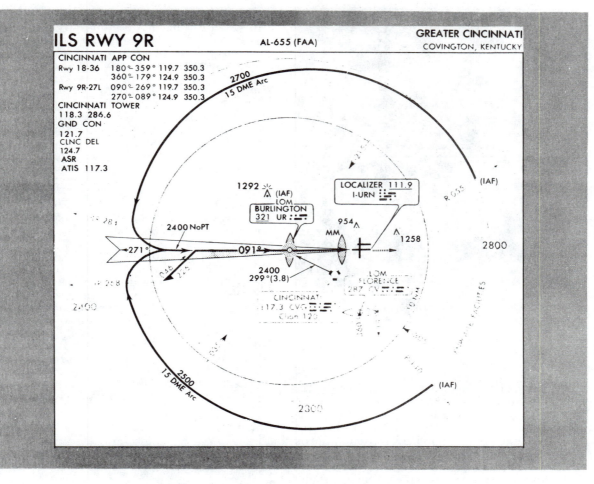

FIGURE 8–20. Localizer interception from DME arc.

the arc. Set the course of the radial to be intercepted as soon as possible and determine the approximate lead. Upon reaching this point, start the intercepting turn. Without an RMI, the technique for radial interception is the same except for azimuth information, which is available only from the OBS and CDI.

The technique for intercepting a localizer from a DME arc is similar to that described above for intercepting a radial. At the depicted lead radial (LR–284 or LR–268 in Fig. 8–20), a pilot having a single VOR/LOCALIZER receiver should set in the localizer frequency. If the pilot has dual VOR/LOCALIZER receivers, one unit may be used to provide azimuth information and the other set to the localizer frequency.

Automatic Direction Finder (ADF)

Knowledge of ADF procedures offers several advantages to the instrument pilot, although many seldom use ADF equipment because of the rela-

tively simpler operation and interpretation of VHF equipment. ADF provides; (a) a backup navigation system in the event of VHF equipment failure; (b) a means of monitoring position en route and providing data for plotting fixes; (c) a navigation system for use in areas and at altitudes where VOR "line-of-sight" signals are unreliable; (d) radio communications (receiver only) on the ground where VHF reception is impossible. Weather broadcasts and clearances can be received, for example, at points outside VHF signal range; and (e) auxiliary and standby navigation information on instrument approaches.

Selection of Station.—An older type ADF receiver is shown in Figure 8–21, and has been described earlier on pages 124 and 125. The receiver illustrated can be tuned to any station between 190–1750 kHz. Included in this range are "H" facilities on Enroute Low Altitude Charts.

Tuning.—Tuning details vary with the type ADF equipment installed in the aircraft. The manufacturer's brochure provided with the particular re-

145

FIGURE 8-21.   ADF receiver.

ceiver will include the necessary operating information. The modern crystal-controlled digitalled-tuned ADF previously discussed on page 125 eliminates manual tuning. The older type ADF (Fig. 8-21) is tuned to a station as follows:

1. Adjust the frequency band selector to the desired band.

2. Rotate the volume knob clockwise to approximately half the range.

3. Select "REC" position on the function switch. This selects the sense antenna for tuning the station for use of the receiver as a nondirectional radio receiver. Tuning with the function switch on "ADF" (automatic) position results in unnecessary hunting of the ADF needle as various station signals are received.

4. Rotate the frequency selector to the desired frequency. If a tuning meter is installed with the receiver, it is essential to tune for maximum tuning meter deflection. Without a tuning meter, adjust the frequency selector for maximum signal clarity and identify the station.

5. Select the "ADF" position on the function switch. The ADF needle will rotate until it points to the station. Note the bearing indicated on the ADF dial and push the "test" button. This will rotate the needle clockwise until the test button is released. If the station is tuned properly and the signal is reliable, the needle will return to the bearing previously noted.

6. Adjust the volume to the desired level. Volume adjustment has no effect on operation of the ADF needle.

ADF Orientation.—Unlike the VOR receiver, which indicates magnetic bearing TO or FROM the station without reference to aircraft heading, the ADF needle points TO the station, regardless of aircraft heading or position. The *relative* bearing indicated is thus the angular relationship between the aircraft heading and the station, measured clockwise from the nose of the aircraft.

A bearing is simply the direction of a straight line between the aircraft and station, or vice-versa. The bearing line measured clockwise from the nose of the aircraft is a *relative bearing;* measured clockwise from true north, it is a *true bearing;* measured clockwise from magnetic north, it is a *magnetic bearing* (Fig. 8-22 and Fig. 8-23). As the illustrations show, a true, magnetic, or compass heading is measured clockwise from the appropriate north, and a relative bearing is measured clockwise from the nose of the aircraft. Thus, the true, magnetic, or compass bearing to the station is the sum of true, magnetic, or compass heading, respectively, and the relative bearing.

You will probably orient yourself more readily if you think in terms of nose/tail and left/right needle indications, visualizing the ADF dial in terms of the longitudinal axis of the aircraft. When the needle points to 0°, the nose of the aircraft points directly to the station; with the pointer on 210°, the station is 30° to the left of the tail; with the pointer on 090°, the station if off the right wing tip (Fig. 8-24). Thus, to turn directly toward station A, turn left 150° since the needle points to the left of the nose/tail line 30° from the tail position. Station **B** is 90° to the right; therefore turn right 90° to head directly toward the station.

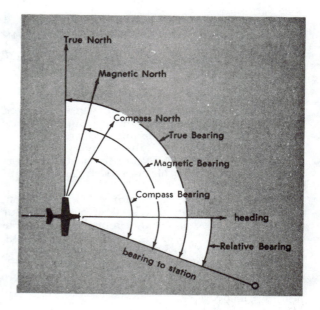

FIGURE 8-22.   ADF bearings.

True bearing to station = TH + rel. bearing.
Magnetic bearing to station = MH + rel. bearing.
Station to aircraft bearings are true, magnetic or compass bearings ± 180°.

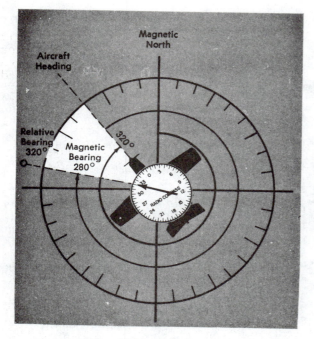

FIGURE 8-23. ADF bearing computations.

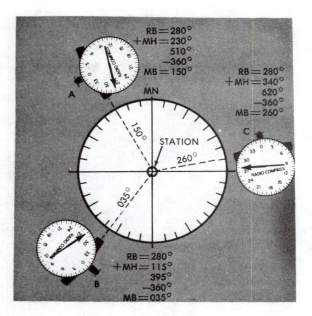

FIGURE 8-25. Determining magnetic bearing to station with ADF.

Magnetic bearing to station = magnetic heading (320°) + rel. bearing (320°) = 640° or 280° (whenever the total is greater than 360°, subtract 360 from the bearing).

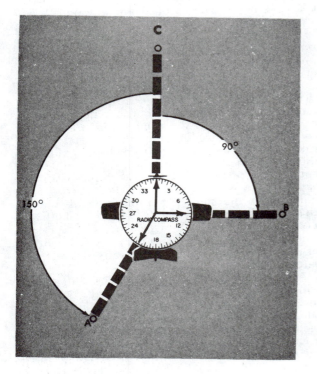

FIGURE 8-24. ADF relative bearings.

Note that (a) the relative bearing shown on the ADF dial does not, by itself, indicate aircraft position, and (b) the relative bearing must be related to aircraft heading to determine direction to or from the station (Fig. 8–25).

Figure 8–25 shows only one of several methods of determining bearings—or lines of position—between aircraft and station. Visualizing the 80° left-of-nose indication at all three positions shown, the magnetic bearing to station can be determined by subtracting the left deflection from the magnetic heading:

	A	B	C
Magnetic heading	230°	115°	340°
Minus left deflection	80°	80°	80°
Magnetic bearing	150°	035°	260°

Homing.—ADF homing is flying the aircraft on any heading required to keep the azimuth needle on 0° until the selected station has been reached (Fig. 8–26). To head the aircraft toward the station, turn to the heading that will zero the ADF needle. The heading indicator, rather than the ADF, should be used to make the turn. At the completion of the initial turn toward the station, check the ADF needle and, if necessary, zero it with small corrections.

For example, Figure 8–26 shows an initial magnetic heading of 050° and a relative bearing of 302°. A left turn of approximately 60° should zero the needle, heading 350°. After the needle is zeroed, it will remain so unless the heading is changed or crosswind affects the aircraft track. If there is no wind, the aircraft will follow a straight track to the station, assuming constant heading. If a crosswind

FIGURE 8-26. ADF homing.

drifts the aircraft, the homing track will be a curve as you keep the ADF needle zeroed.

Approach to the station is indicated by increasingly frequent heading corrections to zero the needle, especially when a strong crosswind exists, and by side-to-side needle deflections very close to the station. Passage directly over the station is shown by a 180° reversal of the ADF needle to the tail position; passage on either side and close to the station is shown by a rapid swing of the needle as it continues to point to the station. Homing is easy, though seldom used during instrument flying. Competent pilots control track by more precise procedures.

Tracking.—A straight geographic flight path can be followed to or from a low (or medium) frequency facility by establishing a heading that will maintain the desired track regardless of wind effect. ADF tracking procedures involve interpretation of the heading indicator and azimuth needle to intercept and hold a desired magnetic bearing.

Inbound Tracking (Fig. 8-27).—To track inbound, turn to the heading that will zero the ADF needle. As you hold this heading, deflection of the ADF needle to left or right shows a crosswind (needle left/wind from left; needle right/wind from right). When a definite change in azimuth (2°-5°) shows that the aircraft has drifted off course, turn in the direction of needle deflection (into the wind) to re-intercept the initial inbound bearing. The angle of interception must always be greater than the number of degrees of drift. The magnitude of any intercepting turn depends upon the observed *rate* of bearing change, true airspeed, and how quickly you want to return to course.

A rapid rate of bearing change, *while heading is constant,* indicates either a strong crosswind or proximity to the station, or both. For example, if you are 60 miles from the station with a 3° left deflection, your aircraft is 3 miles to the right of the desired course. In a slow aircraft, use a large interception angle for quick return to the course. In a very fast aircraft, the same interception angle could result in overshooting the desired course. Likewise, the same 3° needle deflection closer to the station means less deviation from the desired course, and smaller angles of interception result in rapid return to course. Again, when aircraft is 60 miles from the station, a rapid rate of bearing change indicates a strong crosswind; at half that distance, the same rate of bearing change means twice the crosswind effect, or conversely, at half the distance, the same wind effect results in double the rate of bearing change.

At a given angle of interception and with a given wind, rate of closure with the desired track varies directly with true airspeed. At 150 knots TAS as compared with 100 knots TAS, the effectiveness of a given interception angle is proportionately greater for the same wind at the same distance from the station. Having determined the angle of interception for return to the desired track, turn toward the track by that amount. As you make the turn

148

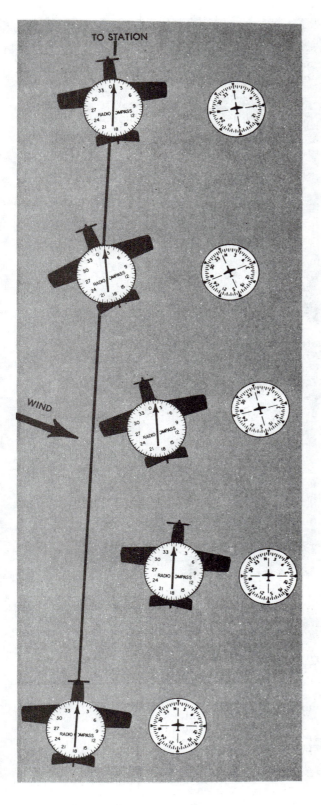

TO STATION

WIND

FIGURE 8-27. ADF tracking-inbound.

with the heading indicator, the azimuth needle rotates opposite the direction of turn, and as the interception angle is established, the needle points to the side of the zero position opposite the direction of turn. As you approach the course on a constant interception heading, the ADF needle continues to rotate as the relative bearing changes. When the needle deflection from zero equals the angle of interception, the aircraft is on the desired track. If you begin the turn to the magnetic bearing of the desired track when these angles are equal, you will overshoot the track. In such a case, you can either drift back to track and then establish an estimated drift correction angle, or bracket the track with successively smaller interception angles.

A quicker technique is to lead the turn to the inbound heading before the track is intercepted. The amount of lead depends upon the distance from station, rate of closure observed as you approach the desired track, number of degrees to be turned, and rate of turn. Since these factors are variable, you will develop effective lead estimates as you become familiar with particular aircraft and practice ADF tracking.

After you are back on track, holding an estimated correction for wind drift, you remain on the desired track as long as the azimuth needle is deflected from zero opposite the direction of drift correction, an amount equal to the drift correction angle. If the needle moves further from the nose position, the drift correction is excessive. Reduce the correction angle allowing the aircraft to drift back on course. This is indicated for any drift correction (or interception) angle when ADF needle deflection and drift correction angle are equal. If the estimated drift correction is insufficient, the azimuth needle will move toward the nose, requiring a further correction to regain track. With careful attention to headings, effective drift correction angles can be established with very little bracketing.

Station Approach and Station Passage.—The same suggestions apply to ADF tracking as have been mentioned in connection with ADF homing and VOR/Localizer procedures. The closer you are to

FIGURE 8-27. ADF tracking—inbound.

1. Turn the aircraft to zero the azimuth needle. Maintain this heading until off-course drift is indicated by left or right needle deflection.
2. When a 5° change in needle deflection is observed, turn 20° in the direction of needle deflection.
3. When the needle is deflected 20° (deflection = interception angle), track has been intercepted. Lead the interception as noted in discussion of tracking. Turn 10° toward the inbound course. You are now inbound with a 10° left drift correction angle.
4. If you observe off-course deflection in the original direction, turn again to the original interception heading.
5. When the desired course has been reintercepted, turn 5° toward the inbound course, proceeding inbound with a 15° drift correction.
6. If the initial 10° drift correction is excessive, as shown by needle deflection away from the wind, turn to parallel the desired course and let the wind drift you back on course. When the needle is again zeroed, turn into the wind with a reduced drift correction angle.

149

the station, the more aggravated are your errors in drift correction and basic instrument flying technique, unless you recognize station approach and prevent yourself from over-controlling the observed track deviations.

When you are close to the station, slight deviations from the desired track result in large deflections of the azimuth needle. It is important, therefore, that the correct drift correction angle be established as soon as possible after interception of an inbound course. With the course "pinned down" and heading corrections kept at a minimum, you will be more alert to signs of station approach than you would be if you were busy "chasing" headings and ADF deflections. Make small heading corrections (not over 5°) as soon as the needle shows a deviation from course, until it begins to rotate steadily toward a wing-tip position or shows erratic left/right oscillations. At this point, hold your last corrected heading constant, and time station passage when the needle shows either wing-tip position or settles at or near the 180° position. The time interval from the first indications of station proximity to positive station passage varies with altitude—a few seconds at low levels to 3 minutes at high altitude.

Outbound Tracking.—Procedures for tracking outbound are identical to those used for inbound tracking. However, the direction of the azimuth needle deflections are different from those noted during inbound track interceptions, as shown in Figure 8–28. When tracking *inbound,* a change of heading toward the desired track results in movement of the azimuth needle *toward* zero. When tracking *outbound,* a change of heading toward the desired track results in needle movement further *away* from the 180° position.

Time/Distance Checks (ADF).—Time and distance to a station may be calculated with radio-compass procedures similar to the VOR procedures already discussed. A variety of methods commonly used are variations of the basic procedures that follow.

Wing-Tip Bearing Change.—To determine the time/distance to the station, use the following steps:

1. After tuning in the station, determine the relative bearing from the position of the ADF needle.

2. Turn the number of degrees necessary to place the needle on 090° or 270°.

3. Note the time, and fly a constant magnetic heading for a specific number of degrees of bearing change. The amount of change flown varies with the observed rate of bearing change. For example, a 10° change at a considerable distance from the station may take unnecessarily long; the time/distance check can be accomplished in this case by timing a 5° change.

4. Apply the observed time interval to the formula, or calculate the time to station by rule of thumb if a 10° bearing change is used (*see* Time/Distance Checks by VOR). For example, you are

FIGURE 8–28. ADF tracking-outbound.

flying a magnetic heading of 180°, TAS 130 knots, ADF relative bearing 090°. Maintaining the magnetic heading for 4 minutes, you observe a relative bearing of 100°. Approximate time to station is as follows:

By formula:

$$\text{Minutes to station} = \frac{60 \times \text{minutes between bearing change}}{\text{Degrees of bearing change}}$$
$$= \frac{60 \times 4}{10}$$
$$= 24 \text{ minutes}$$

150

By rule of thumb (for 10° change):

Minutes to station = 6 × time in minutes between
bearing change.

$$= 6 \times 4$$
$$= 24 \text{ minutes}$$

or Minutes to station = $\dfrac{\text{time in seconds}}{10}$

$$= \dfrac{240}{10}$$
$$= 24 \text{ minutes}$$

To determine the distance from the station, use the formula (see Time/Distance Checks by VOR) or the following computer method:

1. Place the speed index opposite True Air Speed.

2. Read distance from station on miles scale opposite time from station on minutes scale.

Other time/distance checks are applications of the isosceles triangle principle:

Bow-to-beam bearing gives time to station by the following steps:

1. Turn the number of degrees necessary to place the ADF needle on 045° (or 315°).

2. Maintain heading until the needle is on 090° (or 270°).

3. Time/distance flown equals time/distance to station.

The Double-the-angle-on-bow method involves the following steps:

1. Tune in a station between 10° and 45° off the nose position, and note the relative bearing.

2. Fly a constant magnetic heading until the angle on the nose doubles.

3. The time/distance required to double the angle on the nose equals the time/distance to the station.

The accuracy of time/distance checks involves a number of variables, including existing wind, accuracy of timing, and heading control. Time checks, especially those involving a rapid rate of bearing change, demand very precise techniques in basic instrument flying while you maintain heading and check elapsed time.

Interception of Predetermined Magnetic Bearings

Basic ADF orientation, tracking, and time/distance procedures may be applied to the problem of intercepting a specified inbound or outbound magnetic bearing. To intercept an *inbound* magnetic bearing, the following steps may be used (Fig. 8–29):

1. Determine your position in relation to the station by turning to the magnetic heading of the bearing to be intercepted.

2. Note whether the station is to the right or left of the nose position. Determine the number of de-

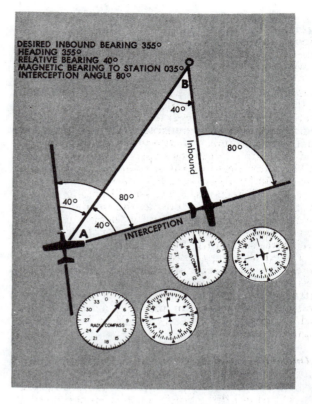

FIGURE 8–29. Interception of predetermined magnetic bearing.

grees of needle deflection from the zero position, and double this amount for the interception angle.

3. Turn the aircraft toward the desired magnetic bearing the number of degrees determined for the interception angle.

4. Maintain the interception heading until the needle is deflected the same number of degrees from the zero position as the angle of interception (minus lead appropriate to the rate of bearing change).

5. Turn inbound and continue with tracking procedures.

Note that this method combines inbound course interception with a time estimate to the station, since the interception leg and the inbound leg are equal sides of an isosceles triangle. The time from the completion of the turn to the interception heading (075°) until interception of the desired inbound bearing is equal to the time-to-station (double-the-angle-on-bow).

Interception of an *outbound* magnetic bearing can be accomplished by the same procedures as for the inbound intercept, except that you substitute the 180° position for the zero position on the azimuth needle.

Application of Basic ADF Procedures

Assume that you have departed airport "X" to fly direct to a destination airport via an inbound magnetic bearing of 020° to the "H" facility located on the airport. See Figure 8–30.

1. You intercept the desired inbound magnetic bearing at a 45° angle and establish the inbound track with a 10° left drift correction angle, heading 010°.

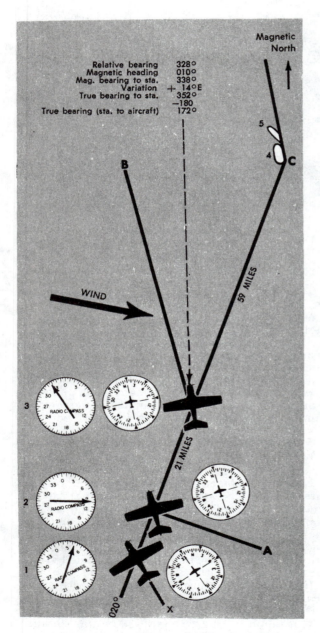

Relative bearing	328°
Magnetic heading	010°
Mag. bearing to sta.	338°
Variation	+ 14°E
True bearing to sta.	352°
	−180
True bearing (sta. to aircraft)	172°

FIGURE 8–30. Application of ADF procedures.

2. *Plotting Position.*—Tuning in nondirectional beacon "A", note the time as the ADF needle indicates 100°. With a 10° left drift correction angle, your position is 90° to the station. The fix can be directly located on the inbound track line drawn on your aeronautical chart. Move your plotter along the track line until the 090 reference line intersects the station.

3. You establish another fix by tuning in nondirectional beacon at "B", noting 9 minutes elapsed time as the ADF shows a relative bearing of 328°. Adding the relative bearing and magnetic heading, the magnetic bearing to the station is 338°. To plot the fix on your chart, the magnetic bearing must be converted to a true bearing *from* the station. Assuming 14°E variation, the true bearing from the station is 172°, which fixes your position 21 nautical miles from the one established 9 minutes earlier. From this data you compute groundspeed as 140 knots and estimate arrival time at your destination after measurement of the remaining distance.

4. Holding should be accomplished in the pattern depicted on the chart unless ATC instructs you otherwise. The depicted holding pattern will normally be aligned with the final approach course to the airport to facilitate letdown and approach to the field. The ADF approach combines the basic procedures you have already studied—orientation, tracking inbound and outbound, and interception of predetermined bearings.

Figure 8–31 illustrates a standard holding pattern (dotted line shows holding entry), as well as the procedure turn for approach to the airport. Holding may or may not be necessary, depending upon traffic and weather conditions. If you hold as illustrated, your entry would be as specified in the *Airman's Information Manual*. The appropriate communications procedures are explained in a later chapter of this text. Assuming a 10° left drift correction angle as you track inbound on the 020° magnetic bearing, proceed as follows:

a. Turn to parallel the outbound course as the ADF needle indicates station passage, applying drift correction appropriate to the known wind. Note the time.

b. Fly the outbound heading for approximately one minute, observing the ADF needle for drift toward, or away from, the inbound holding course. If you apply a 10° left drift correction angle, drift away from course will be shown by movement of the needle farther from the 180° position or by failure of the needle to move toward the tail position as you proceed outbound.

c. Turn toward the inbound course, rolling out on a 125° magnetic heading for a 45° interception of the inbound course. Note the relative bearing immediately. If it is greater than 045°, you have overshot the inbound course and may have difficulty establishing the track before passing the station.

d. Lead the turn to the inbound course (170°) and roll out with drift correction. If you are on course, your drift correction angle will be equal and

152

opposite to the ADF needle displacement from zero.

e. Track inbound, using small corrections. The quicker you establish the desired track, the fewer your holding problems since both basic flight techniques and procedural details will keep you busy.

f. Turn outbound on station passage, noting the time. With no wind, timing the outbound leg would begin as you roll out on a 350° heading with the ADF needle reading 090°. With the wind as shown, your track would be closer to the station than shown in the diagram.

g. Roll out on an outbound heading with a drift correction angle equal to double the amount of inbound drift correction. As you begin outbound timing for one minute, your ADF will indicate approximately 110°, assuming a 20° left drift correction angle. As you maintain the outbound heading, the needle moves toward the 180° position. With experience, you learn to recognize drift by rate of movement of the ADF needle—rapidly toward the tail position if you drift inward or a strong tailwind exists; slowly toward the tail if you drift outward or a strong headwind exists.

h. With correct inbound and outbound drift correction angles, your ADF should read zero, plus or minus the appropriate drift correction angle, as you complete the turn to track inbound.

i. The approach is normally begun directly from the holding pattern, tracking inbound as you descend and execute a low approach to the field.

5. *Procedure Turn and Low Approach.*—When a final approach from a nondirectional beacon holding pattern is not authorized, a procedure turn is required for course reversal. For execution of the procedure turn and approach shown in Figure 8–31, the approach procedure depicted on the approach chart for the airport would be used. At this point, you are concerned with the application of basic navigational techniques to the problem. The associated procedures are shown on the illustration.

To track outbound and reverse course to the final approach, proceed as follows:

a. On station passage, note the time, and turn outbound to intercept the 350° magnetic bearing.

b. Start the procedure turn to 305° as soon as practicable, normally within 2 minutes of station passage. Hold the 305° heading for 40 seconds to 1 minute, depending upon the existing wind.

c. Turn inbound to intercept and track the 170° magnetic bearing to the field.

The suggestions discussed earlier with respect to station approach are of particular importance during the low approach. An ADF instrument approach executed without additional navigation airborne equipment or radar assistance demands a high level of skill in the use of both basic flight

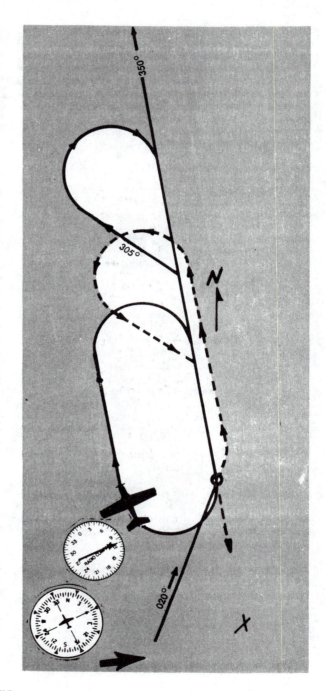

FIGURE 8–31. Transition to ADF approach.

1. Check radio contact with Air Traffic Control before arrival over station. Maintain assigned altitude, or if cleared for approach, descend to initial approach altitude.
2. Turn outbound, reduce speed if necessary, note time, report station passage to ATC, and perform prelanding check.
3. Descend to procedure turn altitude given on approach chart.
4. Procedure turn in direction shown on approach chart.
5. *Inbound*, descend to minimum altitude over final approach fix, then to MDA.
6. *Inbound*, report over final approach fix and complete approach to landing. If field is below minimums, report and execute missed approach depicted on approach chart, or as directed by ATC.

and navigation instruments, as well as facility with communications procedures. It is essential that you be thoroughly familiar with courses, altitudes, and procedural details well *before* you execute the approach in order that you be able to visualize the details in their necessary sequence.

Common Errors in the Use of Navigation Instruments

Other than the specific errors outlined below, the errors underlying most confusion while learning navigation techniques relate to skill in the use of basic flight instruments. You cannot read a VOR or ADF indication while you fumble with pitch, bank, power, and trim control any more than you can read a highway sign or follow a cloverleaf intersection while you stare at your automobile brake pedal.

Mastery of basic flight maneuvers is prerequisite to their application on the aerial highways.

VOR Errors

1. Careless tuning and identification of station.
2. Failure to check receiver for accuracy/sensitivity.
3. Turning in the wrong direction during an orientation. This error is common until you visualize position rather than heading.
4. Failure to check the ambiguity indicator, particularly during course reversals, with resulting "reverse sensing" and corrections in the wrong direction.
5. Failure to parallel the desired radial on a track interception problem. Without this step, orientation to the desired radial can be confusing. Since you think in left/right terms, aligning your aircraft position to the radial/course is essential.
6. Incorrect rotation of the course-selector (OBS) on a time/distance problem.
7. Overshooting and undershooting radials on interception problems. Factors affecting lead should be thoroughly understood, especially on close–in course interception.
8. Overcontrolling corrections during tracking, especially close to the station.
9. Misinterpretation of station passage. On VOR receivers equipped without an ON/OFF flag, a voice communication on the VOR frequency will cause the same to/from fluctuations on the ambiguity meter as shown on station passage. Read the *whole* receiver—TO/FROM, CDI, and OBS—before you make a decision.
10. Chasing the CDI, resulting in homing instead of tracking. Careless heading control and failure to bracket wind corrections makes this error common.

ILS Errors

1. Failure to understand the fundamentals of ILS ground equipment, particularly the differences in course dimensions. Since the VOR receiver is used on the localizer course, the assumption is sometimes made that interception and tracking techniques are identical when tracking localizer courses and VOR radials. Remember that the CDI sensing is sharper and faster on the localizer course.
2. Disorientation during transition to the ILS due to poor planning and reliance on one receiver instead of on all available airborne equipment. Use all the assistance you have available; the single receiver you may be relying on may fail you at a busy time.
3. Disorientation on the localizer course, basically due to the first error noted above.
4. Incorrect localizer interception angles. A large interception angle usually results in overshooting and often disorientation. Turn to the localizer course heading immediately upon the first indication of needle movement, using a small interception angle whenever possible. An ADF receiver is an excellent aid to orientation during an ILS approach.
5. Chasing the CDI and glide path needles, especially when the approach is not sufficiently studied before the flight. Flying the proper headings, altitudes, rate of descent, times and power configuration settings is impossible if your mind is on studying the approach chart.

ADF Errors

1. Improper tuning and station identification. Homing or tracking to the wrong station has been done by many students.
2. Dependence on homing rather than proper tracking, commonly results from reliance on the ADF indications instead of correlating them with heading indications.
3. Poor orientation, due to failure to follow proper steps in orientation and tracking.
4. Careless interception angles, very likely if you rush the initial orientation procedure.
5. Overshooting and undershooting predetermined magnetic bearings, often due to forgetting the course interception angles used.
6. Failure to maintain selected headings. Any heading change is accompanied by an ADF needle change. The instruments must be read in combination *before* any interpretation is made.
7. Failure to understand the limitations of the radio compass and the factors that affect its use.
8. Overcontrolling track corrections close to the station (chasing the ADF needle), due to failure to understand or recognize station approach.
9. Failure to keep heading indicator set with magnetic compass.

IX. RADIO COMMUNICATIONS FACILITIES AND EQUIPMENT

What communications equipment do you need for IFR operations? In uncontrolled airspace, none is required by regulation. What you need is up to your own judgment.

For operations under IFR in controlled airspace, two regulations relate directly to the minimum communications equipment:

a. (FAR 91.33) Your aircraft must be equipped with a two-way radio communications system appropriate to the ground facilities being used.

b. (FAR 91.125) The pilot in command shall have a continuous listening watch maintained on the appropriate frequency and shall report by radio as required.

Information on making radio reports and on the functions and services of Air Traffic Control agencies are considered in Chapter XI.

Ground Facilities

For civil IFR operations in controlled airspace, the ground facilities available for radio communi-

cation include the following components of Air Traffic Control:

1. Clearance delivery.
2. Ground control.
3. Tower control.
4. Departure control.
5. En route control.
6. Approach control.

Communications with these controlling units are normally conducted on VHF frequencies between 118.000 and 136.000 MHz. Flight Service Stations, while not exercising direct control over IFR aircraft, are ground facilities available and used for radio communications. They play an important role in the total ATC system (see pages 193 through 195 for details).

Automatic Terminal Information Service (ATIS) is provided at certain high activity terminal areas. Recorded information on weather, altimeter settings, instrument approaches and runways in use, tower frequencies etc., is broadcast continuously on a specific VHF frequency.

The frequencies with which you should be familiar are listed below. The ILS and VOR frequencies listed may be used as receiving frequencies for communications as well as for navigation.

Air Navigation Aids

108.10–111.95 MHz: ILS localizers
108.00–117.95 MHz: VORs

Communications

118.00–121.40 MHz: Air Traffic Control
121.50 MHz: Emergency
121.60–121.925 MHz: Airport Utility and Ground Control
121.95 MHz: Flying Schools
121.975–123.075 MHz: Private Aircraft to Flight Service Stations
123.10 MHz: Search and Rescue (Temporary Control Towers)
123.125–123.275 MHz: Flight Test
123.30 MHz: Flying Schools
123.325–123.475 MHz: Flight Test
123.50 MHz: Flying Schools–Gliders
123.525–123.575 MHz: Flight Test
123.60–123.65 MHz: FSSs (Airport Advisory Service)
123.675–128.80 MHz: Air Traffic Control
128.825–132.00 MHz: Aeronautical En Route (Operational Control)
132.025–135.975 MHz: Air Traffic Control

Airborne Equipment

Radio communications requirements have increased with the growth of aviation. Implementation of 25 KHz spacing in 1977 now provides 720 VHF channels (118.000–136.000) for air/ground communications. For training, however, you need only a transmitter and receiver suitable for communications with the ground facilities in your training area. Any lightweight equipment which provides the minimum standard frequencies included in the table above, may be sufficient for training but may be inadequate for the instrument rated pilot.

Communications equipment of more recent design reflects the concern of manufacturers for the operational needs of the instrument pilot. Under the best conditions, a pilot flying on instruments must think, decide, and move quickly. Equipment design that contributes to indecision, uncertainty or fatigue creates unnecessary problems when the pilot is flying by reference to instruments.

"One and One–half" Systems

Figure 9–1 illustrates a dual-purpose radio typical of the "one and one-half" systems. These systems incorporate communications and navigation radios in a single compact unit. This is a welcome change from the older installations that required an extensive cockpit search to locate switches, selectors, and associated indicators and too much time to tune and operate. The "one and one-half" radio enables you to communicate with the necessary ground facilities on the transceiver (combined transmitter/receiver) while simultaneously tuned on the separate "one-half" of the set to a VOR station. This radio has controls that are easily identifiable and crystal-tuned frequencies that can be selected with only a glance or two for tuning.

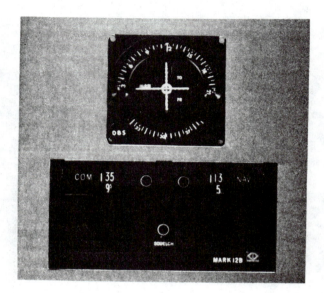

FIGURE 9–1. "One and one-half" system.

Operation of the communications section of these radios is simple. The volume switch on the left is the ON/OFF switch for both COMM and NAV sections. The squelch knob is rotated to reduce background noise. While the set is warming up, set the knob fully clockwise; then turn the control counterclockwise to increase the squelch until the background noise is cut out. Further increase of the squelch setting will decrease receiver sensitivity. If you are tuning in a weak signal, decrease the squelch. Otherwise, once the control is established at a comfortable level, no further adjustment is necessary except to make an occasional check of receiver sensitivity. Transmit/receive frequencies are selected by rotation of the inner and outer knobs on the COMM side of the set.

The "one and one-half" system described has the following communication/navigation frequency coverage:

Communications
Transmit/receive 360 channels   (118.00–135.95 MHz)

Navigation
All VOR and localizer frequencies   (108.00–117.95 MHz)

Expanded NAV/COMM Systems

The advantages of the "one and one-half" system can be expanded with installation of additional radios and centralized control units for rapid selection of receivers and transmitters. The "building block" concept, from which most light aircraft radio design evolves, provides for progressive expansion of your equipment as your training and operational needs increase. For example, if you depart under IFR from an uncontrolled airport and proceed via Victor airway to another uncontrolled airport, your communication/navigation needs may be as little as one VOR frequency and one transmitting frequency for communication with FSS.

When you progress to all-weather IFR flying in and out of unfamiliar terminal areas, your workload can be excessive unless you have sufficient standby equipment for frequent changes of communications channels. Figure 9–2 shows how com-

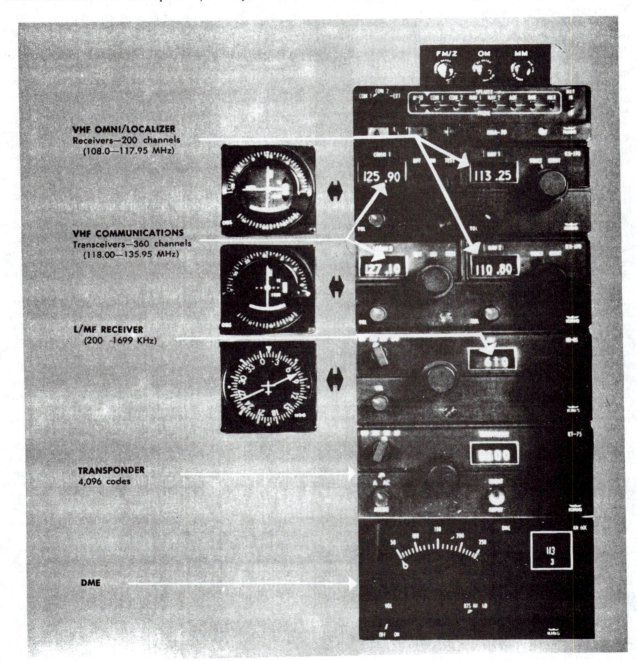

VHF OMNI/LOCALIZER
Receivers—200 channels
(108.0—117.95 MHz)

VHF COMMUNICATIONS
Transceivers—360 channels
(118.00—135.95 MHz)

L/MF RECEIVER
(200 -1699 KHz)

TRANSPONDER
4,096 codes

DME

FIGURE 9–2. Full navigation-communications panel.

157

munications equipment can be grouped for quick reference and operation with minimum distraction from the problem of aircraft control.

Radiotelephone Procedure

From the time you contact ground control for taxi instructions the effectiveness of your coordination with Air Traffic Control will depend upon your competence in communications and your knowledge of traffic procedures under Instrument Flight Rules. Many students have no serious difficulty in learning basic aircraft control and radio navigation, but stumble through even the simplest radio communications. During the initial phase of training in Air Traffic Control procedures and radiotelephone techniques, some students experience difficulty.

Why should talking and listening to a controller pose any problems? The average person takes speaking and listening habits for granted and has had no occasion to develop the specialized skills associated with radio communications. Studies of listening comprehension show that most people listen with low efficiency even when consciously attempting to remember what they hear. Poor listeners are easily distracted. From habit, they tolerate conditions unfavorable to concentration. Their minds wander when they hear anything unexpected or difficult to understand. They are inclined to be more concerned with what they are about to say than what they should be listening to. When in confusing situations, they are more easily aroused emotionally, and may have trouble comprehending what they hear.

These deficiencies are intensified for the pilot in a busy air traffic environment. In addition to attending to cockpit duties demanding rapid division of attention, quick judgment, concentration, and careful planning, you the pilot must be continuously alert to communications from Air Traffic Control. You should be prepared to listen and to transmit in the brief and unmistakably clear terms vital to orderly control.

You attain proficiency in radiotelephone technique just as you do in devleoping any other skill. You should first recognize that radio communications under Instrument Flight Rules, though not difficult, require speaking and listening habits different from those you have been accustomed to. Skill in transmitting and listening will come rapidly once you have studied and practiced the basic terminology.

FAA controllers are intensively trained to speak clearly and concisely in an abbreviated terminology. They use standard words and phrases to save time, reduce radio congestion, and lessen the chances of misunderstanding and confusion. However, the most competent controllers won't "get through" to you under the best conditions unless you are ready to listen and understand.

Communication is a two-way effort, and the controllers expect you to work toward the same level of competency that they strive to achieve. Tape recordings comparing transmissions by professional pilots and inexperienced or inadequately trained general aviation pilots illustrate the need for effective radiotelephone technique. In a typical instance, an airline pilot made a position report in 5 seconds; whereas a private pilot reporting the same fix took 4 minutes to transmit essentially the same information. The difference lay not in equipment and flight experience, but in communication technique. The novice forgot to tune the radio properly before transmitting, interrupted other transmissions, repeated unnecessary data, forgot other essential information, requested instructions repeatedly, and created the general impression of cockpit disorganization. The novice who is embarrassed and concerned about inexperience should remember that every pilot had to make a beginning and was not expected to first communicate like a veteran airline pilot. But the private pilot who learns and practices standardized words and phrases until they become part of the normal radio vocabulary will be able to communicate effectively even under severe reception conditions.

Phonetic Alphabet

It is often necessary in transmitting to identify certain letters and/or groups of letters, or to spell out difficult words, since certain sounds have low intelligibility when mixed with a background of other noises. The standard phonetic alphabet (Fig. 9–3) identifies each letter of the alphabet with a word that is easily understood. These words are pronounced to make the message clear when individual letters are transmitted, and are used to spell out words that are hard to understand on the air.

Phonetic alphabet		Numerals
A—Alpha	N—November	0—Zero
B—Bravo	O—Oscar	1—Wun
C—Charlie	P—Papa	2—Too
D—Delta	Q—Quebec***	3—Tree
E—Echo	R—Romeo	4—Fo-wer
F—Foxtrot	S—Sierra	5—Fife
G—Golf	T—Tango	6—Six
H—Hotel	U—Uniform	7—Seven
I—India	V—Victor	8—Ait
J—Juliett	W—Whiskey	9—Ni-ner
K—Kilo*	X—X-ray	
L—Lima**	Y—Yankee	
M—Mike	Z—Zulu	

* Key-lo ** Lee-mah ***Keh-beck

FIGURE 9–3. Phonetic Alphabet.

Use of Numbers

Numbers are usually of extreme importance in radio messages and are difficult to hear among other noises. The standard pronunciations in Figure 9–3 have been adopted because they have been found most intelligible.

a. Normally, numbers are transmitted by speaking each number separately. For example, 3284 is spoken as "tree too ait fo-wer."

b. There are certain exceptions to the above rule. Figures indicating hundreds and thousands in round numbers, up to and including 9,000 are spoken in hundreds or thousands as appropriate. 500 is spoken as "fife hundred"; 1,200 as "wun thousand too hundred." Beginning with 10,000, the individual digits in thousands of feet are spoken. For 13,000, say "wun tree thousand", for 14,500, say "wun-fo-wer thousand fife hundred."

c. Aircraft identification numbers are spoken as individual digits/letters. 1234Q is spoken as "wun too tree fo-wer Keh-beck."

d. Time is stated in four digits according to the 24-hour clock. The first two digits indicate the hour; the last two, minutes after the hour (Fig. 9–4), as in "wun niner too zero"; "zero niner fo-wer fife."

e. Field elevations are transmitted with each number spoken separately, as in Figure 9–4.

Procedural Words and Phrases

The words and phrases in Figure 9–5 should be studied and practiced until they are readily and easily used and clearly enunciated. To pilots and controllers, their meanings are very specific. Careless or incorrect use can cause both delay and confusion.

Voice Control

Students inexperienced in the use of the microphone are usually surprised at the quality of their own transmissions when they are taped and played back. Words quite clear when spoken directly to another person can be almost unintelligible over the radio. Effective radiotelephone technique sounds self-conscious and unnatural when you practice it, both because the terminology is new and because you are habitually more concerned with *what* you are saying than in *how* it sounds. Maximum readable radiotelephone transmissions depend on the following factors:

1. *Volume.*—Clarity increases with volume up to a level just short of shouting. Speaking loudly, with-

out extreme effort or noticeably straining the voice, results in maximum intelligibility. To be understood, the spoken sound must be louder at the face of the microphone than the surrounding noises. Open the mouth so the tone will carry to the microphone. A higher-pitched tone is easier to hear than a lower one. A distinct and easily readable side tone in your earphones or speaker is a reliable index of correct volume.

2. *Tempo.*—Effective rate of speech varies with the speaker, the nature of the message, and conditions of transmission and reception. Note the following suggestions for improving your rate of transmission:

a. Talk slowly enough so that each word and phrase is spoken distinctly, particularly key words and phrases.

b. Talk slowly enough so the listener will have time, not only to hear, but to absorb the meaning.

3. *Pronunciation and Phrasing.*—As you notice the differences in the transmission of various pilots and controllers, you can readily identify those with exceptional skill. They sound natural and unhurried. The words are grouped for easy readability. They pronounce every word clearly and distinctly without apparent effort, without unnecessary words, and without "uh's" and "ah's." They create the impression of competence that any expert conveys after enough study and practice.

Practice

Many excellent audio training aids are available for practicing radiotelephone procedures. With tapes or records, a microphone, and writing materials, you can develop communications skills under excellent simulated conditions. Practice until you can transmit concisely, hear accurately, and listen critically. Hearing is largely a matter of having an adequate receiver and knowing how to tune it. Critical listening is a more complicated skill. You are ready to listen to a controller when you are thoroughly familiar with your communications equipment and are ready to copy the transmissions, evaluate what is said, and if necessary read it back without neglecting other cockpit duties that may demand your attention. Study of Air Traffic Control procedures under Instrument Flight Rules will enable you to "keep ahead" of communications— just as you keep ahead of your basic flying and

Time	Field elevation
0000—Zero Zero Zero Zero	10 ft.—Field elevation Wun Zero.
0920—Zero Niner Too Zero	75 ft.—Field elevation Seven Fife.
1200—Wun Too Zero Zero	583 ft.—Field elevation Fife Ait Tree.
1645—Wun Six Fower Fife	600 ft.—Field elevation Six Zero Zero.
	1,250 ft.—Field elevation Wun Too Fife Zero.
	2,500 ft.—Field elevation Too Fife Zero Zero.

FIGURE 9–4. Expressing time and field elevation.

Word or phrase	Meanings
Acknowledge	Let me know that you have received and understand this message.
Affirmative	Yes.
Correction	An error has been made in this transmission. The correct version is . . . .
Go ahead	Proceed with your message.
How do you hear me?	Self explanatory.
I say again	Self explanatory.
Negative	That is not correct.
Out	This conversation is ended and no response is expected.
Over	My transmission is ended and I expect a response from you.
Read back	Repeat all of this message back to me exactly as received after I have given "over."
Roger	I have received all of your last transmission. (To acknowledge receipt; shall not be used for any other purpose.)
Say again	Self explanatory.
Speak slower	Self explanatory.
Stand by	If used by itself it means, I must pause for a few seconds. If the pause is longer than a few seconds or if "standby" is used to prevent another station from transmitting, it must be followed by the word "out."
That is correct	Self explanatory.
Verify	Check with the originator.
Words twice	As a request—Communication is difficult: Please say every word twice.

FIGURE 9–5. Radiotelephone words and phrases.

navigation—by knowing what is ahead of you and attending to details in the proper sequence at the appropriate time.

Reminders on Use of Equipment

1. Maintain a "readiness" to communicate. With your flight log handy, charts in order, and other necessary materials readily available, you can eliminate fumbling and confusion. You cannot organize an intelligible message, or listen to one, in a disorganized cockpit.

2. Know your radiotelephone equipment and practice tuning it. Check the knobs, switches and selectors *before* you transmit. Monitor the frequency you are using before transmitting. If you hear nothing on a normally busy terminal frequency, for example, check your volume control; you may be interrupting another transmission.

3. Never subordinate aircraft control to communications. Don't turn your aircraft loose in your haste to transmit.

4. Learn to take notes as you listen. Make written notes of times, altitudes, and other information as you hear it. You have enough to think about in planning ahead without having to waste time thinking back.

X. THE FEDERAL AIRWAYS SYSTEM AND CONTROLLED AIRSPACE

System Details

Up to this point, your instrument training has been concerned largely with problems within the cockpit. While you have been acquiring proficiency in the use of basic flight instruments and NAV/COM equipment, your instructor has kept a watchful eye on other traffic. You have been told what maneuvers to execute, what radials to fly, when and where to go. Instrument flying would be relatively simple if your instrument training ended with mastery of these basic techniques and with a safety pilot aboard to keep you headed in the right direction, safely separated from other traffic. Your problem now is to learn how to use the facilities, services, and procedures established by the Air Traffic System to provide directional guidance, terrain clearance, and safe separation for aircraft operating under Instrument Flight Rules. The extent of this system and the facilities maintained for airspace users can be appreciated by visualizing the tremendous expansion of aviation since 1903 when only one airplane used the national airspace.

Figure 10–1 shows the low-frequency radio facilities serving the Los Angeles-Oakland area in 1934. The navaids provided only one route between those two terminals via the Los Angeles, Fresno, and Oakland range legs.

In 1964, 30 years later, the system in this area included the VOR facilities and routes shown in Figure 10–2 as well as instrument approach aids, radar coverage, and numerous other facilities and services.

By the late-1970's, the Nation's air fleet exceeded 200,000 aircraft, with as many as 90,000 people aloft at any busy hour, most of them converging on, or departing from, major metropolitan areas. In 1977, the 2,491 navigation aids needed to keep these aircraft moving safely throughout the 50 States were listed as follows (exclusive of

161

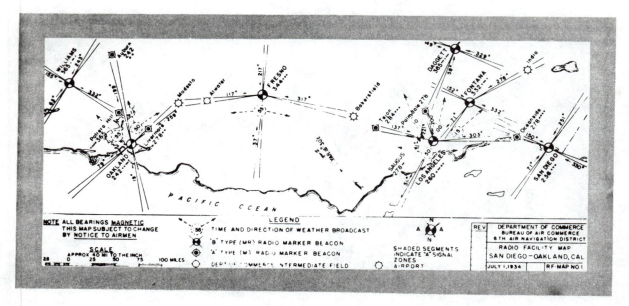

FIGURE 10–1. Navaids during the 1930's.

non-directional beacons, precision approach radar systems, and non-Federal or special use aids):

- 25 Air Route Traffic Control Centers—(includes 2 Center/RAPCONS).
- 104 Air Route Surveillance Radar (ARSR).
- 177 Airport Surveillance Radar (ASR)—(includes 29 military radars which provide service for civil airports).
- 1,034 VOR/VORTACS—(includes 66 non-Federal and 53 military which have been incorporated into the "Common System").
- 650 Instrument Landing System—(includes 5 LDAs, 48 non-Federal, and 6 military ILS's).
- 489 Towers (includes 28 non-Federal and 45 military).
- 12 Combined Station/Towers.

The airways system resembles its automotive counterpart in many ways. Whether you travel by Federal airway or Federal highway, the system must provide a controlling agency, procedural rules, directional guidance, highways between population centers, and a means of access between highways and terminals. The components of the Air Traffic System, the controlling agency, and the procedures established for your use of the system are discussed in this and the following chapter. In a later chapter, you will apply what you have learned to a sample flight planning problem.

Federal Airways

The Federal airways network is based upon the electronic aids already discussed. The navigation system has three component parts: the pilot, the airborne receiver, and the ground navigation facility. When the recognized errors which each con-

tributes are considered, a total system accuracy can be determined. When this accuracy is applied, the area in which obstruction clearance should be provided becomes apparent. Inherent in this concept is the premise that the pilot fly, as closely as possible, the prescribed courses and altitudes.

Obstruction clearance criteria are based on the airborne receiver contributing not more than ±4.2° error to the total system error. Pilot performance must assure a tracking accuracy within ±2.5° (quarter scale) needle deflection. Where these standards are not assured by the pilot, the safety and accuracy normally provided by the criteria are impaired. The VOR and VORTAC facilities are the foundation of the system. Connecting these facilities is the network of routes forming the Victor Airway and Jet Route Systems.

Each Federal Airway is based on a centerline that extends from one navigation aid or intersection to another navigation aid (or through several navigation aids or intersections) specified for that airway. The infinite number of radials transmitted by the VOR permits 360 possible separate airway courses to or from the facility, one for each degree of azimuth. Thus, a given VOR located within approximately 100 miles of several other VORs may be used to establish a number of different airways. For example, 8 radials at Humble VORTAC define 10 low altitude airways (Fig. 10–3).

Three route systems have been established for air navigation purposes: (1) Victor Airway System, (2) Jet Route System, and (3) Area Navigation (RNAV) Route System. The Victor Airway System consists of airways designated from 1,200 feet above the surface (or in some instances higher) to but not including 18,000 feet MSL. The Jet Route System consists of jet routes established from 18,000 feet MSL to FL 450. The RNAV Route Sys-

162

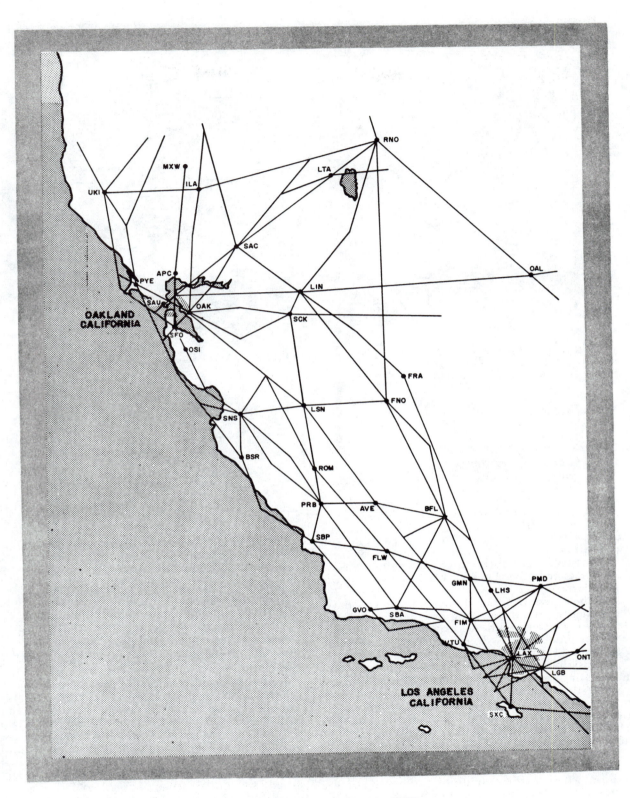

FIGURE 10–2. Navaids during the 1960's.

163

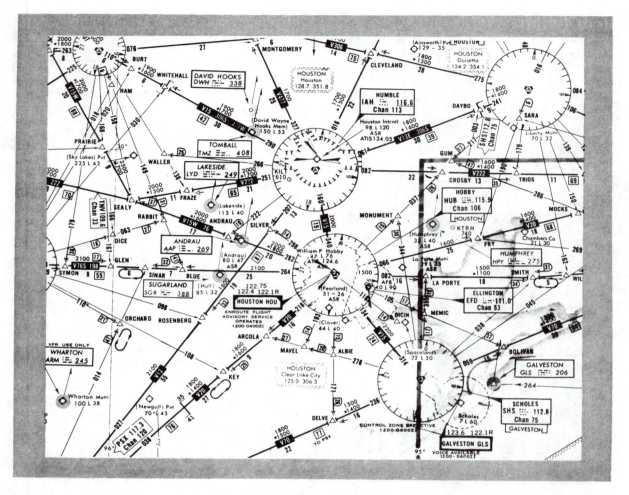

FIGURE 10-3. VOR radials and airways.

tem presently consists of a structure of approximately 76 high altitude routes (18,000 feet MSL to FL 450) embracing the 48 contiguous states. The airspace above FL 450 is for point-to-point operation.

To the extent possible, these route systems have been aligned in an overlying manner to facilitate transition between each. At certain airports, Standard Terminal Arrival Routes (STARs) have been established for application to arriving IFR aircraft.

Like highways, Victor Airways are designated by number—generally north/south airways are *odd;* east/west airways are *even.* When airways coincide on the same radial, the airway segment shows the numbers of all the airways on it. For example, the Humble 290 radial in the chart excerpt (Fig. 10-3), defines three airways V15—306S—477W.

Alternate Victor Airways are used for lateral separation when traffic conditions require it, or as "one-way" routes for efficient control of traffic flow to and from terminal areas. For example, V-14 serves as a normal arrival route into Oklahoma City from Tulsa, Oklahoma. V-14N, lying to the north

of V-14, is an alternate arrival route from Tulsa. V-14S, to the south of V-14, is a normal departure route from Oklahoma City.

Preferred IFR Routes have been established between major terminals to guide pilots in planning their routes of flight, to minimize route changes, and to aid in the orderly management of air traffic using Federal airways. Both high- and low-altitude preferred routes are listed in the *Airport/Facility Directory.*

Terminal Routes (Standard Terminal Arrival Routes [STARs] and Standard Instrument Departures [SIDs])— These Standard Routes have been established and published as an air traffic control aid in certain complex terminal areas. They help reduce verbiage on clearance delivery and control frequencies and provide the pilot with a description of terminal routing. Both SIDs and STARs are currently published in National Ocean Survey booklets. Instructions for pilot use of these coded routes are contained in the *Airman's Information Manual.* Certain complex terminal areas are covered by Area Charts.

164

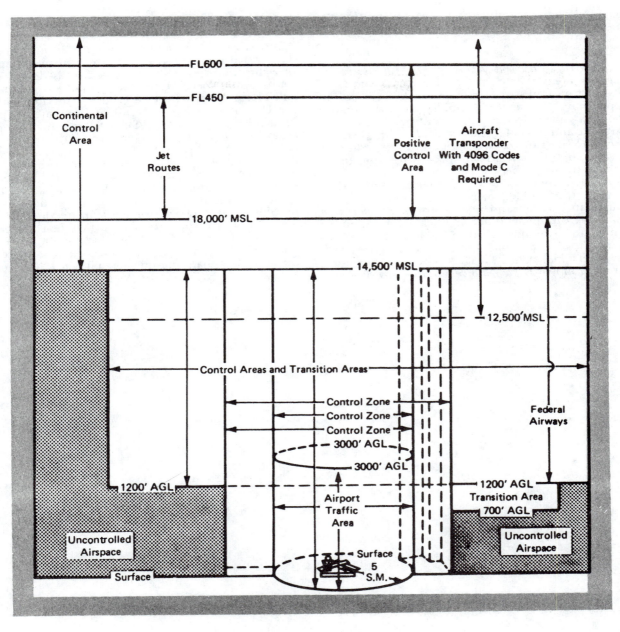

FIGURE 10-4. Controlled airspace.

Controlled Airspace

Considerations of safety, users needs, and volume of flight operations are some of the factors which have dictated the establishment of controlled airspace. Such airspace includes the *Continental Control Area, Control Areas, Control Zones, Terminal Control Areas,* and *Transition Areas.* Figure 10-4 is a three dimensional portrayal of certain features of the airspace structure.

It is essential that you, as an instrument pilot, be well informed regarding the various airspace segments. Refer to the *Airman's Information Manual* for current information.

Radio Navigation Charts

Radio navigation data are shown on many types of aeronautical charts, including the Sectional and WAC charts familiar to the VFR pilot. More specialized charts, compiled and printed by the National Ocean Survey, include several types for use by the instrument pilot.

Standard Instrument Departure (SID) Charts are designed to expedite clearance delivery and to facilitate transition between takeoff and en route operations. These charts, published in two bound booklets, provide departure routing clearance in graphic and textual form. *Standard Terminal Arrival Route (STAR) Charts* are designed to expedite air traffic control arrival route procedures and to facilitate transition between en route and instrument approach operations. These charts, published in one bound booklet, provide arrival route procedures in graphic and textual form. *Enroute Low Altitude Charts* provide aeronautical information for en route navigation (IFR) in the low altitude stratum. *Area Charts,* which are part of this series, furnish terminal data in a larger scale in congested areas. *Enroute High Altitude Charts* provide aero-nautical information for en route instrument navigation (IFR) in the high altitude stratum. *Instrument Approach Procedure Charts* portray the aeronautical data which is required to execute instrument approaches to airports. Each procedure is designed for use with a specific type of electronic navigational aid. These charts reflect the criteria associated with the U.S. Standards for Terminal Instrument Approach Procedures (TERPS). Detailed information regarding their use is contained in Advisory Circular 90–1A, *Civil Use of U.S. Government Instrument Approach Procedure Charts,* which is reproduced in the following pages of this chapter. Regarding helicopter minimums, FAR 97.3 (d-1) states, "Helicopters may also use . . . the Category A minimum descent altitude (MDA) or decision height (DH). The required visibility minimum may be reduced to one-half the published visibility minimum for Category A aircraft, but in no case may it be reduced to less than one-quarter mile or 1,200 feet RVR."

CIVIL USE OF U.S. GOVERNMENT INSTRUMENT
APPROACH PROCEDURE CHARTS
(Reproduced from AC 90–1A)

1. <u>APPLICATION.</u> Civil Instrument Approach Procedures are established by the Federal Aviation Administration after careful analysis of obstructions, terrain features and navigational facilities. Narrative type procedures authorized by the FAA are published in the Federal Register as rule making action under Federal Aviation Regulations, Part 97. Based on this information, the U.S. Coast and Geodetic Survey, and other charting agencies, publish instrument approach charts as a service to the instrument pilot. FAR 91.116a requires use of specified procedures by all pilots approaching for landing under Instrument Flight Rules.   Appropriate maneuvers, which include altitudes, courses, and other limitations, are prescribed in these procedures. They have been established for safe letdown during instrument flight conditions as a result of many years of accumulated experience. It is important that all pilots thoroughly understand these procedures and their use.

2. <u>DEFINITIONS.</u>
   a. MDA – "Minimum descent altitude" means the lowest altitude, expressed in feet above mean sea level, to which descent is authorized on final approach, where no electronic glide slope is provided, or during circle-to-land maneuvering in execution of a standard instrument approach procedure.
   b. DH – "Decision height", with respect to the operation of aircraft, means the height at which a decision must be made, during an ILS or PAR instrument approach, to either continue the approach or to execute a missed approach. This height is expressed in feet above mean sea level (MSL), and for Category II ILS operation the decision height is additionally expressed as a radio altimeter setting.
   c. HAA – "Height above airport" indicates the height of the MDA above the published airport elevation. HAA is published in conjunction with circling minimums for all types of approaches.
   d. HAT – "Height above touchdown" indicates the height of the DH or MDA above the highest runway elevation in the touchdown zone (first 3,000 feet of runway). HAT is published in conjunction with straight-in minimums.
   e. NoPT – means No Procedure Turn Required.
   f. "Precision approach procedure" means a standard instrument approach in which an electronic glide slope is provided (ILS or PAR).
   g. "Non-precision approach procedure" means a standard instrument approach in which no electronic glide slope is provided.
   h. <u>Instrument approach procedure.</u> An instrument approach procedure is one that is prescribed and approved for a specific airport by competent authority and published in an acceptable aeronautical information publication.
      (1) <u>U.S. civil standard instrument approach procedures</u> are approved by the FAA as prescribed under FAR Part 97 and are published in the Federal Register. For the convenience of the user, the aeronautical data prescribed in standard instrument approach procedures are portrayed on instrument approach procedure charts and may be obtained from Coast and Geodetic Survey and other publishers of aeronautical charts.
      (2) <u>U.S. military standard instrument approach procedures</u> are established and published by the Department of Defense and are contained in the DOD Flight Information Publication (FLIP). Civilian requests for military procedures should be directed to the Coast and Geodetic Survey, Washington Science Center, Attn: Distribution Division, Rockville, Maryland 20852.

(3) Special instrument approach procedures are approved by the FAA for individual operators and are not published in FAR Part 97 for public use.

(4) Foreign country standard instrument approach procedures are established and published as contained in that country's accepted Aeronautical Information Publication (AIP).

3. DISCUSSION OF MAJOR CHANGES.

   a. Minimum Descent Altitude (MDA)/Decision Height (DH) Concept.

      (1) IFR landing minimums. FAR sections 91.116 and 91.117, effective November 18, 1967, contain new rules applicable to landing minimums. Ceiling minimums are no longer prescribed in approach procedures as a landing limit. The published visibility is the required weather condition for landing as prescribed in FAR 91.116b. FAR 91 now allows approach down to the prescribed minimum descent altitude (MDA) or decision height (DH), as appropriate to the procedure being executed, without regard to reported ceiling.

      (2) Descent below MDA or DH. No person may operate an aircraft below the prescribed minimum descent altitude or continue an approach below the decision height unless —

         (a) The aircraft is in a position from which a normal approach can be made to the runway of intended landing; and

         (b) The approach threshold of that runway, or approach lights or other markings identifiable with the approach end of that runway, is clearly visible to the pilot.

         (c) If, upon arrival at the missed approach point, or at any time thereafter, any of the above requirements are not met, the pilot shall immediately execute the appropriate missed approach procedure.

         NOTE: The former FAR authorization to descend 50 feet below the applicable minimum landing altitude when clear of clouds is eliminated.

      (3) Conversion of ceiling MDA or DH. Effective November 18, 1967, the Federal Aviation Regulations were amended to provide that if the landing minimums in the instrument approach procedure are stated in terms of ceiling and visibility, the visibility minimum is the applicable landing minimum as prescribed in FAR 91.116b. A ceiling minimum shall be added to the field elevation, and that value is observed as the MDA or DH as appropriate to the procedure being executed.

      (4) Publication of landing minimums. The new Government-produced charts always contain the following information listed in this order: MDA or DH, visibility, HAA or HAT, and military minimums (ceiling and visibility) for each aircraft approach category.

         NOTE: Since the chart is used by both civil and military pilots, the ceiling, as well as visibility, required by the military will be published in parentheses. Civil operators should disregard this information.

         (a) Following are examples of published landing minimums. (Extracted from sample chart Figure 5.)

            1 Straight-in precision. An example of straight-in ILS minimums is shown below. The touchdown zone elevation is 965 feet, whereas the airport elevation is 983 feet.

STRAIGHT-IN TO RUNWAY 14	DH	VIS	HAT	MILITARY
S-ILS 14	1165 /	24	200	(200-½)

It should be noted that the visibility is separated from the DH by a slant line (/) when it is RVR, and separated by a hyphen (-) when it is meteorological visibility. This will help differentiate the two visibility values.

168

RVR is indicated in 100's of feet, and meteorological visibility is in statute miles. If RVR were not authorized, it would appear 1165-½.

2 <u>Straight-in non-precision.</u> When the ILS approach procedure is used but the aircraft does not have a glide slope receiver or the glide slope ground equipment is out of service, localizer minimums apply to the straight-in landing on that runway.

	<u>MDA</u>	<u>VIS</u>	<u>HAT</u>	<u>MILITARY</u>
S-LOCALIZER 14	1500 /	24	535	(600-½)

3 <u>Circling.</u> Visibility for circling is always in a meteorological value of statute miles. Height of the MDA above the airport elevation is provided by HAA.

	<u>MDA</u>	<u>VIS</u>	<u>HAA</u>	<u>MILITARY</u>
Circling	1640 —	1	657	(700-1)

b. <u>Standard Take-off Minimums.</u> FAR 91.116(c) prescribes take-off rules for FAR 121, 129, and 135 operators and establishes standard take-off visibility minimums as follows:

(1) Aircraft having two engines or less - one statute mile.

(2) Aircraft having more than two engines - one-half statute mile.

In cases where departure procedures or non-standard take-off minimums are prescribed, a symbol ▽ is shown on the chart indicating that the separate listing should be consulted. See figures 5, 13, and 17. Ceiling minimums are no longer prescribed for take-off except for those runways where a ceiling minimum is required to enable the pilot to see and avoid obstructions. The ceiling and visibility minimums previously prescribed apply until individual procedures are reissued under the new criteria.

c. <u>Standard Alternate Minimums.</u> Alternate minimums specified for an instrument approach procedure continue to require both ceiling and visibility minimums. FAR 91.83 establishes standard IFR alternate minimums as follows:

(1) Precision approach procedure: ceiling 600 feet and visibility - two statute miles.

(2) Non-precision approach procedure: ceiling 800 feet and visibility - two statute miles.

The standard IFR alternate minimums apply unless higher minimums are specified for the procedure used. These are denoted by a symbol △ on the chart indicating that the separate listing should be consulted. See figures 6, 14, and 18.

d. <u>Inoperative Components, Visual Aids, and Adjustment of Landing Minimums.</u>

(1) <u>Components and Visual Aids.</u>

(a) <u>Precision approach procedure.</u>

ILS (Instrument Landing System) basic components are localizer, glide slope, outer marker and middle marker. PAR (Precision Approach Radar) basic components are azimuth, range, and elevation information.

The following visual aids may supplement the ILS or PAR, and may provide lower visibility minimums:

ALS   Approach Lighting System, 3000' of Standard High Intensity Lights with Sequence Flashers.

SALS   Short Approach Lighting System, 1500' of Standard ALS.

SSALR   Simplified Short Approach Lighting System (1400' of High Intensity Light Bars) plus 1600' of Runway Alignment Indicator Lights (RAIL - Sequence Flashers).

MALSR   Medium Intensity Lighting of Simplified Short Approach Lighting System (1400' of Medium Intensity Light Bars) plus 1600' of Runway Alignment Indicator Lights (RAIL - Sequence Flashers).

TDZL   Touchdown Zone Lights.
RCLS   Runway Centerline Light System.
HIRL   High Intensity Runway Edge Lights.
MIRL   Medium Intensity Runway Edge Lights.

(b) <u>Non-precision approach procedures.</u>

The basic component is the facility providing course guidance, i.e., VOR, NDB, etc. In the case of VOR/DME type procedures, basic components are the VOR and DME facilities.

All of the visual aids listed under precision approach procedures may supplement non-precision procedures plus the following:

MALS   Medium Intensity Approach Light System. Total 1400'.
RAIL   Runway Alignment Indicator Light.
REIL   Runway End Identifier Lights.

(2) <u>Previous approach charts (old chart format).</u>   In many cases, minimums lower than those authorized in the straight-in line are authorized when lighting aids such as REIL, ALS, etc., are installed for the landing runway. Also, minimums higher than those authorized in its straight-in line are required when certain components of an ILS system are inoperative. This information concerning minimums is published as notes below the minimums section.   (Figure 1.)

PREVIOUS APPROACH CHART PRESENTATION

MINIMA						FIELD EL
	65 knots or less 2 eng or less		Over 65 knots 2 eng or less		Over 65 knots Over 2 eng	
	DAY	NIGHT	DAY	NIGHT	DAY	NIGHT
T	300-1	300-1	300-1	300-1	200-½	200-½
C	500-1	500-1	500-1	500-1	500-1½	500-1½
S 21	500-1	500-1	500-1	500-1	500-1	500-1
A	•800-2	800-2	800-2	800-2	800-2	800-2

If Parkersburg FM received, the following minimums are authorized

S 21•	400-1	400-1	400-1	400-1	400-1	400-1

•400-¾ authorized, except for 4-engine turbojet aircraft, with operative REIL or high intensity runway lights.

FACILITY TO AERODROME: 211° 5.8 NM

TIME FROM FACILITY TO MISSED APPROACH					
KNOTS	90	100	110	130	150
MIN: SEC	3:52	3:29	3:10	2:41	2:19

(VOR)

MINIMA						FIELD ELE
	65 knots or less 2 eng or less		Over 65 knots 2 eng or less		Over 65 knots Over 2 eng	
	DAY	NIGHT	DAY	NIGHT	DAY	NIGHT
T	300-1	300-1	300-1	300-1	200-½	200-½
C °	600-1	600-1	600-1	600-1	600-1	500-1½
S 7L•	200-½	200-½	200-½	200-½	200-½	200-½
A	600-2	600-2	600-2	600-2	600-2	600-2

°400-1 required with any component of ILS inoperative, except 700-1 required when glide slope and 7-Mile DME Fix not utilized
†Except for 4-engine turbojet acft, 400-¾ authorized, with operative HIRL or 400-½ with operative ALS.
If glide slope not utilized and 7-Mile DME Fix from PUB VOR received, the following minimums are authorized:

C	600-1	600-1	600-1	600-1	600-1½	600-1½
S 7L†	400-1	400-1	400-1	400-1	400-1	400-1

RATE OF DESCENT ON GLIDE SLOPE					
KNOTS	90	100	110	130	150
FEET/MIN	475	530	585	690	795

(ILS)

Figure 1

(3) <u>Inoperative Components or Visual Aids Table (Pertaining to new chart format).</u>

(a) Since all air navigation facilities have a very low out-of-service time, the lowest landing minimums with all components and visual aids operating are published.

To determine landing minimums when components or aids of the system are inoperative or are not utilized, inoperative components or visual aids tables are published and appear on a separate sheet for insertion in the approach chart binders. This method was selected to reduce chart clutter.

170

INOPERATIVE COMPONENTS OR VISUAL AIDS TABLE

1 ILS and PAR with visibility of ½ mile (RVR 2400) or greater.

Inoperative Component or Aid	Increase DH	Increase Visibility	Approach Category
OM*, MM*	50 feet	By None	ABC
OM*, MM*	50 feet	By ¼ mile	D
ALS	50 feet	By ¼ mile	ABCD
SALS	50 feet	By ¼ mile	ABC

  ·*Not applicable to PAR

2 ILS and PAR with visibility minimum of 1,800 or 2,000 feet RVR.

Inoperative Component or Aid	Increase DH	Increase Visibility	Approach Category
OM*, MM*	50 feet	To ½ mile	ABC
OM*, MM*	50 feet	To ¾ mile	D
ALS	50 feet	To ¾ mile	ABCD
HIRL, TDZL, RCLS	None	To ½ mile	ABCD
RVR	None	To ½ mile	ABCD

  *Not applicable to PAR

3 VOR, VOR/DME, LOC, LDA, and ASR.

Inoperative Visual Aid	Increase MDA	Increase Visibility	Approach Category
ALS, SALS	None	By ½ mile	ABC
HIRL, MALS, REILS	None	By ½ mile	ABC

4 NDB (ADF) and RNG.

Inoperative Visual Aid	Increase MDA	Increase Visibility	Approach Category
ALS	None	By ¼ mile	ABC

5 LOC Approaches

Inoperative Component or Aid	Increase MDA	Increase Visibility	Approach Category
ALS, MM	None	By ¼ mile	D

Figure 2

...tion of the inoperative components or visual aids table. When using
...sed approach charts, the minimums must be adjusted in accordance
...inoperative component or visual aids table. This will be done when
...component or visual aid pertinent to the procedure is inoperative
...'ized.

...or more components inoperative, only the greater or greatest in-
...titude or visibility is required; and the increases are not cumulative.

...ual aid has been installed, but reduced visibility minimums have
...horized, the above tables would not be used. The following note
... below the minimums section.

xample: "Inoperative table does not apply to ALS or HIRL
Runway 12R."   (See figure 14.)

ne following general rules will always apply to inoperative components.

<u>1</u> Operative runway lights are required for night operation.

<u>2</u> When the facility providing course guidance is inoperative, the procedure is not authorized. On VOR/DME procedures: when either VOR or DME is inoperative, the procedure is not authorized.

<u>3</u> When the ILS glide slope is inoperative or not utilized, the published straight-in localizer minimum applies.

<u>4</u> Compass locator or precision radar may be substituted for the ILS outer or middle marker.

<u>5</u> Surveillance radar may be a substitute for the ILS outer marker. DME, at the glide slope site, may be substituted for the outer marker when published on the ILS procedure.

<u>6</u> Facilities that establish a stepdown fix, i.e., 75 MHz FM, off course VOR radial, etc. are not components of the basic approach procedure, and applicable minimums for use, both with or without identifying the stepdown fix, are published in the minimums section.   (See example figure 14.)

<u>7</u> Additional methods of identifying a fix may be used when authorized on the procedure.

<u>8</u> Runway Visual Range (RVR) Minimums.

To authorize RVR minimums, the following components and visual aids must be available in addition to basic components of the approach procedure.

<u>a</u> Precision approach procedures.

(1) RVR reported for the runway.
(2) HIRL.
(3) All weather runway markings.

<u>b</u> Non-precision approach procedures.

(1) RVR reported for the runway.
(2) HIRL.
(3) Instrument runway markings.

<u>c</u> Inoperative RVR minimums. Where RVR visibility minimums are published and the runway markings become unusable, the necessary adjustment will be accomplished by NOTAM and by air traffic advisory.

If RVR minimums for take-off or landing are published in an instrument approach procedure, but RVR is inoperative and cannot be reported for the runway at that time, it is necessary that the RVR minimums which are specified in the procedure be converted and applied as ground visibility in accordance with the table below.

172

RVR	Visibility (statute miles)
1600 feet	1/4 mile
2400 feet	1/2 mile
3200 feet	5/8 mile
4000 feet	3/4 mile
4500 feet	7/8 mile
5000 feet	1 mile
6000 feet	1 1/4 mile

e. **Aircraft Approach Categories.** Minimums are specified for the various aircraft speed/ weight combinations. Speeds are based upon a value 1.3 times the stalling speed of the aircraft in the landing configuration at maximum certificated gross landing weight. Thus they are COMPUTED values. See FAR 97.3 (b). An aircraft can fit into only one category, that being the highest category in which it meets either specification. For example, a 30,000 pound aircraft landing weight combined with a computed approach speed of 130 knots would place the aircraft in Category C. If it is necessary, however, to maneuver at speeds in excess of the upper limit of the speed range for each category, the minimum for the next higher approach category should be used. For example, a B-727-100 which falls in Category C, but is circling to land at a speed in excess of 140 knots, should use the approach category "D" minimum when circling to land. See following category limits and reference table.

Approach Category	Speed/Weight
A :	Speed less than 91 knots; weight less than 30,001 pounds.
B :	Speed 91 knots or more but less than 121 knots; weight 30,001 pounds or more but less than 60,001 pounds.
C :	Speed 121 knots or more but less than 141 knots; weight 60,001 pounds or more but less than 150,001 pounds.
D :	Speed 141 knots or more but less than 166 knots; weight 150,001 pounds or more.
E :	Speed 166 knots or more; any weight.

Reference Table for Determining Aircraft Approach Categories.

Category A

1.3 V_{so} less than 91 knots weight less than 30,001 pounds.

This Category includes civil single engine aircraft, light twins, and some of the heavier twins. Typical heavier aircraft in this Category are:

Make	AIRCRAFT Type/Model	SPEED IN KNOTS 1.3 V_{so}	MAX. LANDING Weight (lbs.)
Aero Commander	680 F	87	8,000
Cessna	310 C	83	4,830
Beechcraft	Queenair 65	90	7,350
Douglas	DC-3	78	26,500

Category B

1.3 V_{so} 91 knots or more but less than 121 knots; weight 30,001 pounds or more but less than 60,001 pounds.

This group includes most of the heavier twin-engine aircraft, some of which are listed as follows:

Make	AIRCRAFT Type/Model	SPEED IN KNOTS 1.3 V_{SO}	MAX. LANDING Weight (lbs.)
Grand Commander		92	8,500
Beechcraft	80	94	8,800
Beechcraft	65-90 Turboprop	100	8,835
Beechcraft	Super 18	97	9,500
Cessna	411 C	95	6,500
Convair	340	107	46,500
Convair	580	110	50,670
Fairchild	F-27	91	36,000

Category C

1.3 V_{SO} 121 knots or more but less than 141 knots; weight 60,001 pounds or more but less than 150,001 pounds.

This Category includes the four-engine propeller aircraft, and two and three engine turbojets, some of which are listed as follows:

Make	AIRCRAFT Type/Model	SPEED IN KNOTS 1.3 V_{SO}	MAX. LANDING Weight (lbs.)
Boeing	727-100	122	135,000
Caravelle	6	139	105,000
Douglas	DC-4	97	63,500
Douglas	DC-6	110	88,200
Douglas	DC-7	115	97,000
Douglas	DC-9-15	135	81,700
Douglas	DC-9-31	126	95,300
Jet Commander	1121	124	16,000
Lear Jet	24	125	11,800
Lear Jet	23	127	11,800
Lockheed	649, 749	93	89,500
Lockheed	1049	112	110,000
Lockheed	Jetstar	128	30,000
Lockheed	188	124	95,600

Category D

1.3 V_{SO} 141 knots or more but less than 166 knots; weight 150,001 pounds or more.
This Category includes the large four-engine turbojet aircraft, some of which are listed as follows:

Make	AIRCRAFT Type/Model	SPEED IN KNOTS 1.3 V_{SO}	MAX. LANDING Weight (lbs.)
Boeing	707/123B	133	190,000
Boeing	720/051B	131	175,000
Boeing	300B	126	207,000
Convair	880M	140	155,000
Convair	990A	160	202,000
Douglas	DC-8-21	136	155,000
Douglas	DC-8-61	144	240,000

f. Legend Pages contain the Plain View Symbols, Profile information, Aerodrome Sketch information, and General Information and Abbreviations. The following figures 3 and 4 are Legend Pages to the Coast and Geodetic Survey instrument approach procedures charts.

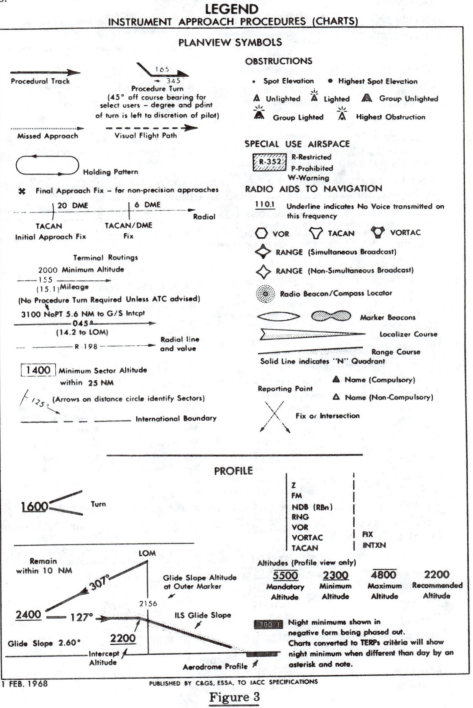

LEGEND
INSTRUMENT APPROACH PROCEDURES (CHARTS)

1 FEB. 1968   PUBLISHED BY C&GS, ESSA, TO IACC SPECIFICATIONS

Figure 3

LEGEND
INSTRUMENT APPROACH PROCEDURES (CHARTS)

AERODROME SKETCH

Runways

Hard Surface   Other Than Hard Surface   Hardstands/Taxiways

Closed Runways and Taxiways   Under Construction   Metal Surface

Over-run   Displaced Threshold

Arresting Gear

uni-directional   bi-directional   Jet Barrier

■ Control Tower
     When Control Tower and Rotating Beacon are co-located, Beacon symbol will be used and further identified as TWR.

★ Rotating Aerodrome Beacon.

☒ U.S. Navy Optical Landing System (OLS) "OLS" location is shown because of its height of approximately 7 feet and proximity to edge of runway may create an obstruction for some types of aircraft.

Ⓗ Helicopter Alighting Area (the prop type symbol is being phased out).

Approach light symbols are shown on a separate legend.

0.8% → UP   Total Runway Gradient
     (shown when runway gradient exceeds 0.3%)

0.8% → DOWN   Take-Off Gradient (shown when runway gradient for first 5000' exceeds 0.5%). This take-off gradient being phased out.

△ Indicates other than standard Alternate Minimums apply for U.S. Army and Civil, refer to tabulation.

▽ Indicates other than standard Take-off Minimums or departures procedures apply for Civil users. Civil users refer to tabulation.
     DOD users refer to Service Directives and DOD produced civil SID publication.

S/S   Sliding Scale applicable to U.S. Army

GENERAL INFORMATION & ABBREVIATIONS

All distances in nautical miles (except Visibility Data which is in statute miles and Runway Visual Range which is in hundreds of feet)

Runway dimensions in feet.

Elevations in feet Mean Sea Level.

All radials/bearings are Magnetic.

ADF	Automatic Direction Finder
ALS	Approach Light System.
BC	Back Course.
CHAN	Channel.
DH	Decision Height.
DME	Distance Measuring Equipment.
HAA	Height Above Aerodrome.
HAT	Height Above Touchdown.
HIRL	High Intensity Runway Lights.
INTXN	Intersection.
LDA	Localizer Type Directional Aid
LDIN	Lead in Light System
LOC	Localizer
MALS	Medium Intensity Approach Light System.
MDA	Minimum Descent Altitude.
NDB	Non-directional Radio Beacon.
NoPT	No Procedure Turn Required Unless ATC advised.
PAR/ASR	Published Radar Minimums at this Aerodrome.
Radar Required	Radar vectoring required for this approach.
Radar Vectoring	May be expected through any portion of the Nav Aid Approach, except final.
RAIL	Runway Alignment Indicator Lights
RBn	Radio Beacon.
REIL	Runway End Identifier Lights.
RCLS	Runway Centerline Light System
Runway Touchdown Zone	First 3000' of Runway.
RVR	Runway Visual Range.
SALS	Short Approach Light System.
(S) SALS	(Simplified) Short Approach Light System.
TAC	TACAN
TDZ	Touchdown Zone
TDZL	Touchdown Zone Lights

1 FEB. 1968   PUBLISHED BY C&GS, ESSA, TO IACC SPECIFICATIONS

Figure 4

g. Revised Format for Government-Produced Instrument Approach Procedure Charts.
Complete revision to instrument approach chart format has been made. Each chart
consists of five sections: margin identification, plan view, profile view, landing minimum
section (and notes), and aerodrome sketch. See figures 5 and 6 below.

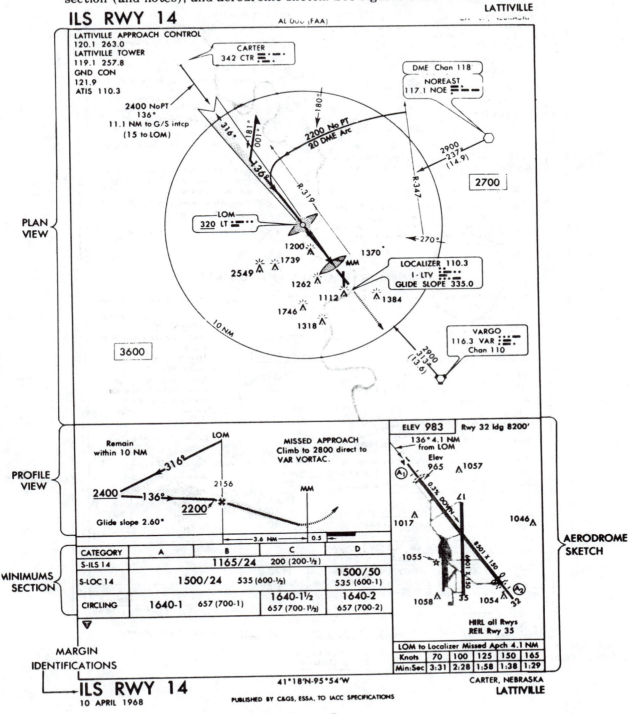

Figure 5

VOR RWY 12R

GRENZALL-WEST
NIXA, MISSOURI

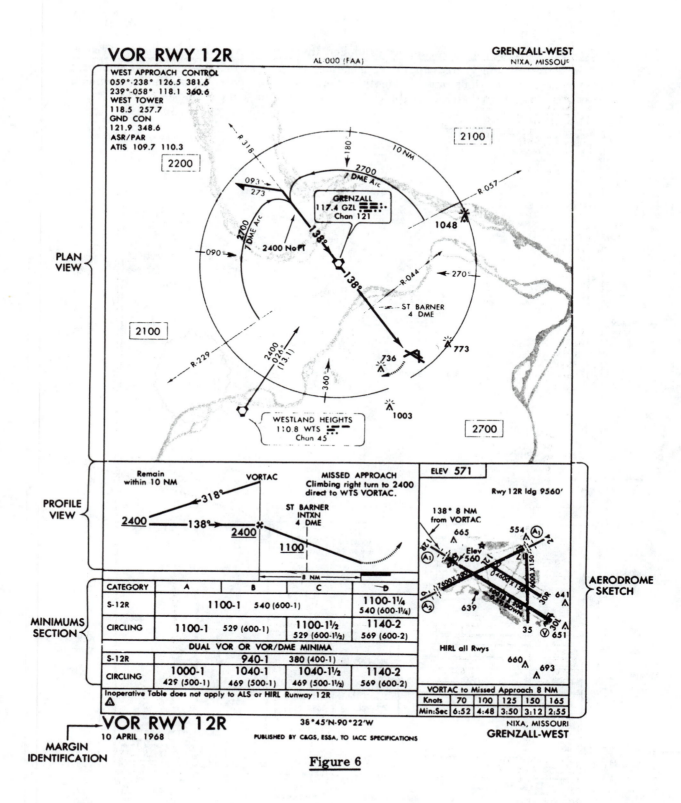

PLAN VIEW

WEST APPROACH CONTROL
059°-238° 126.5 381.6
239°-058° 118.1 360.6
WEST TOWER
118.5 257.7
GND CON
121.9 348.6
ASR/PAR
ATIS 109.7 110.3

2200

2100

R-316

093°
273

090°

2700 7 DME Arc

2400 No PT

138°

138°

GRENZALL
117.4 GZL
Chan 121

2100

10 NM
180

2700
7 DME Arc

2100

R-057

1048

R-044

270°

ST BARNER
4 DME

773

736

1003

R-229

2400
026°
(13.1)

360°

WESTLAND HEIGHTS
110.8 WTS
Chan 45

2700

PROFILE VIEW

Remain within 10 NM

318°

VORTAC

MISSED APPROACH
Climbing right turn to 2400
direct to WTS VORTAC.

2400

138°

2400

ST BARNER
INTXN
4 DME

1100

8 NM

ELEV 571

Rwy 12R ldg 9560'

138° 8 NM
from VORTAC.

665
554
Elev 560
641
639
35
651
660
693

HIRL all Rwys

AERODROME SKETCH

MINIMUMS SECTION

CATEGORY	A	B	C	D
S-12R	1100-1 540 (600-1)			1100-1¼ 540 (600-1¼)
CIRCLING	1100-1 529 (600-1)		1100-1½ 529 (600-1½)	1140-2 569 (600-2)
DUAL VOR OR VOR/DME MINIMA				
S-12R	940-1 380 (400-1)			
CIRCLING	1000-1 429 (500-1)	1040-1 469 (500-1)	1040-1½ 469 (500-1½)	1140-2 569 (600-2)

Inoperative Table does not apply to ALS or HIRL Runway 12R

VORTAC to Missed Approach 8 NM				
Knots	70	100	125	150	165
Min:Sec	6:52	4:48	3:50	3:12	2:55

VOR RWY 12R
10 APRIL 1968

36°45'N-90°22'W

PUBLISHED BY C&GS, ESSA, TO IACC SPECIFICATIONS

NIXA, MISSOURI
GRENZALL-WEST

MARGIN IDENTIFICATION

Figure 6

178

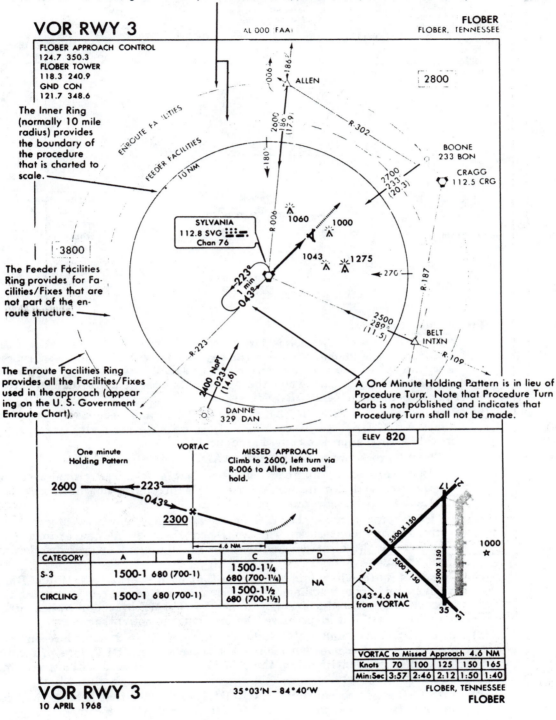

VOR RWY 3

FLOBER APPROACH CONTROL
124.7 350.3
FLOBER TOWER
118.3 240.9
GND CON
121.7 348.6

FLOBER
FLOBER, TENNESSEE

The Inner Ring (normally 10 mile radius) provides the boundary of the procedure that is charted to scale.

The Feeder Facilities Ring provides for Facilities/Fixes that are not part of the enroute structure.

The Enroute Facilities Ring provides all the Facilities/Fixes used in the approach (appearing on the U. S. Government Enroute Chart).

ENROUTE FACILITIES

FEEDER FACILITIES

10 NM

3800

2800

ALLEN

R-302

BOONE
233 BON

CRAGG
112.5 CRG

SYLVANIA
112.8 SVG
Chan 76

1060
1000
1043
1275

270°

R-187

2700
233°
(20.3)

2500
289°
(11.5)

BELT INTXN

R-109

223°
1 min
043°

R-223

R-006

2400 NoPT
023°
(14.6)

DANNE
329 DAN

A One Minute Holding Pattern is in lieu of Procedure Turn. Note that Procedure Turn barb is not published and indicates that Procedure Turn shall not be made.

ELEV 820

One minute Holding Pattern

VORTAC

MISSED APPROACH
Climb to 2600, left turn via R-006 to Allen Intxn and hold.

2600 — 223°
043°
2300

4.6 NM

1000

5500 X 150
5500 X 150
5500 X 150

043°4.6 NM from VORTAC

17

35 / 3

CATEGORY	A	B	C	D
S-3	1500-1 680 (700-1)		1500-1¼ 680 (700-1¼)	NA
CIRCLING	1500-1 680 (700-1)		1500-1½ 680 (700-1½)	

VORTAC to Missed Approach 4.6 NM					
Knots	70	100	125	150	165
Min:Sec	3:57	2:46	2:12	1:50	1:40

VOR RWY 3
10 APRIL 1968

35°03'N – 84°40'W

FLOBER, TENNESSEE
FLOBER

Figure 7

TOP MARGIN IDENTIFICATION

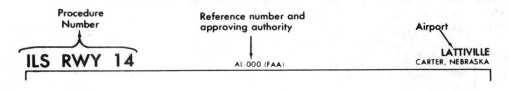

Procedure Number

Reference number and approving authority

Airport

ILS RWY 14

AL 000 (FAA)

LATTIVILLE
CARTER, NEBRASKA

BOTTOM MARGIN IDENTIFICATION

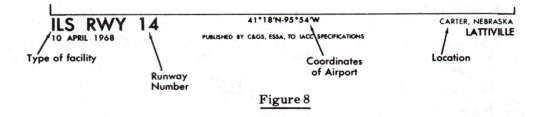

ILS RWY 14
10 APRIL 1968

41°18'N-95°54'W
PUBLISHED BY C&GS, ESSA, TO IACC SPECIFICATIONS

CARTER, NEBRASKA
LATTIVILLE

Type of facility

Runway Number

Coordinates of Airport

Location

Figure 8

(1) **Margin Identification.**

  (a) The procedure identification is derived from the type facility providing final approach course guidance and (1) runway number when the approach course is within 30° of the runway centerline, i.e., ILS Rwy 14, or (2) sequential number for the airport when the approach course is more than 30° from runway centerline, i.e., VOR-1, VOR-2, etc.

  (b) Nondirectional Beacon (NDB), Localizer (LOC) and Localizer Type Directional Aid (LDA) are used to identify more accurately the type facility providing final approach course guidance.

  1 "NDB" procedure number replaces ADF type procedure.

  2 "LOC" procedure number indicates that a localizer provides course guidance and a glide slope (ground facility) has not been installed. (Includes ILS back course procedures.)

  3 "LDA" procedure number is the same as localizer but is not aligned with the runway centerline. The approach chart should be examined to determine the direction and degrees of alignment away from runway centerline.

  (c) VOR/DME procedure number means that both operative VOR and DME receivers and ground equipment in normal operation are required to use the procedure. As stated previously, in the VOR/DME procedure, when either the VOR or DME is inoperative, the procedure is not authorized.

  (d) When DME arcs and DME fixes are authorized in a procedure and the procedure number does not include the three letter "DME" type of facility in the margin identification, the procedure may be used without utilizing the DME equipment.

  (e) VORTAC type procedure is a VOR/DME procedure that is authorized for an aircraft equipped with either VOR/DME or TACAN receiver.

PLAN VIEW
Lattiville Airport
Carter, Nebraska

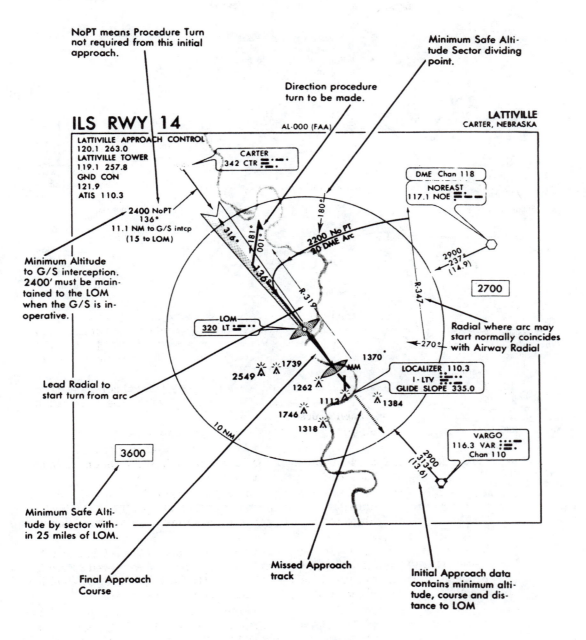

NoPT means Procedure Turn not required from this initial approach.

Direction procedure turn to be made.

Minimum Safe Altitude Sector dividing point.

ILS RWY 14

AL-000 (FAA)

LATTIVILLE
CARTER, NEBRASKA

LATTIVILLE APPROACH CONTROL
120.1 263.0
LATTIVILLE TOWER
119.1 257.8
GND CON
121.9
ATIS 110.3

CARTER
342 CTR

DME Chan 118
NOREAST
117.1 NOE

2400 NoPT
136°
11.1 NM to G/S intcp
(15 to LOM)

2200 No PT
20 DME Arc

316°

181°
001°

136°

R-319°

2900
237°
(14.9)

R-347

2700

Minimum Altitude to G/S interception. 2400' must be maintained to the LOM when the G/S is inoperative.

LOM
320 LT

Radial where arc may start normally coincides with Airway Radial

270°

Lead Radial to start turn from arc

2549 1739
1262
1370°
MM
1113 1384

LOCALIZER 110.3
I - LTV
GLIDE SLOPE 335.0

1746
1318

10 NM

VARGO
116.3 VAR
Chan 110

2900
313°
(13.6)

3600

Minimum Safe Altitude by sector within 25 miles of LOM.

Final Approach Course

Missed Approach track

Initial Approach data contains minimum altitude, course and distance to LOM

Figure 9

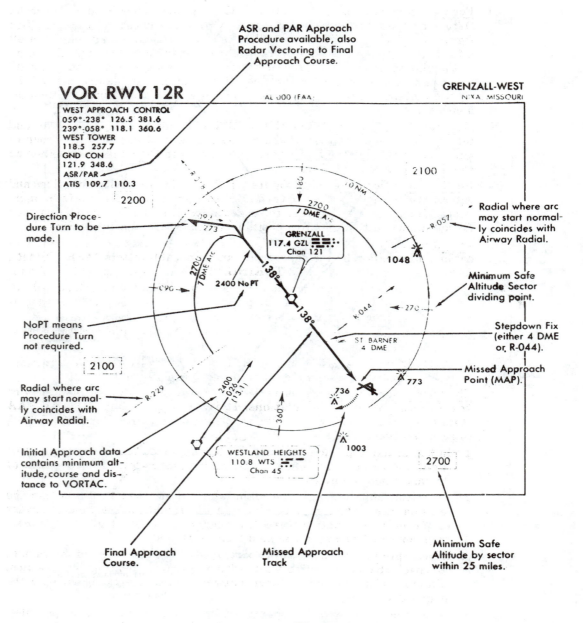

ASR and PAR Approach Procedure available, also Radar Vectoring to Final Approach Course.

VOR RWY 12R

GRENZALL-WEST
NIXA MISSOURI

WEST APPROACH CONTROL
059°-238° 126.5 381.6
239°-058° 118.1 360.6
WEST TOWER
118.5 257.7
GND CON
121.9 348.6
ASR/PAR
ATIS 109.7 110.3

Direction Procedure Turn to be made.

NoPT means Procedure Turn not required.

Radial where arc may start normally coincides with Airway Radial.

Initial Approach data contains minimum altitude, course and distance to VORTAC.

GRENZALL
117.4 GZL
Chan 121

2400 No PT

2100

WESTLAND HEIGHTS
110.8 WTS
Chan 45

Radial where arc may start normally coincides with Airway Radial.

Minimum Safe Altitude Sector dividing point.

Stepdown Fix (either 4 DME or R-044).

Missed Approach Point (MAP).

ST BARNER
4 DME

2700

Final Approach Course.

Missed Approach Track

Minimum Safe Altitude by sector within 25 miles.

Figure 10

182

(2) Plan View (Figures 7, 9, and 10). This is a bird's eye view of the entire procedure. Information pertaining to the initial approach segment, including procedure turn, minimum safe altitude for each sector, courses prescribed for the final approach segment and obstructions, is portrayed in this section. Navigation and communication frequencies are also listed on the plan view.

(a) Format. Normally, all information within the plan view is shown to scale. Data shown within the 10 NM distance circle is always shown to scale. (See figure 7.) The dashed circles, called concentric rings, are used when all information necessary to the procedure will not fit to scale within the limits of the plan view area. These circles then serve as a means to systematically arrange this information in their relative position outside and beyond the 10 NM distance circle. These concentric rings are labeled Enroute Facilities and Feeder Facilities.

(b) Enroute Facilities Ring. (See figure 7.) Radio aids to navigation, fixes and intersections that are part of the Enroute Low Altitude Airway structure and used in the approach procedure are shown in their relative position on this Enroute Facilities Ring.

(c) Feeder Facilities Ring. (See figure 7.) Radio aids to navigation, fixes and intersections used by the air traffic controller to direct aircraft to intervening facilities/fixes between the enroute structure and the initial approach fix are shown in their relative position on this Feeder Facilities Ring.

(d) The availability of RADAR (see figure 10) is indicated below the communications information by the appropriate and applicable letters "ASR", "PAR", "ASR/PAR" or "RADAR VECTORING." These terms are applied as follows:

1 ASR - means Airport Surveillance Radar instrument approach procedures are available at the airport, and also that Radar Vectoring is available for the procedure.

2 PAR - means Precision Approach Radar instrument approach procedures are available.

3 RADAR VECTORING - means Radar Vectoring is available but radar instrument approach procedures are not available.

(e) The term "initial approach" is explained in section 97.3(c) (1) of Part 97 of the Federal Aviation Regulations. It is further explained in the FAA Handbook "U.S. Standard for Terminal Instrument Procedures (TERPS)", page 15, section 3, INITIAL APPROACH.

1 In the initial approach, the aircraft has departed the en route phase of flight, and is maneuvering to enter an intermediate or final segment of the instrument approach.

2 An initial approach may be made along prescribed routes within the terminal area which may be along an arc, radial, course, heading, radar vector, or a combination thereof. Procedure turns and high altitude teardrop penetrations are initial approach segments.

3 Initial approach information is portrayed in the plan view of instrument approach charts by course lines, with an arrow indicating the direction. Minimum altitude and distance between fixes is also shown with the magnetic course.

4 When the term "NoPT" appears, an intermediate approach is provided. These altitudes shown with the term "NoPT" cannot be used as an initial approach altitude for the purpose of determining alternate airports requirements under FAR 91.23(c) and 91.83(b).

(f) <u>When an approach course is published on an ILS procedure</u> that does not require a procedure turn (NoPT), the following applies.

<u>1</u> In the case of a dog-leg track and no fix is depicted at the point of interception on the localizer course, the total distance is shown from the facility or fix to the LOM, or to an NDB associated with the ILS.

<u>2</u> The minimum altitude applies until the glide slope is intercepted, at which point the aircraft descends on the glide slope.

<u>3</u> When the glide slope is not utilized, this minimum altitude is maintained to the LOM (or to the NDB if appropriate).

<u>4</u> In isolated instances, when proceeding NoPT to the LOM and the glide slope cannot be utilized, a procedure turn will be required to descend for a straight-in approach and landing. In these cases, the requirement for a procedure turn will be annotated on the Plan View of the procedure chart.

(g) <u>Procedure turn</u> is the maneuver prescribed when it is necessary to reverse direction to establish the aircraft inbound on an intermediate or final approach course. It is a required maneuver except when the symbol NoPT is shown, when RADAR VECTORING is provided, when a one minute holding pattern is published in lieu of a procedure turn, or when the procedure turn is not authorized. The altitude prescribed for the procedure turn is a <u>minimum</u> altitude until the aircraft is established on the inbound course. The maneuver must be completed within the distance specified in the profile view.

<u>1</u> A barb indicates the direction or side of the outbound course on which the procedure turn is made. Headings are provided for course reversal using the 45° type procedure turn. However, the point at which the turn may be commenced and the type and rate of turn is left to the discretion of the pilot. Some of the options are the 45° procedure turn, the racetrack pattern, the tear-drop procedure turn, or the 80°—260° course reversal. These maneuvers are diagrammed in the FAA Instrument Flying Handbook (AC 61-27A), and the steps numbered under the figures are intended for student practice under no-wind conditions.

<u>2</u> Limitations on procedure turns.

<u>a</u> In the case of a radar initial approach to a final approach fix or position, or a timed approach from a holding fix, or where the procedure specifies "NoPT", no pilot may make a procedure turn unless, when he receives his final approach clearance, he so advises ATC and a clearance is received.

<u>b</u> When a tear-drop procedure turn is depicted and a course reversal is required, this type turn must be executed.

<u>c</u> When a one minute holding pattern replaces the procedure turn, the standard entry and the holding pattern must be followed except when RADAR VECTORING is provided or when NoPT is shown on the approach course. Diagrams of the holding pattern and entries into the pattern also are illustrated in the Handbook 61-27A. As in the procedure turn, the descent from the minimum holding pattern altitude to the final approach fix altitude (when lower) may not commence until the aircraft is established on the inbound course.

<u>d</u> The absence of the procedure turn barb in the Plan View indicates that a procedure turn is not authorized for that procedure.

<u>3</u> A Procedure Turn is not required when the symbol NoPT appears on an approach course shown on the Plan View. If a procedure turn is desired, descent below the procedure turn altitude should not be made since some NoPT altitudes may be lower than the procedure turn altitude.

PROFILE VIEW (Precision)

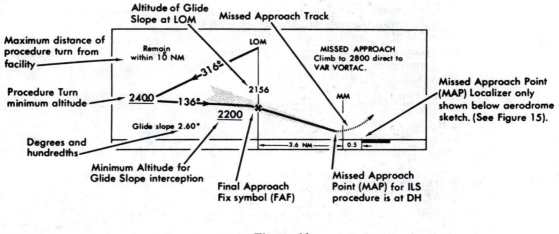

Altitude of Glide Slope at LOM

Missed Approach Track

Maximum distance of procedure turn from facility

Procedure Turn minimum altitude

Degrees and hundredths

Remain within 10 NM

316°

LOM

2156

240.0

136°

Glide slope 2.60°

2200

MM

MISSED APPROACH Climb to 2800 direct to VAR VORTAC.

3.6 NM

0.5

Missed Approach Point (MAP) Localizer only shown below aerodrome sketch. (See Figure 15).

Minimum Altitude for Glide Slope interception

Final Approach Fix symbol (FAF)

Missed Approach Point (MAP) for ILS procedure is at DH

Figure 11

PROFILE VIEW (Non-precision)

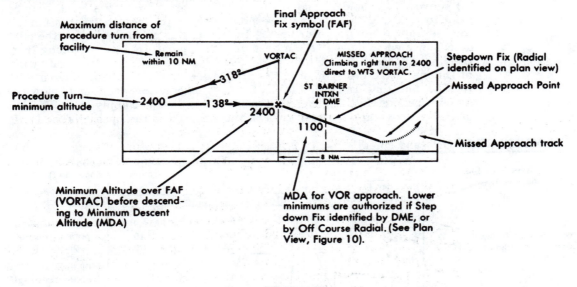

Final Approach Fix symbol (FAF)

Maximum distance of procedure turn from facility

Procedure Turn minimum altitude

Remain within 10 NM

VORTAC

318°

138°

2400

2400

1100

ST BARNER INTXN 4 DME

MISSED APPROACH Climbing right turn to 2400 direct to WTS VORTAC.

8 NM

Stepdown Fix (Radial identified on plan view)

Missed Approach Point

Missed Approach track

Minimum Altitude over FAF (VORTAC) before descending to Minimum Descent Altitude (MDA)

MDA for VOR approach. Lower minimums are authorized if Step down Fix identified by DME, or by Off Course Radial. (See Plan View, Figure 10).

Figure 12

(3) <u>Profile Views (Figures 11 and 12)</u> show a side view of the procedures. These views include the <u>minimum</u> altitude and maximum distance for the procedure turn, altitudes over prescribed fixes, distances between fixes and the missed approach procedure.

(a) <u>Precision approach glide slope intercept altitude.</u> This is a minimum altitude for glide slope interception after completion of procedure turn. It applies to precision approaches and, except where otherwise prescribed, it also applies as a minimum altitude for crossing the final approach fix in case the glide slope is inoperative or not used.

(b) <u>Stepdown fixes in non-precision procedures.</u> A stepdown fix may be provided on the final, i.e., between the final approach fix and the airport for the purpose of authorizing a lower MDA after passing an obstruction. This stepdown fix may be made by an NDB bearing, fan marker, radar fix, radial from another VOR, or by a DME when provided for as shown in figure 12.

(c) Normally, there is only one stepdown fix between the final approach fix (FAF) and the missed approach point (MAP). If the stepdown fix cannot be identified for any reason, the altitude at the stepdown fix becomes the MDA for a straight-in landing. However, when circling under this condition, you must refer to the Minimums Section of the procedure for the applicable circling minimum. See figure 14 for example.

(d) <u>Missed approach point (MAP).</u> It should be specifically noted that the missed approach points are different for the complete ILS (with glide slope) and for the localizer only approach. The MAP for the ILS is at the decision height (DH) while the "localizer only" MAP is usually over the (straight-in) runway threshold. In some non-precision procedures, the MAP may be prior to reaching the runway threshold in order to clear obstructions in the missed approach climb-out area. In non-precision procedures, the pilot determines when he is at the missed approach point (MAP) by timing from the final approach fix (FAF). The FAF has been clearly identified by use of the maltese cross symbol in the profile section. The distance from FAF to MAP and time and speed table, for easy calculation, are found below the aerodrome sketches (figures 15 and 16). This does not apply to VOR/DME procedures, or when the facility is on the airport and the facility is the MAP.

<u>MINIMUMS SECTION</u> (and notes).

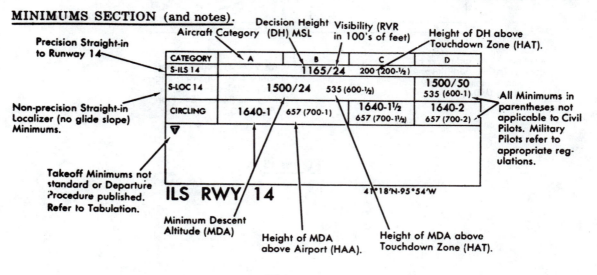

Figure 13

186

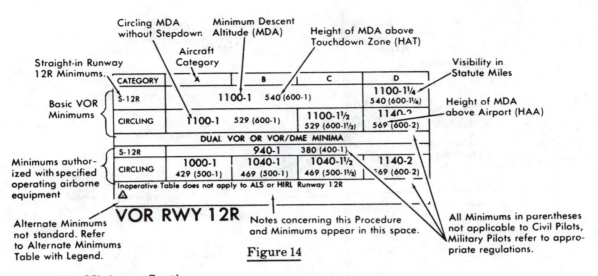

Circling MDA without Stepdown

Minimum Descent Altitude (MDA)

Height of MDA above Touchdown Zone (HAT)

Aircraft Category

Straight-in Runway 12R Minimums.

Visibility in Statute Miles

CATEGORY	A	B	C	D
S-12R	1100-1 540 (600-1)			1100-1¼ 540 (600-1¼)
CIRCLING	1100-1 529 (600-1)		1100-1½ 529 (600-1½)	1140-2 569 (600-2)
DUAL VOR OR VOR/DME MINIMA				
S-12R	940-1 380 (400-1)			
CIRCLING	1000-1 429 (500-1)	1040-1 469 (500-1)	1040-1½ 469 (500-1½)	1140-2 569 (600-2)

Inoperative Table does not apply to ALS or HIRL Runway 12R

Basic VOR Minimums

Minimums authorized with specified operating airborne equipment

Height of MDA above Airport (HAA)

⚠ Alternate Minimums not standard. Refer to Alternate Minimums Table with Legend.

VOR RWY 12R

Notes concerning this Procedure and Minimums appear in this space.

All Minimums in parentheses not applicable to Civil Pilots, Military Pilots refer to appropriate regulations.

Figure 14

(4) <u>Minimum Section.</u>

   (a) The same minimums apply to both day and night operations unless different minimums are specified at the bottom of the minimum box in the space provided for symbols or notes.

   (b) The minimums for straight-in and circling appear directly under each aircraft category. When there is no division line between minimums for each category on the straight-in or circling lines, the minimums apply to two or more categories under the A, B, C, or D.

   (For figure 13, the S-ILS 14 minimums apply to all four categories. The S-localizer 14 minimums are the same for Categories A, B, and C, and different for Category D. The circling minimums are the same for A and B and individually different for C and D.)

   (c) The Nixa, Missouri, Grenzall West Airport, VOR Rwy 12R procedure (figures 12 and 14) authorizes minimums for aircraft with one VOR receiver. Lower minimums are authorized if the aircraft also has DME or dual VOR receivers and St. Barner Intersection is identified. (See figure 14 for dual minimums.)

(5)   <u>Aerodrome Data.</u>

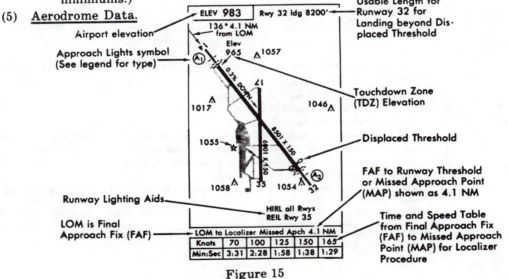

Usable Length for Runway 32 for Landing beyond Displaced Threshold

Airport elevation

Approach Lights symbol (See legend for type)

Touchdown Zone (TDZ) Elevation

Displaced Threshold

FAF to Runway Threshold or Missed Approach Point (MAP) shown as 4.1 NM

Runway Lighting Aids

LOM is Final Approach Fix (FAF)

Time and Speed Table from Final Approach Fix (FAF) to Missed Approach Point (MAP) for Localizer Procedure

ELEV 983   Rwy 32 ldg 8200'

136° 4.1 NM from LOM

Elev 965

HIRL all Rwys
REIL Rwy 35

LOM to Localizer Missed Apch 4.1 NM

Knots	70	100	125	150	165
Min:Sec	3:31	2:28	1:58	1:38	1:29

Figure 15

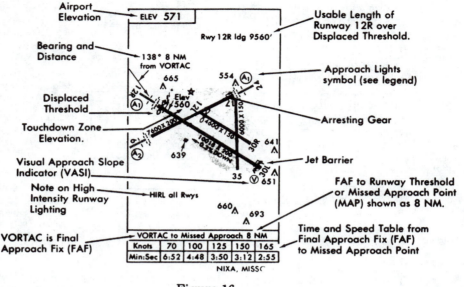

Figure 16

(6) **General Information.**

   (a) During pre-flight planning prior to departure on an IFR flight plan, reference should be made to instrument approach charts to determine:

     <u>1</u> Take-off minimums.

     <u>2</u> Whether an IFR departure procedure for obstruction avoidance has been established.

Instrument approach charts in the old format have take-off minimums and departure procedures published on the chart. Procedures published under the revised format do not contain this information. Take-off minimums are standard (see paragraph 3.b.) unless the symbol ▽ is shown under the minimums box indicating that the separate listing should be consulted. Below is an example of this listing.

INSTRUMENT APPROACH PROCEDURES (CHARTS)
SOUTHEAST UNITED STATES
▽ IFR TAKE-OFF MINIMUMS AND DEPARTURE PROCEDURES

FAR 91.116(c) prescribes take-off rules for FAR 121, 129, and 135 operators and establishes standard take-off visibility minimums as follows:

(1) Aircraft having two engines or less — one statute mile.

(2) Aircraft having more than two engines — one-half statute mile.

Aerodromes within this geographical area with IFR take-off minimums other than standard are listed below alphabetically by aerodrome name. Departure procedures and/or ceiling and visibility minimums are established to assist pilots conducting IFR flight in avoiding obstructions during climb to the minimum enroute altitude.

Take-off minimums and departure procedures apply to all runways unless otherwise specified.

AERODROME NAME	TAKE-OFF MINIMUMS	AERODROME NAME	TAKE-OFF MINIMUMS
CARTER-LATTIVILLE.............................500-2 Carter, Nebraska			

Figure 17

(b) When use of an alternate airport is required in filing an IFR flight plan (FAR 91.83), reference should be made to the instrument approach procedure to be used for the alternate selected to determine alternate airport minimums. Procedures charted in the old format have alternate minimums shown on the chart. Procedures charted in the new format do not contain this information. Alternate minimums are standard (see paragraph 3.c.) unless the symbol △ is shown under the minimums box indicating that alternate minimums are not standard and that the separate listing should be consulted. If the airport is not authorized for use as an alternate, the letters "NA" will follow the symbol under the minimum box. Below is an example of the Alternate Minimums listing.

NOTE: If the pilot elects to proceed to the selected alternate airport, the alternate ceiling and visibility minimums are disregarded, and the published landing minimum is applicable for the new destination utilizing facilities as appropriate to the procedure. In other words, the alternate airport becomes a new destination, and the pilot uses the landing minimum appropriate to the type of procedure selected.

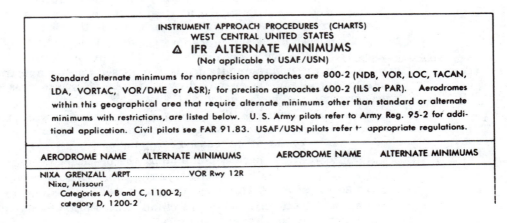

Figure 18

(c) The tables which appear as samples in (a) and (b) above are printed for area chart books, and should be kept with the Legend pages and Inoperative Components or Visual Aids Table at the front of each area chart book.

(d) Straight-in minimums are shown on instrument approach procedure charts when the final approach course of the instrument approach procedure is within 30° of the runway alignment and a normal descent can be made from the IFR altitude shown on the instrument approach procedures to the runway surface. When either the normal rate of descent or the runway alignment factor of 30° is exceeded, a straight-in minimum is not published and a circling minimum applies. The fact that a straight-in minimum is not published does not preclude the pilot from landing straight-in if he has the active runway in sight in sufficient time to make a normal landing. Under such conditions and when Air Traffic Control has cleared him for landing on that runway, he is not expected to circle even though only circling minimums are published. If he desires to circle at a controlled Airport, he should advise ATC.

(e) <u>Circling Minimums.</u> The circling minimums published on the instrument approach chart provide adequate obstruction clearance and the pilot should not descend below the circling altitude until the aircraft is in a position to make final descent for landing. Sound judgement and knowledge of his and the aircraft capabilities are the criteria for a pilot to determine the exact maneuver in each instance since the airport design, the aircraft position, altitude and airspeed must all be considered. The following basic rules apply.

<u>1</u> Maneuver the shortest path to the base or downwind leg as appropriate under minimum weather conditions. There is no restriction from passing over the airport or other runways.

<u>2</u> It should be recognized that many circling maneuvers may be made while VFR flying is in progress at the airport. Standard left turns or specific instruction from the controller for maneuvering must be considered when circling to land.

<u>3</u> At airports without a control tower, it may be desirable to fly over the airport to determine wind and turn indicators, and to observe other traffic which may be on the runway or flying in the vicinity of the airport.

(f) When the missed approach procedure specifies holding at a facility or fix, holding shall be in accordance with the holding pattern depicted on the plan view, and at the minimum altitude in the missed approach instructions, unless a higher altitude is specified by ATC. An alternate missed approach procedure may also be given by ATC.

(g) There are various terms in the missed approach procedure which have specific meanings with respect to climbing to altitude, to execute a turn for obstruction avoidance, or for other reasons. Examples:

'Climb to' means a normal climb along the prescribed course.

'Climbing right turn' means climbing right turn as soon as safety permits, normally to avoid obstructions straight ahead.

'Climb to 2400 turn right' means climb to 2400 prior to making the right turn, normally to clear obstructions.

XI. AIR TRAFFIC CONTROL

There is normally nothing very difficult involved in takeoff, climb, cruise from point to point, and descent solely by reference to instruments. The complications arise when you must execute these maneuvers at precise times, at specified altitudes, over designated routes and geographic positions, and in an orderly sequence with other aircraft. An understanding of the Air Traffic Control system will impress upon you the importance of the training necessary for you to apply the proficiency you have acquired in basic instrument flying and radio navigation techniques.

Federal regulation of civil aviation began with the Air Commerce Act of 1926 and the creation of the Aeronautics Branch in the U.S. Department of Commerce. The Department was concerned with the promotion of air safety, licensing of pilots, development of air navigation facilities, and issuing of flight information. Until the volume of air traffic increased, there was no need for air traffic control, since the likelihood of aircraft colliding in flight was remote.

The need for controlling air traffic was recognized in the 1930's as the aviation industry produced bigger, faster, and safer aircraft, and air transportation became an accepted mode of public travel. A number of large cities, concerned with regulating the increasing air traffic at their airports, built control towers and inaugurated a control service on, and in the immediate vicinity of, the airports. Airline companies, eager to expand and improve their operations, established control centers at Cleveland, Chicago and Newark to provide their pilots with position and estimated time of arrival information during instrument flights between those cities.

In 1936, the Federal Government assumed the responsibility for operation of the centers, employing eight controllers. As aviation has grown, so have the Federal Government functions and the agency charged with the promotion and safety of civil aviation. By the late 1970's, approximately 25,000 ATC personnel provided direction and assistance to over 100 million flights annually.

The number of active aircraft has increased from 29,000, all flying at relatively slow and uniform speeds, to more than 200,000 aircraft operating at various speeds ranging to more than 1,000 miles per hour. The aerial highways have expanded from a few intercity routes to more than 250,000 miles of very high frequency routes utilizing approximately 1,000 VOR and VORTAC stations. A continued increase in traffic volume is expected during the coming decade.

The difficulties associated with mixed IFR and VFR traffic and with diverse pilot training and varying aircraft capabilities, the trend toward automated electronic equipment, and other aspects of control will have a profound effect on flight operations, under both Visual and Instrument Flight Rules.

As an instrument pilot normally operating under the jurisdiction of Air Traffic Control, your understanding of the present system and its operation will better enable you to make full use of ATC services.

Structure and Functions of Air Traffic Service

Air Traffic Service of FAA is responsible for three major general functions: developing plans, establishing standards, and implementing systems for control of air traffic. The two specific functions of immediate concern to the instrument pilot are:

1. Providing preflight and inflight service to all pilots.
2. Keeping aircraft safely separated while operating in controlled airspace.

The preflight and inflight services to pilots are the responsibility of the Flight Service Stations (FSS). An extensive teletype and interphone system permits relay of information from many sources. Many of the services provided by tower and flight service personnel are familiar to the VFR pilot. Aircraft separation is the primary responsibility of both Airport Traffic Control Towers and Air Route Traffic Control Centers (ARTCC). Knowledge of the physical setup and services provided by each type of facility enables the instrument pilot to get information and assistance and to communicate with the appropriate controllers with confidence and efficiency.

Airport Traffic Control Towers

Jurisdiction.—The ATC tower is responsible for control of aircraft on and in the immediate vicinity of airports. Terminals handling a large traffic volume employ specialized personnel for operations; they use light signals, radio, and ASDE radar (Airport Surface Detection Equipment) for control of surface traffic. Less congested airports have fewer controllers to handle the workload with less specialization.

Organization of the tower operations falls into the following units:

Local Control is concerned mainly with VFR traffic in and around the traffic pattern and with ground traffic. The local controller works with the other IFR controllers to integrate VFR and IFR flights

into a smooth, safe traffic flow in and out of the airport.

Ground Control directs the movement of aircraft on the airport surface, working closely with other tower positions. The controller relays clearances from ARTCC to departing IFR flights unless a special position is assigned that function.

Clearance Delivery is accomplished by a separate controller at most busy terminals where heavy ground traffic and frequent IFR departures require division of the workload.

Departure Control originates departure clearances and instructions to provide separation between departing and arriving IFR flights. Although the physical location of this controller varies at different terminals—in the tower at some locations, in separate radar installations at others—there is a close coordination with the Approach Controller and Local Controller.

Approach Control formulates and issues approach clearances and instructions to provide separation between arriving IFR aircraft, using radar if available.

Tower services provide:

1. Control of aircraft on, and in the vicinity of the airport.
2. Coordination with pilots and Air Route Traffic Control Centers for IFR clearances.
3. Air traffic advisories to pilots concerning observed, reported, and estimated positions of aircraft that might present a hazard to a particular flight.
4. Flight assistance, including transmission of pilot reports and requests, and weather advisories.

Approach/Departure Control services provide:

1. Navigation assistance by radar vector for departing and arriving aircraft.
2. DF assistance to lost aircraft, and cooperation with other facilities in Search and Rescue operations.

Some of the larger towers have more than one of the above described positions of operation, each position having its area of responsibility on, or in the vicinity of, the airport. Also, the *Approach Control* function at some highly complex multi-airport metropolitan areas has been established separate from and serving several major or less busy airports.

Air Route Traffic Control Centers

Jurisdiction.—The primary function of an ARTCC is to provide air traffic control service to aircraft operating on IFR flight plans within controlled airspace, principally during the en route phase of flight. When equipment capability and controller workload permit, certain advisory/assistance services may be provided to VFR aircraft.

Organization.—The ARTCC facilities are located throughout the United States at central points in areas over which they exercise control. Each Center controls IFR traffic within its own area and coordinates with adjacent Centers for the orderly flow of traffic from area to area. Each Center's control area is divided into Sectors, based upon traffic flow patterns and controller workload.

Each Sector Controller normally has a sector discrete frequency for direct communications with IFR flights within the sector. As an IFR flight departs, the affected Sector Controller follows the progress of the flight, maintaining a continuing record of route, altitude, and time, and monitors the flight with long-range radar equipment when available. Each Sector Controller has a sector discrete frequency for direct communication with IFR flights within the sector. As an IFR flight progresses to adjacent sectors and centers, and finally to the destination terminal facility, the IFR pilot is requested to change to appropriate frequencies.

The chief functions of the Air Route Traffic Control Centers are to: (1) control aircraft operating under IFR in controlled airspace, (2) provide air traffic advisories to aircraft concerning potential hazards to flight, anticipated delays, and any other data of importance to the pilot for the safe conduct of the flight, (3) provide navigation assistance by radar vectors for detouring thunderstorms and expediting routing, (4) transmit pilot reports and weather advisories to en route aircraft, and (5) provide flight assistance to aircraft in distress.

Air Traffic Control Automation

NAS En Route Stage A

This term refers to ATC's automation of the routine tasks of en route traffic control through the use of computers. The automation is being accomplished in two phases, the flight data processing phase and the radar data processing phase. In the flight data processing phase, the computer takes over the task of processing, printing, distributing, and updating flight plans. In the past, controllers have performed these clerical chores.

The radar data processing phase of en route automation involves bringing vital information about each flight to the radar scope. The controller formerly transferred control information from the flight progress strips to plastic markers called "shrimp boats." These "shrimp boats" were manually kept in association with the displayed radar targets. The controller had to remember which flight progress strip applied to each radar target and "shrimp boat" on the scope—a process which called for heavy concentration and constant verification. Through an electronic process, the computer converts digital information into letters and numbers and projects a bright tag containing all necessary flight data on the radar scope. This alphanumeric display includes flight identification, assigned altitude, Mode C altitude, computer iden-

tification, and a special field that includes control data. Whether an aircraft is climbing or descending is also graphically shown by an arrow pointing up or down. The data tag is attached to the radar target of each aircraft being controlled. A controller "hands off" an aircraft to another controller by making a keyboard entry to the computer, causing the data tag to transfer to the new controller's scope. The tag blinks until the new controller acknowledges the handoff. The Mode C altitude readout is accomplished through the aircraft's transponder and encoding altimeter.

ARTS III

This automated system provides controllers at medium and high activity terminal facilities information similar to NAS En Route Stage A. This includes the display of aircraft flight data and automated handoff capability within the terminal facility with other ARTS–III facilities and with NAS En Route Stage A.

New programs have been added to the system such as Minimum Safe Altitude Warning (MSAW) and Conflict Alert. The former alerts the controller when a controlled aircraft is below or is predicted to descend below a minimum designated altitude or minimum descent altitude (MDA) if past the final approach fix. The latter alerts the controller to unsafe or potentially unsafe proximity between controlled aircraft. These alerts are in the form of a warning message displayed blinking on the controller's radar display accompanied by an aural alarm.

Flight Service Stations (FSSs)

There are approximately 300 Flight Service Stations located within the conterminous United States. Their normal flight service area encompasses an area within 400 miles of the station location. Although FSSs have no direct air traffic authority over either VFR or IFR traffic, they render extensive service to all air traffic. The FSSs are the backbone of the ATC Flight Information System.

FSSs have the following functions: (1) conducting pilot preflight briefing on en route weather and other aeronautical information pertinent to the flight, (2) providing en route communications with pilots on VFR flights, (3) giving emergency assistance to lost VFR and IFR aircraft, (4) relaying ATC clearances, (5) originating, classifying, and disseminating notices to airmen (NOTAMs), (6) broadcasting aviation weather and national airspace information, (7) receiving and closing VFR and IFR flight plans (filed IFR flight plans are forwarded to the appropriate Center), (8) monitoring radio NAVAIDs, (9) performing initial search and rescue operations for missing VFR aircraft, (10) operating the National Weather Teletypewriter Service, (11) taking weather observations (at selected locations), (12) providing airport advisory service at non-tower or part-time tower locations, and (13) conducting the National Pilot Weather Report Program.

Pilot Preflight Briefing.—FSSs aid in fulfilling the requirements of FAR 91.5, which states that the pilot will be familiar with all available information concerning the flight. A complete preflight briefing consists of: (1) a pilot weather briefing, (2) aeronautical information pertinent to the flight, and (3) flight planning assistance, at the pilot's request. You can aid the FSS preflight briefer by providing the following background information: (1) VFR, IFR or VFR/IFR, (2) aircraft identification number, (3) aircraft type, (4) departure point, (5) estimated time of departure, (6) altitude, (7) route of flight, (8) destination, (9) estimated time en route, and (10) estimated time of arrival.

After the briefer has been provided this information, a preflight briefing will be given which will include:

(1) Adverse Weather—The pilot will be advised of any weather conditions that might make it advisable to cancel or postpone the flight. Such conditions include severe thunderstorms, icing conditions, and visibility restrictions.

(2) Synopsis—The synopsis is a brief statement which outlines the primary cause of weather conditions along the pilot's route of flight. This statement may include pressure patterns, wind flow patterns, frontal development, and frontal movement.

(3) Current Weather—The briefer will summarize the existing weather conditions along the pilot's intended route. This may include information from Aviation Weather Reports, Pilot Weather Reports, and Radar Weather Reports.

(4) En Route Forecast—The briefer will give the pilot a summary of the forecast weather conditions along the proposed route. It is the responsibility of the briefer to *interpret* and *summarize* information found in Area Forecasts, Terminal Forecasts, Airmets, Sigmets, forecast amendments, and hazardous weather advisories. This information may include cloud tops, cloud layers, cloud bases, thunderstorms, strong low level wind shear at departure and destination airports, turbulence, and icing.

(5) Destination Forecast—The pilot will be briefed on the weather that can be expected upon arrival at the destination. This information will be obtained from the Terminal Forecast (FT) and will include the portion which is pertinent to the pilot's estimated time of arrival (ETA). If a change is forecast to occur at approximately the pilot's ETA, the briefer will provide weather information to include conditions expected both before and after the change. If no Terminal Forecast is available, an interpretation from the Area Forecast will be used. This, however, will not be identified as an official forecast.

(6) Forecast Winds and Temperatures Aloft—The briefer will provide the pilot with the average wind speed and direction forecast for the intended route. If changes are expected, the pilot will be so advised. This information will be derived from the Winds and Temperatures Aloft Forecast (FD). Temperatures aloft are not routinely given by the briefer unless (a) they are vital for flights during periods of unusually hot or cold weather, (b) an icing potential exists or, (c) they are requested by the pilot. If the pilot's planned altitude is between standard forecast wind levels, the briefer will interpolate to provide accurate wind information.

(7) Pertinent aeronautical information, including NOTAMS.

Notices to Airmen (NOTAMs).—A NOTAM contains information of a time–critical nature that is required for flight planning and not known sufficiently in advance to publicize through aeronautical charts or flight information publications. NOTAM information concerns the establishment, condition or change in, any component, facility, service or procedure of, or hazard in, the National Airspace System. NOTAMS are broken down into the following five categories:

(1) Landing Area NOTAMs—include airport closure; decommissioning of a landing area; conditions which restrict or preclude the use of a runway, taxiway, or ramp; and control zone hours of operation.

(2) Lighting Aid NOTAMs—include information related to airport light systems, approach light systems, and obstruction light outages in proximity of the airport.

(3) Air Navigation Aid NOTAMs—include decommissioning of air navigation aids, radar failure, NAVAID restrictions, and change in hours of operation of a NAVAID.

(4) Special Data NOTAMs—include material not covered under landing area, lighting aids, air navigation aids, or FDC NOTAMs.

(5) FDC NOTAMs—concern compliance with Federal Aviation Regulations and are regulatory in nature. The National Flight Data Center is responsible for their collection, validation, and dissemination. FDC NOTAMs are transmitted to FSSs by teletype. These NOTAMs are *not* provided during preflight briefings unless they are specifically requested.

When disseminated by FSSs, NOTAMs concerning the first four categories listed above are identified as follows:

(1) NOTAM (D)—includes NOTAMs given distant dissemination (in addition to local dissemination) beyond the area of responsibility of the FSS. These include that time-critical information which would affect the pilot's decision to make a flight; for example, an airport closed, terminal radar out of service, en route navigational aids out of service, etc. Dissemination of information in this category will include that pertaining to all navigational facilities and all IFR airports with approved instrument approach procedures. These NOTAMs are stored and repeated hourly at the end of the appropriate Surface Aviation Weather Reports until cancelled.

(2) NOTAM (L)—includes NOTAMs given local distribution via appropriate voice communications,

local teletypewriter or teletautograph circuits, telephone, etc. The information disseminated is primarily of an advisory or "nice-to-know" nature, that can be given to the pilot upon request on an "as-needed" basis before departure, while en route, or prior to landing. An example of such information is, "snowbanks on the sides of the runways."

NOTAMs which are known in sufficient time for publication and are of 7 days duration or longer are normally incorporated into *NOTICES TO AIRMEN* and carried there until cancellation time. FDC NOTAMS are carried in this publication and also in the *National Ocean Survey Approach Procedure Chart* booklets.

Alternate Sources of Aviation Weather and Aeronautical Information.—At many locations, the number of pilots requiring preflight and in-flight weather briefings from FSSs is so great that alternative methods have been made available. After using one of these methods, you can assess the information presented and decide if you need a more detailed briefing.

Pre-recorded Weather Announcements include: (1) TWEBs (Transcribed Weather Broadcasts), (2) PATWAS (Pilot's Automatic Telephone Weather Answering Service), and (3) AAWS (Automatic Aviation Weather Service).

Live Weather Broadcasts include: (1) Scheduled Weather Broadcasts and (2) Unscheduled Weather Broadcasts.

In-flight Services.—FSSs are responsible for providing in-flight services for their flight service area. Having a general knowledge of an area within 400 miles of the station and a detailed knowledge of the 100 mile radius, the FSS specialist is qualified to provide in-flight services to pilots flying under IFR or VFR.

Pilot Weather Briefing Service enables you to obtain a weather briefing for your route of flight and destination by contacting an FSS on the appropriate frequency. An en route weather briefing follows a format which parallels that of a preflight briefing. However, you should understand that due to frequency saturation and other duties performed by the in-flight specialist, your weather briefing may not be as detailed as one you would receive by telephone or in person.

Aeronautical Information such as current NOTAMs, preferred routes, airport data, and communications frequencies may be obtained while en route by contacting an FSS on an appropriate frequency.

An IFR Flight Plan may be filed in flight by contacting the nearest FSS and relaying flight plan information in the numbered sequence that it appears on the flight plan form. This will ensure the receipt of all necessary information for entry of your flight plan into the appropriate Center computer.

Emergency Services can be provided to aircraft in distress by FSS personnel. They assist disoriented pilots through the use of VOR orientation procedures, VHF DF procedures, or a combination of both. FSSs equipped to provide DF procedures may be found in the *Airport/Facility Directory*.

Air/Ground Communications may be conducted with FSSs on designated frequencies. These frequencies are associated with the FSS information boxes on sectional and en route low altitude charts. They also appear in the *Airport/Facility Directory*.

Airport Advisory Service.—Many airports without air traffic control towers or with part-time towers, have FSSs capable of providing airport advisory service to both landing and departing IFR and VFR aircraft. Airport advisory service is provided on 123.6 MHz for the area within five statute miles of an airport having no control tower but where an FSS is located. At locations where airport advisory service is provided by an FSS during the hours the control tower is closed, the local tower control frequency is used. It is recommended that pilots monitor the appropriate frequency when within fifteen miles of the airport. Refer to the *Airman's Information Manual* for services available and recommended phraseologies.

When operating IFR at an airport having a control zone with no operating air traffic control tower and having an FSS located on the field, you may obtain an IFR flight clearance and takeoff clearance through airport advisory service. The FSS specialist will coordinate with the appropriate control facility and relay your clearance instructions.

En Route Flight Advisory Service (EFAS).—Weather information obtained during a preflight briefing cannot state with absolute certainty what conditions you will encounter during flight. National Weather Service forecasters can forecast the immediate meteorological future in general terms, but predicting specific time, location, and severity of weather phenomena is still not possible. Local terrain features can often affect weather patterns. Actual flight conditions can be unexpectedly different from those forecast.

In response to the need for improved in-flight weather availability and dissemination and to provide pilot-to-briefer service of meaningful, real-time weather information, the FAA has implemented EFAS. This service is now available through a nationwide network of 44 FSSs. An EFAS facility should be contacted on 122.0 MHz by using the name of the parent FSS and the words "Flight Watch"; e.g., "Portland Flight Watch." Refer to the *Airman's Information Manual* for further details.

Pilot Weather Report Program (PIREP).—A PIREP is another form of weather observation. No weather observation is more timely than the one you make from the cockpit of your airplane. The EFAS Flight Watch specialist uses PIREPs in accomplishing the goal of providing near real-time weather information directly to pilots in flight. The National Weather Service meteorologist uses PIREPs to update forecasts and to issue advisories; e.g., SIGMETs whenever the situation so warrants. These forecasts and advisories are, in turn, used by the FSS receiving them. They are also disseminated by teletype for use by other facilities.

IFR Control Sequence

To illustrate a typical IFR flight sequence of control, follow an imaginary trip from Will Rogers World Airport, Oklahoma City, Oklahoma to Washington National Airport, Washington, D.C.

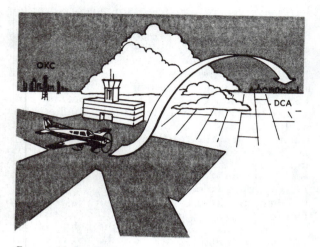

FIGURE 11-1. IFR—Oklahoma City to Washington D.C.

You, as pilot of FASTFLIGHT 5432K, have filed the flight plan either in person or by telephone with the Oklahoma City FSS, giving the information necessary for the Center to coordinate the flight with other IFR traffic. (At airports where no FSS is available, the flight plan may be filed by telephone to an FSS, ATC tower, or ARTCC.) The flight plan should be filed at least 30 minutes prior to the estimated time of departure to preclude possible delay in receiving the departure clearance from ATC. An IFR flight plan can be filed by radio with an FSS after takeoff if VFR conditions are maintained. This is less desirable than filing in person or by telephone.

FIGURE 11-2. Filing the flight plan.

After the flight plan has been filed, the OKC FSS transmits pertinent flight plan data by interphone or teletype to the Fort Worth Air Route Traffic Control Center where it is entered into a computer.

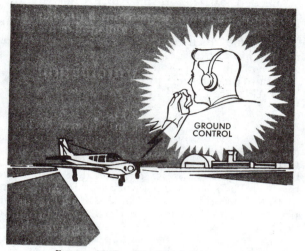

FIGURE 11-3. Copying the clearance.

Prior to taxiing, you should call clearance delivery and request IFR clearance. If there is to be no delay, you will normally be advised at this time. An airport such as Will Rogers, which has "Pre-taxi Clearance Procedures" will probably have your clearance and issue it to you immediately. You could expect your clearance to be issued in the "abbreviated departure clearance" format as follows:

FASTFLIGHT FIVE FOUR THREE TWO KILO—CLEARED TO WASHINGTON NATIONAL AIRPORT AS FILED—FLY RUNWAY HEADING—CLIMB AND MAINTAIN FIVE THOUSAND EXPECT SEVEN THOUSAND ONE ZERO MINUTES AFTER DEPARTURE—DEPARTURE FREQUENCY WILL BE ONE TWO FOUR POINT TWO—SQUAWK ZERO FOUR ONE FOUR.

You should copy the clearance and read it back. This clearance was originated in the Fort Worth Center and the clearance delivery controller is merely relaying it to you. However, certain restrictions may be added as required by the Oklahoma City departure controller.

FIGURE 11-4. Cleared for departure.

After receipt and acknowledgment of the IFR clearance, you should contact ground control and request taxi clearance to the runway in use.

After engine run–up, you should change to tower frequency (118.3 MHz) and advise that FASTFLIGHT five four three two KILO is ready for takeoff. The tower issues the following clearance:

FASTFLIGHT FIVE FOUR THREE TWO KILO—CLEARED FOR TAKEOFF.

After takeoff, the tower controller notifies the Oklahoma City departure controller that FASTFLIGHT 5432K has departed and the pilot will be directed to contact departure control. The departure controller will radar identify the aircraft and issue further instructions to provide separation from other aircraft in the terminal area and establish it on the flight plan route.

FASTFLIGHT FIVE FOUR THREE TWO KILO—OKLAHOMA CITY DEPARTURE CONTROL—RADAR CONTACT—FLY HEADING ZERO FOUR ZERO TO INTERCEPT VICTOR FOURTEEN SOUTH—CLIMB AND MAINTAIN SEVEN THOUSAND.

The phrase, "TO INTERCEPT VICTOR FOURTEEN SOUTH," indicates that you should resume normal navigation upon intercepting the airway, without further clearance. In absence of instructions, "TO INTERCEPT," you should maintain the last assigned heading even though it takes the aircraft through V14S. It is possible that departure control is using this means to provide separation from other aircraft. Normally, the controller would advise, "FASTFLIGHT FIVE FOUR THREE TWO KILO FLY HEADING ZERO FOUR ZERO FOR VECTORS EAST OF VICTOR FOURTEEN SOUTH TO PASS TRAFFIC TEN O'CLOCK SIX MILES SOUTHBOUND, BARON, FIVE THOUSAND."

As 5432K departs the terminal area, you are advised to contact Fort Worth Center on a specified frequency. Since the aircraft has been radar identified, the initial call would be:

FORT WORTH CENTER—FASTFLIGHT FIVE FOUR THREE TWO KILO—LEAVING FIVE THOUSAND.

Fort Worth Center replies:

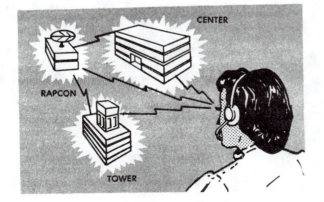

FIGURE 11–5. En route control.

FASTFLIGHT FIVE FOUR THREE TWO KILO—REPORT LEAVING SIX THOUSAND.

Since 5432K is operating in a radar environment, and has been advised "radar contract," the only reports required would be those specifically requested by the controller. However, each time the aircraft is changed to a different control facility, or to a different sector within a facility, you should report altitude on the initial call.

If advised, "RADAR CONTRACT LOST" or "RADAR SERVICE TERMINATED," you should resume normal position reporting procedures. See the *Airman's Information Manual* under "En Route —IFR."

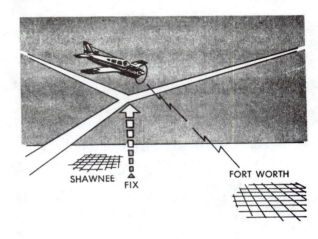

FIGURE 11–6. Position report.

As the flight progresses along airways, the flight data information is passed along from sector to sector within each Center, and from Center to Center along the route. Each controller receives advance notification of this flight and determines if there is any conflict with traffic within the sector. Each controller is responsible for issuing control instructions which will provide standard aircraft separation. This may be accomplished by route changes, altitudes changes, requiring holding, or providing radar vectors off course.

As the flight enters the Washington Terminal area, the Center controller will effect what is known as a "Radar Handoff" to Washington approach control. This is a method whereby one controller points out a target to another controller and thereby passes on the identity and control responsibility without an interruption in radar service. In the absence of a "Radar Handoff," it would be necessary for the approach controller to use one of several other means of identifying the aircraft, such as identifying turns, position reports, or transponder.

When both controllers are satisfied with the identification of 5432K, you will be advised to contact Washington approach control on a specified frequency.

FIGURE 11-7. Positive identification by approach control.

The approach controller will now provide radar navigation to position your aircraft so as to intercept the final approach course prior to the outer marker. You will be advised to descend in sufficient time to reach the proper glide path interception altitude. Your clearance for an ILS approach will be issued when the controller has provided proper spacing between 5432K and other aircraft being controlled and when 5432K is on a course that will intercept the localizer, outside the outer marker, at not more than a 30° angle. This clearance follows:

FASTFLIGHT FIVE FOUR THREE TWO KILO— THREE MILES FROM OUTER MARKER—MAINTAIN TWO THOUSAND FIVE HUNDRED UNTIL ESTABLISHED ON THE LOCALIZER—CLEARED FOR ILS RUNWAY THREE SIX APPROACH—CONTACT TOWER ON ONE ONE NINER POINT ONE.

(NOTE: You should not turn onto the localizer unless this clearance is received.)

You should now turn on the localizer when you intercept it and complete the approach to a landing or to the "MISSED APPROACH POINT."

If traffic conditions at Washington National required a delay, the approach controller would have issued instructions to proceed to a holding point and hold. This clearance would have been:

FASTFLIGHT FIVE FOUR THREE TWO KILO— WASHINGTON APPROACH CONTROL—MAINTAIN SEVEN THOUSAND—PROCEED DIRECT TO ARMEL VORTAC—HOLD WEST OF ARMEL ON VICTOR FOUR—EXPECT FURTHER CLEARANCE AT ONE ONE THREE FIVE.

At the appropriate time, 5432K would have been instructed to depart ARMEL on a specified heading and would have been vectored to final approach as in the preceding example.

Prior to this frequency change, you should have determined that ATIS (Automatic Terminal Information Service) is available at Washington National Airport, and should have tuned in the proper frequency and listened to the information. If you have received the ATIS broadcast, approach control should be so advised. The ATIS provides all the necessary approach, runway, NOTAM, and other pertinent information for landing at Washington National. The controller need provide only necessary control instructions. Your initial call to Washington approach control would be:

WASHINGTON APPROACH CONTROL—FASTFLIGHT FIVE FOUR THREE TWO KILO—SEVEN THOUSAND—INFORMATION BRAVO.

The approach controller's action now depends on the conditions and traffic at the airport. If no approach delay were expected, the reply to 5432K would be:

FASTFLIGHT FIVE FOUR THREE TWO KILO— WASHINGTON APPROACH CONTROL—FLY HEADING ONE TWO ZERO FOR VECTORS TO FINAL APPROACH COURSE—DESCEND AND MAINTAIN THREE THOUSAND.

(NOTE: ATIS information BRAVO advised that ILS approach to runway 36 would be expected.)

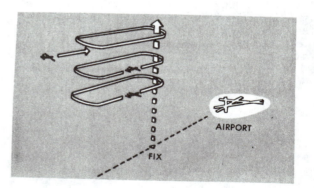

FIGURE 11-9. Stacking.

FIGURE 11-8. ILS approach.

After the approach and landing is completed, unless otherwise instructed, proceed in the landing direction to the nearest turn-off and exit the runway without delay. Do not change to ground control frequency while on the active runway unless so instructed by the tower.

FIGURE 11–10. Cleared to land.

In summary, the foregoing picture of an IFR flight illustrates the need for adherence to carefully established procedures for safe, orderly, and expeditious traffic flow. The pilot and controller must know what to expect of each other, as well as knowing the details of their own special authority and responsibility. The controller, for example, must be aware of the performance capabilities of the various aircraft operating in the system in order to issue clearances and instructions with which the aircraft are capable of complying. Likewise, the instrument pilot should understand the overall traffic problem and the standardized IFR control procedures in order to avoid being unprepared by an unexpected request or change in clearance. In fact, the experienced instrument pilot can usually anticipate what the controller will say. During periods of heavy traffic conditions, when clearances seem complicated and unduly restrictive, the utmost cooperation between the pilot and the controller is especially required.

XII. ATC OPERATIONS AND PROCEDURES

Using the System

Once you understand the overall operation of the traffic control system, the many procedural details can be put into the appropriate sequence as you learn them. The problem now is to review the regulations and procedures involved in using the system under Instrument Flight Rules. Pilot responsibilities relating to air traffic control are stated in the Federal Aviation Regulations, Part 91, General Operating and Flight Rules.

More detailed procedures can be found under "Air Traffic Control" in the *Airman's Information Manual.* The instrument pilot should purchase copies of the Regulations and the AIM and maintain them with current revisions which are included in the subscription prices.

IFR Flight Plan

As specified in FAR 91, if you plan to operate an aircraft in controlled airspace under Instrument Flight Rules, you must file an IFR flight plan and receive an appropriate ATC clearance. If your flight is to be in controlled airspace, your initial contact with Air Traffic Service involves your flight plan. The "Preflight" section of the chapter titled "Air Traffic Control" in the *Airman's Information Manual* provides guidance for completing the FAA Flight Plan, Form 7233-1 (Fig. 12–1). The forms are available at FSSs, flight planning rooms in airport terminal buildings, and at other convenient locations.

Filing in Flight

An IFR flight plan may be filed in the air under various conditions, including:

a. An IFR flight outside of controlled airspace prior to proceeding into IFR conditions in controlled airspace.

b. A VFR flight expecting IFR weather conditions en route in controlled airspace.

c. A flight on a VFR flight plan en route to a destination having high air traffic volume. Even in VFR weather conditions, more efficient handling is provided a flight on an IFR clearance. However,

| DEPARTMENT OF TRANSPORTATION — FEDERAL AVIATION ADMINISTRATION | Form Approved |
| **FLIGHT PLAN** | OMB No. 04-R0072 |

1. TYPE	2. AIRCRAFT IDENTIFICATION	3. AIRCRAFT TYPE/ SPECIAL EQUIPMENT	4. TRUE AIRSPEED	5. DEPARTURE POINT	6. DEPARTURE TIME		7. CRUISING ALTITUDE
VFR					PROPOSED (Z)	ACTUAL (Z)	
IFR							
DVFR			KTS				

8. ROUTE OF FLIGHT

9. DESTINATION (Name of airport and city)	10. EST. TIME ENROUTE		11. REMARKS
	HOURS	MINUTES	

12. FUEL ON BOARD		13. ALTERNATE AIRPORT (S)	14. PILOT'S NAME, ADDRESS & TELEPHONE NUMBER & AIRCRAFT HOME BASE	15. NUMBER ABOARD
HOURS	MINUTES			

| 16. COLOR OF AIRCRAFT | CLOSE VFR FLIGHT PLAN WITH_____FSS ON ARRIVAL |

FAA Form 7233-1 (5-72)   FAA AC 73-2336

FIGURE 12–1. Flight plan form.

acceptance of an IFR clearance does not relieve the pilot of the responsibility for maintaining separation from other traffic when operating in VFR conditions.

d. A flight departing under VFR conditions from an airport where no means of communication with Flight Service is available on the ground.

In any of these situations, the flight plan may be filed with the nearest FSS or directly with the Center. A pilot who files with Flight Service submits the information normally entered during preflight filing, except for "point of departure," together with present position and altitude. The Center will then clear the pilot from present position or from a specified navigation fix. A pilot who files direct with the Center reports present position and altitude, and submits only the flight plan information normally relayed from Flight Service to the Center. You should be aware that traffic saturation frequently prevents Center personnel from accepting flight plans by radio. In such cases, you will be advised to contact the nearest FSS for the purpose of filing your flight plan.

Clearances

Definition.—An ATC clearance is "authorization by Air Traffic Control, for the purpose of preventing collision between known IFR traffic, for an aircraft to proceed under specified traffic conditions within controlled airspace."

As the definition implies, an ATC clearance can be very simple or quite complicated, depending on traffic conditions. Your departure clearance will normally contain the clearance items outlined in the *Airman's Information Manual* under, "ATC Clearance/Separations."

Examples: A flight filed for a short distance at a relatively low altitude in an area of low traffic density might receive a clearances as follows:

FASTFLIGHT FIVE FOUR THREE TWO KILO— CLEARED TO DOEVILLE AIRPORT DIRECT— CRUISE FIVE THOUSAND.

The term "cruise" in this clearance means that you are authorized to fly at any altitude from the minimum IFR altitude up to and including 5,000 feet. You may level off at any altitude within this block of airspace. A climb or descent within the block may be made at your discretion. However, once you have reported leaving an altitude within the block you may not return to that altitude without further ATC clearance. When ATC issues a "cruise" clearance in conjunction with an unpublished route, an appropriate crossing altitude will be specified to ensure terrain clearance until the aircraft reaches a fix, point or route where the altitude information is available. The crossing altitude assures IFR obstruction clearance to the point where the aircraft is on a segment of a published route or instrument approach procedure.

If a flight plan is filed and the clearance received, through Flight Service by telephone or radio, ATC would specify appropriate instructions such as those which follow:

ATC CLEARS FASTFLIGHT FIVE FOUR THREE TWO KILO TO SKYLINE AIRPORT VIA THE CROSSVILLE ZERO FIVE FIVE RADIAL—VICTOR ONE EIGHT—MAINTAIN FIVE THOUSAND—CLEARANCE VOID IF NOT OFF BY ONE THREE THREE ZERO.

Under more complex traffic conditions, you may receive a more involved clearance such as the following:

ATC CLEARS FASTFLIGHT FIVE FOUR THREE TWO KILO TO WICHITA MID-CONTINENT AIRPORT VIA VICTOR SEVEN SEVEN—LEFT TURN AFTER TAKEOFF—PROCEED DIRECT TO THE OKLAHOMA CITY VORTAC—HOLD WEST ON THE OKLAHOMA CITY TWO SEVEN SEVEN RADIAL—CLIMB TO FIVE THOUSAND IN HOLDING PATTERN BEFORE PROCEEDING ON COURSE—MAINTAIN FIVE THOUSAND TO CASHION INTERSECTION—CLIMB TO AND MAINTAIN SEVEN THOUSAND—DEPARTURE CONTROL FREQUENCY WILL BE ONE TWO ONE POINT ZERO FIVE—SQUAWK ZERO FOUR ONE TWO.

None of the foregoing clearances are especially difficult to copy, understand, and comply with—assuming that you—

a. Have properly tuned your radio.
b. Are concentrating on what you hear.

c. Can copy fast enough to keep up with the clearance delivery.
d. Are familiar with the area.

Suppose, on the other hand, that you are awaiting departure clearance at a busy metropolitan terminal (your first IFR departure from this airport). On an average date, the tower at this airport controls departures at a rate of one every 2 minutes to maintain the required traffic flow. Sequenced behind you are a number of aircraft ready for departure, including jet transports.

ATC issues you the following "abbreviated clearance" which includes a Standard Instrument Departure (SID) (Fig. 12–2):

FASTFLIGHT FIVE FOUR THREE TWO KILO—CLEARED TO LA GUARDIA AS FILED—RINGOES EIGHT DEPARTURE PHILLIPSBURG TRANSITION—MAINTAIN EIGHT THOUSAND—DEPARTURE CONTROL FREQUENCY WILL BE ONE TWO ZERO POINT FOUR—SQUAWK ZERO SEVEN ZERO ZERO.

This clearance may be readily copied in shorthand as follows:

CAF/RNGO8/PSB/M80/DPC 120.4/SQ 0700.

The information contained in this clearance for a Standard Instrument Departure is an abbreviation of Air Traffic instructions too complicated and extensive for you to follow and copy, regardless of your proficiency in using clearance shorthand.

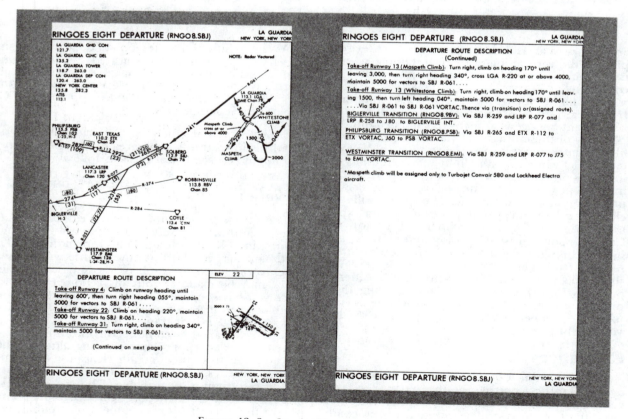

FIGURE 12–2. Standard instrument departure (SID).

202

Study of the route specified in the clearance shows the importance of the Standard Instrument Departure. At common operating speeds in modern light aircraft, the clearance allows no time for extensive reference to your departure chart. You will be too busy flying your aircraft, navigating, and communicating with ATC to familiarize yourself with the clearance data after you have accepted it. You must know the locations of the specified navigation facilities, together with the route and point-to-point times, *before* accepting the clearance.

The Standard Instrument Departure, which you have available during preflight planning, enables you to study and understand the details of your departure before filing your IFR flight plan. It permits you to set up your communications and navigation equipment and to be ready for departure before requesting IFR clearance from the tower. The SID eliminates unnecessarily long delays in clearance delivery that would result in inconvenience and expense to airspace users as well as revisions in flight planning for pilots awaiting departure.

Regardless of the nature of your clearance, it is imperative that you are prepared to understand it, and having accepted it, comply with ATC instructions to the letter. It is your privilege to request a clearance different from that issued by ATC if you consider another course of action more practicable or if your aircraft equipment limitations or other considerations make acceptance of the clearance inadvisable. Though FAR Part 91 does not require you to accept a clearance, it is very specific as to your *privileges and responsibilities*.

1. Responsibility and authority of the pilot in command.

(a) The pilot in command of an aircraft is directly responsible for, and is the final authority as to, the operation of that aircraft.

(b) In an emergency requiring immediate action, the pilot in command may deviate from a rule to the extent required to meet that emergency.

(c) Each pilot in command who deviates from a rule shall, upon the request of the Administrator, send a written report of that deviation to the Administrator.

2. Compliance with ATC clearances and instructions.

(a) When an ATC clearance has been obtained, no pilot in command may deviate from that clearance, except in an emergency, unless he obtains an amended clearance. However, except in positive controlled airspace, this paragraph does not prohibit him from cancelling an IFR flight plan if he is operating in VFR weather conditions. If a pilot is uncertain of the meaning of an ATC clearance, he shall immediately request clarification from ATC.

(b) Except in an emergency, no person may, in an area in which air traffic control is exercised, operate an aircraft contrary to an ATC instruction.

(c) Each pilot in command who deviates, in an emergency, from an ATC clearance or instruction shall notify ATC of that deviation as soon as possible.

(d) Each pilot in command who (though not deviating from a rule of this subpart) is given priority by ATC in an emergency, shall, if requested by ATC, submit a detailed report of that emergency within 48 hours to the chief of that ATC facility.

An ATC clearance presupposes that you are equipped and will comply with the applicable Regulations (Part 91), as follows:

1. **Instruments and equipment IFR flight.** The following instruments and equipment are required: ... Two-way radio communications system and navigational equipment appropriate to the ground facilities to be used. ...

2. **IFR radio communications.** The pilot in command of each aircraft operated under IFR in controlled airspace shall have a continuous watch maintained on the appropriate frequency. ...

3. **Course to be flown.** Unless otherwise authorized by ATC, no person may operate an aircraft within controlled airspace, under IFR, except as follows:

(a) On a Federal Airway, along the centerline of that airway.

(b) On any other route, along the direct course between the navigational aids or fixes defining that route.

However, this section does not prohibit maneuvering the aircraft to pass well clear of other air traffic or the maneuvering of the aircraft, in VFR conditions, to clear the intended flight path both before and during climb or descent.

Departure Procedures

Standard Instrument Departures (SIDs).—To simplify air traffic control clearances and relay and delivery procedures, Standard Instrument Departures have been established for the most frequently used departure routes in areas of high traffic activity. You will normally use a SID (Fig. 12–2) where such departures are available since this is advantageous to both users and Air Traffic Control. The following points are important to remember if you file IFR out of terminal areas where SIDs are in use:

1. SIDs are published in booklet form every 56 days with each issue of the National Ocean Survey Approach and Enroute Charts. Two booklets are issued, one for the eastern half of the United States and one for the western half. The descriptions are both graphic and textual. The *Airman's Information Manual* describes SID procedures.

2. Pilots of IFR civil aircraft operating from locations where SID procedures are effective may expect an ATC clearance containing a SID. The use of a SID requires pilot possession of at least the textual description of the approved effective SID.

3. If you do not possess a preprinted SID or for any other reason do not wish to use a SID, you are expected to advise ATC. Notification may be accomplished by filing "NO SID" in the remarks sec-

tion of the filed flight plan or by the less desirable method of verbally advising ATC.

4. If you accept a SID in your clearance, you must comply with it, just as you comply with other ATC instructions.

Preferred IFR Routes.—In the major terminal and en route environments, preferred routes have been established to guide pilots in planning their routes of flight, to minimize route changes, and to aid in the orderly management of air traffic using the Federal Airways. You file via SID and preferred route for the same reasons that for long automobile trips you drive via expressway and interstate superhighway. The route is quicker, easier, and safer. The *Airport/Facility Directory* lists both high and low altitude preferred routes.

Radar-Controlled Departures.—On your IFR departures from airports in congested areas, you will normally receive navigational guidance from departure control by radar vector. When your departure is to be vectored immediately following takeoff, you will be advised before takeoff of the initial heading to be flown and the frequency on which you will contact departure control. This information is vital in the event that you experience (complete) loss of two-way radio communications during departure.

The radar departure is normally simple. Following takeoff, you contact departure control on the assigned frequency upon release from tower control. At this time departure control verifies radar contact, tells you briefly the purpose of the vector (airway, point, or route to which you will be vectored), and gives headings, altitude, and climb instructions, and other information to move you quickly and safely out of the terminal area. You listen to instructions and fly basic instrument maneuvers (climbs, level-offs, turns to predetermined headings, and straight-and-level flight) until the controller tells you your position with respect to the route given in your clearance, whom to contact next, and to "resume normal navigation."

Departure control will vector you either to a navigation facility or an en route position appropriate to your departure clearance, or you will be transferred to another controller with further radar surveillance capabilities. It is just like having your instructor along to tell you what to do and when to do it. The procedure is so easy, in fact, that inexperienced pilots are often inclined to depend entirely on radar for navigational guidance, unconcerned about the consequences of loss of radar contact and indifferent to common-sense precautions associated with flight planning.

A radar-controlled departure does NOT relieve you of your responsibilities as pilot-in-command of your aircraft. You should be prepared before takeoff to conduct your own navigation according to your ATC clearance, with navigation receivers checked and properly tuned. While under radar control, you should monitor your instruments to ensure that you are continuously oriented to the route specified in your clearance and you should record the time over designated check points.

Departures from Uncontrolled Airports.—Occasionally, you will depart from airports which have neither a Tower nor Flight Service Station. Under these circumstances, it is desirable that you telephone your flight plan to the nearest FAA facility at least 30 minutes prior to your estimated departure time. If weather conditions permit, you could depart VFR and request IFR clearance as soon as radio contact is established with an FAA facility. If weather conditions made it undesirable to attempt to maintain VFR, you could again telephone the facility which took your flight plan and request clearance by telephone. In this case, the controller would probably issue a short range clearance pending establishment of radio contact and might also restrict your departure time to a certain period. For example:

CLEARANCE VOID IF NOT OFF BY 0900.

This would authorize you to depart within the allotted time period and proceed in accordance with your clearance. In the absence of any specific departure instructions, the pilot would be expected to proceed on course via the most direct route.

En Route Procedures

Normal procedures en route will vary according to your proposed route, the traffic environment, and the ATC facilities controlling your flight. Some IFR flights are under radar surveillance and control from departure to arrival; others rely entirely on pilot navigation. Flight proceeding from controlled to uncontrolled airspace are outside ATC jurisdiction as soon as the aircraft is outside of controlled airspace.

Where ATC has no jurisdiction, it does not issue an IFR clearance. It has no control over the flight; nor does the pilot have any assurance of separation from other traffic.

With the increasing use of the national airspace, the amount of uncontrolled airspace is diminishing, and the average pilot will normally file IFR via airways and under ATC control. For IFR flying in uncontrolled airspace, there are few regulations and procedures to comply with. The advantages are also few, and the hazards can be many. For rules governing altitudes and course to be flown in uncontrolled airspace, see FAR 91.

En Route Separation.—For en route control, departure control will advise you to contact Air Route Traffic Control (the appropriate Center) on a specified frequency as you approach the limit of terminal radar jurisdiction. At this point departure control, in coordination with the Center, has provided you with standard separation from other aircraft on IFR clearances. Separation from other IFR aircraft is provided thus:

a. Vertically by assignment of different altitudes.

b. Longitudinally by controlling time separation between aircraft on the same course.

c. Laterally by assignment of different flight paths.

d. By radar—including all of the above.

ATC does NOT provide separation for an aircraft operating—

a. Outside controlled airspace.

b. On an IFR clearance:

(1) With "VFR conditions on top" authorized instead of a specific assigned altitude.

(2) Specifying climb or descent in "VFR conditions."

(3) At any time in VFR conditions, since uncontrolled VFR flights may be operating in the same airspace.

Of more importance to you are the reporting procedures by which you convey information to the Center controller. Using the data you transmit, the controller follows the progress of your flight. The accuracy of your reports can affect the progress and safety of every other aircraft operating in the area on an IFR flight plan because ATC must correlate your reports with all the others to provide separation and expedite aircraft movements.

Reporting Requirements.—Federal Aviation Regulations require pilots to maintain a listening watch on the appropriate frequency and unless operating under radar control, to furnish position reports over certain reporting points. Any unforecast weather conditions or other information related to the safety of flight must also be reported.

If not in "Radar Contact," position reports are required by all flights regardless of altitude, including those operating in accordance with a "VFR conditions-on-top" clearance, over each designated compulsory reporting point (shown as solid triangles) along the route being flown. Along direct routes, reports are required of all flights over each reporting point used to define the route of flight. Reports over an "on request" reporting point (shown as open triangles) are made only when requested by ATC.

Position Reports.—The use of standardized reporting procedures generally makes for faster and more effective communication. A standardized communication with ATC normally complies with the Radiotelephone Contact Procedure comprising call-up, reply, message, and acknowledgment or ending. Use this procedure when making position reports to a Flight Service Station for relay to the center controlling your flight. Your IFR position reports should include the following items:

1. Identification.

2. Position.

3. Time. Over a VOR, the time reported should be the time at which the first complete reversal of the TO/FROM indicator is noted. Over a nondirectional radio beacon, the time reported should be the time at which the ADF needles make a complete reversal, or indicates that you have passed the facility.

4. Altitude or flight level. Include actual altitude or flight level when operating on a clearance specifying "VFR conditions-on-top."

5. Type of flight plan, if your report is made to a Flight Service Station. This item is not required if your report is made direct to an ATC center or approach controller, both of whom already know that you are on an IFR flight plan.

6. Estimated time of arrival (ETA) over next reporting point.

7. The name only of the next succeeding (required) reporting point along the route of flight.

8. Remarks, when required.

During your early communications training, your reports will be clear and concise if you learn and adhere to the procedures outlined in the *Airman's Information Manual*. Often these procedures are abbreviated by both pilots and controllers when clarity and positive identification are not compromised. With increasing experience in ATC communications, you will readily learn to reduce verbiage when high radio congestion makes it advisable.

En route position reports are submitted normally to the ARTCC controllers via direct controller-to-pilot communications channels, using the appropriate ARTCC frequencies listed on the en route chart. Unless you indicate the limitation of your communications equipment, under "Remarks" on your IFR flight plan, ATC will expect direct pilot-to-center communications en route, advising you of the frequency to be used and when a frequency change is required. Failure to provide ATC with frequency information on your flight plan contributes to radio congestion until ATC can assign you a frequency suitable to your equipment limitations.

In order to reduce congestion, pilots reporting direct to an ARTCC follow special voice procedures when making the initial call-up. Whenever an initial center contact is to be followed by a position report, the name of the reporting point should be included in the call-up. This alerts the controller that such information is forthcoming.

Malfunction Reports.—Pilot of aircraft operated in controlled airspace under IFR are required to report immediately to ATC any of the following malfunctions of equipment occurring in flight:

(1) Loss of VOR, TACAN, or ADF receiver capability.

(2) Complete or partial loss of ILS receiver capability.

(3) Impairment of air/ground communications capability.

In each such report, pilots are expected to include aircraft identification, equipment affected, and degree to which IFR operational capability in the ATC system is impaired. The nature and extent of assistance desired from ATC must also be stated.

Additional reports.—The *Airman's Information Manual* specifies the following reports to ATC, without request by the controller:

1. The time and altitude/flight level reaching a holding fix or point to which cleared. (Not required when in "Radar Contact.")

2. When vacating any previously assigned altitude/flight level for a newly assigned altitude/flight level.

3. When leaving any assigned holding fix or point. (Not required when in "Radar Contact.")

4. When leaving final approach fix inbound on final approach. (Not required when in "Radar Contact.")

5. When approach has been missed. (Request clearance for specific action; i.e., to alternate airport, another approach, etc.)

6. A corrected estimate at any time it becomes apparent that an estimate as previously submitted is in error in excess of three minutes. (Not required when in "Radar Contact.")

7. That an altitude change will be made if operating on a clearance specifying "VFR conditions-on-top."

Arrival Procedures

ATC arrival procedures and your cockpit workload are affected by weather conditions, traffic density, aircraft equipment, and radar availability.

Standard Terminal Arrival Routes (STARs).—These routes have been established to simplify clearance delivery procedures for arriving aircraft at certain areas having high density traffic. A STAR (Fig. 12–3) serves a purpose parallel to that of a SID for departing traffic. You should remember the following points regarding STARs:

1. All STARs are contained in one booklet which is published every 56 days with each issue of the National Ocean Survey Approach and Enroute Charts. The descriptions are both graphic and textual. The *Airman's Information Manual* describes STAR procedures.

2. Pilots of IFR civil aircraft destined to locations for which STARs have been published may be issued a clearance containing a STAR whenever ATC deems it appropriate. The use of a STAR requires pilot possession of at least the approved textual description.

3. It is your responsibility to either accept or refuse an issued STAR. If you do not wish to use a STAR, you should advise ATC by placing "NO STAR" in the remarks section of your filed flight plan or by the less desirable method of verbally advising ATC.

4. If you accept a STAR in your clearance, you must comply with it, just as you comply with other ATC instructions.

Uncontrolled Airports (No Tower).—On a flight in an uncongested area into an airport with no tower, the controlling ARTCC advises you to contact the Flight Service Station at or near the destination airport for airport advisory information. This includes the current local altimeter setting, wind direction and velocity, runway information, and known traffic. Further reports are relayed by Flight Service to the Center until you have canceled your IFR flight plan.

Airports With Tower.—Your workload can be much greater on arrival at a terminal area where a combination of low ceiling and visibility, heavy traffic, and type of available approach aids requires considerable delay in the issuance of approach clearances. At an airport equipped with ILS facilities, the local controllers can normally handle an arrival every 2 minutes. At the same airport, with the ILS system unavailable and the VORTAC located 8 miles from the field, the arrival interval may be increased to 10 minutes.

Whatever the reasons for delaying instrument approaches—including arrival intervals, traffic density, deteriorating weather, missed approaches, etc.—holding may be necessary. The order of priority of issuance of approach clearances is normally established on a first-come-first-served basis. The first aircraft estimated over the fixes from which approaches are begun will be the first to receive an approach clearance, followed by the aircraft in the order of their estimated or actual times of arrival over the several fixes.

Holding.—"Holding" is maneuvering an aircraft along a predetermined flight path within prescribed airspace limits with respect to a geographic fix. The fix may be identified visually (without reference to instruments) as a specified location, or by reference to instruments as a radio facility or in-

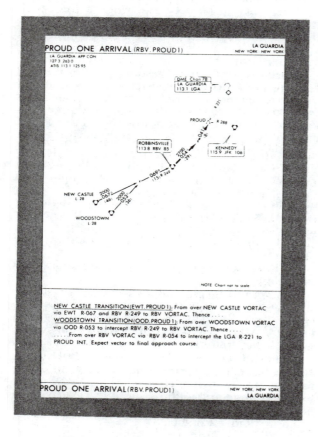

FIGURE 12–3. Standard terminal arrival route (STAR).

tersection of courses. VORs, radio beacons, and airway intersections are used as holding points.

The diagram in Figure 12–4 illustrates control procedures used when a number of aircraft are stacked at an approach fix (Outer Compass Locator) on an ILS front course, with additional aircraft holding in the stack at an outer fix (VOR). Successive arriving aircraft are cleared to the approach fix until the highest altitude/flight level to be assigned is occupied, and thereafter to the outer fix at an appropriate altitude/flight level above the highest level occupied at the approach fix. This permits aircraft subsequently cleared to the approach fix to proceed in descending flight. The illustration shows an interval of 2 minutes between successive approaches. The #1 and #2 aircraft have already passed the Outer Locator (LOM) on final approach, and the #3 aircraft has been cleared for approach and to depart the LOM 2 minutes after the #2 aircraft reported leaving the LOM inbound on final approach.

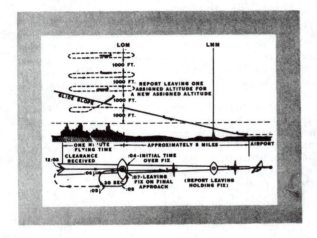

FIGURE 12–4.   ATC procedures—timed approaches.

As Figure 12–4 shows, to fly a holding pattern involves a combination of simple basic maneuvers— two turns and two legs in straight-and-level flight or descending when cleared by ATC. Although these maneuvers are far less difficult than, for example, absolute-rate climbs or descent to predetermined headings and altitudes (see Chapter V, "Attitude Instrument Flying—Airplanes"), holding procedures are a common source of confusion and apprehension among instrument pilot trainees.

There are many reasons for this apprehension, among them the idea that holding implies uncertainty. delay, procedural complications, and generally an increased workload at a time when you are already busy reviewing the details of your instrument approach. Another reason involves the normal psychological pressure attending approach to your destination, when you become increasingly conscious of the fact that your margin of error is narrowing. The closer you get to touchdown, the

more decisions you must make, and the decisions must be quick, positive, and accurate as you have fewer chances to correct the inaccuracies. Like any other flight problem, holding complications become routine after sufficient study of the procedures in their normal sequence.

Standard Holding Pattern (No Wind).—At or below 14,000 feet, the standard holding pattern (Fig. 12–5) is a racetrack pattern requiring approximately 4 minutes to execute. The aircraft follows the specified course inbound to the holding fix, turns 180° to the right, flies a parallel straight course outbound for one minute, turns 180° to the right, and flies the inbound course to the fix.

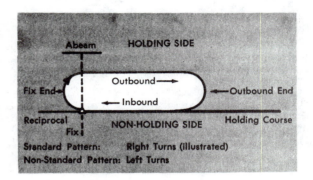

FIGURE 12–5.   Standard holding pattern—no wind.

Nonstandard Holding Pattern.—A nonstandard holding pattern is one in which the fix end and outbound turns are made to the left. Your ATC clearance will always specify left turns when a nonstandard pattern is to be flown.

Standard Holding Pattern With Wind.—In compliance with the holding pattern procedures given in the *Airman's Information Manual,* the symmetrical racetrack pattern cannot be tracked when a wind exists. Pilots are expected to—

a. Execute all turns during entry to and while in the holding pattern at 3° per second, or a 30° bank angle, or a 25° bank angle if a flight director system is used; whichever requires the least bank angle.

b. Compensate for the effect of a known wind except when turning.

Figure 12–6 illustrates the holding track followed with a left crosswind. Further details of compensation for wind effect are given in this manual in Chapter VIII, "Using the Navigation Instruments—Tracking."

The effect of wind is thus counteracted by correcting for drift on the inbound and outbound legs, and by applying time allowances to be discussed under "Time Factors."

Holding Instructions.—If you arrive at your clearance limit before receiving clearance beyond the fix, ATC expects you to maintain the last assigned altitude and begin holding in accordance with the

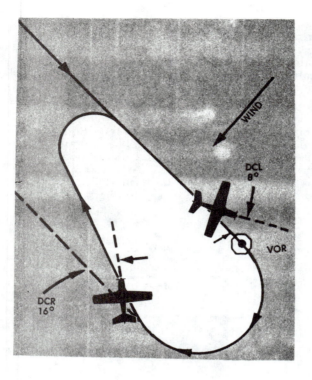

FIGURE 12–6.   Drift correction in holding pattern.

depicted holding pattern. If no holding pattern is depicted, you are expected to begin holding in a standard holding pattern on the course on which you approached the fix. You should immediately request further clearance. Normally, when no delay is anticipated, ATC will issue holding instructions at least 5 minutes before your estimated arrival at the fix. Where a holding pattern is not depicted, the "General Holding Instructions" in the *Airman's Information Manual* state that the ATC clearance will specify the following:

1. Direction of holding from the fix, using magnetic directions and referring to one of eight general points of the compass (north, northeast, east, etc.).

2. Name of the holding fix.

3. Radial, course, magnetic bearing, airway number or jet route on which holding is to be accomplished.

4. Outbound leg in nautical miles if DME is used.

5. Left turns, if nonstandard pattern is to be used.

6. Time to expect further clearance (EFC), or time to expect approach clearance (EAC).

Suitable ATC instructions will also be issued whenever—

1. It is determined that delay will exceed 1 hour.

2. A revised EFC or EAC is necessary.

3. In a terminal area having a number of navigation aids and approach procedures, a clearance limit may not indicate clearly which approach pro-

cedures will be used. On initial contact, or as soon as possible thereafter, approach control will advise you of the type of approach you may anticipate.

4. Ceiling and/or visibility is reported as being at or below the highest "circling minimums" established for the airport concerned. ATC will transmit a report of current weather conditions, and subsequent changes, as necessary.

5. Aircraft are holding while awaiting approach clearance, and pilots thereof advise that reported weather conditions are below minimums applicable to their operation. In this event, ATC will issue suitable instructions to aircraft which desire either to continue holding while awaiting weather improvement or proceed to another airport.

Standard Entry Procedures.—The entry procedures given in the *Airman's Information Manual* evolved from extensive experimentation under a wide range of operational conditions. The standardized procedures should be followed to ensure that you remain within the boundaries of the prescribed holding airspace.

You are expected to reduce airspeed to holding speed 3 minutes prior to your ETA at the holding fix. The purpose of the speed reduction is to prevent overshooting the holding airspace limits, especially at locations where adjacent holding patterns are close together. The *exact* time at which you reduce speed is not important, so long as you arrive *at the fix* at your preselected holding speed within 3 minutes of your submitted ETA. If it takes more than 3 minutes for you to complete a speed reduction and ready yourself for identification of the fix, adjustment of navigation and communications equipment, entry to the pattern, and reporting, make the necessary time allowance.

Technique will vary with pilot experience, cockpit workload, aircraft performance, equipment used, and other factors. With dual VOR receivers, dual transceivers, distance measuring equipment, Integrated Flight System (Flight Director), autopilot, and a copilot to share the workload, holding is far less of a problem than it would be for an inexperienced solo pilot holding with a single obsolescent VOR receiver.

Refer to En Route - IFR in the *Airman's Information Manual* for a discussion of holding pattern entries, turns, and airspeeds.

Time factors.—

Entry time reported to ATC (see "Additional Reports" in this chapter) is the initial time of arrival over the fix.

Initial outbound leg is flown for 1 minute at or below 14,000 feet MSL and for 1½ minutes above 14,000 feet MSL. Timing for subsequent outbound legs should be adjusted as necessary to achieve proper inbound leg time.

Outbound timing begins *over or abeam* the fix, whichever occurs later. If the abeam position cannot be determined, start timing when turn to outbound is completed (Fig. 12–7).

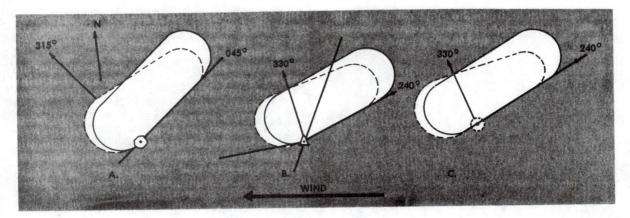

VOR	*AIRWAY INTERSECTION*	*COMPASS LOCATOR*
Outbound timing starts when To/From indicator reverses.	Outbound timing starts at completion of outbound turn, since 330° magnetic bearing cannot be determined.	Outbound timing starts when ADF rel. bearing is 90° minus drift correction angle.

FIGURE 12–7 Holding—outbound timing.

No other time adjustments are necessary unless ATC specifies a time to leave the holding fix, as on a timed approach (see Fig. 12–4). Any necessary reduction in holding time will depend upon the time required to complete a circuit of the pattern. If, for example, a complete circuit requires 4½ minutes, and the fix departure time is 12 minutes after passage over the fix, fly two more patterns (9 minutes) and shorten the outbound leg on the last circuit to provide for a total of 1 minute except for the turns, which at 3° per second will take 2 minutes. Precise timing requires rapid cross-check and planning, in addition to the attention devoted to basic attitude control, tracking, and ATC communications.

Expect Approach Clearance times (EAC) and *Expect Further Clearance times* (EFC) require no time adjustment since the purpose for issuance of these times is to provide for possible loss of two-way radio communications. You will normally receive further clearance prior to your EAC or EFC. If you fail to receive it, request it.

Time leaving the holding fix must be known to ATC before succeeding aircraft can be cleared to the airspace you have vacated (see "Additional Reports" in this chapter). Leave the holding fix—
1. When ATC issues either further clearance en route or approach clearance.
2. As prescribed in FAR 91 (for IFR operations; two-way radio communications failure and responsibility and authority of the pilot in command) or
3. After you have canceled your IFR flight plan, if you are holding in VFR conditions.

The diagram in Figure 12–8 shows the application of the foregoing procedures. Assume approach to the holding fix on the following ATC clearance, estimating Fox 1200:

FASTFLIGHT FIVE FOUR THREE TWO KILO—HOLD EAST OF FOX INTERSECTION ON VICTOR

ONE FOUR ZERO—MAINTAIN SEVEN THOUSAND—EXPECT FURTHER CLEARANCE AT ONE TWO TWO ZERO.

Steps 1–10 show you overheading the fix inbound at 1203, with 17 minutes remaining to hold. If the first complete holding circuit takes 4 minutes, 30 seconds, you should therefore expect further clearance (1220) on the fourth circuit approximately 1 minute from the fix, inbound.

DME Holding.—The same entry and holding procedures apply to DME holding except distances (nautical miles) are used instead of time values. The outbound course of the DME holding pattern is called the outbound leg of the pattern. The length of the outbound leg will be specified by the controller and the end of this leg is determined by the DME odometer reading.

Approaches

Instrument approaches to civil airports.—Unless otherwise authorized, each person operating an aircraft shall, when an instrument letdown to an airport is necessary, use a standard instrument approach procedure prescribed for that airport. Instrument approach procedures are depicted on National Ocean Survey Instrument Approach Procedure Charts.

ATC approach procedures depend upon the facilities available at the terminal area, the type of instrument approach executed, and the existing weather conditions. The ATC facilities, navigation aids, and associated frequencies appropriate to each standard instrument approach are given on the approach chart. Individual charts are published for standard approach procedures associated with the following types of facilities:
1. Nondirectional beacon (NDB).
2. Very high frequency omnirange (VOR).

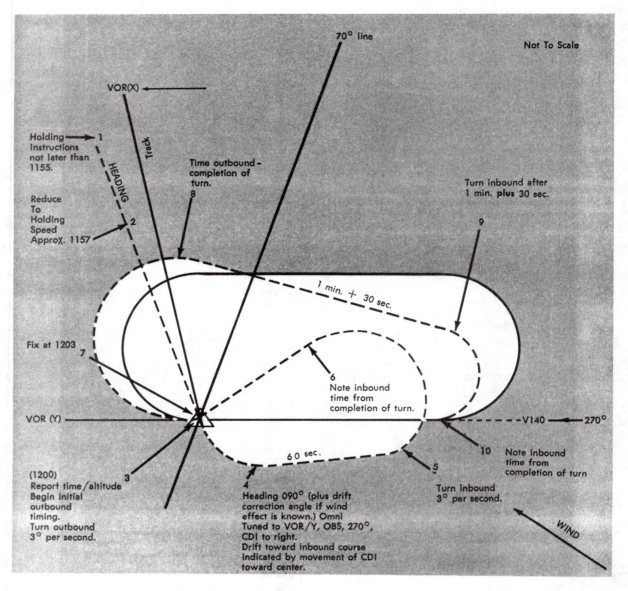

FIGURE 12-8. Holding at an intersection.

3. Very high frequency omnirange with distance measuring equipment (VORTAC or VOR/DME).

4. Instrument landing system (ILS).

5. Localizer type directional aid (LDA).

6. Simplified directional facility (SDF).

Charts are also published for Area Navigation (RNAV) approaches (see Figure 7–21).

Approach to an Airport with Airport Advisory Service but no Tower.—Figure 12–9 shows the approach procedure at an airport where a Flight Service Station is located. When direct communication between the pilot and controller is no longer required, the ARTCC controller will clear you for an instrument approach and advise you to contact the FSS for airport advisory information. During the ap-

proach you will have the benefit of information concerning current weather, known traffic, and any other conditions affecting your flight.

If you are arriving on a "cruise" clearance, ATC will not issue further clearance for approach and landing. The term "cruise" authorizes you to fly at any altitude from the minimum IFR altitude up to and including the altitude specified in the clearance. You may level off at any intermediate altitude within this block of airspace. A climb or descent within the block may be made at your discretion; however, once you start to descend and report leaving an altitude in the block, you may not return to that altitude without an additional clearance. Also, a "cruise" clearance authorizes you to proceed to and make an approach at your destination airport.

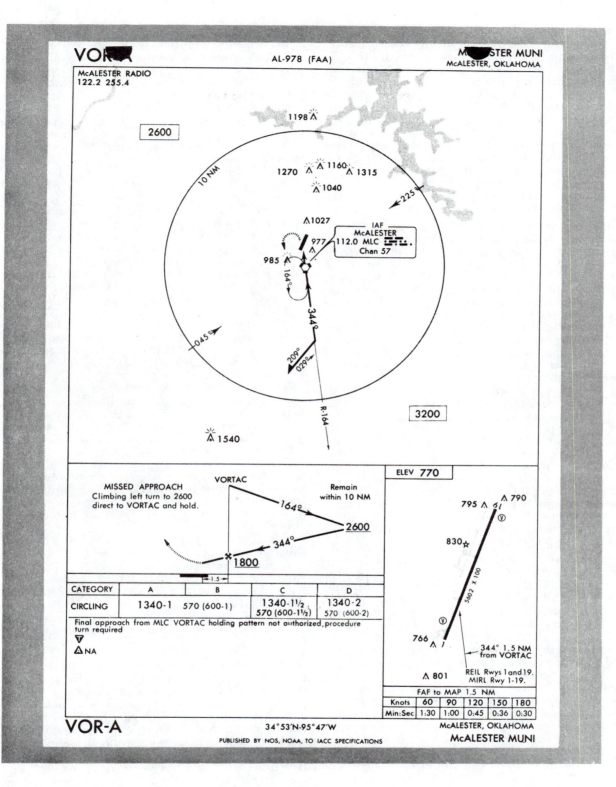

FIGURE 12–9. Instrument approach procedure chart—no tower but advisory service available.

You are required to comply with communications and reporting procedures as on any IFR clearance.

If an approach clearance is required, ARTCC will authorize you to execute your choice of standard instrument approaches (if more than one is published for the airport) with the phrase "CLEARED FOR APPROACH" and the communications frequency change required, if any. Inbound from the procedure turn, you will have no contact with ATC. Accordingly, you must close your IFR flight plan before landing, if in VFR conditions, or by telephone after landing.

Unless otherwise authorized by ATC, you are expected to execute the complete instrument approach procedure shown on the chart.

Approach to an Airport With Tower and Approach Control but No Radar.—Where the approach chart for your destination airport indicates approach control without radar (the notation ASR or RADAR VECTORING will be absent), ARTCC will clear you to an approach/outer fix with the appropriate information and instructions:

1. Name of the fix.
2. Altitude to be maintained.
3. Holding information and expected approach clearance time, if appropriate.
4. Instructions regarding further communications, including:
   a. facility to be contacted.
   b. time and place of contact.
   c. frequency/ies to be used.

If the tower has ATIS, you should monitor that frequency for such information as ceiling, visibility, wind direction and velocity, altimeter setting, instrument approach and runways in use prior to initial radio contact with approach control. The ATIS frequency is listed on the approach chart, en route chart, and in the *Airman's Information Manual.* If there is no ATIS, approach control will, at the time of your first radio contact or shortly thereafter, give you the above information.

Approach to an Airport With Tower, Approach Control, and Radar.—Where radar is approved for approach control service, it is used not only for radar approaches (ASR and PAR) but is also used to provide vectors in conjunction with published instrument approach procedures predicated on radio navaids such as ILS, VOR, and NDB. Radar vectors can provide course guidance and expedite traffic to the final approach course of any established instrument approach procedure.

Approach control facilities that provide this radar service operate in the following manner:

1. Arriving aircraft are either cleared to an outer fix most appropriate to the route being flown with vertical separation and, if required, given holding information; or,
2. When radar hand-offs are effected between ARTCC and approach control, or between two approach control facilities, aircraft are cleared to the airport, or to a fix so located that the hand-off will be completed prior to the time the aircraft reaches the fix.

a. When radar handoffs are utilized, successive arriving flights may be handed-off to approach control with radar separation in lieu of vertical separation.

b. After hand-off to approach control, aircraft are vectored to the appropriate final approach course; e.g., ILS, ADF or NDB.

3. Radar vectors and altitude/flight levels will be issued as required for spacing and separating aircraft; *therefore, you must not deviate from the headings issued by approach control.*

4. You will normally be informed when it becomes necessary to vector you across the final approach course for spacing or other reasons. If you determine that approach course crossing is imminent and you have not been informed that you will be vectored across it, you should question the controller. You should not turn inbound on the final approach course unless you have received an approach clearance. Approach control will normally issue this clearance with the final vector for interception of the final approach course, and the vector will be such as to enable you to establish your aircraft on the final approach course prior to reaching the final approach fix. In the event you are already inbound on the final approach course, you will be issued approach clearance prior to reaching the final approach fix.

5. After you are established inbound on the final approach course, radar separation will be maintained between you and other aircraft and you will be expected to complete the approach using the navaid designated in the clearance (ILS, VOR, NDB, etc.) as the primary means of navigation. Therefore, once you are established on the final approach course, you must not deviate from it unless a clearance to do so has been received from air traffic control.

6. After passing the final approach fix inbound, you are expected to proceed direct to the airport and complete the approach, or to execute the published missed approach procedure.

7. Radar service is automatically terminated when the landing is completed or the tower controller has your aircraft in sight, whichever occurs first.

Figure 12–10 is a reproduction of an instrument approach procedure chart with maximum ATC facilities available.

Radar Approaches.—Initial radar contact for either a surveillance or precision radar approach is made with approach control. You must comply promptly with all instructions when conducting either type procedure. You can determine the radar approach facilities (Surveillance and/or Precision) available at a specific airport by referring to the appropriate Enroute Low Altitude Chart and Instrument Approach Procedure Chart. Surveillance (ASR) and precision (PAR) radar minimums (Fig. 12–11) are listed alphabetically by airport on pages titled, "CIVIL RADAR INSTRUMENT APPROACH MINIMUMS," in the first part of each Instrument Approach Chart booklet. You will note

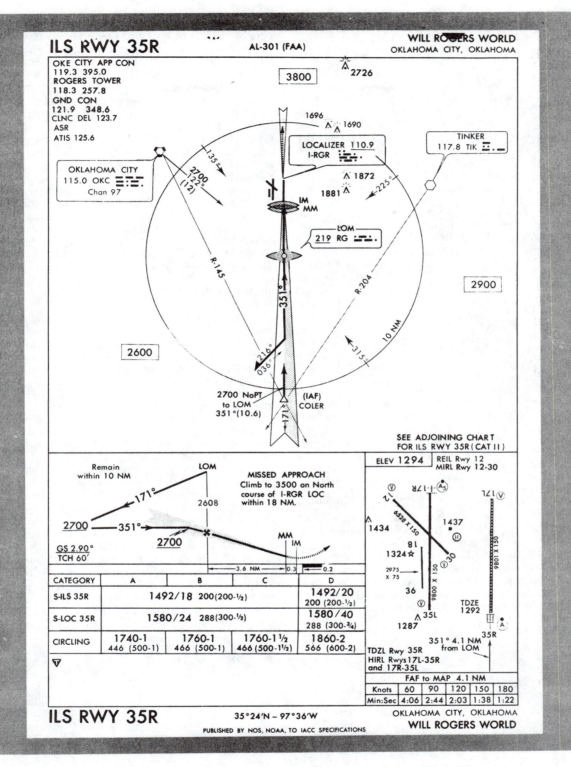

FIGURE 12–10. Instrument approach procedure chart—maximum ATC facilities.

that both straight-in and circling minimums are listed.

Surveillance Approach.—On a surveillance radar approach, the controller will vector you to a point where you can begin a descent to the airport/heliport or to a specific runway. During the initial part of the approach you will be given communications failure/missed approach instructions. Before you begin your descent, the controller will give you the published straight-in MDA. You will not be given the circling MDA unless you request it and tell the controller your aircraft category.

During the final approach, the controller will provide navigational guidance in azimuth only. Guidance in elevation is not possible but you will be advised when to begin descent to the minimum descent altitude (MDA) or if appropriate, to the intermediate "step down fix" minimum crossing altitude and subsequently to the prescribed MDA. In addition, you will be advised of the location of the missed approach point (MAP) and your position each mile from the runway, airport/heliport, or MAP, as appropriate. If you so request, the controller will issue recommended altitudes each mile, based on the descent gradient established for the procedure, down to the last mile that is at or above the MDA. You will normally be provided navigational guidance until you reach the MAP. The controller will terminate guidance and instruct you to execute a missed approach at the MAP, if at that point you do not have the runway or airport/heliport in sight, or, if you are on a point-in-space approach in a helicopter, the prescribed visual reference with the surface is not established. Any time during the approach the controller considers that safe guidance for the remainder of the approach cannot be provided, the approach will be terminated and you will be instructed to execute a missed approach. Also, guidance termination and missed approach will be effected upon pilot request and, for civil aircraft only, the controller may terminate guidance when the pilot reports the runway, airport/heliport, or visual surface route (point-in-space approach) in sight or otherwise indicates that continued guidance is not required. Radar service is automatically terminated at the completion of the radar approach.

Precision Approach.—Duluth International (Fig. 12–11 is one of the few airports that still has PAR. The installations that do have PAR are joint civil/military airports and usually provide service to civilian pilots flying IFR only prior permission, except in an emergency.

A PAR serves the same purpose as an Instrument Landing System (ILS) except guidance information is presented to the pilot through aural rather than visual means. If a PAR is available, it is normally aligned with an ILS. During a PAR approach, you are provided highly accurate guidance in both azimuth and elevation.

The precision approach begins when the aircraft is within range of the precision radar and contact has been established with the PAR controller. Normally this occurs approximately eight miles from touchdown, a point to which your are vectored by surveillance radar or are positioned by a non-radar approach procedure. You will be given headings to fly, to direct you to, and to keep your aircraft aligned with the extended centerline of the landing runway.

Prior to intercepting the glide path, you will be advised of communications failure/missed approach procedures and told not to acknowledge further transmissions. You will be told to anticipate glide path interception approximately 15 to 30 seconds before it occurs, and when to start your descent. The published decision height (DH) will be given only if you request it.

During the final approach, the controller will give elevation information as, "slightly/well above" or "slightly/well below" glide path and course information as "slightly/well right" or "slightly/well left" of course. Extreme accuracy in maintaining and correcting headings and rate of descent is essential. The controller will assume the last assigned heading is being maintained and will base further corrections on this assumption. Range from touchdown is given at least once each mile. If your aircraft is observed by the controller to proceed outside of specified safety zone limits in azimuth and/or elevation and continue to operate outside these prescribed limits, you will be directed to execute a missed approach or to fly a specified course unless you have the runway environment in sight. You will be provided navigational guidance in azimuth

DULUTH INTL	MN Amdt. 11, SEP 29, 1976								
ELEV 1429			DH/	HAT/			DH/	HAT/	
	RWY	CAT	MDA-VIS	HAA	CEIL-VIS	CAT	MDA-VIS	HAA	CEIL-VIS
PAR	9	ABCDE	1627/24	200	(200—½)				
ASR	27	ABC	1820/24	399	(400—½)	DE	1820/50	399	(400—1)
	9	ABC	1840/24	413	(500—½)	DE	1840/50	413	(500—1)
CIRCLING		AB	1880—1	451	(500—1)	C	1880—1½	451	(500—1½)
		D	1980—2	551	(600—2)	E	2360—2	931	(1000—2)
▼ △									

FIGURE 12–11. Radar minimums.

and elevation to the DH. Advisory course and glide path information will be furnished by the controller until your aircraft passes over the runway threshold, at which point you will be advised of any deviation from the runway centerline. Radar service is automatically terminated at the completion of the approach.

No-Gyro Approach Under Radar Control.—If you should experience failure of your directional gyro or other stabilized compass, or for other reasons need more positive radar guidance, ATC will provide a no-gyro vector or approach on request. Prior to commencing such an approach, you will be advised as to the type of approach (surveillance or precision approach and runway number) and the manner in which turn instructions will be issued. All turns are executed at standard rate, except on final approach; then at half standard rate. The controller tells you when to start and stop turns, recommends altitude information and otherwise provides guidance and information essential for the completion of your approach. You can execute this approach in an emergency with an operating communications receiver and primary flight instruments.

Radar Monitoring of Instrument Approaches.—When your instrument approach is being radar monitored, the radar advisories serve only as a *secondary* aid. Since you have selected a navaid such as the ILS or VOR as the *primary* aid for the approach, the minimums listed on the approach chart apply.

At a few FAA radar locations and military airfields, such as Duluth International, instrument approaches have been established on navaids whose final approach course from the final approach fix to the runway coincides with the PAR course. At such locations, your approach will be monitored and you will be given radar advisories whenever the reported weather is below basic VFR minima (1,000 and 3), at night, or at your request. Prior to starting the final approach, you will be advised of the frequency on which the advisories will be transmitted. At some airports it may be the ILS localizer voice channel. If, for any reason, radar advisories cannot be furnished, you will be so advised.

Advisory information derived from radar observations, includes the following:

1. Passing the final approach fix (at this point, you may be requested to report sighting the approach lights or the runway).

2. Trend with respect to elevation and/or azimuth radar position and movement. Whenever your aircraft nears the PAR safety limit, you will be advised that you are well above or below the glidepath, or well left or right of course (glidepath information is given only to those aircraft executing a precision approach; e.g., ILS). Altitude is not transmitted if you are executing a non-precision approach because the descent portions of such approaches generally do not coincide with the depicted PAR glidepath.

3. Advise to execute a missed approach, if, after repeated advisories, your aircraft proceeds outside the PAR safety limit or if a radical deviation is observed, and you are not VFR.

Radar service is automatically terminated upon completion of the approach.

Compliance With Published Standard Instrument Approach Procedures.—Compliance with the approach procedures shown on the approach charts provides necessary navigation guidance information for alignment with the final approach courses, as well as obstruction clearance. Under certain conditions, execution of the complete published procedure is not permissible.

The procedure turn is a required maneuver except in the following instances:

1. When the symbol "NoPT" appears on the approach course on the planview of the approach chart.

2. When RADAR VECTORING is provided.

3. When a one minute holding pattern is published in lieu of a procedure turn.

4. When executing a timed approach from a holding fix.

5. When your approach clearance specifies "Cleared for straight-in (type of approach) approach."

6. When a contact approach has been requested by the pilot and approved by ATC. A "contact" approach is defined as an approach wherein an aircraft on an IFR flight plan, operating clear of clouds with at least 1-mile flight visibility and having received an air traffic control authorization, may deviate from the prescribed instrument approach procedure and proceed to the airport of destination by visual reference to the surface. Approval of your request for a contact approach does not constitute cancellation of your IFR flight plan, and the controller must issue alternative procedures in the event that conditions less than those specified for a contact approach are encountered following approval.

7. At any time you can complete the approach in VFR conditions and cancel your IFR flight plan. Unless you cancel, or unless otherwise authorized by ATC, you are required to comply with the prescribed instrument approach procedure, regardless of weather conditions.

Circling Approaches.—The circling minimums published on the instrument approach chart provide adequate obstruction clearance. During a circling approach, you should maintain visual contact with the runway of intended landing and fly no lower than the circling minimums until you are in position to make a final descent for a landing. Remember that circling minimums are just that—minimums. Nothing prevents you from flying higher. If the ceiling allows it, fly at an altitude that more nearly approximates your VFR traffic pattern altitude. This will make any maneuvering safer and bring your view of the landing runway into a more normal perspective.

Patterns which can be used for circling approaches are shown in Figure 12–12. Pattern "A" can be flown when your final approach course intersects the runway centerline at less than a 90° angle and you sight the runway early enough to establish a base leg. If you sight the runway too late to fly pattern "A," you can circle as shown in "B." You can fly pattern "C" if it is desirable to land opposite the direction of the final approach and the runway is sighted in time for a turn to downwind leg. If the runway is sighted too late for a turn to downwind as shown in "C," you can fly pattern "D."

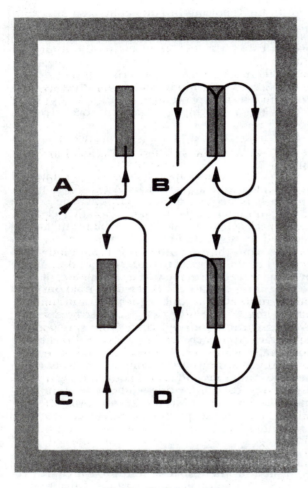

FIGURE 12–12. Circling approaches.

Sound judgment and knowledge of your capabilities and the performance of your aircraft are the criteria for determining the pattern to be flown in each instance, since airport design, ceiling and visibility, wind direction and velocity, final approach course alignment, distance from the final approach fix to the runway, and ATC instructions must all be considered.

Missed Approaches

A missed approach procedure is formulated for each published instrument approach. The missed approach is normally made on a course that most nearly approximates a continuation of the final approach course. A missed approach will be initiated at the point where the aircraft has descended to authorized landing minimums at a specified distance from the facility if visual contact is not established, or if the landing has not been accomplished, or when directed by Air Traffic Control. The procedure is shown on the approach chart in narrative and pictorial form. Since the execution of a missed approach occurs when your cockpit workload is at a maximum, the procedure should be studied and mastered before beginning the approach.

Applicable landing minimums are listed on the approach chart under *circling* or "S" (straight-in). Straight-in minimums apply if landing is to be made on the runway aligned with the final approach course. Circling minimums apply when it is necessary to circle the airport or maneuver for landing, or when no straight-in minimums are specified on the approach chart.

The following subjects are a partial review of those regulations published in FAR Part 91 which prescribes takeoff and landing minimums under IFR.

Landing minimums (91.116). "Unless otherwise authorized by the Administrator, no person operating an aircraft . . . may land that aircraft using a standard instrument approach procedure . . . unless the visibility is at or above the landing minimum prescribed . . . for the procedure used. If the landing minimum in a standard instrument approach procedure . . . "

Descent below MDA or DH (91.117). "No person may operate an aircraft below the prescribed minimum descent altitude or continue an approach below the decision height unless—

(1) the aircraft is in a position from which a normal approach to the runway of intended landing can be made; and

(2) the approach threshold of that runway, or approach lights or other markings identifiable with the approach end of that runway, are clearly visible to the pilot.

If, upon arrival at the missed approach point or decision height, or at any time thereafter, any of the above requirements are not met, the pilot shall immediately execute the appropriate missed approach procedure."

Inoperative or unusable components and visual aids (91.117). "The basic ground components of an ILS are the localizer, glide slope, outer marker, and middle marker. The approach lights are visual aids normally associated with the ILS. In addition, if an ILS approach procedure . . . prescribes a visibility minimum of 1,800 feet or 2,000 feet RVR, high intensity runway lights, touchdown zone lights, centerline lighting and marking, and RVR are aids associated with the ILS for those minimums. Compass locator or precision radar may be substituted for the outer or middle marker. Surveillance radar may be substituted for the outer marker. Except . . . Administrator, if a ground component, visual aid, or RVR is inoperative . . . , the straight-in minimums are increased in accordance with the following tables.* If the related airborne equipment . . . is inoperative . . . , the increased minimums applicable to the related ground component shall be used. If more than one component or aid is inoperative . . . , each minimum is raised to the highest minimum required by any one of the components or aids which is inoperative, ..."

Missed Approach from ILS Front Course.—A missed approach is reported and executed in the following instances:
1. If, at the Decision Height (DH), the runway approach threshold, approach lights, or other markings identifiable with the approach end of the runway, are not clearly visible to the pilot.
2. If a safe landing is not possible.
3. When directed by ATC.

Missed Approach from Radar Approaches.—Prior to starting the final approach of either an ASR or a PAR approach, the pilot will be given missed approach instructions. A missed approach will be reported and executed in the following instances:
1. If, at the missed approach point or DH, as applicable, the runway approach threshold, approach lights, or other markings identifiable with the approach end of the runway, are not clearly visible to the pilot.
2. If a safe landing is not possible.
3. When directed by ATC.

Missed Approach-Localizer, Localizer Back Course, VOR, and ADF Approaches.—For these, the missed approach procedures are related to the location of the final approach fix and are initiated in the following instances:
1. If, at the missed approach point, the runway approach threshold, approach lights, or other markings identifiable with the approach end of the runway, are not clearly visible to the pilot.
2. If a safe landing is not possible.
3. When directed by ATC.
When the final approach fix is not located on the field, the missed approach procedure specifies the distance from the facility to the missed approach point. The "Aerodrome Data" on the approach chart shows the time from the facility to missed approach at various ground speeds, which you must determine from airspeed, wind, and distance values. At this time, you report and execute a missed approach if you do not have applicable minimums.

---

*(See *Inoperative or Unusable Components and Visual Aids Table* in FAR 91.117.)*

Landing

Controllers are responsible for providing current prevailing visibility/RVV/RVR appropriate to the runway in use; however, they are *not* responsible for determining that landing minimums do or do not exist. You, as a pilot, are responsible for determining that the reported visibility meets the landing requirements indicated on the approach chart.

Canceling IFR Flight Plan

You may cancel your IFR flight plan any time you are operating in VFR conditions outside positive controlled airspace by stating "CANCEL MY IFR FLIGHT PLAN" to the controller or air/ground station with which you are communicating. Immediately after cancelling your IFR flight plan, you should change to the appropriate air/ground frequency, VFR transponder code (1200), and VFR altitude/flight level.

ATC separation and information services (including radar services, where applicable) are discontinued. If you desire VFR radar advisory service, you must specifically request it. In addition, you must be aware that other procedures may apply if you cancel your IFR flight plan within an area such as a Terminal Radar Service Area or Terminal Control Area.

If you are operating on an IFR flight plan to an airport with a functioning control tower, your flight plan is cancelled automatically upon landing. If you are operating on an IFR flight plan to an airport with no functioning control tower, you must initiate cancellation of the flight plan. This can be done by telephone after landing if there is no functioning flight service station or other means of direct communications with ATC. If there is no flight service station and air/ground communications with ATC are not possible below a certain altitude, you may cancel your IFR flight plan while still airborne and able to communicate with ATC by radio. If you follow this procedure, you must be certain that the remainder of your flight can be conducted under VFR. Regardless of the procedure followed, it is essential that you cancel your IFR flight plan expeditiously. This allows other IFR traffic to utilize the airspace.

Emergencies

Many inflight emergency procedures are special procedures established to meet situations that have been foreseen and for which an immediate solution is available as a standard procedure. Because of the number of variable factors involved, it is impossible to prescribe ATC procedures covering every possible inflight emergency. You are expected to know thoroughly the emergency procedures formulated to prevent emergencies from developing into accidents.

The emergency for which a published solution is available is just another procedure if you are properly prepared for it. FAR Part 91 prescribes procedures to follow in the event of communications failure. The section in the *Airman's Information Manual* titled "Emergency Procedures" includes radio communications failure and, in addition, a number of other emergency procedures applicable to IFR operations.

XIII. FLIGHT PLANNING

No single detailed procedure can be outlined that is applicable to the planning of all IFR flights. However, the basic elements of preflight action are common to all flight-planning problems, irrespective of the simplicity or complexity of the factors affecting the safe and orderly conduct of the flight. This chapter deals with the computations, sources of aeronautical information, and weather information used in preparation for flight under Instrument Flight Rules.

Your first exercise in flight planning may seem unnecessarily time-consuming and discouraging as you plod through computer operations and a mass of information in search of data relevant to your flight. With practice in the preparation of flight logs, you will become increasingly handy with the computer and familiar with the contents of the appropriate flight planning documents. The exercise that follows later in this chapter lists the steps involved in preparing for a typical IFR flight. At each stage of the exercise, the applicable regulations, charts, and other sources of information are listed.

You should study AC 00-6A, *Aviation Weather*, to obtain a basic knowledge of weather fundamen-tals and refer to AC 00-45B, *Aviation Weather Services* for information about the weather service in general and the details of interpreting and using reports, forecasts, weather maps, and prognostic charts. Many of the charts and tables in AC 00-45B apply directly to flight planning and inflight decisions.

Computer Operations

The amount of computer work necessary to plan an IFR flight depends on a number of factors, including flight plan requirements, weather, type of aircraft, route, ATC services available, and airborne equipment. Your flight plan will require airspeed, time, and fuel estimates normally derived by means of any one of many types of navigation computers.

Pilots are sometimes tempted to be careless about these estimates on the assumption that weather forecasts, routes, and altitudes are subject to change and therefore not worth the time spent on detailed and careful computer operations. If you are tempted to make haphazard "guestimates," bear in mind that it is easier to revise a well-organized flight plan than to improvise in the air. Accurate flight-planned estimates reduce your en route workload and provide greater safety in the event of en route emergencies. In addition, weather conditions can keep you preoccupied enough with aircraft control, navigation, and coordination with Air Traffic Control without the added burden of in-flight attention to computations overlooked or ignored during preflight planning. The more adverse the weather, the more thorough must be your preparation.

As an applicant for the instrument rating, it is assumed that you understand the wind triangle, possess an acceptable navigation computer, and are thoroughly familiar with the instructional booklet that accompanied it at the time of purchase. By use of your computer, you should be able to determine:

1. Altitude change in a certain period of time when the rate of climb or rate of descent is given.

2. Time between two points when groundspeed and distance are given.

3. Density altitude when pressure altitude and temperature are given.

4. True altitude when indicated altitude, pressure altitude, and outside air temperature are given.

5. Groundspeed and track when true heading, true airspeed, and wind are given.

6. Wind when true heading, true track, true airspeed, and groundspeed are given.

7. Total fuel consumed when time and rate of fuel consumption are given.

8. Rate of climb in feet per minute when groundspeed and required climb in feet per mile are given.

Sources of Flight Planning Information

In addition to the Enroute Charts, Area Charts, and Instrument Approach Procedure Charts discussed in Chapter X, the FAA publishes the *Airman's Information Manual, Airport/Facility Directory, Graphic Notices and Supplemental Data,* and *Notices to Airmen (Class II)* for flight planning in the National Airspace System. Each of these publications is revised on a periodic schedule. The revision cycle is based on the relative stability of the different types of information presented. For availability, see "Supplementary Reference Materials" in the Appendix of this handbook.

Because these publications are for all airspace users, much of the information applies to flight operations of no more than casual interest to the student instrument pilot familiar with only typical light plane equipment. For example, "OMEGA," "LORAN," and "CONSOLAN" relate to navigation systems normally of concern only to pilots of sophisticated civil and military aircraft. Specific other information may be important to you only under occasional or rare circumstances. In this category are "Ground-Air Visual Code for Use by Survivors" and "ADIZ Procedures."

The sections of the *Airman's Information Manual* applicable to VFR as well as IFR operations, contain basic operational information especially helpful to inexperienced pilots and those "rusty" on current procedures. Descriptions, diagrams, and general discussions about airport lighting and marking, altimeter settings, radar services, approach lighting systems, and navigation facilities help to clarify these important elements of aeronautical knowledge. Of more immediate importance for the planning and conduct of instrument flights are such listings as "Special Notices," "VOR Receiver Check Points," and "Preferred IFR Routes," found in the *Airport/Facility Directory*. A review of the contents of all the publications listed above will help you determine which material is useful for frequent or occasional reference. As you become more familiar with these publications, you will be able to plan your IFR flights quickly and easily.

Preferred IFR Routes are designed to provide for the systematic flow of air traffic in the major terminal and en route environments. The *Airport/Facility Directory* lists the preferred routes from the major terminals alphabetically, to other major terminals in the airspace system. Although this routing is not mandatory, filing via preferred routes has obvious advantages. Flight planning is simplified because of the probability that the route filed will be approved by ATC. Further, the clearance for a flight via SID and preferred route is in brief form, eliminating the complicated route descriptions familiar to instrument pilots.

Since the preferred routes provide for the most efficient flow of traffic in and out of terminal areas, route changes and traffic delays are minimized. For example, when planning a flight from New Orleans, La., to Dallas, Texas, you find several possible routes shown on the two Low Altitude Charts to be used. A check of the low altitude preferred routes listed shows this entry (Fig. 13–1).

NEW ORLEANS METRO AREA
Dallas............ Walker V114N AEX V114 GGG V94 SCY
SCY296 Seago........................... 0000–2359

FIGURE 13–1.

The preferred route is Walker V114N AEX V114 GGG V94 SCY SCY 296 Seago. Since this preferred route begins with the fix Walker, and ends with the fix Seago, your aircraft may be routed to and from these fixes via a SID, radar vectors, or a STAR. The effective time for the route is from 0000 to 2359 GMT. By thorough study of the navigation and communications data appropriate to your selected route, you avoid uncertainty and confusion during IFR departures from busy terminal areas.

The *Graphic Notices and Supplemental Data* contains a tabulation of Area Navigation (RNAV)

Routes, Military Refueling, Tracks, and Areas, Parachute Jumping Areas, Terminal Area Graphics, and other information that is not subject to frequent change.

The *Notices to Airmen (Class II)* contains NOTAMs which are considered essential to safe flight as well as supplemental data affecting the *Airman's Information Manual, Airport/Facility Directory,* and the *Graphic Notices and Supplemental Data.* It also includes current FDC NOTAMs, which are regulatory in nature, issued to established restrictions to flight, or to amend charts or published instrument approach procedures.

The *Airport/Facility Directory* contains information on airports, communications, navigational aids, instrument landing systems, VOR receiver check points, IFR preferred routes, FSS/Weather Service telephone numbers, ARTCC frequencies, part-time control zones, and various other pertinent, special notices essential to air navigation.

If your preliminary check of weather indicates marginal conditions, the facilities and services available at your destination will determine whether or not you can complete your flight. For complete instrument approach and landing data, refer to the "Instrument Approach Procedure Charts."

As your flight progresses from sector to sector, you will be advised of the frequency to be used and when the frequency change is required. If your communications equipment is limited, the limitations should be specified in your flight plan. For example, if you have 90 channel capability (118.0–126.9 MHz), enter "VHF T/R 90 ch." under "Remarks" on your flight plan. This entry tells ATC that your flight en route can be controlled directly by the centers on Sector Discrete Frequencies below 127.0 MHz.

If your equipment includes only the standard FSS VHF frequencies, enter this limitation on your flight plan so that the ARTCC will communicate to you through Flight Service. This information not only facilitates en route communications; it also affects the separation standards (radar vs nonradar) applied to your flight. The use of radar separation minimums requires instantaneous interference-free controller-to-pilot communications.

Notices to Airmen (NOTAMS)

In addition to the basic flight information found in the publications already discussed, you will be interested in the current information concerning the National Airspace System. This information is distributed in the form of NOTAMS which have been previously described on pages 194 and 195 of this handbook. For further details, refer to the *Airman's Information Manual.*

Flight Planning Problem

The flight planning exercise presented here is not intended as an inflexible procedure for the instrument pilot to follow. Many factors affect the sequence of your preflight activity and the content of your flight log entries. For example, the preflight time and inflight attention to fuel consumption are minor problems for a 1-hour IFR flight in an aircraft with 5 hours of fuel aboard, as compared with fuel management problems in a jet aircraft on a maximum range IFR flight to a destination where the weather is just above minimums. In the first instance, your fuel problem involves only routine inflight checks on fuel consumption for subsequent planning purposes and the usual management of the aircraft fuel system. In the second case, there is little or no margin for error, either in preflight computations or en route record.

The low-time instrument pilot can benefit from experience in the use of all the facilities and sources of information available. Through experience you will find a reliable basis for adapting planning methods to operational needs. The professional corporation pilot familiar with the proposed route and terminal facilities may be concerned primarily with weather and loading data. Other professional pilots limit their preflight computations to those necessary for the IFR flight plan (estimated true airspeed, estimated time en route, and fuel on board). Then they prepare a tentative flight log suitable for quick and continuous inflight computations and revisions. Regardless of their experience and differences in planning methods, they overlook no detail that might invite unnecessary inflight problems.

The following problem involves preparation for an IFR training flight from Fort Worth, Texas (Meacham), to Oklahoma City, Oklahoma (Wiley Post). An instrument approach is planned at Wiley Post. The problem begins with the preliminary check with the weather forecaster and ends with the completed flight plan.

Although the 8 steps and the flight log may need adapting to your particular operational needs, they include the aeronautical knowledge applicable to an IFR flight in controlled airspace. Since the FAA written tests for the Instrument Rating are based on comparable problems, the exercise will assist you in preparing for the tests. Each step discussed in the preflight action is related to the appropriate Federal Aviation Regulations and sources of information related to the planning procedure.

Aircraft equipment, performance and operating data, weight and balance information, and weather reports and forecasts are included. The Enroute Low Altitude Chart Segment on the last page of this handbook applies to this exercise. For completion of this exercise and further practice, you will need, in addition to the chart segment supplied in this handbook, the following "tools of the trade.":

1. Airman's Information Manual;
2. Airport/Facility Directory;
3. Notices to Airmen (Class II);
4. Graphic Notices and Supplemental Data;
5. Aviation Weather, AC 00-6A;
6. Aviation Weather Services, AC 00-45B; and
7. A navigation computer.

AIRCRAFT DATA—FASTFLIGHT N5432K

The aircraft is a 5- to 7-place twin-engine "Fastflight" typical of various light twins in current use. It is appropriately equipped for instrument flight and has the following radio equipment:

One L/MF receiver

One automatic direction finder (ADF)

Dual VHF receivers (both with frequency range 108.0–117.95 MHz) with omni heads of the three-element type (course selector, course deviation indicator, and TO-FROM indicator), and instrument landing equipment (ILS localizer and glide slope receivers).

One marker beacon receiver.

Two 360 channel transceivers (range 118.0–135.95 MHz).

DME

Transponder

EMPTY WEIGHT.—As equipped, 4,940 lbs.

MAXIMUM ALLOWABLE GROSS WEIGHT.— 7,000 lbs.

OIL CAPACITY.—10 gallons (5 gal./engine).

USABLE FUEL.—

Main, 156 gal.

Aux., 67 gal. (38.5 gal. in each of 2 aux.).

FUEL CONSUMPTION.—40 gal./hr. (20 gal./hr./engine).

BAGGAGE COMPARTMENT.—See Weight and Balance information.

CALIBRATED AIRSPEEDS.—

Climb . . . . 145 knots.

Cruise . . . . 165 knots.

Approach . . . . 110 knots.

Stall . . . . 85 knots.

ALTITUDES.—All flight altitudes will be in terms of MEAN SEA LEVEL (MSL) unless otherwise specified.

RADIO CALL.—Fastflight 5432K.

DE-ICING EQUIPMENT.—Aircraft is equipped with propeller anti-icing, and wing, and vertical and horizontal stabilizer de-icers.

COMPASS CORRECTION CARD—

FOR (MH)

0 30 60 90 120 150 180 210 240 270 300 330

STEER (CH)

1 30 58 90 122 153 179 210 240 272 300 330

Preflight Action

As you proceed with the preflight steps, refer to the flight logs and the sources listed within the parentheses. Step 1, for example, refers you to (a) Federal Aviation Regulations, which specify what checks are *required* and (b) *Aviation Weather, AC 00-6A* and *Aviation Weather Services, AC 00-45B*, which explain the meaning of the weather information.

Step 1. Preliminary weather check.—Regardless of how good the current weather looks in your departure area, you may save planning time by making use of forecast services well in advance of your expected departure time. Usually, a detailed forecast is accurate for about 6 hours in advance. Beyond 24 hours, only general weather outlooks are possible. It is therefore important to know the types of forecasts available, their filing times, and their valid times. Familiarization with weather service facilities as you plan practice IFR flights in VFR weather conditions is excellent preparation for all-weather flying capability. (FAR 91. *Aviation Weather, AC 00-6A, Aviation Weather Services, AC 00-45B,* and the weather data on pages 226 and 227.)

Step 2. Tentative route(s) to destination and alternate(s).—If possible, choose preferred routes and select more than one alternate if weather is marginal. Start preparation of flight log (Fig. 13-2). (FAR 91.83 (a) (5); Enroute Chart(s); *Airman's Information Manual; Airport/Facility; Notices to Airmen (Class II);* Winds Aloft Forecasts.)

a. *Proposed Altitude.*—This will depend on factors such as aircraft performance and equipment, winds aloft, freezing level, turbulence, cloud tops, and minimum instrument altitudes. (FAR 91.119; FAR 91.121 (a) and (b).)

b. *Route and Check Points.*—A study of Enroute Low Altitude Chart L-13 indicates that direct BPR and V17 is an appropriate route from Fort Worth to Oklahoma City since no preferred route is listed. En route check points which can be used are Bridgeport VORTAC, Bowie Intersection, Duncan VORTAC, and Alexx Intersection. (FAR 91.123; Enroute Low Altitude Chart segment inside back cover.)

c. *True or Magnetic Courses.*—The courses entered on the sample flight log are true courses. Some pilots reference their computations to true direction; others to magnetic. If you start with magnetic direction in your computations, winds aloft data must be corrected for variation; if you use winds aloft as reported or forecast (true direction/knots), magnetic courses shown on the chart must be corrected for variation.

d. *Distances.*—The first leg (32 NM) entered on the flight log is measured from the departure airport (Meacham) to the first en route fix, Bridgeport VORTAC. Although you can expect a handoff to Oklahoma City Approach Control for a vector to Wiley Post, the entries shown in Figure 13–2 are adequate for flight planning purposes. Your flight plan will supply ATC with the necessary route data in the event of radio communications failure.

e. *Communications/navigation frequencies.*—You may wish to list the VOR frequencies and radials used to establish intersections in the "Reporting Frequencies" column. You may also use this column to note the frequencies as ATC assigns them en route. It is a good idea to record the ARTCC Sector Discrete Frequencies for each Center involved in your flight. For this flight, you should record 126.0—Blue Mound, 135.6—Wichita Falls, and 128.3—Oklahoma City. (FAR 91.125.)

Step 3. Current Instrument Approach Procedure Charts for—

a. Meacham (for the possibility of an emergency return after takeoff).

b. Wiley Post.

c. Alternate airport (Ardmore Municipal). (FAR 91.83; 91.116; Approach Charts appropriate to your aircraft equipment.)

FLIGHT LOG

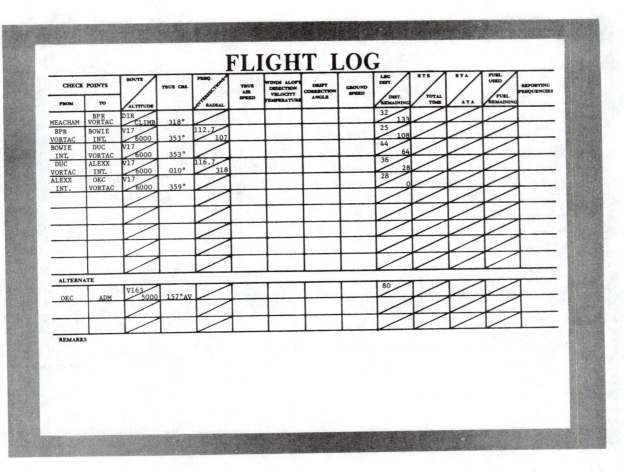

CHECK POINTS FROM	TO	ROUTE / ALTITUDE	TRUE CRS.	FREQ. INTERSECTION / RADIAL	TRUE AIR SPEED	WINDS ALOFT DIRECTION VELOCITY TEMPERATURE	DRIFT CORRECTION ANGLE	GROUND SPEED	LEG DIST. / DIST. REMAINING	ETE / TOTAL TIME	ETA / ATA	FUEL USED / FUEL REMAINING	REPORTING FREQUENCIES
MEACHAM	BPR VORTAC	DIR CLIMB	318°						32 / 133				
BPR VORTAC	BOWIE INT.	V17 6000	353°	112.7 / 107					25 / 108				
BOWIE INT.	DUC VORTAC	V17 6000	353°						44 / 64				
DUC VORTAC	ALEXX INT.	V17 6000	010°	116.7 / 318					36 / 28				
ALEXX INT.	OKC VORTAC	V17 6000	359°						28 / 0				
ALTERNATE													
OKC	ADM	V163 5000	157°AV						80				

REMARKS

FIGURE 13–2. Flight log entries.

Step 4. Current information on facilities and procedures related to your flight, including—

a. *Airport/Facility Directory.* Check airport conditions, including lighting, obstructions, and other notations under "Airport Remarks." Also, check services at destination and alternate.

b. *Notices to Airmen (Class II).* Check FDC NOTAMs in addition to other information listed.

Step 5. Contact Flight Service Station in person or by telephone for preflight briefing.—Refer to page 194 for details concerning the information provided by FSSs during a pilot preflight briefing. (FAR 91.5; current *Airman's Information Manual; Aviation Weather, AC 00-6A; Aviation Weather Services, AC 00-45B;* weather data on pages 226 and 227.)

Step 6. Complete the flight log (Fig. 13–3) to include:—

a. True airspeed, wind data, groundspeed.
b. Estimated time en route.
c. Estimated time between check points.
d. Fuel required.

On the completed flight log (Fig. 13–3), note that the en route times are computed to the tenth of a minute. In actual practice, the figures are rounded off. Note also that the groundspeed (166 knots)

from Meacham to BPR VORTAC is computed on the basis of the winds aloft at 3,000 feet for DAL (210° at 16 knots) and an assumed average temperature of + 8° C. The other true airspeed values are based on 165 knots CAS and on the temperatures given in the winds aloft data for the flight planned altitudes. The only estimated arrival time is logged at BPR VORTAC; the other ETAs are added en route.

The fuel *required* is computed as follows, based on an average consumption of 40 gph:—

	Gallons
a. En route fuel (FTW–OKC)	39.2
b. Fuel to alternate	18.5
c. 45-minute reserve	30.0
d. 10-minute additional allowance for approach at PWA	6.6
Total required	87.7

(FAR 91.23; Aircraft Flight Handbook data in this chapter; weather data for wind forecasts.)

Step 7. Compute weight and balance. To the empty weight and oil data given, enter weights for pilot, instructor, and fuel. Assume 196 gallons total fuel load. The moments are derived from the weight and balance chart (page 228), and the minimum

FLIGHT LOG

CHECK POINTS FROM	TO	ROUTE / ALTITUDE	TRUE CRS.	FREQ. INTERSECTIONS / RADIAL	TRUE AIR SPEED	WINDS ALOFT DIRECTION VELOCITY TEMPERATURE	DRIFT CORRECTION ANGLE	GROUND SPEED	LEG DIST. / DIST. REMAINING	ETE / TOTAL TIME	ETA / ATA	FUEL USED / FUEL REMAINING	REPORTING FREQUENCIES TOTAL FUEL: 196 GALS.
					EXTRA FUEL ESTIMATED FOR TAXI, RUNUP, TAKEOFF, AND CLIMB							3.0 / 193.0	
MEACHAM	BPR VORTAC	DIR CLIMB	318°		162	2116+08	5°L	166	32 / 133	11.6 / 11.6	19:12	7.6 / 185.4	
BPR VORTAC	BOWIE INT.	V17 6000	353°	112.7 / 107	182	2419+07	6°L	189	25 / 108	7.9 / 19.5		5.3 / 180.1	
BOWIE INT.	DUC VORTAC	V17 6000	353°		182	2419+07	6°L	189	44 / 64	14.0 / 33.5		9.3 / 170.8	
DUC VORTAC	ALEXX INT.	V17 6000	010°	116.7 / 318	181	1205+05	2°R	183	36 / 28	11.8 / 45.3		7.9 / 162.9	
ALEXX INT.	OKC VORTAC	V17 6000	359°		181	1205+05	2°R	183	28 / 0	9.2 / 54.5		6.1 / 156.8	
ALTERNATE													
OKC	ADM	V163 5000	157°AV		178	1106+05	1°L	173	80 /	27.8 /		18.6 /	
REMARKS													

FIGURE 13-3. Completed flight log.

and maximum moments (shown under "limits" in the following table) are interpolations between 6,500 and 6,550 pounds. (FAR 91.31; Aircraft Flight Handbook data; Pilot's Weight and Balance Handbook, AC 91–23A.

	Pounds	Moment/1,000
Empty weight	4,940	854.8
Oil	75	15.0
Pilot and Instructor .... (standard weight = 170 lbs.)	340	32.0
Fuel (156 gal. main tank)	936	175.0
Fuel (20 gal. each aux.)	240	43.0
Totals	6,531	1,119.8

Limits.—Minimum 1093 (1092.96)
Maximum 1139 (1138.96)

Step 8. Complete the flight plan (FAA Form 7233–1) and file with FSS at least 30 minutes before estimated departure time (Fig. 13–4).

Instrument Weather Flying

Your first flight under instrument conditions—like your first solo, first night flight, and first simulated instrument flight under the hood—will probably involve some normal apprehensions.

Notwithstanding your temperament, quality of your training, and the thoroughness of your flight planning, the decision to fly under instrument conditions is a commitment for which you *alone* are responsible. What affects your decision to go ahead with an IFR flight or to wait out a weather change for VFR conditions? Your instructor will probably elaborate on the following considerations affecting your judgment.

Flying Experience.—The more experience, the better—both VFR and IFR. Night flying promotes both instrument proficiency and confidence. Progressing from night flying under clear, moonlit conditions to flying without moonlight, natural horizon, or familiar landmarks, you learn to trust your instruments with a minimum dependence upon what you can see outside the aircraft. The more VFR experience you have in terminal areas with high traffic activity, the more capable you can become in dividing your attention between aircraft control, navigation, communications, and other cockpit duties.

The greater your total experience, the greater the number of unexpected situations you have behind you, the fewer surprises you can expect ahead.

224

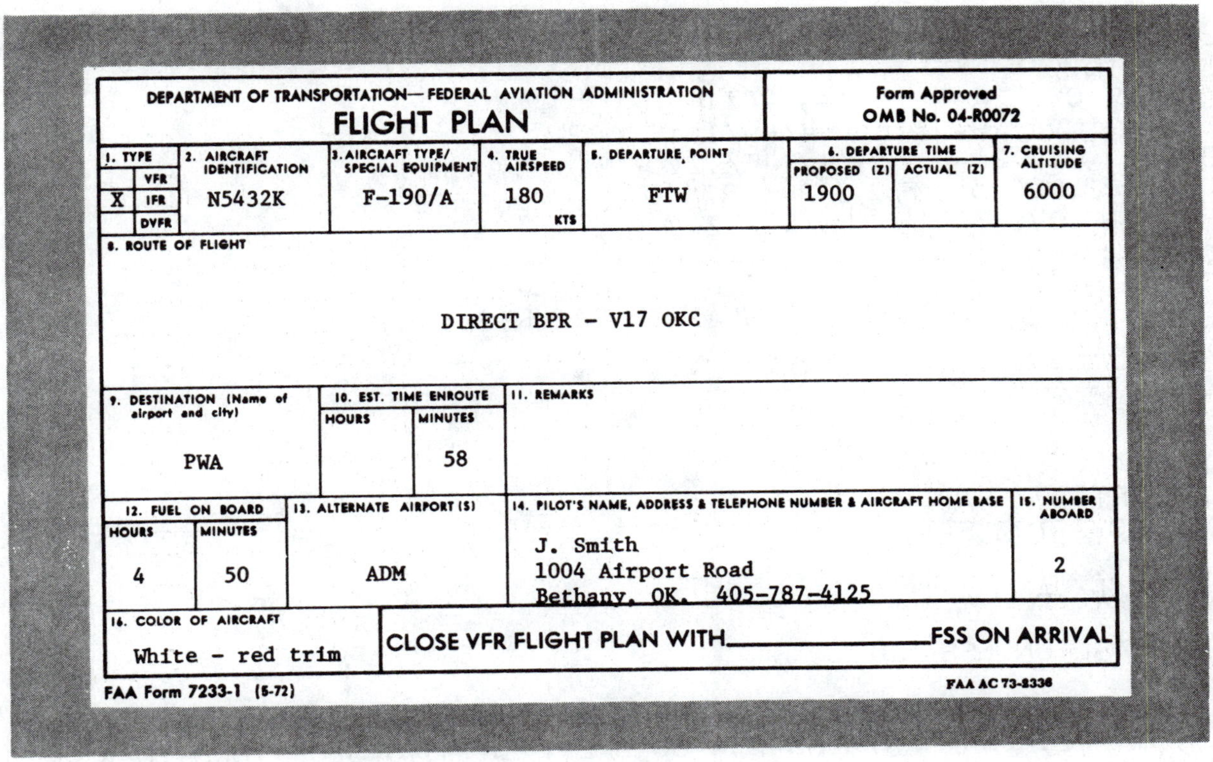

1. TYPE	2. AIRCRAFT IDENTIFICATION	3. AIRCRAFT TYPE/ SPECIAL EQUIPMENT	4. TRUE AIRSPEED	5. DEPARTURE POINT	6. DEPARTURE TIME		7. CRUISING ALTITUDE
VFR					PROPOSED (Z)	ACTUAL (Z)	
X IFR	N5432K	F-190/A	180 KTS	FTW	1900		6000
DVFR							

8. ROUTE OF FLIGHT

DIRECT BPR - V17 OKC

9. DESTINATION (Name of airport and city)	10. EST. TIME ENROUTE		11. REMARKS
	HOURS	MINUTES	
PWA		58	

12. FUEL ON BOARD		13. ALTERNATE AIRPORT (S)	14. PILOT'S NAME, ADDRESS & TELEPHONE NUMBER & AIRCRAFT HOME BASE	15. NUMBER ABOARD
HOURS	MINUTES			
4	50	ADM	J. Smith 1004 Airport Road Bethany, OK. 405-787-4125	2

16. COLOR OF AIRCRAFT	
White - red trim	CLOSE VFR FLIGHT PLAN WITH_____FSS ON ARRIVAL

FAA Form 7233-1 (5-72)　　　　　　　　　　　FAA AC 73-8336

FIGURE 13-4. Flight plan entries.

If you have had the benefit of instrument instruction under instrument weather conditions as well as under the hood, you may have noted that weather flying seemed routine to the instructor. This is the mark of a professional; the unusual is routine because the professional expects it and is ready for it before it happens.

Recency of experience is an equally important consideration. You may not act as pilot-in-command of an aircraft under IFR or in weather conditions less than VFR minimums unless you have met the requirements of FAR 61.57. Remember, these are minimum requirements. Whether they are adequate preparation for *you* is another question.

Airborne Equipment and Ground Facilities.—Here again, regulations specify *minimum* equipment for filing an IFR flight plan. It is your own responsibility to decide on the adequacy of your aircraft and NAV/COM equipment for the conditions expected. A single-engine, well-equipped aircraft in excellent condition and flown by a competent pilot is obviously safer under instrument conditions than a twin, superbly equipped and in perfect condition, in the hands of a reckless or ill-prepared pilot. Whether your aircraft is single-engine or multiengine, its performance limitations, accessories, and general condition are directly related to the weather, route, altitude, and ground facilities pertinent to your flight, as well as to the cockpit workload you can expect.

Weather Conditions.—Departure, en route, arrival, and alternate weather items that should be checked out before determining whether conditions are within your capabilities. Turbulence, icing, and ceiling/visibility at your destination and alternate should be evaluated in terms of their effect on your aircraft, route and altitude, and the cockpit workload that you can safely handle.

IFR flying is a team effort, using a network of facilities manned by many people. Your instrument rating puts you on this team, making air safety your responsibility also.

225

SA 111800
ADM M5 OVC 2R-F 185/49/46/1106/008
FTW M3 OVC 2R-F 169/54/49/1115/003
OKC E3 OVC 2R-F 185/47/45/1208/008
TUL E50 OVC 8 205/50/36/1308/014
PNC E15 OVC 5F 194/48/46/1210/010

AVIATION WEATHER REPORTS (SA)

* * * * * * * * * *

DFW FA 111240
13Z FRI-07Z SAT.
OTLK 07Z-19Z SAT.

NM OK TX AND CSTL WTRS...

HGTS ASL UNLESS NOTED...

SYNS...LO PRES TROF ALG DHT-MRF LN MOVG EWD 15 KTS TO A END-DRT
LN BY 07Z. WRM FNT LRD-PSX-60 S BPT LN MOVG SLOLY NWD TO A
BWD-ACT-LFK LN BY 07Z.

SIGCLDS AND WX...
TX AND OK E OF TROF AND N OF WRM FNT...
CIGS FQTLY BLO 1 THSD VSBY BLO 3 MI IN R-F. TOPS LYRS 200.
CONDS SLOLY IMPVG BCMG CIGS 15-20 OVC VRBL BKN TOPS 150 BY 21Z.
SCTD RW LWRG VSBY TO 1 MI. RW TOPS 250.
OTLK...MVFR CIG RW.

TX E OF TROF AND S OF WRM FNT AND CSTL WTRS...
CIG 15-25 OVC TOPS 120. VSBY 3-5FH. CONDS BCMG 25-30 BKN
VRBL SCT TOPS 120 BY 18Z.
OTLK...MVFR CIG FOG.

TX W OF TROF AND NM...
100-150 SCT 250 SCT.
OTLK...VFR.

ICG...LGT TO MDT MXD ICGICIP ABV FRZG LVL. FRZG LVL 80 NRN NM
NRN OK SLPG TO 125 EXTRM S TX.

AREA FORECAST (FA)

* * * * * * * * * *

Weather data

226

ADM 111515 C10 OVC 3R-F CHC C3X 1R-F. 18Z C12 OVC 4-F. 01Z
    C8 OVC 2L-F. 09Z IFR CIG LF..
FTW 111515 3 SCT C8 OVC 2 1/2R-F 1310 SCT V BKN CHC C3 OVC.
    18Z 10 SCT C14 OVC 1312 VRBL C10 2R-F. 04Z C20 BKN 3210
    BKN V SCT. 09Z VFR..
OKC 111515 C5 OVC 1L-F CHC C12 OVC 3-F. 18Z C15 OVC 4F CHC
    2R-. 22Z C20 BKN 100 BKN LWR BKN V SCT. 04Z 100 SCT
    C250 BKN. 09Z IFR CIG LF..
TUL 111515 C30 OVC 6F SLGT CHC C10 OVC 2F. 18Z C20 BKN 100
    BKN CHC C12 OVC 3R-F. 03Z C10 OVC 3L-F. 09Z MVFR CIG LR..
PNC 111515 C50 OVC CHC C3X1F. 18Z C20 OVC 4F CHC C12 OVC 2R-F.
    23Z C20 BKN 100 BKN LWR SCT V BKN. 04Z 100 SCT C250 BKN.
    09Z VFR..

TERMINAL FORECASTS (FT)

* * * * * * * * * *

FDUS1 KWBC 111740
DATA BASED ON 111200Z

VALID 120000Z FOR USE 1800-0300Z. TEMPS NEG ABV 24000

FT   3000   6000   9000   12000   18000   24000

DAL 2116 2419+07 2321-01 2223-06 2438-21 2253-33
OKC 0907 1205+05 1406-01 1612-07 1820-21 1927-33

WINDS AND TEMPERATURES ALOFT FORECAST (FD)

* * * * * * * * * * *

DFW WA 111735
111735-112335

AIRMET BRAVO 4. FLT PRCTN. OVR OK AND TX AND CSTL WTRS
GENLY E AND N OF A AMA-BWD-GLS LN DUE CIGS BLO 10 VSBY
BLO 3 MI. IMPVG FM W BUT CONTG BYD 2335Z.

AIRMET (WA)

* * * * * * *
Weather data
227

PASSENGERS

SEAT NO.	WEIGHT	MOMENT/1000
Co-P	170	16
4	170	22
5	170	22
1	170	29
2	170	29
3	170	29

FUEL

GALS.	WEIGHT	MOMENT/1000
10	60	12
20	120	24
30	180	36
40	240	48
50	300	59
60	360	71
70	420	83
80	480	94
90	540	105
100	600	116
110	660	127
120	720	138
130	780	148
140	840	159
150	900	169
156	936	175

L & R OUTBOARD FUEL SYSTEM

GALS.	WEIGHT	MOMENT/1000
10	60	11
20	120	21
30	180	32
40	240	43
50	300	53
60	360	64
67	402	72

BAGGAGE

WEIGHT	MOMENT/1000
25	5
50	10
75	15
100	20
125	25
150	30
175	35
200	40
225	45

WEIGHTS AND MOMENTS TO DETERMINE ALLOWABLE LIMITS

167.40 Min. To 174.40 Max.
(Stay Within Min. and Max. Limits)

Weight	Minimum Moment/1000	Maximum Moment/1000
5500	921	959
5550	929	968
5600	937	977
5650	946	985
5700	954	994
5750	963	1003
5800	971	1012
5850	979	1020
5900	988	1029
5950	996	1038
6000	1004	1046
6050	1013	1055
6100	1021	1064
6150	1030	1073
6200	1038	1081
6250	1046	1090
6300	1055	1099
6350	1063	1107
6400	1071	1116
6450	1080	1125
6500	1088	1134
6550	1096	1142
6600	1105	1151
6650	1113	1160
6700	1122	1168
6750	1130	1177
6800	1138	1186
6850	1147	1195
6900	1155	1203
6950	1163	1212
7000	1172	1221

Weight and balance table

228

APPENDIX

Contents

Clearance Shorthand

The shorthand system given here is recommended by the Federal Aviation Administration. Applicants for the Instrument Rating may use *any* shorthand system, in any language, which ensures accurate compliance with ATC instructions. No shorthand system is required by regulation and no knowledge of shorthand is required for the written test; however, because of the vital necessity for safe coordination between the pilot and controller, clearance information should be unmistakably clear.

As an instrument pilot, you should make a written record of all ATC clearances and instructions that consist of more than a few words; and any portions that are complex, or about which there is any doubt, should be verified by a repeat back. Safety demands that you receive correctly and do not forget any part of your clearance.

Occasionally ATC will issue a clearance that differs from the original request. In such cases, the pilot must be particularly alert to be sure that he receives and understands the clearance given.

The following symbols and contractions represent words and phrases frequently used in clearances. Most of them are regularly used by ATC personnel. Learn them along with the location identifiers which you will use.

By using this shorthand, omitting the parenthetical words, you will be able, after some practice, to copy long clearances as fast as they are read.

WORDS AND PHRASES	SHORTHAND
ABOVE	ABV
ABOVE (ALTITUDE--HUNDREDS OF FEET)	7O (underlined)
ADVISE	ADV
AFTER (PASSING)	<
AIRWAY (DESIGNATION)	V26
AIRPORT	A
ALTERNATE INSTRUCTIONS	( )
ALTITUDE 6,000--17,000	60-170
AND	&
APPROACH	AP
APPROACH CONTROL	APC
AT	@
(ATC) ADVISES	CA
(ATC) CLEARS OR CLEARED	C
(ATC) REQUESTS	CR
BACK COURSE	BC
BEARING	BR
BEFORE (REACHING, PASSING)	>
BELOW	BLO
BELOW (ALTITUDE--HUNDREDS OF FEET)	7O (overlined)
CENTER	CTR
CLEARED AS FILED	CAF
CLEARED TO LAND	L
CLIMB TO (ALTITUDE--HUNDREDS OF FEET)	↑7O
CONTACT	CT
CONTACT APPROACH	CAP
CONTACT (DENVER) APPROACH CONTROL	(den
CONTACT (DENVER) CENTER	(DEN
COURSE	CRS
CROSS	X
CRUISE	→

Clearance shorthand

230

WORDS AND PHRASES	SHORTHAND
DELAY INDEFINITE- - - - - - - - - - - - - - - - - - -	DLI
DEPART- -	DP
DEPARTURE CONTROL - - - - - - - - - - - - - - - - -	DPC
DESCEND TO (ALTITUDE--HUNDREDS OF FEET) - - - - - -	↓70
DIRECT- -	DR
DIRECTION (BOUND)	
EASTBOUND- - - - - - - - - - - - - - - - - - -	EB
WESTBOUND- - - - - - - - - - - - - - - - - - -	WB
NORTHBOUND - - - - - - - - - - - - - - - - - -	NB
SOUTHBOUND - - - - - - - - - - - - - - - - - -	SB
INBOUND- - - - - - - - - - - - - - - - - - - -	IB
OUTBOUND - - - - - - - - - - - - - - - - - - -	OB
DME FIX (MILE)- - - - - - - - - - - - - - - - - - -	21
EACH- -	EA
ENTER CONTROL AREA- - - - - - - - - - - - - - - - -	△
ESTIMATED TIME OF ARRIVAL - - - - - - - - - - - - -	ETA
EXPECT- -	EX
EXPECT APPROACH CLEARANCE - - - - - - - - - - - - -	EAC
EXPECT FURTHER CLEARANCE- - - - - - - - - - - - - -	EFC
FAN MARKER- -	FM
FINAL -	F
FLIGHT LEVEL- - - - - - - - - - - - - - - - - - - -	FL
FLIGHT PLANNED ROUTE- - - - - - - - - - - - - - - -	FPR
FOR FURTHER CLEARANCE - - - - - - - - - - - - - - -	FFC
FOR FURTHER HEADINGS- - - - - - - - - - - - - - - -	FFH
FROM- -	FR
HEADING -	HDG
HOLD (DIRECTION)- - - - - - - - - - - - - - - - - -	H-W
HOLDING PATTERN - - - - - - - - - - - - - - - - - -	⬭
ILS APPROACH- - - - - - - - - - - - - - - - - - - -	ILS

Clearance shorthand

WORDS AND PHRASES	SHORTHAND
INITIAL APPROACH	I
INTERSECTION	XN
JOIN OR INTERCEPT AIRWAY/JET ROUTE/TRACK OR COURSE	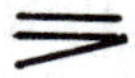
LEFT TURN AFTER TAKEOFF	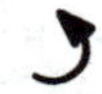
LOCATOR OUTER MARKER	LOM
MAINTAIN OR MAGNETIC	M
MAINTAIN VFR CONDITIONS ON TOP	VFR
MIDDLE COMPASS LOCATOR	ML
MIDDLE MARKER	MM
NONDIRECTIONAL BEACON APPROACH	NDB
OUT OF (LEAVE) CONTROL AREA	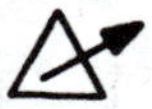
OUTER MARKER	OM
OVER (STATION)	OKC
ON COURSE	OC
PRECISION RADAR APPROACH	PAR
PROCEDURE TURN	PT
RADAR VECTOR	RV
RADIAL (080° RADIAL)	080R
REMAIN WELL TO LEFT SIDE	LS
REMAIN WELL TO RIGHT SIDE	RS
REPORT CROSSING	RX
REPORT DEPARTING	RD
REPORT LEAVING	RL
REPORT ON COURSE	R-CRS
REPORT OVER	RO
REPORT PASSING	RP
REPORT REACHING	RR
REPORT STARTING PROCEDURE TURN	RSPT
REVERSE COURSE	RC
RIGHT TURN AFTER TAKEOFF	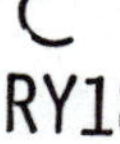
RUNWAY (NUMBER)	RY18

Clearance shorthand

WORDS AND PHRASES	SHORTHAND
SQUAWK -	SQ
STANDBY- -	STBY
STRAIGHT-IN APPROACH -. - - - - - - - - - - - - - - - - - - -	SI
SURVEILLANCE RADAR APPROACH- - - - - - - - - - - - - - -	ASR
TAKEOFF (DIRECTION)- -	T→N
TOWER- -	Z
UNTIL- -	U
UNTIL ADVISED (BY) -	UA
UNTIL FURTHER ADVISED- - - - - - - - - - - - - - - - - - - -	UFA
VIA- -	VIA
VICTOR (AIRWAY NUMBER) - - - - - - - - - - - - - - - - - -	V14
VISUAL APPROACH- -	VA
VOR- -	⊙
VORTAC -	Ⓣ
WHILE IN CONTROL AREA- - - - - - - - - - - - - - - - - - - -	△

EXAMPLE

An example of a clearance written in shorthand:

    CAF M RY HDG RV V18 SQ 0700 DPC 120.4

Translated it reads: (Aircraft number), cleared as filed, maintain runway heading for radar vector to Victor 18, squawk 0700 just before departure, departure control frequency--120.4.

Clearance shorthand.

Supplementary Reference Material

Persons studying for the instrument rating, as well as qualified instrument rated pilots, will find the publications and materials listed below to be useful in augmenting their knowledge of instrument flying. In addition to these, there are many excellent textbooks, charts, and other reference materials available from commercial publishers.

Advisory Circulars and Flight Information Publications

ADVISORY CIRCULARS

00–6A—*Aviation Weather*

Provides an up-to-date and expanded text for pilots and other flight operations personnel whose interest in meteorology is primarily in its application to flying. (Supt. Docs.)

00–45B—*Aviation Weather Services*

Supplements AC 00–6A, Aviation Weather, in that it explains the weather service in general and the use and interpretation of reports, forecasts, weather maps, and prognostic charts in detail. It is an excellent source of study for pilot certification examinations. (Supt. Docs.)

61–8D—*Instrument Rating Written Test Guide*

Reflects the current operating procedures and techniques in a background setting appropriate for applicants preparing for the Instrument Pilot Airplane and Instrument Pilot Helicopter written tests. (Supt. Docs.)

61–56A—*Flight Test Guide—Instrument Pilot Airplane*

Assists the applicant and the instructor in preparing for the flight test for the Instrument Pilot Airplane Rating. (Supt. Docs.)

61–64A—*Flight Test Guide—Instrument Pilot Helicopter*

Assists the applicant and the instructor in preparing for the Instrument Pilot Helicopter Rating. (Supt. Docs.)

91–23A—*Pilot's Weight and Balance Handbook*

Provides an easily understood text on aircraft weight and balance for pilots who need to appreciate the importance of weight and balance control for safety of flight. Progresses from an explanation of basic fundamentals to the complete application of weight and balance principles in large aircraft operations. (Supt. Docs.)

In addition, the following Advisory Circulars pertain to areas of knowledge listed in the "Study Outline" and are available from FAA free of charge: 00–24A, 20–32B, 60–4, 60–6A, 91–8A, and 91–25A.

FLIGHT INFORMATION

Airman's Information Manual (AIM) Basic Flight Information and ATC Procedures. Issued semi-annually, January and July.

Graphic Notices and Supplemental Data. Issued quarterly.

Notices to Airmen (Class II). Issued every 14 days.

Descriptions of the contents, source of supply, prices and stock numbers where applicable, for all Advisory Circulars and the other flight information publications listed above, are contained in **AC 00–2, Advisory Circular Checklist** available free of charge from:

U.S. Department of Transportation
Publications Section, M-443.1
Washington, D.C. 20590

IFR and VFR Pilot Exam-o-Grams

These brief instructional aids are prepared on subject areas in which applicants for airman written examinations have shown a lack of knowledge. They are an excellent media for providing guidance information to applicants preparing for the various written tests.

Exam-O-Grams may be obtained from:
Superintendent of Documents
U.S. Government Printing Office
Washington, D.C. 20402.

FEDERAL AVIATION REGULATIONS (FARs)

Part 1. Definitions and Abbreviations.
Part 61. Certification: Pilots and Flight Instructors.
Part 91. General Operating and Flight Rules.
Part 95. IFR Altitudes.
Part 97. Standard Instrument Approach Procedures.

Federal Aviation Regulations are sold by the Superintendent of Documents. **AC 00–44, Status of Federal Aviation Regulations,** lists the FAR Parts, their Changes, prices, stock numbers, and ordering information. AC 00–44 is available free of charge from:

U.S. Department of Transportation
Publications Section, M-443.1
Washington, D.C. 20590

If you wish to be placed on the free mail list to receive revised copies of either AC 00–2 or AC 00–44, send your name and address to:

U.S. Department of Transportation
Distribution Requirements Section, M-482.2
Washington, D.C. 20590

Aeronautical Charts and Airport/ Facility Directory

En Route Low and High Altitude Charts. These charts provide necessary aeronautical information for en route instrument navigation in the established airway structure.

Area Charts. These charts are part of the En Route Low Altitude Chart series. They furnish terminal data on a larger scale in congested areas.

Instrument Approach Procedures Charts. Each of these charts depict an instrument approach procedure, including all related data, and the airport diagram.

Standard Instrument Departures (SIDs). These charts are collated in two booklets, "East" and "West." They are designed for use with En Route Low and High Altitude and Area Charts. They furnish pilots departure routing clearance in graphic and textual form.

Standard Terminal Arrival Routes (STARs). These charts are collated in one booklet and are designed for use with En Route Low and High Altitude Charts. They furnish pilots preplanned instrument flight rules (IFR) air traffic control arrival route procedures in graphic and textual form.

The National Ocean Survey publishes and distributes the Airport/Facility Directory and aeronautical charts of the United States. Charts for foreign areas are published by the U.S. Air Force Aeronautical Chart and Information Center (ACIC) and are sold to civil users by the National Ocean Survey.

A "Catalog of Aeronautical Charts and Related Publications," listing their prices and instructions for ordering, may be obtained free on request from:

Department of Commerce
National Ocean Survey
Distribution Division (C–44)
Riverdale, Maryland 20840

Orders for the Airport/Facility Directory and for specific charts or publications should be accompanied by check or money order made payable to, NOS, Department of Commerce.

Study Outline for the Instrument Pilot Written Test

This study outline covers the areas of aeronautical knowledge which pertain to Instrument Pilot Written Tests. The outline expands the general aeronautical knowledge requirements set forth in Federal Aviation Regulations Part 61, and is based on airman activity for flight under Instrument Flight Rules.

REFERENCE CODE:

AC—Advisory Circular
AW—Aviation Weather (AC 00–6A)
AWS—Aviation Weather Services (AC 00–45B)
AIM—Airman's Information Manual
AFD—Airport/Facility Directory
NOTAM—Notices to Airmen
EOG—IFR Exam-O-Grams
IFH—Instrument Flying Handbook (AC 61–27C)
BHH—Basic Helicopter Handbook (AC 61–13B)
IAPC—Instrument Approach Procedure Charts
PHB—Pilot's Handbook of Aeronautical Knowledge (AC 61–23B)

I. FLIGHT PLANNING

   A. Certificates and Ratings
      1. Requirements for certificates and ratings (61.3)
      2. Eligibility for instrument rating (61.65)
      3. Where instrument rating required (61.3(e), 91.97)
      4. Recency of experience (61.57)

   B. Preflight Action for Flight
      1. Familiarization with all available information (91.5; EOG–31; AFD)
      2. Fuel requirements (91.23)

   C. Preflight Action for Aircraft (EOG–31)
      1. Responsibility for airworthiness (91.29)
      2. Equipment required
         Instruments and equipment (91.33)
         Transponder (91.24, 91.90)
         ELT (91.52)
      3. Tests and inspections
         VOR (91.25; EOG–22; AIM)
         Altimeter system (91.170)
         Transponder (91.177)
         Aircraft (91.169)
      4. Portable electronic devices (91.19)

   D. Flight Plan (AIM)
      1. When required (91.97, 91.115)
      2. Information required (91.83)
      3. Alternate airport requirements (91.83)

   E. Route Planning
      1. Preferred routes (AFD); SIDs and STARs; En Route Charts
      2. Airport/Facility Directory
      3. NOTAM
      4. FDC NOTAMs (NOTAM)
      5. Special Notices (NOTAM, AFD)
      6. Area Navigation Routes (NOTAM)
      7. Direct Routes (AIM, Airspace; 91.119, 91.121(b))
      8. Restrictions to En Route Nav. Aids (AFD)
      9. Substitute Route Structure (EOG–39)

   F. Flight Planning (Ch. XIII—IFH)
      1. Wind correction angle-heading
      2. GS
      3. ETE/ETA
      4. Fuel estimates

   G. Aircraft Performance (Aircraft Owner's Handbook; VFR EOG–33; EOG–32)
      1. Takeoff distance
      2. Climb performance
      3. Cruise performance (VFR EOG–38)
      4. Fuel flow
      5. Landing performance
      6. Airspeed: IAS, CAS, EAS, TAS
      7. Placards and instrument markings
      8. Hovering

   H. Aircraft Operating Limitations (documents in aircraft, AC 60–6A)
      1. Weight and balance (EOG–21; AC 91–23A)
      2. Instrument limit markings and placards (91.31)
      3. Maximum safe crosswind (VFR EOG–27)
      4. Turbulent air penetration

   I. Aircraft Systems (Ch. IV—IFH)
      1. Pitot-static system (EOG–10; IFH)
      2. Vacuum/gyroscopic (EOG–24)
      3. Electric/gyroscopic
      4. Compass

J. Fundamentals of Weather
1. Composition of the atmosphere (Ch. 1–AW)
2. Temperature (Ch. 2–AW)
3. Pressure (Ch. 3–AW)
4. Circulation (Ch. 4–AW)
5. Moisture (Ch. 5–AW)
6. Stability and wind (Ch. 6–AW)
7. Clouds (Ch. 7–AW)
8. Air masses and fronts (Ch. 8–AW)
9. Turbulence (Ch. 9–AW)

K. IFR Weather Hazards
1. Icing (Ch. 10–AW)
2. Thunderstorms (Ch. 11–AW; AIM)
3. Fog and obstructions to vision (Ch. 12–AW)

L. Aviation Weather Observations and Reports
1. Aviation weather reports (SA) (AWS–2)
2. Pilot weather reports (PIREPs, UA) (AWS–3)
3. Radar weather reports (RAREPs) (AWS–3) Radar summary chart AWS–7)
4. Surface analysis (AWS–5)
5. Weather depiction chart (AWS–6)
6. Upper wind chart (AWS–9)
7. Freezing level chart (AWS–10)
8. Stability chart (AWS–11)
9. Constant pressure charts (AWS–13)

M. Aviation Weather Forecasts
1. Terminal (FT) (AWS–4; EOG–5)
2. Area (FA) (AWS–4; EOG–5)
3. Winds and temperatures aloft (FD) (AWS–4) and chart (AWS–9)
4. Severe weather (AWS–4), Hurricane advisories (WH); convective outlook (AC); Weather Watch (WW); severe weather outlook chart (AWS–12)
5. TWEB route forecast and synopsis (AWS–4)
6. Inflight advisories (WS, WA, WAC) (AWS–4)
7. Prognostic charts: Surface (AWS–8); Significant Weather (AWS–8); Constant Pressure (AWS–14); Tropopause and Wind Shear (AWS–15)

N. Weather Tables and Conversion Graphs (AWS–16)
1. Icing intensities
2. Turbulence intensities
3. Locations of probable turbulence

4. Standard temperature, speed, and pressure conversions
5. Density altitude

O. Weather Facilities
1. FSS weather service (AFD; EOG–19), Telephone numbers (AFD), Remote weather radar display (AFD), Scheduled weather broadcast (AFD)
2. ATIS (AIM)
3. Weather Service Forecast Offices (AIM); TWEB, PATWAS (AFD)

II. DEPARTURE
A. Authority and Limitations of Pilot
1. Pilot in command (91.3, 91.4, 91.67, 91.75, 91.87(h))
2. Emergency action (92.3(b)), Deviation from rules
3. Required reports, Emergency deviation (91.3(c), 91.75(c)), Malfunction of equipment (91.33(c), 91.129)

B. Flight Plan
1. Where to file (AFD)
2. When to file (AIM—Flight Plan)

C. Departure Clearance (AIM—Departures; EOG–35)
1. "Cleared as filed"
2. Amended clearance
3. Pretaxi clearance procedure
4. Clearance delivery (AFD)

D. Taxi and Takeoff Procedures (AIM—Departure and Airport Operation)
1. Taxi limits (AIM; EOG–26, 28)
2. ATC control sequence (AIM)
3. Airport advisory service (AIM; AFD)
4. ATIS (AIM; AFD)

E. Departure Procedures (AIM)
1. Obstruction clearance minimums (approach chart book)
2. Departure control procdures (non-radar)
3. Departure control procedures (radar)
4. SIDs
5. Speed adjustments
6. Terminal area limitations

F. VOR Accuracy Check (AIM; EOG–22; 91.25)
1. VOT (AFD, L-chart legend)
2. VOR ground checkpoints (AFD)
3. VOR airborne checkpoints (AFD)
4. VOR dual receiver check

G. Pretakeoff Instrument Check (IFH; AC 91–46)
   1. Prestart instrument indications
   2. Taxi test

H. Transponder (EOG–25; AIM)
   1. Operation
   2. Switching code
   3. Emergency use

I. Airport Facilities (AFD, NOTAM, Charts)
   1. Service (AFD, NOTAM)
   2. Runways (EOG–26, 28; AIM)
   3. Airport lighting (AIM; EOG–33)
   4. Communications (AFD)

J. FSS Facility (AIM; EOG–39; chart legend)
   1. Flight plan service
   2. Traffic advisories (AFD)
   3. Communications (AFD)
   4. Weather advisories (AFD; AWS–1)

K. Departure Control Facility
   1. Communications (AFD; IAPC)
   2. Geographical area

III. EN ROUTE

A. En Route Limitations (AIM)
   1. Altitude limitations (91.119; EOG–8): MEA, MOCA, MCA, MRA, MAA
   2. Cruising altitudes (91.121, 91.109)
   3. Courses to be flown (91.123, 91.67)
   4. Altimeter settings (91.81)
   5. Positive Control Airspace (91.97)
   6. Special Use Airspace (91.95; AIM; En Route Chart)

B. En Route Procedures (AIM; Ch. XI—IFH)
   1. Radar environment—vectors, reporting, handoffs
   2. Nonradar environment—reporting, handoffs
   3. Altitude: cruise, maintain, climb, descend, VFR on top
   4. Delays: clearance limits, holding
   5. Securing weather info (AWS–1)

C. ATC Clearances
   1. Phraseology (Ch. IX—IFH; AIM; EOG–11, 34, 35)
   2. Responses and read backs (AIM; 91.125)

D. Oxygen Requirements (91.32)
   1. Pilot and crew requirements
   2. Passenger requirements

E. Emergencies (AIM; EOG–2)
   1. Difficulty with communications
   2. Malfunction of equipment

   3. LOC (EOG–7 & 14)
   4. RNAV (EOG 30)
   3. Lost
   4. Lost communications (91.127; EOGs 36, 37, 38)
   5. Malfunction reports (91.129, 91.33(e))
   6. Deviation from clearance (91.75(c))

F. Radio Orientation (Ch. VIII—IFH)
   1. VOR (EOG–7 & 14)
   2. NDB (EOG–23)

G. Establishing Radio Fixes and Waypoints (Ch. VIII—IFH)
   1. VOR radials
   2. VOR—DME (Ch. VII—IFH; AC 90–62; AC 170–3B)
   3. ADF (EOG–23)
   4. ADF-VOR/LOC
   5. RNAV (EOG–30)

H. En Route Computer Operations
   1. GS
   2. ETE/ETA
   3. Altitude or speed conversion
   4. Fuel

I. Attitude Instrument Flying (Ch. V and VI—IFH; AC 91–43)
   1. Interpretation of flight instruments
   2. Aircraft control: pitch, bank, power
   3. Basic maneuvers: straight and level, climbs and descent, turns (EOG–18)
   4. Unusual attitudes
   5. Flight patterns

J. Unusual Flight Conditions
   1. Thunderstorms (AC 00–24; page 105—AW)
   2. Structural icing (Ch. 10—AW)
   3. Induction icing (Ch. 10—AW; PHB)
   4. Use of anti/deicing equipment
   5. Frost
   6. Clear air turbulence

K. Radio Navigation Facilities (Ch. VIII—IFH; AIM)
   1. VOR/VORTAC
   2. NDB
   3. LOC
   4. DF
   5. RADAR

L. Airway Route System (En Route Chart Legend; AIM; EOG–8)
   1. Victor/jet airway limits
   2. Route identification: military, substitute, unusuable
   3. Altitude limits: MOCA, MEA, MRA, MCA, MAA

4. Reporting points: compulsory, non-compulsory
5. Fixes, waypoints
6. Geographical limit: VOR changeover points, altimeter setting boundary, time zone boundary
7. Airspace designation

M. Special Use Airspace (AIM, chart legends)
   1. Prohibited area
   2. Restricted area
   3. Military operations area
   4. Warning area
   5. Alert area—intensive student jet training area

N. ARTCC Facility (Ch. XI—IFH; AIM)
   1. ARTCC remote frequencies (En Route Chart)
   2. Geographical area of control (En Route Chart)
   3. Advisories, services, assistance

O. En Route Weather Services (AFD)
   1. EFAS (AWS-1)
   2. TWEB (AWS-1)
   3. ARTCC significant weather advisories

P. Fixed-Wing Aerodynamic Factors (Ch. III—IFH; AC 61- 23B)
   1. Aerodynamic forces
   2. Straight and level
   3. Turns
   4. Climbs
   5. Descents
   6. Stalls

Q. Rotary-Wing Aerodynamic Factors (BHH)
   1. Vibrations (Ch. 2)
   2. Dissymmetry of lift (Ch. 2)
   3. Translation (Ch. 2)
   4. Rotor disc-loading, coning, and flapping (Ch. 9)
   5. Settling with power (Ch. 9)
   6. Ground resonance (Ch. 9)
   7. Speed limitations (Ch. 9)
   8. Autorotation particulars (Ch. 11)
   9. Factors affecting performance (Ch. 11)

R. Physiological Factors (Ch. II—IFH; AIM)
   1. Physiologic altitude effects: hypoxia, aerotitis, aerosinusitis (AC 91-8A)
   2. Hypoxic effects: alcohol, hyperventilation, drugs, carbon monoxide (AC 20-32B)
   3. Sensations of instrument flying (AC 60-4)
   4. Spatial disorientation (AC 60-4)

IV. ARRIVAL

A. Approach Control (AIM; Ch. XII—IFH)
   1. Radar control: STARs, vectors, approach clearances
   2. Non-radar control
   3. Aircraft speed (91.70)
   4. Procedure turns/holding patterns
   5. Visual and contact approaches

B. Holding Procedures (AIM)
   1. Holding pattern entry
   2. Shuttle
   3. Changing altitude
   4. Timing
   5. Adjustments and corrections

C. Precision Approaches (AC 90-1A; IFH; AIM)
   1. Initial approach/procedure turn (91.116(h))
   2. Vectors to final approach (91.116(f))
   3. Intermediate approach
   4. Final approach
   5. Glide slope
   6. Decision height (91.117(b))
   7. Inoperative components (91.117(c))
   8. Reports

D. Non-Precision Approach (AC 90-1A; AIM)
   1. Initial approach/procedure turn (91.116(h))
   2. Vectors to final approach (91.116(f))
   3. Intermediate approach
   4. Final approach
   5. Minimum descent altitude (91.117(b))
   6. Inoperative components (91.117(c))
   7. Reports

E. Missed Approach (91.117(b); AC 90-1A; AIM)
   1. Precision approach
   2. Non-precision
   3. Loss of visual cues
   4. Low approach (practice approaches)

F. Landing Procedures (AIM)
   1. Noncontrolled airport (91.89)
   2. Controlled airport (91.87)
   3. Landing minimums (91.116(b), 97.3 (d-1))
   4. Close flight plan (91.83)

G. Logging of Flight Time
   1. Instrument flight time (61.51(4))
   2. Conditions for simulated instrument flight (91.21)

3. Information required (61.51(4)); Instrument approaches; Safety pilot
4. Pilot in command (61.51(2))

H. Radio Orientation on Approach (Ch. VIII—IFH)
1. Relation to LOC on front and back course (Ch. VII—IFH; EOG–7)
2. Glide slope (Ch. VII—IFH)
3. LOC and glide slope (EOG–7); Ch. VII—IFH)
4. Marker beacons (Ch. VII—IFH)
5. Compass locators (EOG–23)
6. NDB (EOG–23)
7. VOR/VORTAC (EOG–7)
8. LOC type; LDA, SDF (AIM)

I. Wake Turbulence (AIM; AC 90–23D)
1. Landing hazards
2. Takeoff hazards
3. Inflight hazards
4. Wake turbulence theory

J. Terminal Area (IAPC; AFD)
1. Approach control facility: frequencies, area
2. FSS (AIM): airport advisories, flight plan service, weather service

K. Instrument Approach Procedure Chart—Planview (AC 90–1A; IAPC legend)
1. Facility frequencies and services
2. Procedural tracks
3. Fixes and markers
4. Obstructions
5. Special use airspace
6. Radio aids
7. Minimum altitudes

L. Instrument Approach Procedure Chart—Profile (AC 90–1A; IAPC legend)
1. Altitude limits
2. Descent pattern/glide slope
3. Facilities/fixes

M. Instrument Approach Procedure Chart Aerodrome Sketch (AC 90–1A; IAPC legend)
1. Runway configuration and specifications
2. Approach light systems
3. Elevations: Obstacles, TDZE, and aerodrome
4. Airport taxi chart

N. Instrument Approach Procedure Chart—Minimums Section (AC 90–1A; IAPC legend)
1. Aircraft category
2. DH/MDA
3. HAT
4. HAA
5. Minimum visibility: miles/RVR
6. IFR takeoff minimums and departure procedures
7. IFR alternate minimums
8. Civil RADAR instrument approach minimums

O. Approach Facilities (AIM; IFH; Chart Legends)
1. ILS
2. LDA
3. SDF
4. VOR/VORTAC
5. NDB
6. Marker beacons, compass locators
7. VASI (91.87(d) (3))

Instrument Flight Instructor Lesson Guide (Airplanes)

U.S. Department of Transportation
Federal Aviation Administration

MIKE MONRONEY AERONAUTICAL CENTER
FAA ACADEMY

Preface

To the Instrument Flight Instructor

The Instrument Flight Instructor Lesson Guide has been prepared for use with the FAA Instrument Flying Handbook, AC 61–27C. Although the guide deals with basic instrument flying in airplanes, the instructor can modify it for use in helicopter instrument training. The seventeen lessons on Attitude Instrument Flying are arranged in what is considered to be a logical learning sequence. To ensure steady progress, teach the course lesson-by-lesson, and be sure the student has mastered each before advancing to the next. Lessons may be combined when giving refresher training. As all experienced instrument instructors know, the student will learn more rapidly during the early stage of instrument training if a considerable part of the time is spent "open hood." The student is thus allowed to associate aircraft attitude relative to outside visual references with the indications of the various flight instruments individually and in combination. This teaching procedure makes it clear that the pilot uses exactly the same control techniques during visual and instrument flight. Remember, the largest single learning factor in Attitude Instrument Flying is that of interpreting the flight instruments to determine the attitude of the aircraft.

To the Student Instrument Pilot

At the beginning of your instrument flight training, your instructor will brief you on the concept of Attitude Instrument Flying and explain each of the flight instruments used in Pitch Control, Bank Control, and Power Control. Your instructor will point out similarities each instrument has to outside references and explain the limits and errors inherent in each instrument. After a thorough demonstration, you will practice using each instrument individually and in combination with other instruments. This procedure is followed for the first three lessons on Pitch Control, Bank Control, and Power Control in level flight. After a short time, you will be making a logical cross-check and not merely scanning the instruments. Approximately 6 hours of flight time plus the necessary ground school is usually required to cover the first three basic lessons. Your instructor will monitor your progress closely during this early training to guide you in dividing your attention properly. The importance of this "division of attention" or "cross-check" cannot be emphasized too much. This, and proper instrument interpretation, enables the instrument pilot to accurately visualize the aircraft's attitude at all times. To properly understand this guide, the terms "Primary Instrument" and "Supporting Instrument" must be clearly understood. For clarification of these terms, refer to Chapter V of the FAA Instrument Flying Handbook AC 61–27C.

> NOTE: The instrument maneuvers presented in this guide are based on an airplane equipped with a turn coordinator. If the airplane flown has a turn needle, the descriptions apply if "turn needle" is substituted for "miniature aircraft of the turn coordinator." Power settings and airplane performance figures used in this guide are for illustrative purposes only. Exact power settings and performance information must be obtained experimentally or from performance charts for each airplane flown.

Contents

Lesson 1

Cockpit Check

1. *Publications.*—Enroute Navigation Charts, Appropriate Pilot's Handbooks, Terminal Area Charts, Approach Charts, Computer, and Flight Log.
2. *Suction Gauge or Electrical System.*—For suction-driven gyro instruments, be sure the suction gauge is within prescribed limits. For electrically-driven instruments, check generators and inverters for proper operation.
3. *Pitot Head.*—Cover removed and heat checked.
4. *Airspeed Indicator.*—Check reading, should be zero. Check calibration card.
5. *Heading Indicator.*—Uncaged, if applicable. Checked against a known heading, and operating properly.
6. *Attitude Indicator.*—Uncaged if applicable. Checked and operating properly. Set miniature aircraft.
7. *Altimeter.*—Set to current altimeter setting. Check for error.
8. *Turn Coordinator.*—Miniature aircraft operating properly. Ball moves freely in the race.
9. *Vertical-Speed Indicator.*—Should indicate zero. If it doesn't and is not adjustable, interpret ground indication as zero.
10. *Magnetic Compass.*—Bowl full of fluid. Card moves freely. Checked against known heading.
11. *Clock.*—Operating and set to correct time.
12. *Carburetor Heat.*—Check for operation and return to cold position.
13. *Engine Instruments.*—Check for proper markings and readings.
14. *Radio Equipment.*—Checked for proper operation.
15. *Trim and Throttle Friction.*—Trim set for takeoff and throttle friction adjusted.
16. *De-Icing and Anti-Icing Equipment.*—Check operation.

Pitch Control

1. *Attitude Indicator*
   a. Adjust miniature aircraft for level flight at normal cruise.
   b. Demonstrate similarity between the natural horizon and the horizon bar by placing the nose of the aircraft first above the horizon, then below it.
   c. Discuss the limits of operation.
   d. Demonstrate why the attitude indicator must be caged and uncaged in level flight (if a caging device is available). Stress the importance of fully uncaging the instrument.
   e. Reliable pitch attitude is indicated within approximately 30° in climbs and dives. In excess of 30°, the horizon bar is no longer visible or may lag. The extreme limits vary with instrument design.
   f. Acceleration and deceleration error.
      (1) Increase power rapidly from low to high—show loss of altitude while maintaining a level attitude on the attitude indicator.
      (2) Reduce power rapidly from high to low—show gain of altitude while maintaining a level attitude on the attitude indicator.
      (3) Hold altitude during power changes—show that the bar moves down on acceleration and moves up on deceleration.
   g. Comparison of movement of the miniature aircraft and the nose of the aircraft. The instrument gives a *direct* indication of pitch.

247

(1) Adjust the miniature aircraft with the wings exactly centered on the horizon bar.

(2) Change pitch attitude to ½ bar climb—student compares the movement of the aircraft's nose to the actual horizon.

(3) Change pitch attitude to ½ bar descent—student compares to actual horizon.

(4) Emphasize smooth control pressures and that ½ bar is recommended for small corrections.

h. Student practice.

(1) Maintaining level flight, keeping wings centered on horizon bar.

(2) Making small pitch changes not to exceed ½ bar width.

(3) Place aircraft in moderate climbs and descents and have student return to level flight.

(4) Stress importance of smoothness and of not over-controlling.

2. *Altimeter*

a. Constant altitude.

(1) Maintain straight and level flight at a constant power setting. Point out that pitch attitude must also remain constant.

(2) Raise the nose of the aircraft until the altimeter indicates a climb—show the relationship between increased pitch attitude and gain of altitude.

(3) Lower the nose of the aircraft until the altimeter indicates a descent—show the relationship between decreased pitch and loss of altitude.

b. Determining pitch attitude by the altimeter.

(1) Place the miniature aircraft well above the horizon bar. Point out the rapid change of the altimeter and the large change of pitch attitude shown on the attitude indicator.

(2) Make small changes in pitch attitude—show slow change in altitude. Visualize the approximate change in pitch attitude by interpolating the rate of altimeter movement.

c. Lag in the altimeter.

(1) Make an abrupt pitch change and point out the momentary lag in the altimeter.

(2) Make small, smooth pitch changes and point out that the altimeter, for practical purposes, has no lag.

d. Proper technique for correcting altimeter movement.

(1) Change pitch attitude to stop altimeter.

(2) Change pitch attitude to return smoothly to desired altitude.

e. Cross-check (division of attention) between altimeter and attitude indicator.

(1) The cross-check is simple. Maintain level flight on the attitude indicator with frequent reference to the altimeter to determine that the altitude is being maintained. If an error is noted, correct it by making an appropriate correction on the attitude indicator. Guard against over-controlling.

(2) During level flight, the altimeter is *primary* for pitch and all changes in pitch are made so as to maintain a constant altitude.

f. Student practice.

(1) Maintaining a constant altitude.

(2) Maintaining level flight by use of the attitude indicator and altimeter.

(3) Lose or gain 50 feet by changing pitch attitude not more than ½ bar (emphasize small pitch changes).

(4) Return to the original altitude, using the above technique.

(5) Repeat this exercise until the student has acquired the proper cross-check and control technique.

3. *Vertical-Speed Indicator*—Point out that the instrument reads zero when a constant altitude is maintained. The vertical-speed indicator is used both as a *trend* and a *rate* instrument.

a. Use of the vertical-speed indicator as a *trend* instrument. Observe the vertical-speed indicator and altimeter as small pitch changes are made. Note that the vertical-speed indicator shows a trend up or down before the altimeter shows a climb or descent.

b. Use of the vertical-speed indicator as a *rate* instrument in climbs and descents.

    (1) Establish a small attitude change and allow the vertical-speed indicator to "settle down" on a rate. The attitude change will give a particular vertical speed which will vary with different aircraft.

    (2) Caution the student not to "chase the needle," but to make small pitch changes, then wait for the needle to settle down. As a demonstration, put the aircraft into a climb or descent. With the needle of the vertical-speed indicator in motion, apply control pressures in the opposite direction to stop the trend. Have the student note that when the altimeter stops, the aircraft is passing through level flight attitude, and that simultaneously, the needle of the vertical-speed indicator is stopping and reversing its direction of movement.

c. Use of the vertical-speed indicator to correct for deviations in altitude.

    (1) Raise the nose ½ bar. With a pitch attitude change of this magnitude, the vertical-speed indicator indicates a climb of about 200 feet per minute in low speed flight. (Explain that the relation between the attitude-indicator and the vertical-speed indicator depends on airspeed.)

    (2) For altitude corrections of 100 feet or less, use no more than a 200 feet per minute rate of climb or descent. A vertical speed in excess of this indicates over-controlling.

    (3) For altitude corrections of more than 100 feet, make a correspondingly larger correction.

    (4) Lower the nose ½ bar. Show that the vertical-speed indicator indicates a rate of descent of about 200 feet per minute.

d. Cross-check of pitch instruments.

    (1) Resume level flight. Cross-check the attitude indicator, altimeter, and vertical-speed indicator to detect any change in pitch attitude. Any deviation from zero by the vertical-speed indicator shows a need for a pitch change.

    (2) Descend 50 feet below the desired altitude, then enter a climb of 200 feet per minute and return to the desired altitude.

    (3) Climb 50 feet above the desired altitude, then enter a descent of 200 feet per minute and return to the desired altitude.

e. Student practice.

    (1) Attitude control with the vertical-speed indicator only.

    (2) Attitude control with the attitude indicator and the vertical-speed indicator.

    (3) Attitude control with the attitude indicator, vertical-speed indicator, and the altimeter.

    (4) Have the student climb 100 feet at a rate of 200 feet per minute.

    (5) Have student resume level flight, then descend at 200 feet per minute to the desired altitude.

    (6) Cross-check altimeter, attitude indicator, and vertical-speed indicator to maintain level flight.

    (7) Stress proper corrective pressures when correcting altitude.

    (8) Emphasize precision (correct small errors).

4. *Airspeed Indicator*

a. Use of airspeed indicator to determine attitude.

    (1) At constant power in level flight, point out that when altitude is constant, airspeed remains constant.

    (2) Make small changes in pitch and point out slow changes in airspeed.

    (3) Make extreme changes in pitch and point out fast changes in airspeed.

(4) At cruising airspeed in level flight, have student climb or dive aircraft. Point out apparent lag. Explain that lag is caused by the time required for the aircraft to accelerate or decelerate after pitch has been changed.

(5) Explain that there is no appreciable lag incorporated in the design of the instrument.

b. Cross-check the attitude indicator, vertical-speed indicator, and airspeed indicator. As each instrument is added to the cross-check, the speed of the cross-check must be increased to afford adequate coverage of all instruments. (NOTE: Encourage the use of peripheral vision.)

c. Student practice. With a constant power setting, hold constant airspeed in level flight by use of:

(1) The airspeed indicator alone.

(2) All available pitch instruments.

5. *Elevator Trim*

a. Application of elevator trim in pitch control.

(1) Place aircraft in level flight, out of trim.

(2) Point out pressures required to maintain desired pitch attitude.

(3) Adjust trim to relieve pressure—show that aircraft flies "hands off."

(4) In level flight, change airspeed. Point out the necessity of first holding pressure and relieving pressure with elevator trim.

b. Student practice. Use of elevator trim in level flight.

(1) With all pitch instruments.

(2) Without the attitude indicator.

NOTE.—The instructor should aid the student in rudder and bank control throughout this lesson.

Lesson 2

Bank Control

1. *Attitude Indicator*

a. Point out the similarity of the horizon bar to the natural horizon while banking. The instrument gives a *direct* indication of bank.

(1) Roll from one bank to another and point out the similarity of the apparent movement of the miniature aircraft and the real aircraft. To aid the student's understanding, tell him to imagine himself in the miniature aircraft.

(2) Point out the banking scale at the top of the instrument. Rolling from one bank to another, show how the pointer indicates the degree of bank.

(3) If the aircraft is flying right-side-up, the bank indices will be next to the reference marks on the case of the instrument.

(4) If the aircraft is inverted, the bank indices will be at the bottom of the case (non-tumbling instrument).

b. Demonstrate the banking limits of the instrument.

c. Precession of the horizon bar. Make a steep turn of 180°. After returning to level flight at the completion of the turn, point out that pitch and bank errors may be as much as 5°.

d. Caging and uncaging (if a caging device is available).

(1) Cagé and uncage in a banked attitude—show error.

(2) Emphasize the importance of uncaging the instrument in level flight.

(3) Stress the importance of fully uncaging the instrument after caging it, otherwise its limits may be greatly reduced.

e. Cross-check. Point out that while cross-checking the attitude indicator, both pitch and bank should be checked at the same time.

f. Student practice.

(1) Bank control with the attitude indicator alone.

(2) Occasionally place the aircraft in a bank and have the student level the wings.

(3) Pitch and bank control using all the pitch instruments and the attitude indicator for bank control.

2. *Heading Indicator*

   a. Banks and turns.

     (1) In coordinated flight, turning means banking. The heading indicator gives an *indirect* indication of bank.

     (2) Roll into a shallow bank. The heading indicator moves slowly in the direction of the bank.

     (3) Increase the bank and point out the corresponding increase in the rate of turn on the heading indicator.

   b. Limits of the heading indicator.

     (1) The limits of the heading indicator vary with instrument design. Until recently, these limits have generally been 55 degrees of pitch and bank. If the limits of the instrument are exceeded, it gives an unreliable indication.

     (2) Due to precession caused by internal friction, the instrument should be checked at least every 15 minutes during flight and reset to the correct heading. An error of 3 degrees in 15 minutes is acceptable for normal operation.

   c. Correcting headings.

     (1) When correcting a heading, do not exceed in bank the number of degrees to be turned. For example, if the heading error is 10°, do not exceed a 10° bank when correcting.

     (2) The bank should *never* exceed that required to produce a standard rate turn or a maximum of 30°.

   d. Cross-check. Include the heading indicator in the cross-check to maintain straight-and-level flight. When available, the heading indicator is always *primary* for bank in straight flight.

   e. Student practice.

     (1) Maintaining straight flight with the heading indicator alone.

     (2) Maintaining straight flight by use of the heading indicator and the attitude indicator.

     (3) Maintaining straight and level flight by the use of all pitch instruments together with the heading indicator and attitude indicator of the bank group.

3. *Turn Coordinator (miniature aircraft)*

   a. When the miniature aircraft is level (proper trim), it indicates that the airplane is flying straight with the wings level. Demonstrate that the roll rate of the miniature aircraft is proportional to the airplane's rate of roll. Also, point out that the miniature aircraft indicates the airplane's rate of turn when the roll rate is reduced to zero.

   b. Roll from one turn to another. The miniature aircraft shows the roll rate of the airplane.

   c. Point out that when the airplane is banked in coordinated flight, it is also turning. This turn is indicated by the miniature aircraft.

   d. In straight-and-level unaccelerated flight, when the heading indicator is not available, the magnetic compass is *primary* for bank, closely supported by the miniature aircraft of the turn coordinator.

   e. Referring to the attitude indicator, place the airplane in a very shallow bank (approximately 2°) and point out the position of the miniature aircraft of the turn coordinator. Point out the corresponding movement of the heading indicator.

   f. Emphasize keeping the miniature aircraft level to maintain straight flight.

4. *Turn Coordinator (ball instrument)*
   a. Using turns of approximately a standard rate, demonstrate slipping and skidding turns. Point out that the ball on the low side of center indicates that the airplane's wing is low relative to the position of the miniature aircraft.
   b. Student practice. Visual, then under the hood, emphasizing cross-check (division of attention).
      (1) Bank control using the turn coordinator.
      (2) Maintaining straight-and-level flight with all pitch and bank instruments.

5. *Rudder and Aileron Trim*
   a. Emphasize maintaining attitude and trimming off pressures.
   b. Demonstrate how the need for trim can be determined by a proper interpretation of instrument indications.
   c. Make power changes and have the student maintain straight-and-level flight, keeping the aircraft properly trimmed.
   d. The cross-check for need of trim should be continued throughout flight.
   e. Trim technique—partial panel and full panel.
      (1) Partial panel—relax control pressures in straight-and-level flight. If the miniature aircraft of the turn coordinator indicates a turn, but the ball is centered, aileron trim is needed. If the miniature aircraft and ball move simultaneously, rudder trim is needed.
      (2) Full panel—relax control pressures in straight-and-level flight. If the heading indicator shows a turn before a bank is shown on the attitude indicator, rudder trim is needed. If a bank is shown on the attitude indicator before a turn is shown on the heading indicator, aileron trim is needed. Refer to the miniature aircraft and ball of the turn coordinator to confirm this interpretation.

Lesson 3

Power Control and Trim

1. *Effect of Power Changes*
   a. In level flight, increase power and point out that the nose has a tendency to rise and yaw left. Hold forward elevator pressure to maintain level flight and relieve the pressure with trim. The position of the ball indicates the need for rudder trim.
   b. In level flight, reduce power and point out that the nose has a tendency to drop and yaw right. Hold back pressure to maintain level flight. The position of the ball indicates the need for rudder trim.
   c. Increase and decrease power, demonstrating that little banking tendency exists if proper rudder pressure and trim are applied.
   d. Student practice. Make large power changes and have the student practice trim control in straight-and-level flight.

2. *Airspeed Changes*—The terms *Low Cruise*, *Normal Cruise*, and *High Cruise* used in this section refer to speeds which can be established for an airplane used in instrument training or during actual instrument flight. Normal Cruise and High Cruise are en route speeds. Low Cruise is maintained during holding patterns and the approach phase of an instrument flight. Airspeed changes should be practiced first in a "clean" configuration, then as proficiency increases, while extending the flaps and landing gear. Some of the performance

figures and approximate pitch attitudes for a representative general aviation single-engine airplane follow:

	MP	RPM	MPH-(IAS)	Approx. Pitch Att.
High Cruise	23"	2300	160	½ bar low
Normal Cruise	21"	2300	140	level
Low Cruise	17"	2300	110	½ bar high
500 FPM Climb	23"	2500	110	2 bars high
500 FPM Descent	13"	2500	110	½ bar low
Low Cruise—Gear Down	22"	2500	110	½ bar high
500 FPM Climb—Gear Down	25"	2500	110	2 bars high
500 FPM Descent—Gear Down	15"	2500	110	½ bar low

   a. Decrease airspeed—from High Cruise to Normal Cruise or from High Cruise or Normal Cruise to Low Cruise.

      (1) Reduce manifold pressure 3 to 5 inches (or 200 to 300 RPM on an aircraft with a fixed pitch propeller) below power required for desired cruise. Stress smooth and accurate throttle movement in all power changes. When the throttle is moved to the approximate correct position, the manifold pressure gauge is included in the cross-check and a final adjustment is made. Re-emphasize the need for proper rudder and elevator trim.

      (2) Pitch must be changed to maintain a constant altitude as airspeed changes. Remind student of acceleration and deceleration errors of the attitude indicator.

      (3) The manifold pressure gauge is the primary power instrument while the airspeed is changing. As the airspeed approaches desired cruise, the airspeed indicator becomes primary for power. Power should then be increased to the approximate setting that will maintain desired cruise airspeed.

   b. Increase airspeed—from Slow Cruise to Normal Cruise or High Cruise, or from Normal Cruise to High Cruise. Increase power 3 to 5 inches (or 200 to 300 RPM on an aircraft with a fixed pitch propeller) above the power required to maintain desired cruise. Trim. The manifold pressure gauge is primary for power while the airspeed is changing. As desired cruise airspeed is approached, the airspeed indicator becomes primary for power and the manifold pressure is adjusted to maintain it. Trim.

3. *Control of Altitude and Airspeed in Straight-and-Level Flight*

   a. Altitude is maintained with pitch control and airspeed is maintained with power control. The need for a pitch or power change is indicated by a cross-check between the altimeter and the airspeed indicator.

   b. If the altitude is correct and the airspeed is either high or low, change power to attain the desired airspeed. When the altitude is low and the airspeed is high (or when the altitude is high and the airspeed is low), only a pitch change may be needed to attain the desired altitude and airspeed. When both altitude and airspeed are high or low, a change in both pitch and power is needed.

4. *Interpretation and Cross-Check of Pitch, Bank, and Power Instruments in Straight-and-Level Flight*

   a. The altimeter is primary for pitch; the heading indicator (or magnetic compass, if the heading indicator is not available) is primary for bank; and the airspeed indicator is primary for power control. During power changes, your cross-check must be particularly efficient and accurate.

   b. Student practice changing airspeed in straight-and-level flight:

      (1) With all available pitch, bank, and power instruments.

      (2) Without the heading indicator.

      (3) Without the heading indicator and attitude indicator.

Lesson 4

Constant Airspeed Climbs and Descents

1. *Climbs—Entry from Normal Cruise Airspeed*
   a. Enter constant airspeed climb from normal cruise airspeed.
   b. As the climb power and climb pitch attitude are established, the attitude indicator becomes primary for pitch at the approximate climb attitude. At this time, the manifold pressure (or tachometer) is primary for power. The vertical-speed indicator will show an immediate upward trend and will stop on a rate appropriate to the stabilized airspeed and attitude. The airspeed indicator becomes primary for pitch when the airspeed stabilizes on a constant value.
   c. Emphasize trim as power and pitch are changed.
   d. Demonstrate the use of the vertical-speed indicator as an aid in maintaining a desired airspeed by adjusting the pitch attitude on the attitude indicator to change the vertical-speed 200 feet per minute to gain or lose 5 knots in airspeed.
   e. In climbs as well as in level flight, the vertical-speed indicator is used as an aid in pitch control.

2. *Level-off from Climbs at Cruise Airspeed*
   a. Lead the altitude by approximately ten percent of the vertical speed shown, i.e., for 500 feet per minute, use a 50-foot lead.
   b. As the level-off is started, the altimeter becomes primary for pitch.
   c. Cross-check the attitude indicator, the altimeter, and vertical-speed indicator.
   d. Leave the power at climbing power until the airspeed approaches normal cruise airspeed, adjusting pitch as necessary to maintain altitude.
   e. Emphasize trim.

3. *Student Practice.* Enter climbs from normal cruise airspeed and level-off at normal cruise airspeed:
   a. With all available instruments.
   b. Without the attitude indicator and heading indicator.

4. *Climbs—Entry from Climb Airspeed*
   a. As the power is increased to climb power, the airspeed indicator immediately becomes primary for pitch.
   b. As power is increased, adjust the pitch attitude on the attitude indicator to maintain a constant airspeed.
   c. Use the relationship between the airspeed and the vertical-speed for pitch control.

5. *Level-Off from Climbs at Climb Airspeed*
   a. Lead the altitude by approximately ten percent of the vertical speed.
   b. As the level-off is started, the altimeter becomes primary for pitch.
   c. Simultaneously lower pitch attitude and reduce power to maintain altitude and airspeed.
   d. Trim.

6. *Student Practice.* Enter climbs from climb airspeed and level off at climb airspeed:
   a. With all available instruments.
   b. Without the attitude indicator and heading indicator.

7. *Descents—Entry*
   a. Reduce power to descending power setting. Maintain altitude until the airspeed approaches descending airspeed.

b. When the airspeed approaches that desired, the airspeed indicator becomes primary for pitch and remains so throughout the descent. Adjust pitch attitude to maintain airspeed. This establishes the descent.

c. Demonstrate the use of the vertical-speed indicator as an aid in maintaining the desired airspeed by adjusting the pitch attitude on the attitude indicator to change the vertical speed 200 feet per minute to gain or lose 5 knots in airspeed.

8. *Level-Off from Descents at Cruise Airspeed*

a. At approximately 150 feet above the desired altitude, advance power to cruise power setting.

b. The vertical-speed indicator is primary for pitch until the normal lead for level-off is reached. At this time, the altimeter becomes primary for pitch. Properly executed, cruise airspeed should be reached as the level-off is completed.

c. Trim is particularly important, since the nose tends to rise when the power is applied.

9. *Level-Off from Descents at Descent Airspeed*

a. At approximately 50 feet above the desired altitude, advance the power to a setting which will hold the airspeed constant. Simultaneously adjust pitch attitude to maintain airspeed.

b. As the level-off is started, the altimeter becomes primary for pitch and the airspeed indicator becomes primary for power.

c. Trim.

10. *Student Practice.* Enter descents and execute level-off from descents at cruising and descending airspeed:

a. With all available instruments.

b. Without the attitude indicator and heading indicator.

Lesson 5

Turns and Heading Indicator Turns

1. *Standard Rate Turns at Cruising Airspeed*

a. Turn entry and recovery.

(1) In level flight, enter a turn. As the turn is established on the attitude indicator, it becomes primary for bank. When the approximate desired bank is reached, the miniature aircraft of the turn coordinator becomes primary for bank and the attitude indicator becomes supporting for bank. The altimeter is primary for pitch and the airspeed indicator is primary for power.

(2) Loss of vertical lift. Pitch attitude must be changed to hold a constant altitude. Apply corrections only when the instruments show need for correction.

(3) When the desired bank is reached, it may be necessary to hold slight aileron and rudder pressure opposite the direction of turn to maintain the desired bank. Emphasize maintaining a constant bank angle.

(4) Power is adjusted as necessary to maintain a constant airspeed.

(5) Recovery to straight-and-level flight. The roll-out is accomplished by reference to the attitude indicator. When the normal lead for roll-out is reached, the heading indicator (if available) becomes primary for bank. Adjust the pitch attitude and power as necessary to maintain the desired altitude and airspeed.

b. Turn entry with rudder alone.

(1) Enter a turn using only rudder. Show the resulting skid, displacement of the ball, and the effect on airspeed.

(2) Show that the aircraft is turning faster than the bank indicates.

c. Turn entry with aileron alone.

(1) Enter a turn using only aileron. Show yaw caused by aileron drag and that coordinated use of rudder and aileron eliminates its effect.

(2) When correcting for a slip or skid, the angle of bank will have to be changed to maintain a constant rate turn.

d. Angle of bank for standard rate turn.

Airspeed in Knots (True)	Approximate Angle (to nearest degree) for 3°/Second
80	12°
90	14°
100	15°
110	17°
120	18°
130	20°
140	21°
150	22°

NOTE.—A rule-of-thumb to find the amount of bank needed for a standard rate turn is to divide the airspeed by 10 and add one-half the answer. For 100 knots, the angle of bank required is:

$$\frac{100}{10} = 10 + 5 \text{ (one-half of 10)} = 15°$$

(1) Make turns at low cruise airspeed, using correct bank for standard rate.

(2) Make turns at normal cruise airspeed, using correct bank for standard rate.

(3) Make turns at high cruise speed, using correct bank for standard rate.

e. Student practice turns.

(1) First without the hood, then with the hood.

(2) Full and partial panel.

2. *Climbing and Descending Turns*

a. Entry.

(1) The entry may be made in three ways: enter the climb/descent then the turn; enter the turn then the climb/descent; enter the climb/descent and turn simultaneously.

(2) Point out that these maneuvers require simultaneous use of bank and pitch techniques previously learned individually for level turns and straight climbs and descents.

(3) When climbing or descending airspeed is reached, the airspeed indicator becomes primary for pitch.

(4) The manifold pressure gauge is primary for power, and as the approximate desired bank is reached, the miniature aircraft of the turn coordinator becomes primary for bank.

(5) Emphasize trim.

b. Level-off

(1) Combine techniques previously described for climb and descent level-offs and turn recovery.

(2) The student may stop the turn, then level-off, or level-off then stop the turn, or level-off and stop the turn simultaneously.

c. Student practice. Make climbing and descending turns, leveling-off at various airspeeds:

(1) With all available instruments.

(2) Without the attitude indicator.

3. *Turns to Predetermined Headings*

a. Enter a coordinated standard rate turn. Show the student that the aircraft will turn as long as the wings are banked and point out that the rollout must be started before reaching the desired heading.

b. As a guide for rollout on a desired heading, use a lead of 1° for each 2° of bank being held. Never exceed in bank the number of degrees to be turned, and in no case exceed a standard rate of turn.

c. With the attitude indicator covered, have the student change heading 30° using a standard rate turn.

d. With all instruments available, show the proper bank to use when changing heading less than 15°.

e. Student practice. Make turns to various headings:
   (1) With all available instruments.
   (2) Without the attitude indicator.

Lesson 6

Instrument Takeoff

1. *Cockpit Check*
   a. Stress the importance of a complete and careful cockpit check.
   b. Emphasize the importance of setting the miniature aircraft properly.
   c. Emphasize setting the trim properly.

2. *Taxi to Takeoff Position*
   a. Accurately align the aircraft with the runway, being sure that the nose wheel or tail wheel is straight.
   b. Set the heading indicator with the nose index on the 5° mark nearest the published heading of the runway. Be sure the instrument is uncaged.
   c. Hold the aircraft stationary with brakes.

3. *Takeoff*
   a. Advance the power to a setting that will provide partial rudder control.
   b. Release the brakes and advance the throttle smoothly to takeoff power.
   c. During the takeoff roll, the heading indicator is primary for directional control. Control direction with rudder. (Use brakes as a last resort.)
   d. As you reach a speed where elevator control becomes effective (approximately 15 to 25 knots below takeoff speed), note acceleration error and establish takeoff attitude on the attitude indicator (approximately a 2-bar width).
   e. As the aircraft approaches flying speed and immediately after leaving the ground, the pitch and bank attitudes are controlled by reference to the attitude indicator. When the altimeter and vertical-speed indicator show a climb, you are airborne. Continue to maintain heading by reference to the heading indicator.
   f. Continue to maintain the pitch and bank attitudes by reference to the attitude indicator.
   g. Maintain a stable climb as indicated by the altimeter and vertical-speed indicator and at 100 feet call for gear retraction.
   h. When the gear is retracted, maintain a pitch attitude on the attitude indicator that will give a continuous climb on the vertical-speed indicator and a smooth increase in airspeed.
   i. The heading indicator becomes primary for bank when the vertical-speed indicator and altimeter indicate a climb.
   j. Retract the flaps as soon as a safe altitude and airspeed is reached.
   k. When climbing airspeed is reached, reduce power to the climb setting. At this time, the airspeed indicator becomes primary for pitch and the manifold pressure gauge (or tachometer) becomes primary for power.
   l. The climb-out is accomplished as a constant airspeed climb.
   m. The trim is set prior to takeoff. Do not alter the trim until after the aircraft is definitely airborne, then relieve control pressures with trim as necessary.

4. *Student Practice*. Instrument takeoffs to be practiced:
   a. Without the hood.
   b. With the hood.

Lesson 7

Rate Climbs and Descents

1. *Climbs at a Definite (Indicated) Rate*
   a. While maintaining straight-and-level flight, change to climb airspeed.
   b. Enter a climb from an exact altitude with climbing airspeed.
   c. Advance the power to the approximate setting that will result in a 500-foot per minute rate of climb. Simultaneously adjust pitch attitude to maintain a constant airspeed.
   d. As the power is advanced in the climb entry, the airspeed indicator becomes primary for pitch and remains so until the vertical speed approaches a rate of climb of 500 feet per minute. At this time, the vertical-speed indicator becomes primary for pitch and remains so for the remainder of the climb. The airspeed indicator again becomes the primary instrument for power.
   e. The heading indicator is primary for bank throughout the maneuver.
   f. Show that any deviation in vertical speed indicates the need for a pitch change, and that the airspeed is controlled by the use of power.
   g. Show how pitch and power changes must be coordinated closely. For example:
      (1) If the vertical speed is correct but the airspeed is high, reduce power.
      (2) If the vertical speed is high and the airspeed is low, reduce pitch.
      (3) If the vertical speed is low and the airspeed is low, increase both pitch and power.
      (4) If the vertical speed is high and the airspeed is high, reduce both pitch and power.
   h. Emphasize trim throughout.

2. *Level-Off from a Climb at a Definite (Indicated) Rate*. Follow the same procedure that was described previously for level-off from a constant airspeed climb.

3. *Descents at a Definite (Indicated) Rate*
   a. Enter a descent from an exact altitude and descending airspeed.
   b. Reduce power to the approximate setting for a 500-foot per minute rate of descent, simultaneously adjusting pitch attitude to maintain a constant airspeed.
   c. As the power is reduced in the descent entry, the airspeed indicator is primary for pitch and remains so until the vertical speed approaches a rate of descent of 500 feet per minute. At this time, the vertical-speed indicator becomes primary for pitch and remains so for the remainder of the descent. As the vertical-speed reaches 500 feet per minute, the airspeed indicator becomes the primary instrument for power.
   d. The heading indicator is primary for bank throughout the maneuver.
   e. Show how pitch and power changes must be coordinated (see examples given for climbs).
   f. Emphasize trim.

4. *Level-Off from a Descent at a Definite (Indicated) Rate*. Follow the same procedure that has been described previously for level-off from constant airspeed descents.

5. *Student Practice*. Make climbs and descents at a definite indicated rate.

6. *Calibration of the Vertical-Speed Indicator*
   a. Establish a climb or descent at a 500-foot per minute indicated rate.

b. Each 15 seconds, check the altimeter for a 125-foot altitude change.

c. If the altitude change is more or less than 125 feet, adjust the vertical speed accordingly.

d. Repeat the procedure until a vertical speed is determined that will produce the desired rate.

e. Any error found during calibration should be considered during subsequent rate climbs or descents.

7. *Student Practice.* Calibrate the vertical-speed indicator during both climbs and descents.

8. *Climbs at a Definite (Absolute) Rate*

a. Establish climbing airspeed.

b. As the clock second hand passes any cardinal point (12, 3, 6, or 9), enter the climb using the same technique that has been described for the entry into a climb at a definite indicated rate.

c. The primary pitch, bank, and power instruments are the same as those which are primary during climbs at a definite indicated rate.

d. Since the aircraft does not start climbing immediately after power is applied, the altimeter is approximately 20 to 30 feet behind the clock. This lag is maintained throughout the climb.

e. Use the first 30 seconds to establish the proper vertical speed and trim.

f. Check the clock and altimeter every 15 seconds thereafter for 125 feet of altitude change.

g. Show the student how to correct for any errors.

9. *Level-Off from a Climb at a Definite (Absolute) Rate.* Follow the same procedures that were described previously for level-off from a constant airspeed climb.

10. *Student Practice.* Make climbs and descents at a definite absolute rate.

Lesson 8

Vertical S, S–1, and S–2

1. *Vertical S.*—This maneuver is a series of climbs and descents at a definite indicated rate.

a. Climbing or descending airspeed should be established prior to entry.

b. During the reversal of vertical direction, lead the altitude 40 to 60 feet in descents and 20 to 30 feet in climbs.

c. Change the altitude 500 feet, 400 feet, 300 feet, then 200 feet, returning to the original altitude each time. After the 200-foot altitude change, return to the original altitude and level-off at climbing or descending airspeed (low cruise).

d. Performing the Vertical S.

(1) From an exact altitude and climbing or descending airspeed, adjust power and pitch attitude to enter a climb or descent.

(2) As the power is adjusted in the entry, the airspeed indicator becomes primary for pitch.

(3) As the vertical speed approaches 500 feet per minute, the vertical-speed indicator becomes primary for pitch and remains so until the reversal of the vertical direction is started. As the vertical speed reaches 500 feet per minute, the airspeed indicator again becomes the primary instrument for power.

(4) As the reversal of the vertical direction is started, the airspeed indicator becomes primary for pitch and remains so until the vertical speed approaches the desired rate of 500 feet per minute.

(5) Stress the importance of trim and cross-check.

2. *Vertical S–1.*—This maneuver is a combination of the vertical "S" and a standard rate turn.
   a. Enter in the same manner as a climbing or descending turn.
   b. Reverse the direction of turn with each return to entry altitude.
   c. Emphasize trim and smooth control technique.

3. *Vertical S–2.*—This maneuver differs from the Vertical S–1 in that the direction of turn is reversed with each reversal of vertical direction.

4. *Student Practice.* Perform Vertical S, S–1, and S–2:
   a. With all available instruments.
   b. Without the attitude indicator.

Lesson 9

Magnetic Compass

1. *Turning Errors*
   a. The magnetic compass gives erroneous turn indications when the aircraft is flying near headings of north or south.
   b. The magnitude of error varies with angle of bank and proximity to north or south headings. The error becomes progressively smaller as east or west headings are approached. The error also depends on the latitude at which the aircraft is flying.
   c. All methods of compensating for turn error in medium latitudes are based on using a definite and constant bank between 15° and 18°.

2. *Northerly Turning Error*
   a. Fly a north heading long enough for the compass to settle down (wings must be level).
   b. Enter a turn toward the west. The compass immediately indicates a turn in the opposite direction, i.e., toward the east. (Return to the north heading.)
   c. Enter a turn toward the east. The compass indicates a turn toward the west. (Return to the north heading.)
   d. Enter a very shallow banked turn toward the west. The compass indicates momentarily that a straight course is being maintained. Point out that the wings must be level to avoid turn errors. Repeat the demonstration in a shallow turn toward the east.
   e. Enter a steep turn. The compass lags excessively and may swing completely around in the opposite direction from the turn.

3. *Southerly Turning Error*
   a. Fly a south heading and let the compass settle down (wings must be level).
   b. Enter a turn toward the west. The compass indicates a much faster turn in the same direction. (Return to the south heading.)
   c. Enter a turn toward the east. The compass indicates a much faster turn in the same direction.
   d. The wings must be level to avoid compass turn errors.

4. *Acceleration and Deceleration Error*
   a. Fly a heading of east.
   b. Increase airspeed in level flight to show acceleration error—compass indicates a turn toward north.
   c. Reduce airspeed in level flight to show deceleration error—compass indicates a turn toward the south.
   d. Lower the nose at a constant power setting—show acceleration error.
   e. Raise the nose at a constant power setting—show deceleration error.
   f. Fly a heading of west and repeat the above demonstration.

g. Explain that the magnitude of the error depends on the rate of acceleration or deceleration. To read the compass accurately on easterly and westerly headings, the airspeed must be constant.

h. Acceleration and deceleration errors are not present in constant airspeed climbs and descents.

i. Show that acceleration and deceleration errors are not present on north and south headings.

j. Show that turn errors are not present on east and west headings.

5. *Turns to Magnetic Compass Headings*
   a. Turn to a heading of north, using 15° to 18° of bank. Lead the heading an amount equal to the latitude plus half the angle of bank.
   b. Turn to heading of south, using 15° to 18° of bank. Over-shoot the heading an amount equal to the latitude minus half the angle of bank.
   c. From south, then from north, turn to a heading of east. Lead the heading approximately 5° when turning from a heading of south to east and approximately 10° when turning from a heading of north to east.
   d. Turn to a heading of west, using the procedure given above.
   e. Show that lead or lag must be interpolated when turning to intermediate headings.

6. *Student Practice.* Make turns to magnetic compass headings:
   a. Without the heading indicator.
   b. Without the heading indicator and attitude indicator.

Lesson 10

Timed Turns

1. *Calibration of the Miniature Aircraft of the Turn Coordinator*
   a. With all instruments available, establish a standard rate turn as indicated by the miniature aircraft of the turn coordinator.
   b. As the clock second hand passes a cardinal point (12, 3, 6, or 9), check the heading indicator.
   c. Check for a turn of 30° each 10 seconds (no lag, since timing is started after turn is established).
   d. Make necessary changes in indicated rate (miniature aircraft position) to produce a standard rate turn.
   e. Calibrate miniature aircraft of turn coordinator both right and left.
   f. Note exact deflection of miniature aircraft and use during all timed turns.

2. *Timed Turns with All Instruments Available*
   a. Enter a standard rate turn when the clock second hand passes a cardinal point (12, 3, 6, or 9).
   b. The first 30 seconds is used to establish the turn properly.
   c. Check the heading indicator to see whether the rate of turn is proper. It should indicate a turn of 90° minus the number of degrees lag for the angle of bank used (lag will be approximately one-half the degree of bank).
   d. Demonstrate how the angle of bank is increased or decreased to compensate for any error.
   e. After the first 30 seconds, the heading indicator should be checked against the clock every 15 seconds.
   f. Time is started when pressure is applied to roll into a turn and is stopped when pressure is applied to roll out.
   g. With all instruments available, roll out on the desired heading regardless of time.

3. *Timed Turns without the Heading Indicator and Attitude Indicator*
   a. Enter a standard rate turn, using the miniature aircraft of the turn co-ordinator as the primary bank instrument while in the turn.
   b. Turn for 30 seconds, using a constant miniature aircraft position.
   c. At the end of 30 seconds, roll out of the turn at the same rate you made the roll-in.
   d. With the wings level and the miniature aircraft of the turn coordinator indicating zero rate of turn, the magnetic compass should indicate that a turn of 90° has been made.
   e. For small changes in heading, use a half-standard-rate turn as indicated by the miniature aircraft of the turn coordinator.

4. *Student Practice.* Make timed turns at different airspeeds:
   a. With all available instruments.
   b. Without the heading indicator.
   c. Without the heading indicator and attitude indicator.

Lesson 11

Steep Turns

1. *Demonstrate Steep Turns*
   a. Explain that any turn greater than standard rate is considered a steep turn.
   b. Stress value of steep turn to increase student's ability to react quickly and smoothly to rapid changes in attitude.
      NOTE—Student should use normal rate of roll-in and roll-out.
   c. Point out that entry, turn, and recovery procedures are the same as those used in normal turns.
   d. To maintain altitude as bank increases, the nose of the aircraft must be raised to compensate for the decrease of vertical lift.
   e. With the increase in drag, the airspeed tends to decrease, so power must be added to maintain the desired airspeed.

2. *Performance of Steep Turns—Full Panel*
   a. Enter a turn of more than a standard rate.
   b. The altimeter is primary for pitch. To maintain altitude, make a pitch change only when the pitch instruments show the need for a change.
   c. The airspeed indicator is primary for power. Add power when the airspeed indicator shows a need for it.
   d. Cross-check the attitude indicator, altimeter, and vertical-speed indicator for pitch control. Refer to the attitude indicator when making pitch corrections, taking precession error into consideration.

3. *Performance of Steep Turns—Partial Panel*
   a. Use the turn coordinator to maintain a constant rate of turn.
   b. Control pitch by reference to the altimeter/vertical-speed indicator combination.

4. *Recovery*
   a. Should be smooth with a normal rate of roll.
   b. Since vertical lift increases, pitch attitude and power should be reduced as required to maintain altitude and airspeed.

5. *Student Practice.* Make steep turns:
   a. With all available instruments.
   b. Without the attitude indicator and heading indicator.

Lesson 12

Recovery From Unusual Attitudes

1. *General Considerations*

   Assume that an unusual attitude exists if the rate of movement of the instruments is not normal. When an unusual attitude is detected, prompt corrective action is essential. In moderate unusual attitudes, the pilot can normally reorient himself by establishing a level flight indication on the Attitude Indicator. However, recoveries should be made primarily by reference to the airspeed indicator, altimeter, turn coordinator, and the vertical-speed indicator for these reasons; (1) many aircraft are equipped with spillable attitude indicators, and (2) the gyroscopic instruments may become inoperative, or, in extreme attitudes, difficult to interpret.

2. *Rules for Recovery*

   Check the trend of the airspeed indicator and altimeter to determine whether the nose is low or high. Determine the direction of turn by reference to the turn coordinator. Make corrective control applications almost simultaneously. Emphasize proper interpretation of attitude to ensure proper control sequence. The example given below is the recommended sequence for most situations.

   a. If the nose is low:
      (1) Reduce the power to prevent excessive airspeed and loss of altitude.
      (2) Level the wings by applying coordinated aileron and rudder pressures to level the miniature aircraft of the turn coordinator and center the ball.
      (3) Apply elevator pressure to correct the pitch attitude to level flight.

   b. If the nose is high:
      (1) Apply power.
      (2) Apply forward elevator pressure to lower the nose and prevent a stall.
      (3) Correct the bank by applying coordinated aileron and rudder pressure level the miniature aircraft of the turn coordinator and center the ball.

   c. The pitch attitude will be approximately level when the airspeed and altimeter needles stop their movement and the vertical-speed indicator reverses its trend.

   d. The airplane's bank attitude will be approximately level when the miniature aircraft of the turn coordinator is level.

   e. Do not use the attitude indicator until you verify that it is reliable.

   f. Start a climb or descent back to the original altitude and heading as soon as you attain full control of the aircraft and have a safe airspeed.

3. *Student Practice*

   a. Recovery from nose-low unusual attitudes:
      (1) With all available instruments.
      (2) Without the attitude indicator and heading indicator.

   b. Recovery from nose-high unusual attitudes:
      (1) With all available instruments.
      (2) Without the attitude indicator and heading indicator.

Lesson 13

Change of Airspeed In Turns

1. *Change from Normal to Low Cruise Airspeed after Turn is Established*

   a. Establish a standard rate turn at normal cruise airspeed.

   b. Reduce power 3″ to 5″ (or 200 to 300 RPM on an aircraft having a fixed pitch propeller) below power required for low cruise airspeed.

263

c. Point out the increase in pitch attitude required to maintain altitude as the airspeed decreases.

d. Point out the reduction in bank required to maintain a standard rate turn as the airspeed decreases.

e. Point out the similarity to change of airspeed in straight-and-level flight.

f. The altimeter is primary for pitch and the miniature aircraft of the turn coordinator is primary for bank.

g. While the airspeed is changing, the manifold pressure gauge (or tachometer) is primary for power. As the airspeed approaches the desired value, the airspeed indicator becomes primary for power.

h. Stress trim as the airspeed changes.

2. *Change from Low to Normal Cruise Airspeed after Turn is Established.* The procedure parallels that given above *except*—

a. The power must be overshot 3″ to 5″ (or 200 to 300 RPM on an aircraft having a fixed pitch propeller).

b. The pitch is lowered to maintain altitude.

c. The bank is increased to maintain a standard rate turn.

3. *Change Airspeed and Enter Turn Simultaneously.* The procedure is the same as that described above, *except* the turn entry and power change are started simultaneously.

4. *Student Practice.* Make changes of airspeed in turns:

a. After the turn has been established.

b. Entering turn and changing airspeed simultaneously.

c. With all available instruments.

d. Without the attitude indicator and heading indicator.

Lesson 14

Climbs and Descents to Predetermined Altitudes and Headings

1. *Climbs to Predetermined Altitudes and Headings (Climb 1,000 feet and turn 360°)*

a. Change airspeed to climbing airspeed in straight-and-level flight.

b. When the clock second hand indicates the starting time (12, 3, 6, or 9), change pitch, bank, and power simultaneously. Enter a standard rate climbing turn (3° per second and 500 feet per minute).

c. Control bank as in timed turns, checking heading every 15 seconds after the first 30 seconds.

d. Control pitch as in rate climbs, checking altitude every 15 seconds after the first 30 seconds.

e. Consider lag in heading and altitude. Maintain lag throughout the maneuver.

f. Roll-out on correct heading and level-off on correct altitude, regardless of time.

2. *Descents to Predetermined Altitudes and Headings (Descend 1,000 feet and turn 360°)*

a. Change airspeed to descending airspeed in straight-and-level flight.

b. Make a descending turn paralleling procedures outlined above for climb.

3. *Student Practice.* Make climbs and descents to altitudes and headings:

a. With all available instruments.

b. Without the heading indicator and attitude indicator.

Lesson 15

Pattern "A"

The purpose of both Pattern "A" and Pattern "B" is to further develop the pilot's ability to control the aircraft without deliberate thought. These patterns help prepare the student for the holding patterns and procedure turns he will fly during radio navigation. Initial practice should be on cardinal headings for simplification; however, as proficiency increases the student should be able to accomplish the patterns on any heading. The instructor may make various changes in the patterns, or, the patterns may be flown over a navigational facility, correcting for drift on each leg.

1. *Brief Student Thoroughly Prior to the Flight*

2. *Performance of Maneuver in the Aircraft*
   a. This maneuver should be performed first with all available instruments, then on partial panel.
   b. Start Pattern "A" and demonstrate through the first three turns, then have the student continue.
   c. Timing should start when the clock second hand is on a cardinal point, preferably the 12 o'clock position.
   d. The timing for this pattern is consecutive in that the time for each leg is started when control pressure is applied to recover from the preceding turn.
   e. After recovery from turns, allow sufficient time for the compass card to stop oscillating, then note the heading and correct if necessary. An exception is the 30-second leg. If you note an error in heading here, compensate for it by lengthening or shortening the time allotted for the next turn.

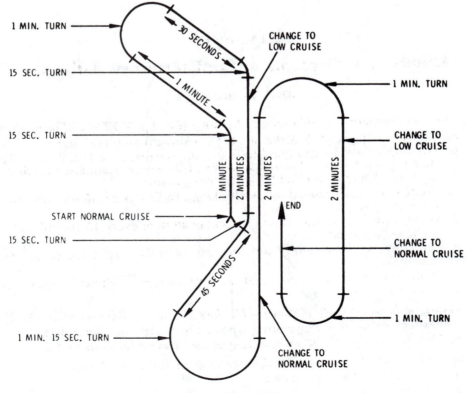

FIGURE 1.   Pattern "A".

f. The turn coordinator and magnetic compass must be observed closely at all times. To correct a heading, use a timed turn (for small heading changes, use a half-standard rate turn).

g. An efficient cross-check is required during airspeed changes so that corrections may be applied immediately.

Lesson 16

Pattern "B"

1. *Brief Student Thoroughly Prior to the Flight*

2. *Performance of Maneuver in the Aircraft*
   a. Do not demonstrate unless absolutely necessary.
   b. All available instruments are used.
   c. Roll out on headings regardless of time.
   d. When changing airspeed in turns, *simultaneously* change bank and power, also pitch if applicable.
   e. The descending final turn is made at an absolute rate.
   f. The final descent is made to a minimum altitude set by the instructor, or until the time expires, whichever comes first.
   g. The emergency pull-up is made as a normal go-around procedure, climbing to the original altitude.

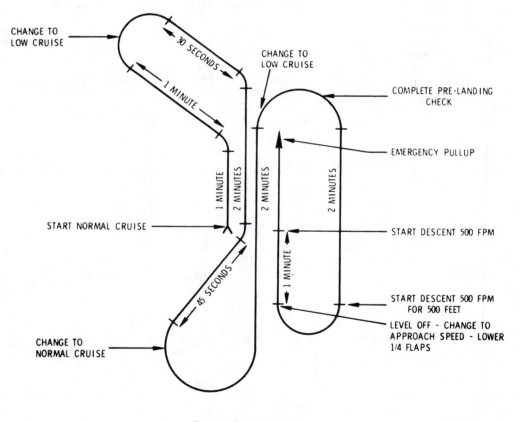

FIGURE 2. Pattern "B".

Lesson 17

Radar Approach (PAR)

1. *Brief Student Thoroughly Prior to Flight*
2. *Radar Pattern*
   a. Position the aircraft on a downwind leg and on interphone simulate the initial call-up, the surveillance radar controller, and the final controller.
   b. The student reads back all headings and altitudes given, and acknowledges all other transmissions *except* when instructed otherwise by the final approach controller.
   c. Perform the pre-landing check on the downwind leg. Change airspeed to initial approach airspeed and set flaps as appropriate.
   d. Make all heading changes in the pattern with a standard rate turn.
   e. Turn to base leg and complete the final cockpit check.
   f. Turn to the final approach heading, reduce airspeed to approach speed, and make final flap setting. Maintain altitude and heading while changing airspeed and setting flaps.
   g. Enter a normal 500-foot per minute rate descent when so instructed by the controller.
   h. Final approach corrections:
      (1) If above or below the glide path, make an approximate pitch correction and monitor the airspeed indicator for the need of power change.
      (2) When changing headings, do not exceed in bank angle the number of degrees to be turned.
      (3) Stress the importance of making immediate and precise corrections when so instructed by the controller.

3. *Student Practice*
   a. The instructor acts as the surveillance radar controller and the final controller and has the student perform a simulated precision radar approach at altitude.
   b. Repeat the above to a landing runway. At simulated PAR minimums, the instructor will take over and land the aircraft or have the student perform a missed approach.

INDEX